INDIAN FINANCIAL MARKET

THEORY & PRACTICE

INDIAN FINANCIAL MARKET

THEORY & PRACTICE

Prof. Nalinіprava Tripathy
Indian Institute of Management, Shillong,
INDIA.

Himalaya Publishing House

MUMBAI • NEW DELHI • NAGPUR • BENGALURU • HYDERABAD • CHENNAI • PUNE • LUCKNOW • AHMEDABAD
• ERNAKULAM • BHUBANESWAR • INDORE • KOLKATA • GUWAHATI

First Edition : 2011

Published by : Mrs. Meena Pandey for **Himalaya Publishing House Pvt. Ltd.**, "Ramdoot", Dr. Bhalerao Marg, Girgaon, **Mumbai - 400 004.** Phone: 022-23860170/23863863, Fax: 022-23877178 **E-mail: himpub@vsnl.com; Website: www.himpub.com**

Branch Offices :

New Delhi : "Pooja Apartments", 4-B, Murari Lal Street, Ansari Road, Darya Ganj, New Delhi - 110 002. Phone: 011-23270392, 23278631; Fax: 011-23256286

Nagpur : Kundanlal Chandak Industrial Estate, Ghat Road, Nagpur - 440 018. Phone: 0712-2738731, 3296733; Telefax: 0712-2721215

Bengaluru : No. 16/1 (Old 12/1), 1st Floor, Next to Hotel Highlands, Madhava Nagar, Race Course Road, Bengaluru - 560 001. Phone: 080-32919385; Telefax: 080-22286611

Hyderabad : No. 3-4-184, Lingampally, Besides Raghavendra Swamy Matham, Kachiguda, Hyderabad - 500 027. Phone: 040-27560041, 27550139; Mobile: 09848130433

Chennai : No. 85/50, Bazullah Road, T. Nagar, Chennai - 600 017. Phone: 044-28144004/28144005

Pune : First Floor, "Laksha" Apartment, No. 527, Mehunpura, Shaniwarpeth (Near Prabhat Theatre), Pune - 411 030. Phone: 020-24496323/24496333

Lucknow : Jai Baba Bhavan, Church Road, Near Manas Complex and Dr. Awasthi Clinic, Aliganj, Lucknow - 226 024. Phone: 0522-2339329, 4068914; Mobile: 09305302158, 09415349385, 09389593752

Ahmedabad : 114, "SHAIL", 1st Floor, Opp. Madhu Sudan House, C.G. Road, Navrang Pura, Ahmedabad - 380 009. Phone: 079-26560126; Mobile: 09327324149, 09314679413

Ernakulam : 39/104 A, Lakshmi Apartment, Karikkamuri Cross Rd., Ernakulam, Cochin - 622011, Kerala. Phone: 0484-2378012, 2378016; Mobile: 09344199799

Bhubaneswar : 5 Station Square, Bhubaneswar - 751 001 (Odisha). Mobile: 09861046007

Indore : Kesardeep Avenue Extension, 73, Narayan Bagh, Flat No. 302, IIIrd Floor, Near Humpty Dumpty School, Narayan Bagh, Indore - 452 007 (M.P.). Mobile: 09301386468

Kolkata : 108/4, Beliaghata Main Road, Near ID Hospital, Opp. SBI Bank, Kolkata - 700 010, Phone: 033-32449649, Mobile: 09910440956

Guwahati : House No. 15, Behind Pragjyotish College, Near Sharma Printing Press, P.O. Bharalumukh, Guwahati - 781009, (Assam). Mobile: 09883055590, 09883055536

DTP by : HPH, Editorial Office, Bhandup (Avinash)

Printed at : A to Z Printer, New Delhi.

Dedicated to my Dearest
OM SIRIDI SAI
Who bestow on me the inspiration and strength
to take up this work

Prof. Naliniprava Tripathy

PREFACE

The world today is dominated by new ideas and new economic thinking. Financial markets have grown considerably in developed and developing countries over the last two decades. It has also seen a concurrent transformation and restructuring of the international financial market. These organizational changes incorporated the liberalization of the economy, integration of capital markets, increasing dominance of institutional investors, the development of new financial techniques and instruments and the growth of the emerging markets.

The Indian financial market has experienced tremendous growth interms of primary issues and trades on the secondary market in recent years. But there is a large gap existing between the practice and research done by the academic community and required by the practitioners. Hence, there is a need to explore the real performs happening in the Indian Financial market, which is useful to the professional student community, practitioners, regulators and research scholars. Towards this endeavour, this book has been design to discuss the application of theory and practice of financial market for bridging the gap between the academic population and the practitioners.

The prime objective of the book is to provide MBA, M.Com., MFC, CFAs, CAs, and Ph.D. Students, Researchers, Practitioners, Academicians, an insight into the operational efficiency of financial market and financial service institutions with latest trends. This book contains eighteen chapters covering the entire gamut of development that are taking place in the financial market and institutions.

I feel quite confident that the Chapters that are included in this volume would go a long way of great value and useful to students, research scholars, academic community as well as corporate world. The text is presented in a lucid manner and simple language to meet the specific needs of the target group. The text will no doubt act as a catalyst, motivator, and facilitator thereby leading the students to pursue a career in financial market in today's competitive financial world.

I hope, this book will definitely create sustained interest in the minds of the students and researchers in particular and guide the industry as regards to the characteristics which are to be incorporated into the product to strengthen anticipating investor's needs in purchase decision. The financial world is simply too unpredictable. The book has tried here to provide some inputs and tools to help the industry as well as investors make better decision, which should lead to improved results.

I would like to thank Himalaya Publishing House Pvt. Ltd. For publishing this book. I wish to express my appreciation to Mr. Bijoy Kumar Ojha, Himalaya Publishing House Pvt. Ltd. for bringing out the book in a record time. Last but not the least, I have to keep in record that I am solely responsible for errors/omissions that have crept in advertently in the publication. At the same time, I would welcome suggestions from readers in this regard.

Prof. Naliniprava Tripathy

CONTENTS

	Subject	Page No.
CH-1	Market Efficiency of Indian Stock Markets	1 - 33
CH-2	Derivatives Trading on Indian Stock Market	34 - 61
CH-3	Expiration and Week effect on Indian Derivative Market	62 - 82
CH-4	Currency Derivatives in Indian Stock Market	83 - 92
CH-5	Commodity Market in India	93 - 117
CH-6	Behavior Dynamics of Indian IPO Market	118 - 132
CH-7	Stock Market, Market Capitalization and Net FII Investments in India	133 - 141
CH-8	Indian Stock Market, Trading Volume, Exchange Rate, and Standard Gold Rate	142 - 152
CH-9	FII Investment and Indian Stock Market Performance	153 - 179
CH-10	Dividend Policies and Practices in Indian stock market	180 - 200
CH-11	Indian Stock Market Reaction to Announcement of Bonus Issue	201 - 213
CH-12	GDR Market in India	214- 232
Ch-13	Emerging Market and Developed Market	233 - 250
CH-14	Performance Evaluation of Mutual Funds in India	251 - 280
CH-15	Mutual Fund Investors Behavior Model in Indian Stock Market	281 - 292
CH-16	A Service Quality Model for Customers in Public Sector Banks	293 - 299
CH-17	Holistic Approach for Debit Card Consumers in India	300 - 322
CH-18	Inclusive Growth: Role of Insurance Industry in India	323 - 340
	References	341 - 358

1

Market Efficiency of Indian Stock Markets

Indian Stock market is being regarded as the barometer of the health of the economy. This chapter explores the daily nifty movements as well as wide range of economic events. This chapter concludes that the market would react very sharply to economic, political and policy issues. Hence. the market participants should take care of their portfolio while investing in volatile months.

INTRODUCTION

The Indian authorities have been prioritizing the development of the financial market as a top item on the economic agenda. The vision of the financial market is aiming to help and facilitate the development of the Indian economy as well as sustaining its competitiveness in the international financial market arena. To achieve this goal, the Indian financial market strategic objectives are providing an effective source of financing, creating a favorable investment environment with a diverse investor base, providing a world-class infrastructure with low transaction cost, encouraging an establishment of strong and qualified institutional intermediaries and promoting "Good Corporate Governance" and any necessary measures that serve the appropriate needs of investors. Indian financial market has been going through a fascinating phase and it throws open excellent business opportunities to the financial service sectors.

Financial market is classified into two categories, i.e., money market and capital market. Money market deals with short-term loans and capital market deals with long-term loans. Capital market supplies funds for financing the fixed capital requirement of trade and commerce as well as the long-term requirements of the Government. The long-term funds are made available through various instruments such as debentures, preference shares, and common shares. The capital market is classified into two categories, namely, (i) primary market or new issue market, and (ii) secondary market or stock exchange. As a rule, only when a country's primary market is alone, it is possible to ensure a good degree of activity in the secondary market because it is the primary market which ensures a continuous flow of securities to the secondary market. On the contrary, if secondary market is only active but not transparent and disciplined, it becomes difficult to develop and sustain the cult of equity and related investment in the primary market. This is because the liquidity which the secondary market imparts to such investments in the hands of the investors is adversely affected.

A stock exchange is often the most important component of a stock market. Supply and demand in stock markets is driven by various factors which affect the price of stocks. At the stock exchange, share prices rise and fall depending, largely, on market forces. Share prices tend to rise or remain stable when companies and the economy in general show signs of stability and growth. An economic recession, depression, or financial crisis could eventually lead to a stock market crash. Therefore, the movement of share prices and stock indexes is an indicator of the general trend of the economy. The stock market is an important institution for capitalist countries because it encourages investment in corporate securities, providing capital for new businesses and income for investors. In 1990s, large numbers of ordinary persons have come to own stock through pension funds, deferred employee savings plans, investment clubs, or mutual funds.

The financial system in most western countries has undergone a remarkable transformation. One feature of this development is disintermediation. A portion of the funds involved in saving and financing flows directly to the financial markets instead of being routed via banks' traditional lending and deposit operations. The general public's heightened interest in investing in the stock market, either directly or through mutual funds, has been an important component of this process. The trend towards form of saving with a higher risk has been accentuated by new rules for most funds and insurance, permitting a higher proportion of shares to bonds. Similar tendencies are also found in other industrialized countries. In all developed economic systems, such as the European Union, the United States, Japan and other first world countries, the trend has been the same: saving has moved away from traditional bank deposits to more risky securities of one sort or another.

Statistics show that in recent decades shares have made up an increasingly large proportion of households' financial assets in many countries. In the 1970s, in Sweden, deposit accounts almost 60 per cent of households' financial wealth, as against less than 20 per cent in the 2000s. The major part of this adjustment in financial portfolios has gone directly to shares. But now a good deal takes the form of various kinds of institutional investment for groups of individuals, e.g., pension funds, mutual funds, hedge funds, insurance investment of premiums, etc.

IMPORTANCE OF STOCK MARKETS

Stock markets constitute an important part of the total infrastructure for every society that has passed the stage of largely domestic economies. The financial system performs three main tasks: first, it handles transfer of payments; second, it channels savings to investments with a good return for future consumption; and third, it spreads and reduces economic risks in relation to the players' targeted returns. Moreover, an unforeseen risk, or catastrophic risks, is not being capable of being spread, or insured against. The smooth functioning of all these activities facilitates economic growth in that lower cost and enterprise risks promote the production of goods and services as well as employment. In this way, the financial system contributes to increase prosperity. The stock market is one of the most important sources for companies to raise money. Experience has shown that the price of shares and other assets is an important part of the dynamics of economic growth. Rising share prices, for instance, tend to be associated with increased business investment and *vice versa*. Share prices also affect the wealth of households and their consumption. Therefore, central banks tend to keep an eye on the control and behavior of the stock market for smooth operation of financial system functions.

BRIEF HISTORY OF MARKET EFFICIENCY

The concept of market efficiency was first anticipated at the beginning of the century by Bachelier (1900). Bachelier recognizes that past, present and even discounted future events are reflected in market price, but often show no apparent relation to price changes. Eugene Fama defined Market Efficiency that security prices reflect all available information. Reilly and Brown in 1997 defined an efficient market as one in which stock prices adjust rapidly when new information arrives and, therefore, the current prices of stocks have already reflected all information about the stock. Thus, the market leaves no pattern to exploit the trading opportunities and to make economic gains. High liquidity in the market is an important requisite for determining market efficiency as market with low liquidity is not in a condition to adjust to the information quickly. To test the market efficiency, we need to look at the pattern of short-term movements of the combined market returns and try to identify the principle governing those returns. If the market is efficient, then we can say that no particular pattern is followed and they follow a random walk process. If a model is able to identify the pattern, then historical data can be used to predict the future data.

Efficient Market Hypothesis

Under the efficient market hypothesis (EMH), investors cannot earn abnormal profits on the available information set other than by chance. The term 'market efficiency' is used to explain the relationship between information and share prices in the capital market. It examines the degree, the pace, and the accuracy of the available information being incorporated into security prices.

Stock Price Reflects Information

If one spots that XYZ's stock pattern will guarantee pure profit, he/she shall exploit it by borrowing as much as one can to invest in XYZ stock. This process of exploiting actually makes the opportunity vanish because, then XYZ stock price is bid up; when you think it is hot. Higher prices mean lower expected return. Also the price is bid down when one thinks it is cold. Lower prices mean higher expected return. This means that, the fact that one has figured out a stock price movement is very likely to be reflected by the stock price. The more greedy (which is rational) one is, the faster the pattern will be eliminated. One should also realize that, there exists an "army" of intelligent, well-informed security analysts, arbitrageurs, traders, who spend their lives looking for securities which are mispriced or follow a price moving pattern based on information. This army has high-tech computers, subscription to professional database, and up-to-date information on thousands of firms, state-of-the-art analytical technique among some of the facilities. They can assess, assimilate and act, very quickly. In this intense search, the professional investors may "police" the market so efficiently that they drive the prices of all assets. This price then reflects all available information.

What does this mean?

- Competition for finding any mispriced securities is high.
- This competition always kills the "sure-profit" pattern because if there was one, it would have been exploited by someone who had spotted it before. Thus, "no arbitrage" should hold in this market.
- The first one makes profit, but here net profit ≠ gross profit.
- Prices are unpredictable. This means that stock prices should reflect "all available information".
- Thus, stock prices change by reacting only to "new information".
- This fact that the information is new means that the stock prices are unpredictable.

Unpredictability arises due to:

- Stock prices should have reflected all available information, which is not necessarily true.
- Stock prices should be unpredictable.

TYPES OF MARKET EFFICIENCY

There are three types of market efficiencies:

♦ Weak Form of Efficiency

It is also known as '*Random Walk*' theory. It means that there is no point in studying historical data prices as the current prices fully incorporates all the information of the past. In other words, it says that there is no need to do technical analysis of the historical data. Random Walk is the path of a variable over time that exhibits no predictable patterns at all. If price,. p, moves in a random walk, the value of p in any period will be equal to the value of p in the period before, plus or minus some random variable. The random walk hypothesis (RWH) states that the present market price is the best indicator of the future market prices with an error term that is stochastic in nature. In an efficient market, it is not possible to make profit based on the past information. Hence, the prediction of future price conditional on the past prices on an average should be zero. The more efficient a market is the more random and unpredictable the market returns would be. In the most efficient market, the future prices is totally random and the prices formation is assumed to be a stochastic process.

There have been four major methods to test this weak form of market efficiency:

- Serial Correlation test
- Filter test
- Cyclical test
- Volatility test

◆ Semi-strong Form of Market Efficiency

It says that the current market prices of the stocks fully reflect all the information present to the public like corporate reports, Dividend Policy, forthcoming stock splits, technical breakthroughs, resignation of top executives and so on. Thus, any effort by analysts and investors to analyze the reports to gain from the stock market will be ineffective as the information is already incorporated in the stock prices. Hence, it is too late for the investors to wait for the announcement of the reports. The testing of Semi-strong form of EMH includes the testing of market reaction to accounting information, stock split, and block trading. If semi-strong efficiency is true, it undermines the work of millions of fundamental analysts whose trading rules cannot be applied to produce abnormal returns because all publicly available information is already reflected in the share price. The analyst try to estimate the value of the stocks based on the information available and then compare it with the prices in the market to watch gain. The information can be following:

- Growth projections
- Industry environment
- Company announcements
- Details of company's financials
- Technological and social change

◆ Strong Form of Market Efficiency

It says that all the information is useless in the stock market even the information available privately. In other words, the current stock prices instantaneously and fully reflect all known information about the securities including the privately available inside information. The focus lies on the phenomenon of 'Insider Trading'. It is possible to trade share with the knowledge of information not in the public domain and make abnormal profits. This will make investors believe that the market is an unfair scenario and hence they will be reluctant to invest which in turn will not be good for the society as a whole. Insider trading is considered to be a bad thing and hence is illegal in many countries including India.

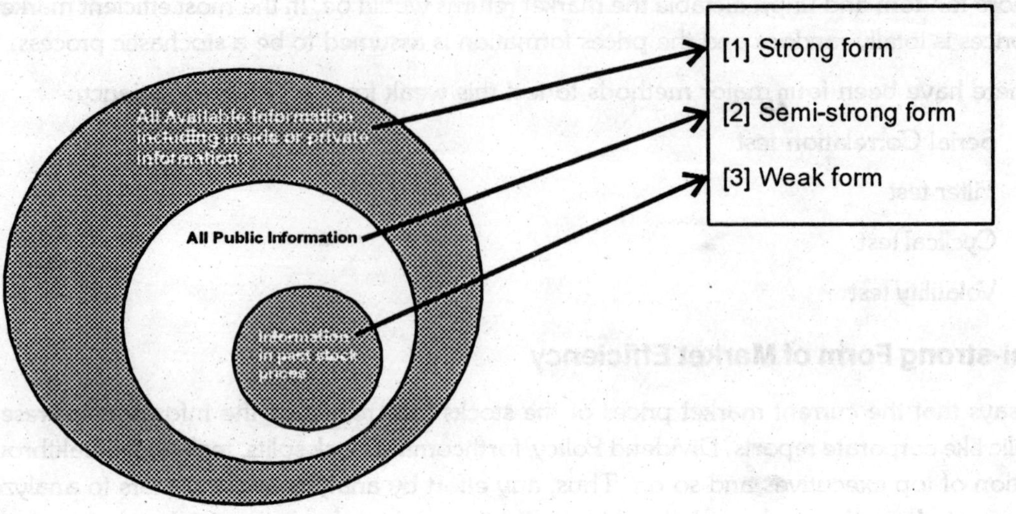

Fig. 1

STOCK EXCHANGES

Though a number of other exchanges exist, NSE and the BSE are the two most significant stock exchanges in India. Between them, they are responsible for the vast majority of share transactions.

NSE: National Stock Exchange

This Mumbai-based stock exchange is the largest stock exchange in India in terms of daily turnover and number of trades — for both equities and derivative trading. NSE is expected to become the biggest stock exchange in India in terms of market capitalization by 2009-end. The NSE's key index is the S&P CNX Nifty, popularly known as the Nifty, an index of fifty major stocks which have been weighted by market capitalization.

NSE is mutually-owned by a set of leading financial institutions, banks, insurance companies and other financial intermediaries in India. Its ownership and management operate as separate entities. There are at least 2 foreign investors namely NYSE Euronext and Goldman Sachs who have a stake in the NSE. In October 2007, the equity market capitalization of the companies listed on the NSE was US $ 1.46 trillion, which made it the second largest stock exchange in South Asia. It is also the third largest Stock Exchange in the world in terms of the number of trades in equities. Further, it is the second fastest growing stock exchange in the world with a recorded growth of 16.6%.

It has consistently remained in the forefront of modernization of India's capital and financial markets. Following are some of the reasons why NSE is among the most important stock exchanges of the world:

- It is the first national, anonymous, electronic limit order book (LOB) exchange to trade securities in India.
- It set up "National Securities Clearing Corporation Ltd.", the first clearing corporation in India.
- It co-promoted the "National Securities Depository Ltd.", the first depository in India.

- Setting up of S&P CNX Nifty.
- It pioneered the commencement of Internet Trading in February 2000.
- It was the first exchange to propose the exchange of traded derivatives, particularly on an equity index, in 1996. After four years of policy and regulatory debate, it was permitted to start trading equity derivatives.
- It is the only exchange to trade GOLD ETFs (exchange traded funds) in India.
- NSE became the first stock exchange to get approval for Interest rate futures as recommended by SEBI-RBI committee, on 31 August, 2009, a futures contract based on 7% 10 Year GOI bond (NOTIONAL) was launched with quarterly maturities.

WHY IT IS IMPORTANT TO STUDY EFFICIENCY OF INDIAN STOCK MARKET?

The stock market of India have witnessed a radical transformation in last decade. The adoption of international quality trading, settlement mechanisms and reduction of transactions costs have made the investors, domestic and foreign, more optimistic which in turn evidenced a considerable growth in market volume and liquidity. The market features a developed regulatory framework, a modern market infrastructure, removal of barriers to the international equity investment, better allocation and mobilization of resources and increased transparency. All these infer better efficiency of Indian stock market. Despite this transformation, Indian stock market has recently shown greater volatility due to global financial crisis which has affected the informational efficiency of markets. With fall in stock prices on news that Lehman Brothers, Merrill Lynch, and many other investment bankers and companies collapsed, Indian stock market has seen its worst time with the global financial crisis. Mostly all the industrial sectors have experienced a consistent low in their stock prices. The Sensex which had reached historically high levels in the beginning of 2008, declined to its levels three years back. Similar trend has also been observed for the S&P CNX Nifty. The movements in Sensex and CNX Nifty between January 2007 and July 2009 are shown in the following Figure 2.

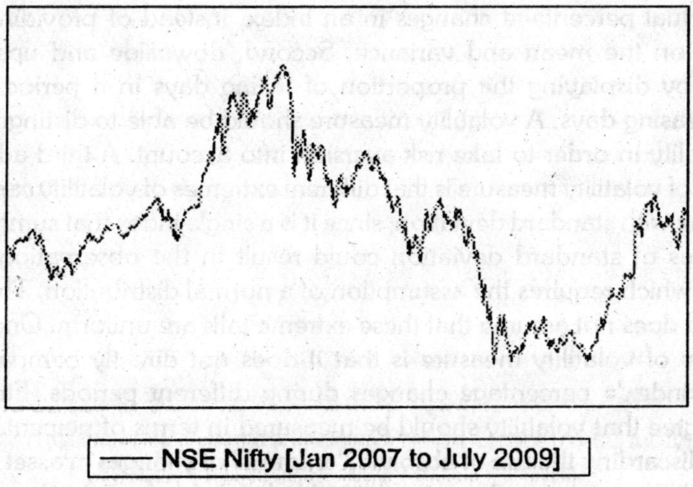

Fig. 2

However, Indian stock market showed remarkable resistance to the winds from the international financial implosion. Now, the stock market of India has returned to its previous growth track in spite of a greater degree of volatility. In this context, it is very much essential to study the efficiency of Indian stock market as the possibility of undervaluation or overvaluation of a sizable amount of stock prices is there.

WHAT IS STOCK MARKET VOLATILITY?

Considerable attention has been paid to overall stock market volatility after stock market crash of October 19, 1987. Volatility is a measure of fluctuations in share price. Volatility is an important factor in the comparison of risk and reward between stocks and other asset classes. This comparison helps to determine the appropriate strategic asset allocation for an investor. One well-known conclusion of empirical studies pertaining to security markets is that the volatility of asset returns tends to change over time. While changing volatility is apparent in most markets, it is perhaps most evident in stock markets. There are two fundamentally different approaches for the determination of volatility. On one hand, it is possible to determine the historical volatility by measuring the (standard deviation) prices for any particular security or index over a given period of time. On the other hand, one might look for the volatility which is currently implied by option prices, i.e., the implied volatility, based on the assumptions of the trades involved. A drawback to using the standard deviation of returns is that it assumes that stock market returns are normally distributed. Standard deviation can reflect only an index's historical volatility. To gain any knowledge about future volatility, an investor has to make the assumption that future volatility is represented by the distribution of historical volatility results. One way to avoid this assumption is to allow investors to tell us what their expectations are for volatility in the future. In an effort to neutralize some of the disadvantages of using the standard deviation, investors can use another potential proxy for stock market volatility, the "percentage of days of volatility." The percentage of days of volatility is a measurement of the percentage of days in a period when an index level goes up or down a certain percentage or more. There are advantages to using the percentage of days of volatility measure over standard deviation. First, although it uses historical information instead of expectations of volatility, it does not assume that the data are normally distributed. This measurement summarizes the actual percentage changes in an index, instead of providing an estimate of the distribution based on the mean and variance. Second, downside and upside volatility can be shown separately by displaying the proportion of falling days in a period separately from the percentage of increasing days. A volatility measure should be able to distinguish between positive and negative volatility in order to take risk aversion into account. A third advantage to using the percentage of days of volatility measure is that different extremes of volatility can be tested separately. This cannot be done with standard deviation, since it is a single index that summarizes total volatility. Measuring extremes of standard deviation could result in the observation of "three-standard-deviation events," which requires the assumption of a normal distribution. The percentage of days of volatility method does not assume that these extreme tails are uniform. One disadvantage of the percentage of days of volatility measure is that it does not directly compare the differences in magnitude of the index's percentage changes during different periods. Finance academicians, however, widely agree that volatility should be measured in terms of percentage changes in prices or rates of return, discarding the use of absolute "amount" of changes in asset prices. Point changes usually exceed percentage change because the index levels from where the prices move are often greater than 100. Thus, the point changes mostly favored by press overestimate and create a false impression regarding magnitude of volatility among investors. Present study here also relies on percentage not on point changes of prices, the approach that is rightly followed by financial economists. The percentage changes in prices, in fact, reflect the rates of return.

International Comparison:

Table 1

Average Daily Return and Volatility of International Indices during 2010

Country	***Index***	***Return***	***Volatility***
Developed Market			
Australia	All Ordinaries	-0.1	1.2
France	CAC 40	-0.1	1.7
Germany	Dax	0.0	1.2
Hong Kong	Hang Sang	0.1	1.2
Japan	Nikkei 225	-0.2	1.7
Singapore	Straits Times	0.1	1.0
UK	FTSE 100	-0.2	1.1
USA	Dow Jones Indus Avg	-0.1	1.5
USA	Nasdaq Composite	-0.2	1.8
Emerging Market			
India	Sensex 30	0.2	1.2
India	S&P CNX Nifty	0.2	1.2
Argentina	Indice Bolsa General	0.0	1.5
Brazil	Bovespa	-0.2	1.5
Chile	Stock Market select	0.2	0.8
China	Shanghai SE Composite IX	-0.4	1.5
Colombia	IGBC General	0.1	0.5
Egypt	Hermes	-0.3	1.2
Hungary	Budapest Stock Exchange	-0.2	1.4
Indonesia	Jakarta Composite	0.2	1.3
Malaysia	FTSE Bursa Malaysia KLCI	0.1	0.6
Mexico	Bolsa	-0.1	1.3
Pakistan	Karachi 30	0.2	1.6
Russia	Russian Traded	-0.2	2.0
South Korea	Kospi Index	0.2	0.9
South Africa	FTSE/JSE Africa All Share	-0.2	1.3
Taiwan	Taiwan Taiex	0.0	1.3
Thailand	Stock Exchange of Thai	0.3	1.0
Turkey	ISE National 100	0.0	1.0

Source: SEBI Bulletin, July 2010

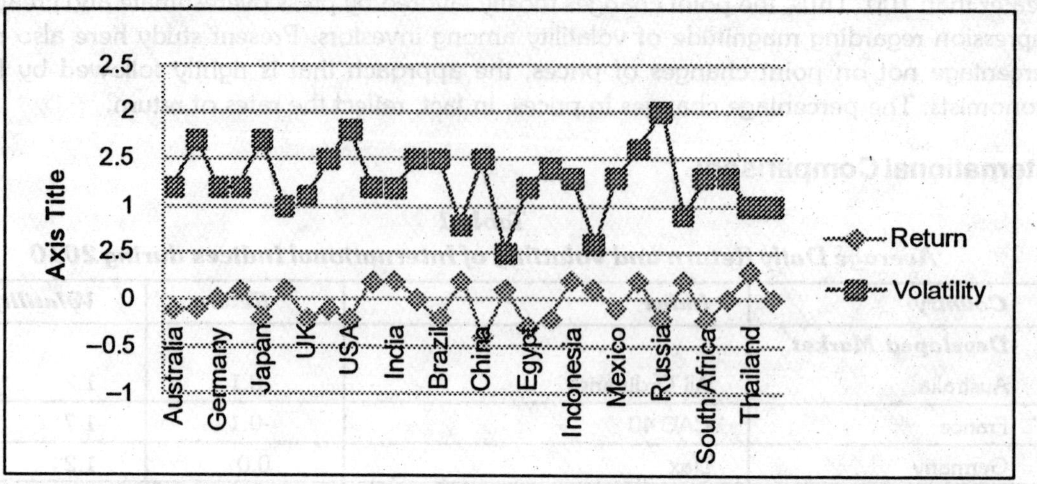

Fig. 3: Average Daily Return and Volatility of International Indices during 2010

It is evident from Table 1 and Fig. 3 that the average daily return of Hang Sang index and Straits Times Index are 0.1 per cent followed by Dow Jones Indus AVE Index is –0.1 per cent. All developed market are showing negative average daily return. But the average return of stock exchange of Thai Index is 0.3 per cent followed by Jakarta composite index (0.2 per cent), Sensex (0.2 per cent), S&P Nifty of India also showing positive return. The performance of emerging is comparatively is better than developed market. The volatility of developed market is also high in comparison to emerging market.

LITERATURE REVIEW

Since the last decade, India has gradually as an important destination of global investors' investment in emerging markets. But the highly fluctuating nature of such flows has been a matter of concern for economics receiving these investments. Indian stock markets have been notoriously well known for significant price fluctuations in short time spans. Stock market volatility can have a wide repercussion on the economy as a whole. Policy makers therefore rely on market estimates of volatility as a barometer of the vulnerability of financial markets. The existence of excessive volatility or "noise" also undermines the usefulness of stock prices as a "signal" about the true intrinsic value of a firm, a concept that is core to the paradigm of informational efficiency of markets. Further, volatility estimation and forecasting have become a compulsory risk management exercise for economies and many financial institutions around the world. Understanding volatility is, therefore, central to risk management in an economy. It can be used to measure the market risk of a single instrument or an entire portfolio of instruments. An important aspect of volatility is its emphasis on the variability, rather than the direction of price movement. The fluctuation in the market prices is a major concern to investors. Stock prices and there volatility, which has become prevalent feature of securities markets, adds to the concern. The index number of stock prices has been widely used by researches around the world for measuring volatility of stock returns.

A number of studies have been carried out to measure the volatility of the market. For an emerging and transition economy, this is an interesting one since these economies operate in unique economic, technological and social environments. Hence, it is important to investigate the extent of volatility behavior of the index. A comprehensive literature survey was done to understand past works carried out in this area. Though there have been a few studies done related to this area, most of the studies have been done on developed markets and few have done on the Indian market. Broadly, the researchers examined the volatility patterns of different time periods ranging from 80s to early 2000. After reviewing the past studies, it has been felt that there is a need to measure to the extent of volatility during period 1991 to 2008. Malay and Madhusudan (1995) have examined two key issues: (a) What is the average level of volatility and whether it has increased in the current period; (b) Whether the present trend of share price movement is likely to impair the development process of our economy. In each instance, the conclusion is essentially the same, i.e., stock market volatility has increased in the study period. Dilbagh S. Broca (1995) has developed and tested a methodology for identifying changes in the volatility of aggregate share prices prevalent on the Bombay stock exchange as represented by the Sensex. Application of the "control chart" approach on daily Sensex returns over 1990-1992 reveals several volatility changes, some of which either signal the onset/decline of speculative manias witnessed in recent years or coincide with release of budget news. Broca (1993a, 1993b, 1994 and 1995) and conclude that there is mixed evidence of return and volatility spillover between the US tried to measure the level of average volatility and examined the effects of volatility on the growth process of an economy. Harvinder Kaur (2004) has examined the volatility in the Indian stock market and Indian markets. Seth and Saloni (2005) examined the volatility of common stock from the period 1980 to 2003. Standard deviations of daily returns and monthly returns are calculated to gauge the size of the volatility. The study concludes that the stock market returns follow a deterministic path implying that stock returns oscillate between excess and under return, passing through the mean stock return. Hence, the acceptable limits of volatility for the decision making of investors, depending on the type of investors can be made.

The issue of volatility and risk has become increasingly important in recent times to financial practitioners, market participants, regulators and researchers. Keeping in view, the present study has been carried out to measure the extent of volatility of nifty, volatility spikes and to understand the volatility behavior of the Indian stock markets.

LET US TAKE CASE OF S&P CNX NIFTY FOR TESTING VOLATILITY BEHAVIOUR OF MARKET

The stock market indices are fairly representative of various industry sectors and trading activity mostly revolves around the stocks comprising the indices. S&P CNX Nifty is a well-diversified 50 stock index accounting for 23 sectors of the economy. S&P CNX Nifty average total traded value of all nifty stocks was approximately 58% of total value of all stocks on the NSE. Nifty stocks represented about 60% of the total market capitalization on March 31, 2005. It is also taken to be an indicator of the performance of the overall economy or a particular sector of the economy. The stock price data of Nifty has been collected from NSE website, which is maintained by National Stock Exchange of India. Additionally, leading financial dailies such as *The Economic Times*, *Business Line*, *Business Standard*, *Prowess* and business magazines etc. have also been referred for this chapter.

The following methods have aided in analyzing and interpreting the data. A brief description has been provided of all the methods used.

In the present chapter, volatility has been measured as the standard deviation of the rates of return. The rate of return is the logarithmic difference of prices of two successive periods. Symbolically, it may be stated as follows:

$$r_t = \log\left(\frac{p_t}{p_{t-1}}\right) * 100$$

Where log is natural logarithm

p_t and p_{t-1} are the prices for the two successive periods

Daily and monthly volatility have been annualized by multiplying them with the square root of the number of trading days and the number of months in a year, respectively. While annualizing the returns, the multiplier used is the number of trading days and the number of months in a year respectively.

Standard Deviation

The standard deviation of a probability distribution, random variable, or population or multi set of values is defined as the square root of the variance.

The standard deviation is measured in the same units as the values of the population. For a population of distances in meters, the standard deviation is also measured in meters, whereas the variance is measured in square meters.

At least 75% of the values in any population are at most two standard deviations away from the mean. The actual percentage depends on the distribution; for example, it is approximately 95% if the population has a normal distribution.

The standard deviation is the root mean square (RMS) deviation of the values from their arithmetic mean. Standard deviation may serve as a measure of uncertainty. Standard deviation is the most common measure of statistical dispersion, measuring how widely spread the values in a data set is:

Standard Deviation of a Random Variable

The standard deviation of a random variable X is defined as:

$$\sigma = \sqrt{E\left((X - E(X))^2\right)} = \sqrt{E(X^2) - (E(X))^2}$$

Where E(X) is the expected value of X

Not *all* random variables have a standard deviation.

The standard deviation of return [r] from a sample of n observations is the square root of the average squared deviation of returns from the average of the sample. Thus

$$\sigma_p = \left\{ \frac{1}{n} \sum_{t=1}^{n} (R_{pt} - R_p)^2 \right\}^{1/2}$$

Where $R_{pt} = \log_e (p_t/p_{t-1})$

The logarithmic standard deviation is expressed in percentage terms after multiplying it by 100.

A large standard deviation indicates that the data points are far from the mean and a small standard deviation indicates that they are clustered closely around the mean.

Normality Tests

Many statistical tests have been proposed to find out whether a sample is drawn from a normal distribution or not. Here, we discuss the Jarque-Bera test which is based on the classical measures of skewness and kurtosis."The Jarque-Bera statistic has an asymptotic chi-square distribution with two degree of freedom and can be used to test the null hypothesis that the data are from a normal distribution. The null hypothesis is a joint hypothesis of both the skewness and excess kurtosis being 0, since samples from a normal distribution have an expected skewness of 0 and an expected excess kurtosis of 0. As the definition of JB shows, any deviation from this increases the JB statistic."

Skewness

Skewness is a measure of the asymmetry of the probability distribution of a real-valued random variable. Roughly speaking, a distribution has positive skew (right-skewed) if the right (higher value) tail is longer or fatter and negative skew (left-skewed) if the left (lower value) tail is longer or fatter. The two are often confused, since most of the mass of a right (or left) skewed distribution is to the left (or right) of its respective tail.

Skewness, the third standardized moment, is written as γ_1 and defined as

$$\gamma_1 = \frac{\mu_3}{\sigma^3},$$

Where μ_3 is the third moment about the mean and σ is the standard deviation. Equivalently, skewness can be defined as the ratio of the third cumulant k_3 and the third power of the square root of the second cumulant k_2:

$$\gamma_1 = \frac{\kappa_3}{\kappa_2^{3/2}}$$

For a sample of *n* values, the *sample skewness* is

$$g_1 = \frac{m_3}{m_2^{3/2}} = \frac{\sqrt{n}\Sigma_{i=1}^{n}(\chi_i - \overline{\chi})^3}{\left(\Sigma_{i=1}^{n}(\chi_i - \overline{\chi})^2\right)^{3/2}},$$

Where x_i is the ith value, $\overline{x}$ is the sample mean, m_3 is the sample third central moment, and m_2 is the sample variance.

Given samples from a population, the equation for the sample skewness g_1 above is a biased estimator of the population skewness. The usual estimator of skewness is

$$G_1 = \frac{k_3}{k_2^{3/2}} = \frac{\sqrt{n(n-1)}}{n-2} g_1,$$

Where k_3 is the unique symmetric unbiased estimator of the third cumulant and k_2 is the symmetric unbiased estimator of the second cumulant. Unfortunately G_1 is, nevertheless, generally biased. Its expected value can even have the opposite sign from the true skewness.

The skewness of a random variable X is sometimes denoted Skew[X]. If Y is the sum of n independent random variables, all with the same distribution as X, then it can be shown that Skew[Y] = Skew[X] /n.

Skewness has benefits in many areas. Many simplistic models assume normal distribution, i.e., data is symmetric about the mean. But in reality, data points are not perfectly symmetric. So, an understanding of the skewness of the dataset indicates whether deviations from the mean are going to be positive or negative.

Kurtosis

Kurtosis is a measure of the "peakedness" of the probability distribution of a real-valued random variable. Higher kurtosis means more of the variance is due to infrequent extreme deviations, as opposed to frequent modestly-sized deviations.

The fourth standardized moment is defined as μ_4/σ^4, where μ_4 is the fourth moment about the mean and σ is the standard deviation. This is sometimes used as the definition of kurtosis in older works, but is not the definition used here.

Kurtosis is more commonly defined as the fourth cumulant divided by the square of the variance of the probability distribution,

$$\gamma_2 = \frac{k_4}{k_2^2} = \frac{\mu_4}{\sigma^4} - 3,$$

which is known as excess kurtosis. The "minus 3" at the end of this formula is often explained as a correction to make the kurtosis of the normal distribution equal to zero. Another reason can be seen by looking at the formula for the kurtosis of the sum of random variables. Because of the use of the cumulant, if Y is the sum of n independent random variables, all with the same distribution as X, then Kurt[Y] = Kurt[X]/n, while the formula would be more complicated if kurtosis were defined as μ_4/σ^4.

More generally, if $X_1, \ldots, X_n$ are independent random variables all having the same variance, then

$$\mathrm{kurt}\left(\sum_{i=1}^{n} X_i\right) = \frac{1}{n^2}\sum_{i=1}^{n} \mathrm{Kurt}(Xi)$$

Whereas this identity would not hold if the definition did not include the subtraction of 3.

A high kurtosis distribution has a sharper "peak" and fatter "tails", while a low kurtosis distribution has a more rounded peak with wider "shoulders".

Distributions with zero kurtosis are called mesokurtic. A distribution with positive kurtosis is called leptokurtic. In terms of shape, a leptokurtic distribution has a more acute "peak" around the mean (that is, a higher probability than a normally distributed variable of values near the mean) and "fat tails" (that is, a higher probability than a normally distributed variable of extreme values). A distribution with negative kurtosis is called platykurtic. In terms of shape, a platykurtic distribution has a smaller "peak" around the mean (that is, a lower probability than a normally distributed variable of values near the mean) and "thin tails" (that is, a lower probability than a normally distributed variable of extreme values).

In statistics, the Jarque-Bera test is a goodness-of-fit measure of departure from normality, based on the sample kurtosis and skewness. The test is named after Carlos Jarque and Anil K. Bera. The test statistic *JB* is defined as

$$JB = \frac{n}{6}\left(S^2 + \frac{1}{4}K^2\right)$$

Where *n* is the number of observations (or degrees of freedom in general); *S* is the sample skewness, and *K* is the sample kurtosis:

$$S = \frac{\hat{\mu}_3}{\hat{\sigma}^3} = \frac{\frac{1}{n}\sum_{i=1}^{n}(\chi_i - \overline{\chi})^3}{\left(\frac{1}{n}\sum_{i=1}^{n}(\chi_i - \overline{\chi})^2\right)^{3/2}}$$

$$K = \frac{\hat{\mu}_4}{\hat{\sigma}^4} - 3 = \frac{\frac{1}{n}\sum_{i=1}^{n}(\chi_i - \overline{\chi})^4}{\left(\frac{1}{n}\sum_{i=1}^{n}(\chi_i - \overline{\chi})^2\right)^2} - 3,$$

where $\hat{\mu}_3$ and $\hat{\mu}_4$ are the estimates of third and fourth central moments, respectively, $\overline{\chi}$ is the sample mean, and is the estimate of the second central moment, the variance.

When the GARCH model is estimated, the normality test is obtained using the standardized residuals $\hat{\upsilon}_1 = \hat{\varepsilon}_1 / \sqrt{\hbar_1}$. The normality test can be used to detect misspecification of the family of ARCH models.

Selecting Forecasting Models:

Normally, it is easy to use unit root tests as investigative tools for selecting forecasting models. Difference stationary and trend stationary models of economic and financial time series often imply very different predictions, so deciding about the model is extremely important for forecasters. Forecasters face three choices: always difference the data, never difference, or use a unit root pretest. There are several preliminary steps for using time series data in econometric analyses. Initially it is essential to determine the form in which the data can be used for any subsequent estimation; in many instances using macroeconomic data in their levels leads to serious econometric problems. Time series data typically contains a trend, which must be removed prior to undertaking any estimation. The traditional detrending procedure separates the trend from the cyclical component of the series. This procedure is appropriate for trend stationary (TS) time series. However, many macroeconomic time series are difference stationary (DS). DS type time series are non-stationary and they contain unit roots. The DS type sequences must be differenced prior to any meaningful econometric estimation. If ordinary least squares (OLS) estimation techniques are applied to indifferences, DS type sequences, resulting error terms are serially correlated. The actual determination of whether a variable is TS or DS is based upon the results of unit root tests. Numerous unit root tests have been presented in economic literature; the most common test, and the chapter here utilized is the augmented Dickey-Fuller test. If one can reject the null hypothesis that a series possesses a unit root, then the series is TS, or integrated of order zero (I(0)). If one cannot reject the null of a unit root, then the series is DS. Subsequent unit root tests on differenced DS series determine the form in which the data may be used in regressions. The most common occurrence is that first differences of DS series are stationary; in this case the series is said to be integrated of order one (I(1)) and no further differencing of the data or unit root testing is required.

When multiple individual time series variables are found to be integrated of order one, an additional test is required to determine whether long-term relationships exist among the variables. Co-integration tests indicate the presence of such stable long-term relationships. Different estimation procedures are required for co-integrated variables than for non-co-integrated DS series.

Moreover, economic and finance theory often suggests the existence of long-run equilibrium relationships among non-stationary time series variables. If these variables are I(1), then co-integration techniques can be used to model these long-run relations. Hence, pre-testing for unit roots is often a first step in the co-integration modeling.

This chapter used Unit Root Tests and PP test for the study. The most popular unit root rest is the ADF (Augment Dickey- Fuller, 1979) test. PP proposes a non-parametric method of controlling for higher-order serial correlation in a series.

The initial step in the estimation involves the determination of the time-series property of each variable individually by conducting unit root tests.

Statistical Issues with Unit Root Tests:

Conceptually, the unit root tests are straightforward. In practice, however, there are a number of difficulties:

- Unit root tests generally have non-standard and non-normal asymptotic distributions.

- These distributions are functions of standard Brownian motions, and do not have convenient closed form expressions. Consequently, critical values must be calculated using simulation methods.
- The distributions are affected by the inclusion of deterministic terms, e.g., constant, time trend, dummy variables, and so different sets of critical values must be used for test regressions with different deterministic terms.

Dicky and Fuller (1979) consider three different regression equations that can be used to test for the presence of a unit root.

$$X_t = p X_{t-1} + e_t$$

$$X_t = a_0 + p X_{t-1} + e_t$$

$$X_t = a_o + p X_{t-1} + a_{1t} + e_t$$

The difference between the three regressions concerns the presence of the deterministic elements a_0 and a_{1t}. Equation '1' is a pure random walk model, equation '2' adds an intercept/drift term and equation '3' includes both a drift and linear time trend.

If p=1, the series contains a unit root. In this test the null hypothesis is H_0: p=1 in which case it is said X has a unit root. The alternative is H_1: p<1. If the alternative hypothesis is correct, then X is stationary. But if the null hypothesis is correct, then the variable is non-stationary so the tests do not apply here.

The Augmented Dickey-Fuller test simply includes AR (p) terms of the Δ Xt, term in the three alternative models.

$$\Delta X_t =_\gamma X_{t-1} + \sum_{i=1}^{p} \beta_i \Delta X_{t-1} + e_t$$

$$\Delta X_t = \alpha_{0\gamma} X_{t-1} + \sum_{i=1}^{p} \beta_i \Delta X_{t-1} + e_t$$

$$\Delta X_t = \alpha_{0\gamma} X_{t-1} + a_{2t} + \sum_{i=1}^{p} \beta_i \Delta X_{t-1} + e_t$$

The difference between the three regressions again concerns the presence of the deterministic elements a_0 and a_{2t}. If γ=0, the series contains a unit root.

Phillips-Perron (PP) Test:

The non-parametric corrections for serial correlation of the Dickey-Fuller [DF] statistics by Phillips (1987) and Phillips and Perron (1988) are widely used in practice. Here how these unit root tests can be generalized in order to obtain trace statistics for the null hypothesis of no cointegration with limiting distributions free of nuisance parameters are addressed.

PP proposes a non-parametric method of controlling for higher-order serial correlation in a series. The test regression for the PP test is AR (1) process:

$\Delta yt=\alpha+\beta y_{t-1}+\ \varepsilon t$

The PP test makes a correction to the t-statistics of the γ coefficient from the AR (1) regression to account for the serial correlation in ε. The correction is non-parametric since it use an estimate for the sectrum of ε at frequency zero that is robust to Heteroskedasticity and auto correlation of unknown from. The Newey-West Heteroskedasticity auto correlation consistent estimate:

$$W^2=\gamma+2\sum_{j=1}^{q}\left(1-\frac{j}{q+1}\right)rj$$

$$\gamma_j=\frac{1}{T}\sum_{t=j+1}^{t}\bar{\epsilon}_t\bar{\epsilon}_{t-j}$$

Where q is the truncation lag. The PP t-statistics is computed as:

$$t_{pp}=\frac{\gamma o^{1/2}t_b}{W}-\frac{(W^2-\gamma o)TS_b}{2W\bar{\sigma}}$$

Where t_b S_b are the t-statistics and standard error of β and σ is the standard error of the test regression.

ANALYSIS

This chapter here employs unit root test to examine the time series properties of concerned variables. Unit root test speaks of whether a series is stationary or non-stationary. For the test of unit root the present study employees, the Augmented Dicky Fuller (ADF) and Phillips-Perron (PP) Test both with trends and intercept. The results are shown in the Table-2.

Table 2
Unit Root Tests

	ADF	*Phillips-Perron*
With intercept	– 30.45737(0)	– 58.32414(0)
With trend and intercept	– 30.49723(0)	– 58.34098(0)

It is evident from the Table 2 that all the variables considered is stationary. This is because the calculated values of all the variables exceed the critical value at 1%, 5% and 10% significance level in both ADF and PP tests. Hence, the null hypotheses of a unit root are rejected and conclude that all the variables are stationary.

The summary statistics for the S&P CNX Nifty are given in Table 3. All returns are calculated as the first difference of the log of the daily closing price and Fig. 4 graphs the returns on the Nifty index over time. It is found from the Table 3 that the kurtosis is high indicating that the dataset distribution exhibits Leptokurtosis, i.e., the frequency distribution assigns a higher probability to returns around zero as well as very high positive and negative returns. So, Jarque-Bera statistics shows that all the three series are leptokurtic, exhibit non-normality and indicate the presence of heteroskedasticity.

Table 3
Descriptive Statistics

Particulars	***S&P CNX Nifty***
Mean	0.028292
Median	0.040772
Maximum	5.248913
Minimum	–5.669220
Standard Deviation	0.752782
Skewness	–0.172668
Kurtosis	8.766839
Jarque-Bera	5758.696
Probability	0.000000

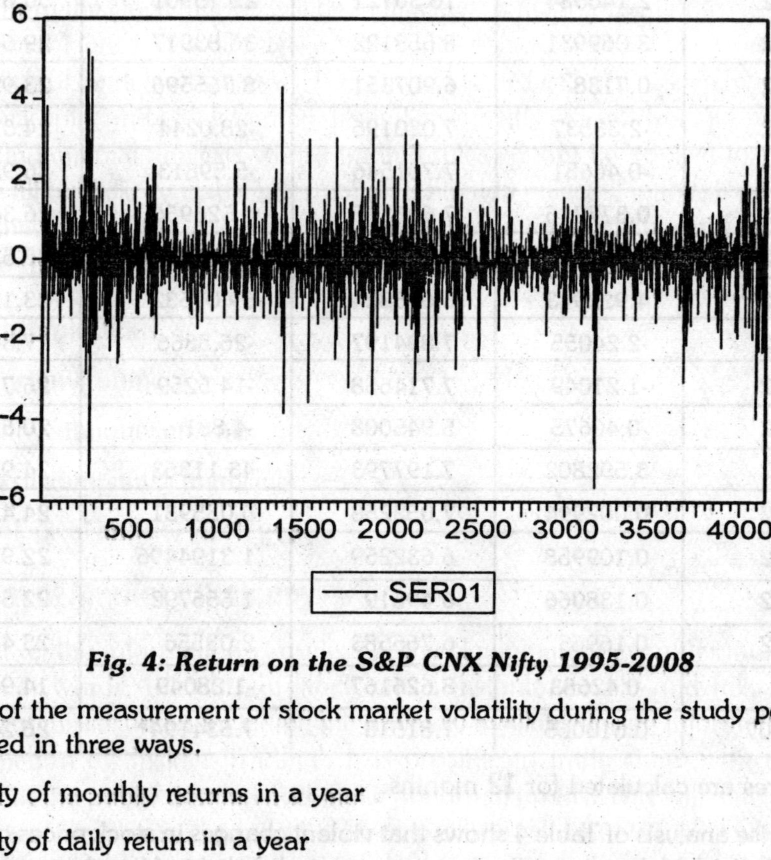

Fig. 4: Return on the S&P CNX Nifty 1995-2008

The result of the measurement of stock market volatility during the study period, i.e., 1991-2008 is generated in three ways.

- Volatility of monthly returns in a year
- Volatility of daily return in a year
- Volatility of daily return in a month

The daily returns have been calculated as the difference between the natural logarithms of the daily closing prices on the consecutive trading days in percentages, while the monthly returns have been calculated as the difference between the natural logarithms of the closing prices on the first and the last trading day of the month.

Volatility of Monthly Returns in a Year:

Table 4 presents the average monthly returns, volatility of monthly returns and their annualized values for Nifty. In Fig. 3, the percentage standard deviations are shown in the vertical and the horizontal axis represents the time period.

Table 4
S&P CNX Nifty: Volatility of Monthly Returns in a Year (1991-2008)

Year	*No. of Months*	*Average Returns (%)*	*Monthly Volatility (%)*	*Annualized Returns (%)*	*Annualized Volatility (%)*
(1)	*(2)*	*(3)*	*(4)*	*(5) = (3) * (2)*	*(6) = (4) * sqrt. (2)*
1991	12	4.217158	8.062941	50.6059	27.93083
1992	12	2.146584	16.36721	25.75901	56.69764
1993	12	3.069931	8.558122	36.83917	29.64619
1994	12	0.7138	6.907351	8.565596	23.92775
1995	12	-2.33537	7.020196	-28.0244	24.31866
1996	12	-0.46651	7.781546	-5.59813	26.95605
1997	12	0.377246	7.606315	4.526956	26.34903
1998	12	-1.39344	7.368712	-16.7213	25.52596
1999	12	4.922943	6.675824	59.07532	23.12572
2000	12	-2.24055	7.894197	-26.8866	27.34629
2001	12	-1.21049	7.714658	-14.5259	26.72435
2002	12	-0.40675	5.945008	-4.881	20.5941
2003	12	3.592802	7.197793	43.11363	24.93387
2004	12	0.002994	7.052258	0.035931	24.42973
2005	12	0.109958	6.632259	1.3194496	22.97481
2006	12	0.138066	6.49619	1.656792	22.50346
2007	12	0.16963	6.766583	2.03556	23.44013
2008	3	-0.42683	8.626167	-1.28049	14.94095
Overall	207	0.610065	7.81518	7.534194*	26.242528*

These figures are calculated for 12 months.

The year-wise analysis of Table 4 shows that violent changes in stock prices occurred in 1992, during which Harshad Mehta securities scam came into limelight. After decreasing sharply in the years immediately after 1992, volatility has increased steadily ever since. For the total period, the overall monthly volatility of Nifty was 7.81518%. The corresponding annualized volatility of Nifty was 26.242528%. While the monthly volatility has been in the range of 5% and 16% approximately, the annualized volatility has been in the range of 20% and 56% approximately.

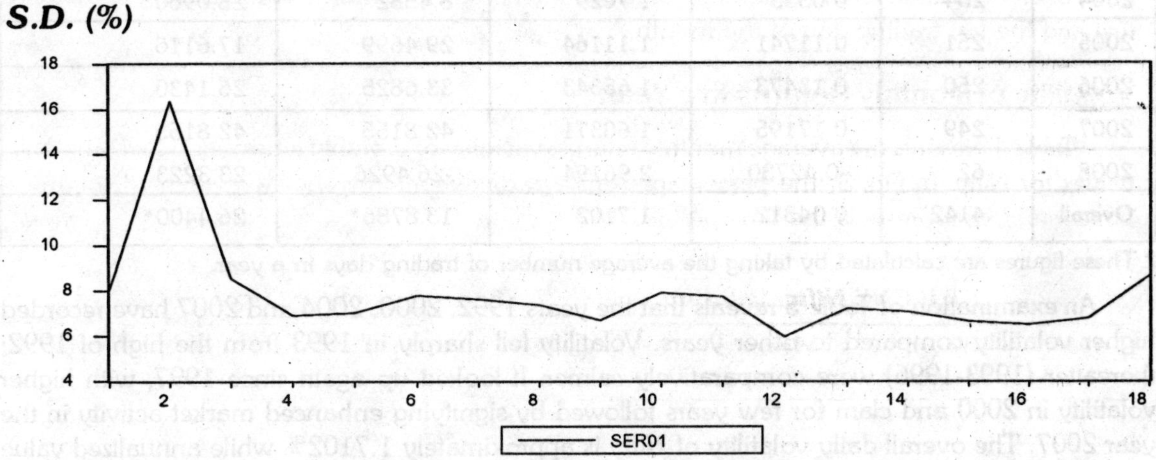

Fig. 5: Yearly Volatility of Monthly Return (%)

Volatility of Daily Returns in a Year:

An attempt has been made here to measure volatility of daily returns in a year. Table 5 shows the average daily return, volatility of daily returns and their annualized values for S&P CNX Nifty.

Table 5

S&P CNX Nifty: Volatility of Daily Returns in a Year (Jan. 1991-Dec. 2008)

Year	*No. of Trading Days in a Year*	*Average Daily Returns (%)*	*Daily Volatility (%)*	*Annualized Returns (%)*	*Annualized Volatility (%)*
(1)	*(2)*	*(3)*	*(4)*	*(5) = (3) * (2)*	*(6) = (4)*sqrt.(2)*
1991	206	0.2733	1.6851	56.2998	24.1857
1992	190	0.1505	3.3156	28.595	45.7023
1993	213	0.1585	1.7435	33.7605	25.4455
1994	230	0.0380	1.3801	8.74	20.9302
1995	236	-0.1120	1.2447	-26.432	19.1214
1996	250	-0.0039	1.5290	-0.975	24.1756
1997	244	0.0571	1.7805	13.9424	27.8122
1998	250	-0.0807	1.7807	-20.175	28.1553
1999	254	0.2007	1.8407	50.9778	29.3359
2000	250	-0.0928	1.9507	-23.2	30.8432
2001	248	-0.0685	1.6330	-16.988	25.7165
2002	251	0.0142	1.0627	3.5642	16.8363
2003	254	0.2117	1.2344	53.7718	19.6730

2004	254	0.0333	1.7629	8.4582	28.0960
2005	251	0.11741	1.11164	29.4699	17.6116
2006	250	0.13473	1.65343	33.6825	26.1430
2007	249	0.17195	1.60371	42.8155	42.8155
2008	62	-0.42730	2.96194	-26.4926	23.3223
Overall	4142	0.04312	1.7102	13.8786*	26.4400*

* These figures are calculated by taking the average number of trading days in a year.

An examination of Table 5 reveals that the years 1992, 2000, 2004 and 2007 have recorded higher volatility compared to other years. Volatility fell sharply in 1993 from the high of 1992; thereafter (1993-1996) were comparatively calmer. It looked up again since 1997, with higher volatility in 2000 and clam for few years followed by signifying enhanced market activity in the year 2007. The overall daily volatility of Nifty is approximately 1.7102% while annualized value was approximately 26.4400%. For each year, the daily volatility was in the range of 1.0627% and 3.3156%. The annualized volatility ranged approximately from 16.8363% to 45.7023%.

Volatility of Daily Returns in a Month:

In the previous sections, volatility of monthly returns in a year and volatility of daily returns in a year have been presented. This section presents measurements of volatility of daily returns in a month. In the literature of financial economics, there is enough evidence of using monthly stock price index to measure volatility. For example, a study by Schwert shows that in the long run, both monthly and daily stock price indices reveal identical trends. But, the information relating to intra-month movement of stock prices gets lost by the use of monthly stock price index and hence is less informative. Minute measurement of volatility based on daily stock price index would be helpful for a better understanding of the pattern of volatility of the Indian stock market. Therefore, volatility of daily returns in each month has been calculated for the Nifty. For one month, on the basis of daily returns within that month, standard deviation has been calculated.

The table 6 presents the data pertaining to the volatility of daily returns in each month for the period January 1991 to December 2008. A close observation of the table reveals that volatility has varied across months in a year and across years. The most volatile year of all the years was 1992. Majority of the months in the year 1992 were the most volatile as compared to the corresponding months in other years. Similarly, the year 2008 for the first three months is volatile months.

Further among the month's average values, April has been the most volatile followed by March, May and February. This trend could be attributed to the fact that most hectic economic activities during the year particularly the presentation of budgets, both Union and Railway. There is a lot of speculation before and after presentation of budgets. After the presentation of the budget, the market reacts to the actual announcements made as part of the budget.

Table 6
S&P CNX Nifty: Volatility of Daily Returns in a Month (Jan 1991 to Dec 2008)

Months	Volatility (%)																	
	1991	1992	1993	1994	1995	1996	1997	1998	1999	2000	2001	2002	2003	2004	2005	2006	2007	2008	Average
Jan	1.79	1.38	1.55	2.23	1.45	0.99	2.06	1.53	2.06	1.94	1.20	1.00	0.79	2.19	1.66	0.94	1.15	*3.36	1.62
Feb	*2.45	*3.12	2.03	*2.44	1.67	*2.59	1.20	1.00	1.73	1.89	1.59	1.52	0.86	1.64	0.77	0.80	1.56	*2.45	1.41
March	2.24	*4.78	2.07	1.55	1.62	1.28	*2.48	1.46	1.39	1.82	*2.97	0.91	1.12	1.36	1.08	0.93	1.99	*3.06	1.49
April	1.27	*5.63	2.21	0.94	1.25	1.65	1.63	1.57	*3.35	*3.60	2.28	1.11	1.39	1.30	1.23	1.67	1.74		1.53
May	1.07	*5.37	1.67	1.09	1.24	1.49	0.84	1.38	2.19	*2.43	0.89	1.35	0.76	*4.42	0.67	*2.76	0.85		1.42
June	1.44	*2.36	1.58	1.27	0.75	1.06	0.86	*3.12	1.35	1.39	1.25	1.13	0.96	1.45	0.73	*3.21	0.84		1.36
July	1.98	*2.41	1.46	0.62	1.14	1.54	1.40	1.88	1.60	1.76	1.03	0.98	1.06	1.26	0.93	1.93	1.15		1.31
Aug	1.46	*2.38	1.74	0.94	0.79	1.06	1.55	1.57	1.34	1.08	0.54	0.86	1.55	1.01	0.98	0.71	2.05		1.18
Sep	1.83	1.70	1.65	0.82	0.66	1.08	0.95	1.31	1.33	2.00	*2.62	0.73	1.83	0.84	1.19	1.06	1.06		1.11
Oct	1.81	1.68	0.95	0.62	0.75	1.76	*3.10	1.85	2.09	1.61	1.22	0.84	1.56	0.91	1.51	0.92	*2.45		1.49
Nov	1.22	2.20	1.23	1.14	1.35	1.30	1.70	1.20	1.36	1.40	1.20	0.69	1.16	0.69	0.95	0.60	1.72		1.24
Dec	1.09	*2.60	2.13	1.13	1.04	1.79	1.40	1.49	1.44	1.45	1.24	0.92	0.88	0.75	1.08	1.51	1.67		1.32

The following Table 7 presents the most volatile months of the Nifty during the study period. It is clear from the table that April 1992 stands out as the most volatile month followed by May 1992.

Table 7
S&P CNX Nifty: Top 26 Volatile Months

Sl. No.	Month	Monthly Volatility (%)
1	April 1992	5.637
2	May 1992	5.37952
3	March 1992	4.78288
4	May 2004	4.42853
5	April 2000	3.60736
6	January	3.37092
7	April 1999	3.35151
8	June 2006	3.21781
9	February 1992	3.12250
10	June 1998	3.12203
11	October 1997	3.10101
12	March 2006	3.06213
13	March 2001	2.97104
14	May 2006	2.76948
15	September 2001	2.62725
16	December 1992	2.60735
17	February 1996	2.59843
18	March 1997	2.48594
19	February 1991	2.46757
20	February 2008	2.45816
21	October 2007	2.45623
22	February 1994	2.44084
23	May 2000	2.43007
24	July 1992	2.41092
25	August 1992	2.38352
26	June 1992	2.36318

Overall for Nifty, 8 of the most volatile months belong to the year 1992, 3 of the most volatile months are in the year 2008, two each to 1997, 2000, 2001 and one each to 1991, 1994, 1996, 1998, 1999 and 2004. Thus, 1992 was the most volatile year in the history of the Indian stock market followed by 2004 and 2000. Except for these three years, however, the market was generally cool and steady.

SPIKE VOLATILITY

It is a useful concept to look at market volatility in the absence of extreme but short-lived "spikes" in volatility. Whereas small changes in stock prices may be the result of investors' liquidity needs or portfolio rebalancing considerations, large price changes are more likely to reflect the expected value of new information. If large price swings cannot be attributed to the arrival of new information, then the market can hardly be described as an efficient one. These extreme variations interrupt the normal rhythm of stock price movement temporarily and increase the concern of investors. In real markets, volatility spikes may vary more in amplitude, but this is implied by randomness in the daily moves themselves and in varying periods spent at elevated volatility. Volatility spikes can be caused by company-specific developments or wider systematic events. Wider systemic events would appear as correlated volatility spikes across multiple stocks or asset classes. Here is a Table 8 of the 28 days with intraday volatility greater than 10%.

Table 8

Volatility Rank	*Historical Context*	*Date*	*Intraday Volatility*	*Gain Loss*
7	Crash of 1929	10/24/1929	14.85%	–2.09%
6	Crash of 1929	10/28/1929	14.97%	–13.47%
3	Crash of 1929	10/29/1929	18.85%	–11.73%
9	Crash of 1929	10/30/1929	12.97%	12.34%
23	Crash of 1929	11/6/1929	10.44%	–9.92%
17	Crash of 1929	11/7/1929	11.14%	2.61%
8	Crash of 1929*	10/6/1931	14.83%	14.87%
14	Crash of 1929	12/18/1931	11.68%	9.35%
27	Crash of 1929	6/1/1932	10.13%	0.42%
19	Great Depression*	8/3/1932	10.76%	9.52%
24	Great Depression*	8/8/1932	10.22%	8.16%
21	Great Depression*	8/12/1932	10.58%	–8.40%
22	Great Depression	9/14/1932	10.48%	–5.68%
16	Great Depression	7/20/1933	11.49%	–7.7%
4	Great Depression	7/21/1933	16.86%	–7.84%
26	Great Depression	10/19/1937	10.16%	0.89%
20	1961-1962 Bear Market	5/29/1962	10.72%	4.69%
1	Crash of 1987	10/19/1987	29.01%	–22.61%
2	Crash of 1987*	10/20/1987	27.92%	5.88%
28	Tech Crash	7/24/2002	10.06%	6.35%
13	Financial Crisis of 2008	10/9/2008	11.73%	–7.33%
5	Financial Crisis of 2008	10/10/2008	15.64%	–1.49%

10	Financial Crisis of 2008	10/13/2008	12.28%	11.08%
18	Financial Crisis of 2008	10/16/2008	10.98%	4.68%
12	Financial Crisis of 2008	10/28/2008	11.76%	10.88%
11	Financial Crisis of 2008	11/13/2008	11.96%	6.67%
25	Financial Crisis of 2008	11/20/2008	10.18%	–5.56%
15	May 6, 2010*	5/6/2010	11.63%	–3.20%

The Table 8 shows the rank order in the range of intraday volatility. Volatility generally moved inversely with the market price through the crash and initial phase of the Great Depression. The crash of 1987 makes the evidence volume in a couple of categories. The back-to-back spikes in volatility were by far the largest in the history of the Dow. And the first spike is associated with the single largest per cent decline in Dow history (22.61%). It's clear that program trading played a major role in the crash, but overvaluation, illiquidity, and market psychology were additional factors. The most dramatic spike in volatility occurred during the weeks following the Lehman collapse on September 15· 2007. The volatility subsided as the year-end approached, but a smaller wave of volatility appeared at the beginning of 2009 and peaked around the March 9th bottom and the initial weeks of recovery.

Till now, volatility has been measured by standard deviation of daily/monthly returns. However, in order to capture tendency of the stock market to make infrequent extremely large moves, one should count the number of days during a given period in which it moved, i.e., daily return was more than some threshold in either direction. Theoretically, 'spikes' are those price changes that lie outside the ±3 standard deviation limit. The extreme tails of the normal curve represent plus or minus three standard deviations.

Table 5 presented earlier shows that the mean of the daily returns on the Nifty for the entire study period was about 0.0556% and the standard deviation was about 1.7102%. The three standard deviation limit for Nifty was (3*1.7102%) 5.1306.

The following Table 9 shows the frequency of occurrence of spikes for the Nifty.

Table 9

S&P CNX Nifty: Number of Daily Returns in Excess of ± 5.1306

Year	*Positive*	*Negative*	*Total*
1991	2	1	3
1992	7	8	15
1993	—	2	2
1994	2	—	2
1995	—	—	—
1996	2	—	2
1997	3	2	5
1998	1	2	3
1999	2	2	4
2000	3	3	6

2001	1	3	4
2002	—	—	—
2003	—	—	—
2004	1	2	3
2005	—	—	—
2006	1	2	3
2007	1	—	1
2008	4	6	10
Total	30	33	63

It is observed from the Table 9 that there are 63 days out of 4142 trading days on which daily returns are outside the plus or minus 5.1306 limits, which are the spikes that occurred in the stock market barometer Nifty volatility. It is evident from the Table 9 that 1992 tops the list with highest number of spikes, followed by 2008 and 2000. By comparing Tables 1 and 2, it can be said that the years with more frequent spikes had higher overall volatility also. After 1992, there has been considerable decrease in volatility until 1996 after which, increase in volatility is seen since 1997 with higher volatility in 2000.

The following Table 10 presents the particulars relating to spike volatility together with the dates of its occurrence.

Table 10

S&P CNX Nifty: Spike Volatility Dates (Jan 1991 to Dec 2008)

Year	*Day & Month*	*Positive Change*	*Year*	*Day & Month*	*Negative Change*
1992	24th March	12.08607	2004	17th May	13.0539
1992	13th May	11.6434	1992	28th April	12.52194
1992	2nd March	9.946212	1992	12th May	11.72716
1997	1st March	9.933932	2008	21st January	9.10461
1992	30th March	9.065425	1992	6th May	8.929421
1992	29th February	8.954364	1997	31st March	8.84046
1991	19th February	8.832196	1997	28th October	8.196282
2004	18th May	7.969092	2004	14th May	8.1927
1999	16th April	7.539398	1992	11th May	7.719514
2000	3rd January	7.277061	1999	17th April	7.70989
1998	17th June	7.042027	1998	5th October	7.358534
1997	29th October	6.957376	2000	4th April	7.20226
2000	7th April	6.926125	2006	18th May	7.01312
1992	8th April	6.900494	1997	10th March	6.64573
2008	25th January	6.720522	1991	7th March	6.514379
2006	15th June	6.114284	2001	13th March	6.30954

1991	25th July	6.10983	2008	22nd January	6.12572
1992	22nd April	6.05767	1993	27th February	5.992382
2008	23rd January	6.021992	1992	29th April	5.878366
2001	14th March	5.996017	2000	24th July	5.85803
2008	25th March	5.643747	1998	15th June	5.759159
2000	26th April	5.48509	1993	9th March	5.630631
1994	7th February	5.484838	2001	14th September	5.49996
1996	2nd February	5.457069	1992	6th April	5.397466
2007	23rd October	5.437785	2000	2nd May	5.33703
1994	21st February	5.413385	2008	3rd March	5.31742
1999	7th October	5.384801	2001	17th September	5.29714
2008	14th February	5.381575	1999	26th April	5.29562
1996	9th February	5.241379	1992	10th December	5.294482
1997	15th January	5.170764	2008	17th March	5.2494
			2006	22nd May	5.23329
			2008	11th February	5.28018
			2008	17th March	5.23309

Table 10 lists the dates on which the daily return is more than ± 5.1306. The list of dates is dominated by the year 1992, which has 7 positive and 8 negative excessive return entries for Nifty. The year 2008 comes next wherein four positive and six negative highly volatile days followed by the year 2000 there are six entries, each of three positive and negative returns for Nifty. From the above table, one may note that the largest positive and negative returns during the period occurred are March, April and May, i.e., around the presentation of union budget. The largest one-day price change in Nifty occurred on 24th March 1992 (+12.08607). The largest negative change in the value of Nifty occurred on 17th May 2004 (–13.0539) when political turmoil happened in the Indian politics. It has been understood that the relative contribution of 'noise' and 'news' is causing abnormal price oscillations.

Table 11 presents the information related to the dates on which the large price swings occurred and the reasons for it.

Table 11

Events Reported Around Extreme Daily Returns

Sl. No.	Date	Daily Return (%)	Event Reported
1.	19th February 1991	8.83	The Govt. decided to postpone the presentation of Union Budget.
2.	7th March 1991	–6.52	Prime Minister Mr. Chandrasekhar resigned on 6/3/91.
3.	25th July 1991	6.11	Presentation of Union Budget (1991-92) on 24th July, 91.

4.	29th February 1992	8.95	None.
5.	2nd March 1992	9.95	Market-friendly union budget (1992-93).
6.	10th March 1992	–6.65	RBI Governor directed mutual funds to offload stocks to stop the runaway boom in the market.
7.	24th March 1992	12.09	Removal of curbs on trading on the Calcutta stock exchange.
8.	30th March 1992	9.07	Softening of trading restrictions on the BSE.
9.	6th April 1992	–5.40	None.
10.	8th April 1992	6.90	None.
11.	22nd April 1992	6.06	Trading restored on BSE after a gap of 9 days. [The deadlock on the registration issue was resolved as agitated brokers got assurance from the BSE President].
12.	28th April 1992	–12.52	BSE authorities call for a confidential report from SBI on the alleged involvement of the leading operator in the market.
13.	29th April 1992	–5.88	The multi-crore securities scam came into lime-light.
14.	6th May 1992	–8.93	The RBI appointed a committee to inquire into securities transactions of banks and Financial Institutions. BSE initiated a probe into Harshad Mehta transactions in the market.
15.	11th May 1992	–7.72	Govt. ordered a CBI inquiry on SBI, United Commercial Bank and National Housing Bank *vis-à-vis* Harshad Mehta's securities scam.
16.	12th May 1992	–11.73	BSE imposed ban on forward sales in 15 specified stocks and cuts margins.
17.	13th May 1992	11.64	Sharp recovery on short sales ban and cut in the daily margins on purchases.
18.	10th December 1992	–5.29	Trading resumes after the market was officially closed for three days on account of the developments at Ayodhya. Fresh outbreak of violence triggered by the demolition of the Babri Mosque in Ayodhya on 6th December 1992.
19.	27th February 1993	–5.99	None.
20.	9th March 1993	–5.63	None.
21.	7th February 1994	5.49	None.
22.	21st February 1994	5.41	None.
23.	2nd February 1996	5.46	None.
24.	9th February 1996	5.24	None.

25.	15th January 1997	5.17	None.
26.	1st March 1997	9.93	Presentation of Union budget (1997-98) on 28.02.97 FII investment ceiling raised from 24% to 30%.
27.	31st March 1997	–8.84	Announcement by the congress president withdrawing the party's support to the ruling United Front Government, President asks Prime Minister to prove majority before April 7th.
28.	28th October 1997	–8.20	Worldwide meltdown in stock markets. Worst ever-in Hang Seng and Dow Jones.
29.	29th October 1997	6.96	Recovery in global equity markets. Dow Jones turns around, calms markets worldwide.
30.	15th June 1998	–5.76	Reports of Southeast Asian financial turmoil. Japanese yen and Dow Jones plunks down.
31.	17th June 1998	7.04	SEBI bans short sales to arrest further fall in equities. General recovery in Southeast Asia.
32.	5th October 1998	–7.36	None.
33.	16th April 1999	7.54	National Lok Dal and DMK parties agree to support the ruling BJP-led coalition during the impending vote of confidence.
34.	17th April 1999	–7.71	BJP-led coalition loses vote of confidence in the parliament.
35.	26th April 1999	–5.30	The president dissolves the Lok Sabha.
36.	7th October 1999	5.38	BJP-led coalition (NDA) heads towards majority in the General elections.
37.	3rd January 2000	7.28	None.
38.	4th April 2000	–7.20	Reports of the income tax department issuing notices to FIIs who route investment through Mauritius. Also, NASDAQ composite index falls sharply the previous day.
39.	7th April 2000	6.93	The Government decides to withdraw Income tax notices served earlier to the FIIs. Also, NASDAQ rebounded sharply the previous day.
40.	26th April 2000	5.49	SEBI raises margins on net sales positions, bars payment of carry forward charges to naked short-sellers and relaxes daily circuit filter limit to 12%.
41.	2nd May 2000	–5.34	None.
42.	24th July 2000	–6.31	RBI hikes bank rate by 1%.
43.	13th March 2001	–6.31	The talk of corporatization of brokers and protection of investors by the Govt.

44.	14th March 2001	5.60	
45.	14th September 2001	–5.50	Possible US retaliation after the September 11th attack on WTC.
46.	17th September 2001	–5.30	Uncertainty on how the US markets would behave when they reopened terrorist attack on 11th September.
47.	14th May 2004	–8.19	Statements of political parties on economic agenda of the new government formation.
48.	17th May 2004	–13.05	Political turmoil in Indian politics.
49.	18th May 2004	7.97	SEBI press release on settlement and risk management measures and RBI decision to reduce the margins for bank financing.
50	15th May 2006	6.11	BSE inducts Citibank as Clearing Bank.
51	18th May 2006	–7.01	Revision in BSE Indices, Introduction of Dollex-100 Index and computation, BSE inducts Kotak Mahindra Bank as Clearing Bank.
52	22nd May 2006	–5.24	***Change in margins:*** The exchanges are revising the applicable exposure/extreme loss margins in respect of stocks in the cash and derivatives market segments from the current limit of 10% or 1.5 times the standard deviation, whichever is higher to 5% or 1.5 times the standard deviation, whichever is higher. Similarly in respect of index products in the Derivatives segment, the applicable limit is revised from 6% to 3%.
53	23rd Oct 2007	5.45	Revision in BSE Mid-cap and BSE Small-cap Indices, Revision in BSE Indices, Bombay Stock Exchange and Deutsche Börse agree over index cooperation, Bombay Stock Exchange Ltd. resolved 421 investors complaints against companies during the month of September 2007.
54	21st Jan 2008	–9.10	BSE clarification on Trading Halts.
55	22nd Jan 2008	–6.13	Temporary stoppage in trading in F&O segment on January 22, 2008.
56	23rd Jan 2008	6.02	Replacement of scrip(s) in BSE Indices.
57	25th Jan 2008	6.72	Rescheduling of Settlement Activities on Friday, January 25, 2008.
58	11th Feb 2008	–5.29	Bombay Stock Exchange Ltd. resolved 734 investor's complaints against companies during the month of January, 2008.

59	18th Feb 2008	5.39	Revision of scrip in group 'A'.
60	7th March 2008	–5.32	BSE to suspend trading in securities of 10 companies for non-compliances of various clauses of the Listing Agreement, Exclusion from BSE Small-cap Index.
61	13th March 2008	–5.24	Bombay Stock Exchange Ltd. resolved 731 investor's complaints against companies during the month of February, 2008.
62	17th March 2008	–5.25	Replacement of scrip in BSE Indices
63	31st March 2008	5.64	Index based market wide circuit breaker for the Quarter 1st April 2008 to 30th June 2008.

Source: The Economic Times, Business Line, Harvinder Kaur, *op.* cit. pp. 113-118, www.bseindia.com

CONCLUDING OBSERVATION

On the basis of the analysis of Nifty during the period 1991 to 2008, it is seen that the stock market volatility is highest during 1992 followed by 1993, 2000 and 2008. The Nifty fell sharply after 1992 till 1995, after which it started increasing again. This result is confirmed by the analysis of volatility of monthly returns in a year as well as volatility of daily returns in a year. The largest number of spikes occurred in the years 1992, 2000, 1997 and 2008 the most volatile years. These abnormal years, months and days are studied further in detail to find the logical reasons for the excessive or under returns on the specific day for the market. The reasons associated for the unusual returns are unique in its kind and implies that the market would react very sharply to economic, political and policy issues. Hence the market participants should take care of their portfolio while investing in these volatile months.

REVIEW QUESTIONS

1. What is a financial market? Discuss the significance of this market?
2. What is efficient market hypothesis? What are its important features?
3. Why do we need to determine the efficiency of stock market? Justify your answers.
4. How is stock market discrepancy evaluated?
5. Why NSE is among the most important stock exchanges of the world?
6. Quiz
   (a) The capital market is classified into ____ categories: _____ market and _____ market.
   (b) _____ and _____ is an indicator of the general trend of the economy.
   (c) The concept of market efficiency was first anticipated at the beginning of the century by ____.
   (d) ______ is used to explain the relationship between information and share prices in the capital market.
   (e) The NSE's key index is the S&P CNX Nifty, popularly known as _______.
   (f) Which is also the third largest Stock Exchange in the world in terms of the number of trades in equities?

(g) _____ is an important factor in the comparison of risk and reward between stocks and other asset classes.

(h) ______ reflect only an index's historical volatility.

(i) A distribution with positive kurtosis is called _____.

(j) Unit root tests generally have _____ and ______ asymptotic distributions.

(k) Which is one in which stock prices adjust rapidly when new information arrives and, therefore, the current prices of stocks have already reflected all information about the stock?

(l) Which hypothesis states that the present market price is the best indicator of the future market prices with an error term that is stochastic in nature?

2

Derivatives Trading on Indian Stock Market

This chapter investigates the impact of introduction of index futures derivative and index option derivative on Indian stock market by using ARCH and GARCH model to capture the time varying nature of volatility presence in the market. This chapter concludes that financial derivative products are not responsible for increase or decrease in spot market volatility, but there could be other market factors which influenced the market volatility.

INTRODUCTION

The continuous integration of India with the global economy has brought with slew of opportunities. The rate of financial innovations seen throughout the world has been phenomenal. In this innovational era, a lot of innovative products and processes have been introduced in the financial markets. One innovation in this era that has received a lot of attention worldwide is the derivatives. Starting from a very small part of business on various stock exchanges, derivatives today account for the largest amount of business on most major stock exchange in the world. The average daily volume of derivatives trade on the New York Mercantile Exchange today is to the tune of staggering US $ 1.5 trillion. Introduction of derivatives was made in a phased manner allowing investors and traders sufficient time to get used to the new financial instruments.

Stock markets are extremely volatile and hence the risk factor is an important concern for financial agents. To reduce this risk and to improve the depth of the financial markets, the risk management tool like derivatives appears into the picture. Financial derivatives, especially stock market derivatives, first emerged in the US in the early 1980s and quickly spread to the major financial centers and other markets. During the last decade, many countries across the world have introduced derivative products in their financial markets. The impact of introduction of derivative products on the underlying stock market volatility received major attention all over the world. There are conflicting claims about the impact of derivative trading on the market volatility. Derivative products like index options, stock options, index futures and stock futures, have become important instruments of price discovery, portfolio diversification and risk hedging in stock markets all over the world in recent times. There was also strong empirical evidence that the introduction of derivatives had been bringing significant gains in both trading volumes and market capitalization. It is also argued that the introduction of derivatives was expected to bring in greater participation from risk-averse investors resulting in increased volume of trades and liquidity in the markets. Derivative instruments made spot price discovery more reliable and analysts pointed out that these instruments caused any arbitrage opportunities to disappear led to better price discovery. Institutional investors would be able to hedge their risks effectively against unfavorable market movements by using derivatives. On the other hand, other studies claim that volatility increases after the introduction of derivative trading due to increased speculative activities. Many researchers have proposed the hypothesis that derivative markets lead the price movements in cash segment. The popular assertion is that derivative securities tend to destabilize the underlying spot markets. The concern over how derivative trading affects the spot market has been an interesting subject for investors, academicians, regulators and exchanges in world over.

The derivatives market has recently attracted more attention against the backdrop of the financial crisis, fraud cases and the near failure of some market participants. Although the financial crisis has primarily been caused by structured credit-linked securities that are not derivatives, policy makers and regulators have started to think about strengthening regulation to increase transparency and safety both for derivatives and other financial instruments.

WHAT IS DERIVATIVE?

Derivatives have probably been around for as long as people have been trading with one another. Forward contracting dates back at least to the 12th century, and may well have been around before then. Merchants entered into contracts with one another for future delivery of specified amount of commodities at specified price. A primary motivation for pre-arranging a buyer or seller for a stock of commodities in early forward contracts was to lessen the possibility that large swings would inhibit marketing the commodity after a harvest. Derivatives are totally different from securities. They are financial instruments that are mainly used to protect against and administer risks, and very often also serve arbitrage or investment purposes, providing a variety of advantages compared to securities. A derivative is a contract between a buyer and a seller entered into today regarding a transaction to be fulfilled at a future point in time. Derivatives must be distinguished from securities, where transactions are fulfilled within a few days. Some securities have derivative-like characteristics — such as certificates, warrants, or structured credit-linked securities — but they are not derivatives.

A derivative security is a financial contract whose value is derived from the value of something else, such as a stock price, a commodity price, an exchange rate, an interest rate, or even an index of prices. A derivative provides risk protection with minimal upfront investment and capital consumption. It allows investors to trade on future price expectations. It has very low total transaction costs compared to investing directly in the underlying asset. It allows fast product innovation because new contracts can be introduced rapidly. It can be tailored to the specific needs of any user. Derivatives are traded for diversity of reasons. The first is to eliminate uncertainty by exchanging market risks, commonly known as hedging. Hedgers use futures or options markets to reduce or eliminate the risk associated with price of an asset. A derivative enables a trader to hedge some pre-existing risk by taking positions in derivatives markets that counterbalance potential losses in the underlying or spot market. Corporate and financial institutions use derivatives to protect themselves against changes in raw material prices, exchange rates, interest rates etc. 92 per cent of the world's 500 largest companies manage their price risks using derivatives. In India, most derivatives users portray themselves as hedgers. Another motive for derivatives trading is speculation. Speculators use futures and options contracts to get extra leverage in betting on future movements in the price of an asset. They can increase both the potential gains and potential losses by usage of derivatives in a speculative venture. Speculators face the risk of losing money from their derivatives trades, as they do with other securities. A third type of trader, called arbitrageurs, profit from discrepancies in the relationship of spot and derivatives prices, and thereby help to keep markets efficient. Arbitrageurs are in business to take advantage of a discrepancy between prices in two different markets. If, for example, they see the futures price of an asset getting out of line with the cash price, they will take offsetting positions in the two markets to lock in a profit. Derivatives is also used as an investment. Derivatives are an alternative to investing directly in assets without buying and holding the asset itself. They also allow investments into underlying risks that cannot be purchased directly.

THE NEED FOR A DERIVATIVE MARKET

- The derivatives market performs a number of economic functions.
- They help in transferring risks from risk-averse people to risk-oriented people.
- They help in the discovery of future as well as current prices.
- They catalyze entrepreneurial activity.
- They increase the volume traded in markets because of participation of risk-averse people in greater numbers.
- They increase savings and investment in the long run.

DERIVATIVES CAN BE DIFFERENTIATED ALONG THREE MAIN DIMENSIONS

Type of derivative and marketplace:

Derivatives can be traded bilaterally OTC or multilaterally on exchanges.

Types of underlying: Underlying can be financial instruments themselves, physical assets, or any risk factors that can be measured. Common examples are fixed income, foreign exchange, credit risk, equities and equity indices or commodities.

Types of product: The three main types are forwards (or futures), options and swaps. They differ in terms of their dependence on the price of the underlying.

EXCHANGE-TRADED AND OVER-THE-COUNTER DERIVATIVE INSTRUMENTS

The OTC derivatives markets have witnessed spiky growth over the last few years, which have accompanied the transformation of commercial, and investment banking and globalization of financial activities. While both exchange-traded and OTC derivative contracts present many benefits, the former have rigid structures compared to the latter. OTC contracts, such as forwards and swaps, are bilaterally negotiated between two parties. The terms of an OTC contract are flexible, and are often customized to fit the specific requirements of the user. OTC contracts have substantial credit risk, which is the risk that the counterparty that owes money defaults on the payment. An exchange-traded contract, such as a futures contract, has a standardized format that indicates the underlying asset to be delivered, the size of the contract, and the logistics of delivery. They trade on organized exchanges with prices determined by the contact of many buyers and sellers. In India, two exchanges offer derivatives trading: the Bombay Stock Exchange (BSE) and the National Stock Exchange (NSE). However, NSE now accounts for almost all exchange-traded derivatives in India. Contract performance is guaranteed by a clearing house, which is a wholly owned subsidiary of the NSE. Margin requirements and daily marking-to-market of futures positions considerably diminish the credit risk of exchange-traded contracts, relative to OTC contracts.

The OTC derivatives markets have the following features compared to exchange-traded derivatives:

- The management of counterparty risk is decentralized and located within Individual institutions,
- There are no formal centralized limits on individual positions, leverage, or margining,
- There are no formal rules for risk and burden-sharing,
- There are no formal rules or mechanisms for ensuring market stability and integrity, and for safeguarding the collective interests of market participants, and
- The OTC contracts are generally not regulated by a regulatory authority and the exchange's self-regulatory organization, although they are affected indirectly by national legal systems, banking supervision and market surveillance.

TYPES OF DERIVATIVES

Derivatives are financial products whose value is derived out of one or more basic products. The important financial derivatives are forwards, futures, options and swaps. A forward contract is the most simple of derivative securities. It is an agreement to buy or sell an asset in the future at a certain price. A future is essentially a legal binding contract to buy or sell a pre-specified quality and quantity of a specific commodity on a predetermined future delivery date at an agreed price. Financial futures usually fix the exchange rate, interest rate or the stock index levels at which the contracted financial transactions would take place at a future date. Forwards and futures are available in practically all types of products both financial as well as non-financial. Futures contract is an exchange-traded product while a forward contract is an over-the-counter product. The holder of the contract has the right to buy the product in consideration in the future at a pre-decided price.

The holder of a currency option has the right to buy or seller fixed amount of a certain currency at a predetermined rate of exchange during a certain given period of time, but no obligation to do so. The option to buy is called "call" and the option to sell is called "put" while the predetermined rate is called "strike or exercise". The currency options are bought and sold on traded exchanges and also through the OTC market. In the option exchange, currencies options are sold and bought in the form of standard contracts having constant amount periods and strike prices. Options have been associated with all kinds of products like stocks, currencies, commodities as well as weather and energy. Swap is another exciting trading instrument. It is a combination of forwards by two counterparties. The market of currency swaps has been developing at a rapid pace during last decade. Swap enables companies to obtain desired form of financing in terms of interest rates and currencies.

Forward Contracts

A forward contract is an agreement to buy or sell an asset on a specified date for a specified price. One of the parties to the contract assumes a long position and agrees to buy the underlying asset on a certain specified future date for a certain specified price. The other party assumes a short position and agrees to sell the asset on the same date for the same price. Other contract details like delivery date, price and quantity are negotiated bilaterally by the parties to the contract. The forward contracts are normally traded outside the exchanges.

The salient features of forward contracts are:

- They are bilateral contracts and hence exposed to counterparty risk.
- Each contract is custom designed, and hence is unique in terms of contract size, expiration date and the asset type and quality.
- The contract price is generally not available in public domain.
- On the expiration date, the contract has to be settled by delivery of the asset.
- If the party wishes to reverse the contract, it has to compulsorily go to the same counterparty, which often results in high prices being charged.

However, forward contracts in certain markets have become very standardized, as in the case of foreign exchange, thereby reducing transaction costs and increasing transactions volume. This process of standardization reaches its limit in the organized futures market.

Limitations of Forward Markets

Forward markets worldwide are badly affected by several problems:

- Lack of centralization of trading,
- Illiquidity and
- Counterparty risk

The forward market is like a real estate market in that any two consenting adults can form contracts against each other. This often makes them design terms of the deal which are very convenient in that specific situation, but makes the contracts non-tradable. Counterparty risk arises from the possibility of default by any one party to the transaction. When one of the two sides to the transaction declares bankruptcy, the other suffers. Even when forward markets trade standardized contracts, and hence avoid the problem of illiquidity, still the counterparty risk remains a very serious issue.

Futures Contracts

Futures markets were designed to solve the problems that exist in forward markets. A futures contract is an agreement between two parties to buy or sell an asset at a certain time in the future at a certain price. But unlike forward contracts, the futures contracts are standardized and exchange traded. To facilitate liquidity in the futures contracts, the exchange specifies certain standard features of the contract. It is a standardized contract with standard underlying instrument, a standard quantity and quality of the underlying instrument that can be delivered, (or which can be used for reference purposes in settlement) and a standard timing of such settlement. A futures contract may be offset prior to maturity by entering into an equal and opposite transaction.

The main standardized items in a futures contract are:

- Quantity of the underlying
- Quality of the underlying
- The date and the month of delivery
- The units of price quotation and minimum price change
- Delivery center

Futures are a significant improvement over the forward contracts as they eliminate counterparty risk and offer more liquidity.

Table 1
Forwards vs. Future

Futures	*Forwards*
Trade on an organized exchange	OTC in nature
Standardized contract terms	Customized contract terms
More liquid	Less liquid
Requires margin payments	No margin payment
Follows daily settlement	Settlement happens at end of period

Payoff for Futures

Futures contracts have linear payoff, just like the payoff of the underlying asset. If the price of the underlying rises, the buyer makes profits. If the price of the underlying falls, the buyer makes losses. The magnitude of profits or losses for a given upward or downward movement is the same. The profits as well as losses for the buyer and the seller of a futures contract are unlimited. The payoff for a person who buys a futures contract is similar to the payoff for a person who holds an asset. He has a potentially unlimited upside as well as a potentially unlimited downside. Take the case of a speculator who buys a two-month gold futures contract on the NCDEX when it sells for

₹ 18000 per 10 gms. The underlying asset in this case is gold. When the prices of gold in the spot market goes up, the futures price too moves up and the long futures position starts making profits. Similarly, when the prices of gold in the spot market goes down, the futures prices too move down and the long futures position starts making losses. In the above example, the investor enters into a two-month futures contract at ₹ 18000 per 10 gms of gold and holds the contract till expiry. On the expiry day, if the final settlement price is declared as ₹ 18500 per 10 gms, the investor will have made a profit of ₹ 500 per 10 gms through the term of the contract. On the other hand, if prices of gold have fallen, the final settlement price may be ₹ 17500 per 10 gms. In that event, the investor would have made a loss of ₹ 500 per 10 gms. The investor bought futures when gold futures were trading at ₹ 18000 per 10 gms. If the price of the underlying gold goes up, the gold futures price too would go up and his futures position starts making profit. If the price of gold falls, the futures price falls too and his futures position starts showing losses.

The payoff for a person who sells a futures contract is similar to the payoff for a person who shorts an asset. He has a potentially unlimited upside as well as a potentially unlimited downside. Take the case of a speculator who sells a two-month chilli futures contract when the contract sells at ₹6500 per quintal. The underlying asset in this case is red chilli. When the prices of chilli move down, the chilli futures prices also move down and the short futures position starts making profits. When the prices of chilli move up, the chilli futures price also moves up and the short futures position starts making losses. In the above example, the investor sells a chilli futures contract for ₹ 6500 per quintal. If the prices rise to ₹ 7000 per quintal on expiry date, the investor stands to make a loss of ₹ 500 per quintal at the end of the term of the contract. If the prices fall to ₹ 6000 per quintal, the investor makes profit of ₹ 500 per quintal. The investor sold chilli futures at ₹ 6500 per quintal. If the price of the underlying red chilli goes down, the futures price also falls, and the short futures position starts making profit. If the price of the underlying red chilli rises, the futures too rise, and the short futures position starts showing losses.

Forwards vs. Future

Factors which favor futures trading

- ***Easy entry and exit:*** The facility to easily enter into and exit from the contract encourages participation from those who do not have specifications of physical delivery in the terms of quantity, maturity date and position limits which generally are the speculators and arbitrageus.

- ***Anonymity and transparency in dealing:*** Since the deals occur online on the exchange platform, there is transparency in pricing and arriving at the deal.

Factors which discourage futures trading

- ***Mismatch of contract size:*** Since the futures contracts are standardized with a fixed amount of quantity that may not match the actual requirement of the participants many times. As a result, the participants may prefer to take positions in OTC market where the contracts can be customized to their required amount or size.

- ***Mismatch in maturity:*** Another difficulty the hedgers may face in case of futures is the mismatch between the date of requirement and the maturity date of the contract. The hedgers who are actually interested to take the delivery will find it difficult when the date of maturity of the contract does not match with the date of their requirement.

- ***Position limits:*** Another important factor that may be discouraging the participation in futures is the position limits. The exchange fixes the upper limit on the position taken by each participant. The details of the limits fixed by the exchanges are given in Table 2. Because of these limitations, the participants cannot take position beyond this limit and to the extent they need and hence it becomes a constraint.

Table 2

Clients	***Trading Members***	***Banks***
Higher of 6% of total open interest or USD 10 million	Higher of 15% of the total open interest or USD 50 million	Higher of 15% of the total open interest or USD 100 million

- ***No physical delivery:*** Lack of physical delivery option and only cash settlement in futures trading becomes a problem for hedgers when they have payment obligations in foreign currency. Hence, this may discourage participants, who need physical delivery of foreign currency.
- ***Restriction on the participation of FIIs:*** Another important factor that discourages the active trading in futures is the restriction of foreign institutional investors (FIIs) participation. According to guidelines of the Reserve Bank of India, trade participation of FIIs in futures trading is not yet allowed.

The Futures Basis

The difference between the spot price and the futures price is called the basis. As a futures contract nears expiration, the basis reduces to zero. If the futures price is above the spot price during the delivery period, the trader can short his futures contract, and buy the asset from the spot market and make the delivery. Hence, the demand for the contract will increase and futures prices will fall leading to the convergence of the future price with the spot price. If the futures price is below the spot price during the delivery period, all parties interested in buying the asset will take a long position, causing the demand for the particular asset to increase and the futures price would rise nullifying the arbitrage opportunity.

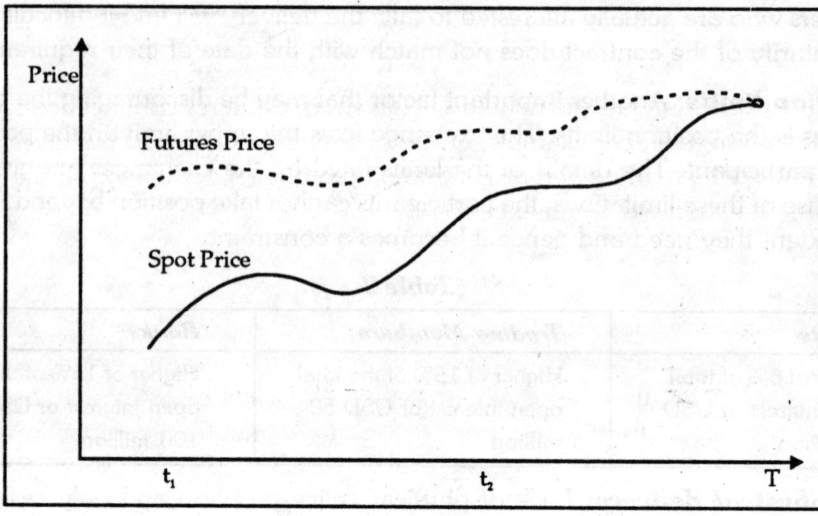

Fig. 1

As the date of expiration comes near, the basis reduces - there is a convergence of the futures price towards the spot price. On the date of expiration, the basis is zero. If it is not, then there is an arbitrage opportunity. Arbitrage also arises when the basis or the spreads (difference between prices of two futures contracts) during the life of a contract are incorrect. There is nothing but cost of carry related arbitrage that drives the behaviour of the futures price in the case of investment assets. In the case of consumption assets, we need to factor in the benefit provided by holding the physical commodity.

Options Contracts

Options are fundamentally different from forward and futures contracts. An option gives the holder of the option the right to do something. The holder does not have to exercise this right. In contrast, in a forward or futures contract, the two parties have committed themselves to doing something. Whereas it costs nothing except margin requirements to enter into a futures contract, the purchase of an option requires an up front payment. An option on a futures contract is the right, but not the obligation, to buy or sell a particular futures contract at a specific price on or before a certain expiration date. There are two types of options: call options and put options. Each offers an opportunity to take advantage of futures price moves without actually having a futures position.

A call option gives the holder the right but not the obligation to buy an asset by a certain date for a certain price. A put option gives the holder the right but not the obligation to sell an asset by a certain date for a certain price.

Call Option

A call option gives the holder (buyer) the right to buy (go long) a futures contract at a specific price on or before an expiration date. For example, a September Japanese Yen 85 call option gives the holder (buyer) the right to buy or go long a yen futures contract at a price of 85 anytime between purchase and September expiration. Even if yen futures rise substantially above 85, the call holder will still have the right to buy yen futures at 85.

Put Option

A holder of a put option has the right to sell (go short) a futures contract at a specific price on or before the expiration date. For example, an October Japanese Yen 70 put gives the put holder the right to sell October Japanese Yen at 70. Should the futures decline to 64, the put holder still retains the right to go short the contract at 70.

Option Buyer

An option buyer can choose to exercise his or her right and take a position in the underlying futures. A call buyer can exercise the right to buy the underlying futures and a put buyer can exercise the right to sell the underlying futures contract. In most cases though, option buyers do not exercise their options, but instead offset them in the market before expiration, if the options have any value.

Option Seller

An option seller (i.e., someone who sells an option that he or she didn't previously own) is also called an option writer or grantor. An option seller is contractually obligated to take the opposite futures position if the buyer exercises his or her right to the futures position specified in the option the buyer has purchased. In return for the premium, the seller assumes the risk of taking a possibly adverse futures position.

Puts and Calls

Puts and calls are separate option contracts; they are not the opposite side of the same transaction. For every put buyer there is a put seller, and for every call buyer there is a call seller. The option buyer pays a premium to the seller in every transaction. The following is a list of the rights and obligations associated with trading put and call options on futures.

Table 3

Call Buyers	*Call Sellers*
pay premium	collect premium
have right to exercise, resulting in a long futures position	have obligation if assigned, resulting in a short position in the underlying futures contract
have time working against them	have time working in their favour
have no performance bond requirements	have performance bond requirements

Table 4

Put Buyers	*Put Sellers*
pay premium	collect premium
have right to exercise, resulting in a short futures position	have obligation if assigned, resulting in a long position in the underlying futures contract
have time working against them	have time working in their favour
have no performance bond requirements	have performance bond requirements

Exercise Price

Also known as the strike price, the exercise price is the price at which the option buyer may buy or sell the underlying futures contracts. Exercising the option results in a futures position at the designated strike price. Strike prices are set above and below the existing futures price and additional strikes are added if the futures move significantly up or down.

Premium

The premium is the price that the buyer of an option pays and the seller of an option receives for the rights conveyed by an option. Thus, ultimately the cost of an option is determined by supply and demand. Various factors affect options premiums, including strike price level in relation to the futures price level; time remaining to expiration; and market volatility.

Exercise

Exercise refers to the process whereby the option buyer asserts his right and goes long the underlying futures (in the case of exercising a call) or short the underlying futures (in the case of exercising a put).

Offset

The buyer is under no obligation to exercise an option on a futures contract. As a matter of fact, many traders choose to offset their position prior to expiration. Traders will offset their position if they wish to take profits before expiration or limit losses on the downside. Buyers can offset their options by instructing their broker to sell their option before expiration. An option seller can offset a position by buying back or "covering" a short position. Options on futures, like futures themselves, trade both on the stock exchange floor, where a market normally exists to offset options positions, and on the electronic trading platform, where many options can be traded virtually around-the-clock throughout the trading week.

Payoff for Options:

The optionality characteristic of options results in a non-linear payoff for options. In simple words, it means that the losses for the buyer of an option are limited; however the profits are potentially unlimited. The writer of an option gets paid the premium. The payoff from the option written is exactly the opposite to that of the option buyer. His profits are limited to the option premium; however his losses are potentially unlimited. A call option gives the buyer the right to buy the underlying asset at the strike price specified in the option. The profit/loss that the buyer makes on the option depend on the spot price of the underlying. If upon expiration, the spot price exceeds the strike price, he makes a profit. Higher the spot price more is the profit he makes. If the spot price of the underlying is less than the strike price, he makes loss. If he lets his option expire unexercised, his loss in this case is the premium he paid for buying the option.

Consider the profits/losses for the buyer of a three-month call option on gold at a strike of ₹ 17000 per 10 gms. As can be seen, as the prices of gold rise in the spot market, the call option becomes in-the-money. If upon expiration, gold trades above the strike of ₹ 17000, the buyer would exercise his option and get profit. The profits possible on this option are potentially unlimited. However, if the price of gold falls below the strike of ₹ 17000, he lets the option expire. His losses are limited to the extent of the premium he paid for buying the option.

A call option gives the buyer the right to buy the underlying asset at the strike price specified in the option. For selling the option, the writer of the option charges a premium. The profit/loss that the buyer makes on the option depend on the spot price of the underlying. Whatever is the buyer's profit is the seller's loss. If upon expiration, the spot price exceeds the strike price, the buyer will exercise the option on the writer. Hence, as the spot price increases, the writer of the option starts making losses. Higher the spot price more is the loss he makes. If upon expiration the spot price of the underlying is less than the strike price, the buyer losses. If he lets his option expire unexercised, the writer gets to keep the premium. Consider the profits/losses for the seller of a three-month call option on gold with a strike of ₹ 17000 per 10 gms. As the price of gold in the spot market rises, the call option becomes in-the-money and the writer starts making losses. If upon expiration, gold price is above the strike of ₹ 17000, the buyer would exercise his option on the writer who would suffer a loss. The loss that can be incurred by the writer of the option is potentially unlimited, whereas the maximum profit is limited to the extent of the upfront option premium of ₹ 500 charged by him.

Payoff for Buyer of Put Options: Long Put

A put option gives the buyer the right to sell the underlying asset at the strike price specified in the option. The profit/loss that the buyer makes on the option depend on the spot price of the underlying. If upon expiration, the spot price is below the strike price, he makes a profit. Lower the spot price more is the profit he makes. If the spot price of the underlying is more than the strike price, he makes loss. If he lets his option expire unexercised, his loss in this case is the premium he paid for buying the option.

Let us consider the profits/losses for the buyer of a three-month put option on cotton. As can be seen, as the price of cotton in the spot market falls, the put option becomes in-the-money. If at expiration, cotton prices fall below the strike of ₹ 6000 per quintal, the buyer would exercise his option and get profit. However, if spot price of cotton on the day of expiration of the contract is above the strike of ₹ 6000, he lets the option expire. His losses are limited to the extent of the premium he paid for buying the option, ₹ 400 in this case.

Payoff for Writer of Put Options: Short Put

A put option gives the buyer the right to sell the underlying asset at the strike price specified in the option. For selling the option, the writer of the option charges a premium. The profit/loss that the buyer makes on the option depends on the spot price of the underlying. Whatever is the buyer's profit is the seller's loss. If upon expiration, the spot price happens to be below the strike price, the buyer will exercise the option on the writer. If upon expiration the spot price of the underlying is more than the strike price, the buyer lets his option expire unexercised and the writer gets to keep the premium.

Now consider the profits/losses for the seller of a three-month put option on cotton. As the price of cotton in the spot market falls, the put option becomes in-the-money and the writer starts making losses. If upon expiration, cotton prices fall below the strike of ₹ 6000 per quintal, the buyer would exercise his option on the writer who would suffer a loss to the extent of the difference between the strike price and spot cotton-close. The profit that can be made by the writer of the option is limited to extent of the premium received by him, i.e., ₹ 400 whereas the losses are limited to the strike price since the worst that can happen is that the price of the underlying asset falls to zero.

Table 5

Future	*Options*
Exchange traded, with innovation	Same as futures
Exchange defines the product	Same as futures
Price is zero, strike price moves	Strike price is fixed, price moves
Linear payoff	Non-linear payoff

Using Futures versus Using Options

Options are different from futures in several interesting senses. At a practical level, the option buyer faces an interesting situation. He pays for the option in full at the time it is purchased. After this, he only has an upside. There is no possibility of the options position generating any further losses to him (other than the funds already paid for the option). This is different from futures, which is free to enter into, but can generate very large losses. This characteristic makes options attractive to many occasional market participants, who cannot put in the time to closely monitor their futures positions. More generally, options offer "non-linear payoffs" whereas futures only have "linear payoffs". By combining futures and options, a wide variety of innovative and useful payoff structures can be created.

Factors Driving the Growth of Financial Derivatives

1. Increased volatility in asset prices in financial markets.
2. Increased integration of national financial markets with the international markets.
3. Marked improvement in communication facilities and sharp decline in their costs.
4. Development of more sophisticated risk management tools, providing economic agents a wider choice of risk management strategies.
5. Innovations in the derivatives markets, which optimally combine the risks and returns over a large number of financial assets leading to higher returns, reduced risk as well as transaction costs as compared to individual financial assets.

GROWTH OF DERIVATIVE MARKET

Derivatives in India have permitted by Reserve Bank of India and Securities Exchange Board of India. The introduction of swaps in the Indian market by RBI in 1999 can be regarded as the first seal step in the development of the derivative market in India. Since 1999, RBI has allowed banks and financial institutions to enter into swap deals. The basic motive for banks and financial institutions is the risk mitigation and risk management. Derivatives trading commenced in India in June 2000 after Securities Exchange of India (SEBI) granted the final approval to this effect in May 2001. SEBI permitted the derivative segments of two stock exchanges, National Stock Exchange (NSE) and Bombay Stock Exchange (BSE), and their clearing corporation to commence trading and settlement in approved derivatives contracts. To begin with, SEBI approved trading in index futures contracts based on S&P CNX Nifty and BSE-30(Sensex) index. On June 9, 2000, the Bombay Stock Exchange (BSE) introduced India's first derivative instrument — the BSE-30(Sensex) index futures. The plan to introduce derivatives in India was initially unresolved by the National Stock Exchange (NSE) in 1995. Since the involvement of foreign institutional investors (FIIs) participation had been very low in Indian stock market due to the absence of derivatives for hedging risk, the main purpose of introducing derivative instruments was to encourage greater amount of participation of them. However, there was no consensus of opinion on the issue among industry analysts and the media. The pros and cons of introducing derivatives trading were debated intensely. The lack of transparency and inadequate infrastructure of the Indian stock markets were cited as reasons to avoid derivatives trading. Derivatives were also considered risky for retail investors because of their poor knowledge about their operation. In spite of the opposition, the path for derivatives trading was cleared with the introduction of Securities Laws (Amendment) Bill in Parliament in 1998.

The trading in BSE Sensex options commenced on June 4, 2001 and the trading in options on individual securities commenced in July 2001. But the volumes in this segment are not as high. The important reason being the lack of understanding of the products by common investors as well as a large number of corporate and inability to predict volatility of the stock price as well as changes in the interest rate accurately. Futures contracts on individual stocks were launched in November 2001. The National Stock Exchange of India Limited (NSE) commenced trading in derivatives with the launch of index futures on June 12, 2000. The futures contracts are based on the popular benchmark S&P CNX Nifty Index. The Exchange introduced trading in Index Options (also based on Nifty) on June 4, 2001. NSE also became the first exchange to launch trading in options on individual securities from July 2, 2001. Futures on individual securities were introduced on November 9, 2001. Futures and Options on individual securities are available on 258 securities stipulated by SEBI. The Exchange has also introduced trading in Futures and Options contracts based on CNX-IT, BANK NIFTY, CNX NIFTY JUNIOR, CNX 100, NIFTY MIDCAP 50 and S&P CNX DEFTY indices. NSE started trading in the equities segment (Capital Market segment) on November 3, 1994 and within a short span of 1 year became the largest exchange in India in terms of volumes transacted. The most recent development in the history of derivatives market in India and related to the introduction of currency options by RBI on July 7, 2003. This development has meant that banks and corporate can trade in options. The exchange-traded derivatives witnessed a volume of ₹ 4,42,343 core during 2002-2003 as against ₹ 1,03,847 crore during the 2001-2002. While NSE accounted for about 99.5% of total turnover, BSE accounted for about 0.5% in 2002-2003. The market witnessed higher volumes from June 2001 with introduction of index options, and still higher volumes with the introduction of stock options in July 2001. There was a spurt in volumes in November 2001 when stock futures were introduced. It is believed that India is the largest market in the world for stock futures. It is observed that futures are more popular than options, contracts on securities are more popular than those on indices; call options are more popular than put options; and near-month contracts are more popular than not-so-near-month contracts. The index futures, stock futures index options and stock options accounted for 10%, 65%, 2% and 23% respectively of total turnover during 2002-2003. The global derivatives markets are now three times more than the current equity markets. SEBI permitted the Indian stock exchanges to trade on single index futures on 31 Indian stocks during 2001. The list has been increased to 53 scripts in 2003. NSE is now one of the prominent exchanges amongst all emerging markets, in terms of equity derivatives turnover. Between April 2002 and March 2006, the total turnover of the derivatives segment increased by 4,633 per cent, while the average daily turnover increased by 4,587 per cent. Trading volumes in the equity segment have grown rapidly with average daily turnover increasing from ₹ 17 crore during 1994-95 to ₹ 14,148 crore during FY 2007-08. During the year 2007-08, NSE reported a turnover of ₹ 3,551,038 crore in the equities segment. National Stock Exchange of India Limited has been awarded 'Derivatives Exchange of the Year' by Asia Risk Magazine in December 2006 due to best practice, quality service and innovation in derivatives and risk management in the Asia-Pacific region. The meteoric growth of the cash and derivative segments of the NSE is graphically highlighted in Fig. 2 Experience with the launch of equity derivatives market in India has been extremely positive by world standards. With the introduction of derivative instruments, analysts felt that Indian corporate would be able to raise finance from global markets at better terms. They would also be able to take advantage of low interest rates prevailing in global markets. It could be also easy to encourage greater participation of foreign institutional investors (FIIs) in the Indian stock markets. Apart of it, foreign institutions very often faced currency and market risk, while operating in the Indian markets. The currency risk could be hedged through the dollar rupee futures while the market risk could be hedged through stock index futures. On the other hand, certain threats are also associated with derivative trading. This market segment provides good speculative opportunities and excessive speculative trading increases the volatility of the market (http:www.nseindia.com).

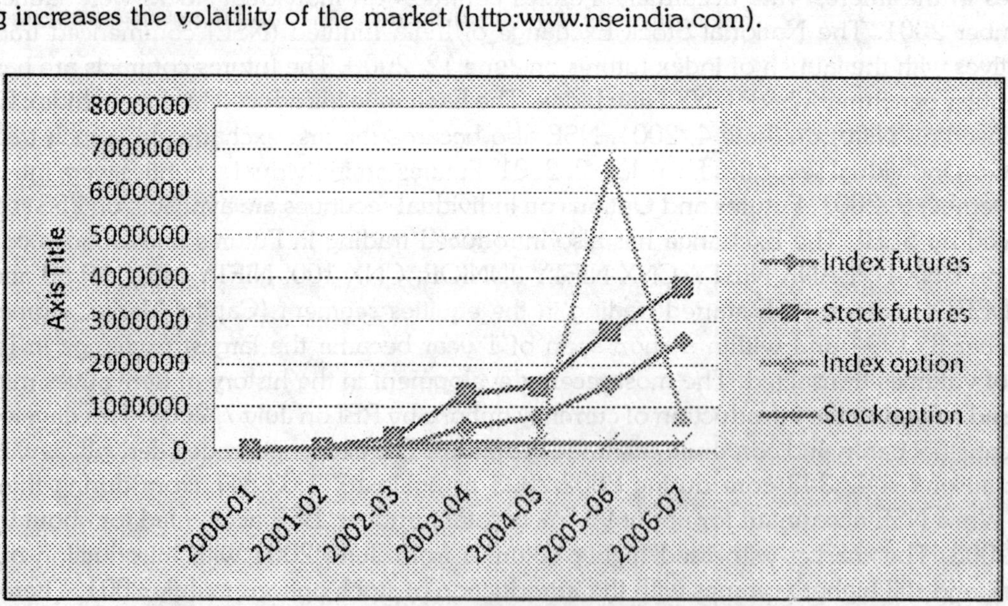

Fig. 2: Turnover in NSE Derivative Market

LITERATURE REVIEW:

The effect of introduction of derivatives on the volatility of the spot markets and in turn, its role in stabilizing or destabilizing the cash markets has remained an active topic of analytic and empirical interest. One of them argues that derivatives trading increases the corresponding spot market volatility, while others finds the opposite effect on return volatility of the underlying instruments. There is wide disagreement among researchers at the empirical front regarding trading on the volatility of prices of underlying assets. A number of studies show that derivative trading can destabilize the underlying spot market. Edwards (1988) studied whether stock Index futures trading destabilized the spot market in the long run. Using variance ratio F tests for the period June 1973 to May 1987, he concluded that the introduction of futures trading did not induce a change in spot volatility in the long run. Harris (1989) examined volatility after introduction of Index futures by comparing daily return volatilities during the pre futures (1975-1982) and post futures (1982-1987) period between S&P 500 and a non-S&P 500 group of stock controlling for differences in firm attributes. He found that increased volatility was a common phenomenon in different markets and Index futures by themselves may not be a cause. Ross (1989) suggests that derivative trading increases the volatility in the cash market. He argues that derivative trading improve the overall price efficiency of equity market through noise reduction. However, the non-arbitrage condition between spot and derivatives market segments implies that the variance of the price change will be equal to the information flow. The implication of this is that the volatility of asset price increases as the rate of information flow increases. Thus, if futures increase the flow of information, then in absence of arbitrage opportunity, the volatility of spot price must increase. Lee and Ohk (1992), on the other hand, presents evidence that futures trading affect cash market volatility only in more matured markets including Japan, UK and the US, but not in less developed markets such as Australia or Hong Kong. Mayhew Stewart (2000) focused on how the introduction of derivative securities affects the underlying market. In most cases, the resulting models predicted that speculative trading and derivative markets stabilize the underlying market and make spot markets more liquid and more informationally efficient. Huseyin Gulen and Stewart Mayhew (2000) studied the stock market volatility before and after introduction of index futures in 25 countries. They examined whether spot market volatility after the introduction was related to futures market volume and open interest. They found that futures' trading was related to an increase in conditional volatility in US and Japan, but for the rest of the countries they found no significant effect. It was further found that, except for US and Japan, volatility tended to be lower in periods when open interest was high. Benilde Maria Do Nascimen Oliveira *et al.* (2001) analyzed the impact of futures introduction in the Portuguese stock market. The authors used GARCH model to measure the futures trading impact on the spot market volatility. They found that introduction of the PSI-20 index futures trading increased the Portuguese spot market volatility and that there was no improvement on the market efficiency front. Board John *et al.* (2001) examined the effect of futures market volume on spot market volatility in two parallel markets, viz., the equity (spot or cash) market and the market for futures on equity index by using GARCH and stochastic volatility models. They found that there was no evidence that futures trading instantly destabilized the spot market or that an increase in volume in one market, relative to the other, instantly destabilized the other market. The stochastic volatility analysis showed that there is a positive influence on spot market volatility which indicates that spot market volatility has increased. Ali F. Darrant, *et al.* (2002) examined the role of futures trading in spot market fluctuations. The Exponential Generalised Autoregressive Conditional Heteroscedasticity was used to measure volatility and relationship between volatility in the spot and futures markets for the period November 1987 to November 1997. They concluded that index futures trading could not be blamed for the volatility in the spot market. Pilar Corredor and Rafael Santamania examined the effect of the introduction of derivatives (futures and options) in the Spanish market on the volatility and on the trading volume of the underlying index. The period of analysis covers October 1990 to December 1994 and they used GARCH, EGRCH and GJR models to find out the conditional volatility. The findings of the study are that the level of volatility had decreased when derivative markets were introduced but the trading volume of the Ibex 35 had increased. They concluded that the introduction of derivatives did not present a problem for the spot market because their impact was beneficial and possessing characteristics similar to the Spanish market. Kiran Kumar Kotha and Mukhopadhyay Chiranjit (2003) studied the impact of futures introduction on underlying NSE Nifty volatility by using a CUSUM plot and GARCH family of techniques to capture the time varying nature of volatility and volatility-clustering phenomenon's presence in the data. The results reported that the introduction of index futures trading had no effect on the mean level of returns of Nifty. Nagaraj K.S. and Kiran Kumar Kotha's (2004) studied the impact of Index Futures trading on the spot market volatility by using GARCH model. The study found that the market had become more efficient in assimilating the information into the market after the introduction of index futures. Furthermore, the study indicated that Monday and Friday are significant in terms of day of week effect of the market and also that volatility of the spot market has declined. Y.P. Singh and S. Bhatia (2006) studied the futures trading impact the spot market volatility by using the GARCH (1, 1) model. The study proved that the daily spot market volatility in India has marginally declined since the introduction of futures trading in India. The market efficient has also improved after introduction of derivative products in the Indian capital markets. The study also found that there is a marginal decline in daily volatility on the expiration day of the derivative contracts. These results are quite contrary to the earlier studies results.

LET US TAKE CASEOF S&P CNX NIFTY, S&P CNX NIFTY JUNIOR AND S&P 500 INDEX FOR STUDYING THE VOLATILITY BEHAVIOUR:

The stock market indices are fairly representative of various industry sectors and trading activity mostly revolves around the stocks comprising the indices. The present chapter has been carried out with the three-benchmark indices: S&P CNX Nifty, S&P CNX Nifty Junior and S&P 500 index for studying the volatility behavior. Daily closing prices were obtained from NSE website for Nifty and Nifty Junior; similarly S&P 500 index from Prowess.

S&P CNX Nifty is a well-diversified 50 stock index accounting for 21 sectors of the economy. It is used for a variety of purposes such as benchmarking fund portfolios, index-based derivatives and index funds. It is also used for a variety of purposes such as historical comparison of returns on money invested in the stock market against other forms of investment such as gold or debt. It is also taken to be an indicator of the performance of the overall economy or a particular sector of the economy. Nifty stocks represent about 61.70% of the total market capitalization as on Sep 30, 2008. The stock price data of Nifty and Nifty Junior have been taken from NSE website, which is maintained by National Stock Exchange of India for a period of October 1995-December 2006. The database contains all the actively traded stocks at any given time on the NSE. Similarly, S&P 500 data has been collected from prowess. Returns are proxied by the log difference change in the price index. For the dataset, daily returns are calculated for Nifty, Nifty Junior and S&P 500 index by using the following formula.

$$R_t = \ln (P_t/P_{t-1})*100$$

P_t and P_{t-1} are the prices at time t, and t-1 respectively and R_t is the return for time t.

In the recent past, financial market volatility modeling, especially temporal variation has been a fascinating topic in financial market research. The impact on financial derivatives on the spot market volatility has to be examined by using a suitable and appropriate model. It is well-accepted fact that many financial time series contain a unit root, i.e., the series are non-stationary and it is generally acknowledged that stock index and stock index futures series might not be exception. Stationary time series is one whose mean, variance and covariance are unchanged by time shift. Non-stationary time series have time varying mean or variance or both. Knowledge of non-stationarity of the time series is significant in the modeling of economic relationships because standard statistical techniques that assume stationarity may give invalid inferences in the presence of stochastic trends. In case of non-stationary data, ordinary least squares can produce spurious results. Such a model would be termed as 'spurious regression'. Therefore, prior to modeling any relationship, non-stationarity must be tested. This eliminates any possibility of being trapped in spurious regression. The data considered for the study is time series, which is non-stationary whereas the examination of first difference often reveals wide swings, which is predominantly the volatility effect suggesting that the variance of the time series varies over time. For application of GARCH and ARCH model on Nifty, the initial step in the estimation involves the determination of the time-series property of each variable individually by conducting unit root tests. The most popular unit root test is the ADF (Augment Dickey-Fuller, 1979) test.

Volatility of the stock markets is measured by using Standard Deviation or GARCH model. GARCH model has been a preferred measure of volatility by many researchers. The GARCH model provides for Heteroscedasticity in the observed returns. It is a time-series modeling technique that uses past variance and the past variance forecasts to forecast future variances. The ordinary regression model proved to be inefficient because of the untenability of one of its key assumptions that the errors have the same variance throughout sample. It is called Homoscedasticity. If the error variance is not constant, the data is said to be Heteroscedasticity. It is observed that the model that takes into account the changing variance can make more efficient use of the data.

Financial time series usually exhibits a characteristic called volatility clustering which means that large changes tend to follow large changes and small changes tend to follow small changes. GARCH model accounts for certain characteristics like thick tails and volatility clustering that are commonly associated with financial time series. Graphical analysis and computation of some basic statistics like Kurtosis and Skewness can help to provide relevant empirical evidence of the presence of volatility clustering tendencies. The thick tail phenomena in the data are known as excess kurtosis. Time series data that exhibit a thick tail distribution is often referred to as Leptokurtic. Generally, the presence of Leptokurtic tendencies on the time series returns suggests the presence of volatility clustering; hence the modeling of such phenomena is recommended through the adjustment of

Autoregressive Conditional Heteroscedasticity. The Generalized Autoregressive Conditional Heteroscedasticity (GARCH) model is a variation of the Autoeegressive Conditional Heteroscedasticity (ARCH) model developed by Engle in 1982. Bollerslev originally proposed the GARCH model in 1986. A distinguishing feature of this model was that the error variance might be correlated over time because of the phenomenon of volatility clustering. Following Antonion and Holmes (1995) and others, the return series is modeled as a univariate GARCH process. Today, the most widely used model to estimate the conditional (hence time-varying) variance of stock and stock-index returns is the Generalized Autoregressive Conditional Heteroscedasticity (GARCH) model. In analyzing the behavior of volatility due to derivative products, it is necessary to eliminate the influences of other factors. The GARCH (1, 1) is estimated for measuring volatility. The GARCH (1, 1) framework has been found to have the best specification in both the works.

ARCH

The ARCH (q) process captures the conditional heteroscedasticity of financial returns by assuming that today's conditional variance is a weighted average of past-squared unexpected returns:

$$h_t = \alpha_0 + \alpha_1 \varepsilon_{t-1}^2 + \alpha_2 \varepsilon_{t-2}^2 + ... + \alpha_q \varepsilon_{t-q}^2$$

Where $\alpha_0 > 0$, α_1, $\alpha_2 .... \alpha_q$ > and $e_{t1}\ I_{t-1} \sim N$ (0, ht)

If a major market movement occurred yesterday, the day before or up to q days ago, the effect will be to increase today conditional variance because all parameters are constrained to be non-negative. In fact, the ARCH model with exponentially declining lag coefficients is equivalent to a GARCH (1, 1) model.

The GARCH (1, 1) Model

Any GARCH Model consists of two distinct specifications. The first is the conditional mean equation. The simple GARCH models used in practice take the simple possible conditional equation.

$$R_t = R_{t-1}\beta + \varepsilon_t$$

Where R_t is the daily return on Nifty and R_{t-1} is the lagged return, β is a fixed parameter vector and e_t is the residual error term for the day t. e_t is treated as a collective measure of news at times t. A positive e_t suggests the arrival of good news, while a negative e_t suggests the arrival of bad news. The second equation in a GARCH model is the conditional variance equation. The conditional variance equation is a function of three terms:

$$ht = \alpha_0 + \sum_{i=1}^{q} \beta i \varepsilon_{t-1}^2 + \sum_{j=1}^{p} \beta j h_{t-1}$$

Where α_0 is mean. News about volatility from the previous period, measured as the lag of the squared residual from the mean equation ε_{t-1}^2 (the ARCH term). Last period's forecast variance is

h_{t-1} (the GARCH term). GARCH (1, 1) refers to the presence of a first-order GARCH term (the first term in parentheses) and first-order ARCH term (the second term in parentheses). An ordinary ARCH model is a special case of a GARCH specification in which there are no lagged forecast variances in the conditional variance equation. The GARCH (1, 1) model is represented as given below.

$$R_{Nifty} = \alpha_0 + \alpha_1 R_{Nifty,\,t-1} + \alpha_2 R_{Nifty\ junior,\,t} + \alpha_3 R_{S\&P\ 500,\,t-1} + \sum_{J=4}^{7} \alpha_i Day_i + \mu_t$$

Where $R_{Nifty,\,t}$ is the daily return on the S&P CNX Nifty index calculated as the first difference of the log of the index, $R_{Nifty,\,t-1}$ is the lagged Nifty return, $R_{Nifty\ Junior,\,t}$ is the return of Nifty Junior, $R_{SP500,t-1}$ is the lagged S & P 500 index return, and DAY_j are day-of-the-week dummy variables for Monday to Friday except Thursday. It is essential to remove domestic market wide factors influence on Nifty returns to isolate the impact of derivative products introduction into the Indian capital market. In order to do this, Nifty Junior, a proxy variable which do not have derivative products but captures market wide influence of domestic markets in India has been included in the above conditional mean equation. In GARCH, the residuals (u_t) from the conditional mean equation are assumed to be distributed in N (0, h_t) where the conditional volatility h_t is given by the following equation:

$$h_t = y_0 + y_1 \in_{t-1}^2 + y_2 h_{t-1} + y_3 D_t$$

Where D_t is a dummy variable that takes a value of "0" before introduction of index options, index futures, stock options and stock futures period and value of "1" in the post introduction period. Relevant to the first research question about the impact of the introduction of derivatives on spot market volatility is estimated by using dummy variable D_t, which captures the differences in volatility between the time before the introduction of derivatives instruments and thereafter. The study formulated null hypotheses H_0: P=1 in which case it is said that value of dummy coefficients of derivative product y_3 y_4 y_5 y_6 do not have an impact over spot market volatility. The alternative is H_1: P<1 If the alternative hypothesis is correct then derivative instruments is having impact over spot market volatility. If the coefficients on the dummy are statistically significant then the introduction of derivatives has an impact on the spot market volatility. A significant negative value for y_3, y_4, y_5 y_6 would indicate that derivatives introduction decreases the volatility. Similarly, a positive value suggests increase of volatility.

In order to answer the second research question, similarly H_0: P=1 in which case it is said the value of y_1, y_2 do not have an impact on change in the assimilation of information after introduction of derivatives in the market. The alternative is H_1: P<1 If the alternative hypothesis is correct then it is said there is change in the assimilation of information after introduction of derivatives in the market. y_1 reflects the impact of recent news (shocks), y_2 reflects the impact of old news (persistence volatility). For a GARCH process to be stable, it is necessary that y_0 and y_1 and y_2 are greater than zero. The sum of ARCH snd GARCH coefficients (y_1 +y_2) is very close to one or <1 indicating that volatility shocks are quite persistent.

Asymmetrical Response to the Arrival of News

Though ARCH and GARCH models responds to good and bad news and quite useful in forecasting and modelling volatility, they lack in capturing "leverage effect" and information asymmetry. The rational and underlying logic of asymmetric or leverage effect is that the distribution of stock return is highly asymmetric. Bad news is followed by larger increase in price volatility than good news (positive returns) of the same size. It is known that the magnitude of the response of asset prices to shocks dependents on whether the shock is negative or positive. To demonstrate this point, Engle and Ng (1990) mapped the relationship between the conditional variance of asset returns to exogenous shocks which resulted in what they termed a news impact curve. They found evidence of asymmetry is stock returns. In an attempt to explain the asymmetry of volatility in speculative prices, Black (1976) posited that when stock price falls the value of the associated company's equity declines. As a result, the debt-equity ratios of firms tend to rises, thereby signalling that the company has become riskier. Increased risk is considered an indicator for higher volatility. Used in this context, it is widely accepted that the statistically interpretation of Black's leverage effect implies that negative surprises increases predictable volatility in asset markets more than positive surprises. Another alternative explanation of the asymmetry volatility response is based on the time-varying risk premium (Campbell and Hentschel, 1992; Wu, 2001). According to them, if volatility is priced; an expected increase in volatility raises the required return on equity, leading to an immediate stock price decline. Schwert (1989) also agreed with this explanation. Schwert (1989) and Black (1976) had shown that the returns are negatively correlated with volatility. This implied that the returns were more volatile in response to bad news compared to the good news. Bekaert and Wu (2000) shown, when combining these two explanations in an empirical model, often the coefficient linking volatility to expected return is insignificant and the sign is different depending on the study. Also that the leverage effect alone does not adequately explain the changes in volatility after a decrease in the asset prices. Finally third explanation, described as following-the-herd effect (De Goeij and Marquering, 2004) is based on a psychological behaviour. Investors might pay less attention to the market fundamentals during a stock market crash and therefore sell their stocks if everybody else is selling. The negative relationship between stock returns and volatility was discussed in Jinho, Chang-Jin and Nelson (2007). Some scholars argue that the asymmetry effect may stem from the feedback from volatility to stock price as changes in volatility trigger change in risk premiums.

Nelson (1991) proposed an exponential GARCH model or EGARCH model which is the earliest extension of the GARCH model that incorporates asymmetric effects in returns from speculative prices based on a logarithmic expression of the conditional variability of variable under analysis. Later on, the Threshold ARCH (TARCH) model was introduced by Zakoian (1994). The TARCH model developed by Glosten *et al.* (1993) is considered to be most suitable in estimating the impact of positive and negative shocks on volatility. To answer the third research question regarding leverage effect and changes in the asymmetric pattern of the impact of positive and negative return shocks on conditional volatility, we estimated the volatility equation by using EGARCH, TARCH, PGARCH and Component ARCH Model.

The TARCH Model

The TARCH model is another volatility model that allows asymmetric effects. TARCH or Threshold ARCH was introduced independently by Zakeian (1994) and Glosten *et al.* (1993). The conditional variance is

$$h = \omega + \sum_{i=1}^{q} \alpha_i \varepsilon_{t-1} + \gamma\varepsilon_{t-1} d_{t-1} + \sum_{j=1}^{p} \beta j h_{t-j}$$

Where $d_t = 1$ if $\varepsilon_t < 0$ and $d_t = 0$ otherwise. In this model, is used to capture the asymmetrical effect of good news such as favourable business cycle conditions and demand supply conditions and bad news such as political instability, oil prices shocks and increase inflation volatility. In this model, α is ARCH term and β is GARCH term. Accordingly, good news ($\varepsilon_t<0$), and bad news ($\varepsilon t>0$), have differential effects on the conditional variance. Good news has an impact on α, while bad news has an impact $\alpha+$. The presence of leverage effects can be tested by the hypothesis that ($\gamma>0$). The impact is asymmetric if $\gamma \neq 0$. Negative γ implied positive return shocks generate less volatility than negative return shocks.

The EGARCH Model

Glosten *et al.* (1994) illustrated how to allow the effects of good and bad news to have different effects on volatility in their TARCH model. In the volatility equation, positive and negative shocks can have different effects on subsequent volatility. The first asymmetric GARCH model that precipitated considerable academic interest was the EGARCH or exponential GARCH model proposed by Nelson (1991). The conditional variance equation in the EGARCH (1, 1) model is

$$\log h_t = \omega + \beta * \log h_{t-1} + \alpha * \frac{|\varepsilon_{t-1}|}{\sqrt{h_{t-1}}} + \gamma * \frac{|\varepsilon_{t-1}|}{\sqrt{h_{t-1}}}$$

Where, h_t is an asymmetric function of past ε_t.

Note that the left hand side is the lag of the conditional variance. This implies that the leverage effect is exponential, rather than quadratic and that forecasts of the conditional variance are guaranteed to be non-negative. In this model specification, β is the GARCH term that measures the impact of last period's forecast variance. A positive β indicates volatility clustering implying that positive stock price changes are associated with further positive changes and *vice versa*. α is the ARCH term that measures the effect of news about volatility from the previous period on current period volatility. The presence of leverage effects can be tested by the hypothesis $\gamma<0$. The impact is asymmetric if $\gamma \neq 0$.

If γ is negative, implying that bad news has a bigger impact on volatility than good news of the same magnitude. The sum of the ARCH & GARCH coefficients indicates the extent to which a volatility shock is persistent over time. A persistent volatility shock raises the asset price volatility.

The Power GARCH (PGARCH) Model

PGARCH differs from the other models by relating the conditional standard deviation to the previous values rather than conditional variance. In line with Davidian and Carroll (1987), who argued that, standard deviation specifications are more robust than variance specifications. Taylor (1986) and Schwert (1989) introduced the standard deviation GARCH model, where the standard deviation is modeled rather than the variance. This model, along with several other models, is generalized in Ding *et al.* (1993) with the Power ARCH specification. In the PGARCH (1, 1) model, the power parameter of the standard deviation can be estimated rather than imposed, and the optional parameters are added to capture asymmetry of up to order:

$$\sigma_t^{\delta} = \omega + \alpha(|\varepsilon_{t-1}| + \gamma\varepsilon_{t-1})^{\delta} + \beta\sigma_{t-1}^{\delta}$$

Where α, β are standard GARCH parameters and γ are the leverage parameters and $\overline{0}$ is the parameter for the power term. As in EGARCH, asymmetric effects are incorporated here when, the asymmetric effects are present if $\gamma \neq 0$. Parameter $\overline{0}$ could be fixed in the PGARCH models before estimation. Usually choices for this parameter are $\overline{0}=1$ (then PGARCH model is robust to outliers) and $\overline{0}=2$. Coefficients $\overline{0}$ plays the role of a Box-Cox power transformation of the conditional standard deviation process. If $\overline{0}=2$ and $\gamma=0$, PGARCH reduces to a GARCH model. When $\overline{0}=2$, PGARCH reduces to an EGARCH model. When $\overline{0}=1$, PGARCH reduces a TARCH model.

The Component ARCH Model:

There are two equations in component models: permanent or transitory equations. The variables in the permanent equation will have an impact on the long-run movements in volatility, while the variables in the transitory equation will affect the short-run levels of volatility.

The Conditional Variance in the GARCH Model:

$$h = \varpi + \alpha(\varepsilon_{t-1}^2 - \varpi) + \beta(h_{t-1} - \varpi)$$

The component model allows mean reversion to a varying level qt, modelled as:

$$h - q_t = \alpha(\varepsilon_{t-1}^2 - q_{t-1}) + \beta(h_{t-1} - q_{t-1})$$

$$q_t = \omega + p(q_{t-1} - \omega) + \phi(\varepsilon_{t-1}^2 - h_{t-1})$$

Here h is still the volatility, while q_t takes the place of ω and is the time-varying long-run volatility. q_t describes the long-run component which converges to ω with powers of p. Typically, p is between .99 and 1 so that q_t approaches very slowly. g $\gamma > 0$ implies transitory leverage effects in the conditional variance.

ANALYSIS

This chapter tried to find out whether the nature of the GARCH process is changed as a result of the derivative products introduction. The Indian stock markets have witnessed changes like rolling settlement system, electronic trading system, and creation of futures and options segment etc. These changes could have contributed to improve the efficiency of the market operations. Hence, to explore this, the GARCH (1, 1) model is estimated separately for the pre-index futures and post-index futures, pre-index options and post-index options. This facilitates obtaining more information about the effect of the introduction of index derivative products in the Indian stock market. The conditional mean and variance equations are similar except that the dummy variable for derivative products would not be there in conditional variance equation. The results of these two equations are helpful in analyzing the information efficiency in the pre-and post-derivative products period, examining the persistence of volatility and the changes in the day-of-week effect.

Table 6

Estimates of the GARCH (1, 1) Model before the Introduction of Index Futures

	Particulars	*Coefficient*	*t-Statistic*	*Prob.*
α_0	Intercept	–0.010343	–0.196482	0.8442
α_1	Lagged Nifty Return	–0.03459**	–2.355926	0.0185
α_2	Nifty Junior Return	0.862942*	66.5254	0.0000
α_3	Lagged S&P 500 Return	0.116363*	5.88259	0.0000
α_4	Dummy-Monday	–0.140195**	–1.950164	0.0512
α_5	Dummy-Tuesday	0.018224	0.479469	0.6316
α_6	Dummy-Wednesday	–0.030494	–1.323961	0.1855
α_7	Dummy-Friday	0.015306	0.967904	0.3331
y_0	ARCH (0)	0.018371*	3.309349	0.0000
y_1	ARCH (1)	0.074674*	5.42106	0.0000
y_2	GARCH (1)	0.907286*	57.03493	0.0000

* Statistically significant at 1% level

** Statistically significant at 5% level

The GARCH analysis of before introduction of derivatives products has exhibited in Table 6 explains that there is an impact of Nifty Junior, Lag S&P 500 and Lag Nifty on Nifty. It is observed that Monday coefficient is significant at 5% level. It indicates that before the introduction of index futures, Monday effect was there in the market as it happens to be opening day of the week and there may be weekend effect also. The output of conditional variance equation y_1 and y_2 are related to efficiency of news. y_1 relates to the impact of yesterday's market specific changes today. It can be inferred that recent news has an impact on price changes. y_2 coefficient reflects the impact of old news on yesterday's variance and as such it indicates the level of persistence in the information effect on volatility. Persistence of volatility means that today's volatility due to information arriving today will affect tomorrow's volatility and volatility of the days to come.

Table 7

Estimates of the GARCH (1, 1) Model after Introduction of Index Futures

	Particulars	*Coefficient*	*t-Statistic*	*Prob.*
α_0	Intercept	–0.040276	–0.784469	0.4328
α_1	Lagged Nifty Return	–0.014684	–1.020877	0.3073
α_2	Nifty Junior Return	0.68205*	66.44498	0.0000
α_3	Lagged S&P 500 Return	0.068489*	3.843142	0.0001
α_4	Dummy-Monday	0.019376	0.264724	0.7912
α_5	Dummy-Tuesday	0.054594	1.400666	0.1613
α_6	Dummy-Wednesday	–0.020677	–0.823774	0.4101
α_7	Dummy-Friday	0.028116**	1.934983	0.053
y_0	ARCH (0)	0.032364**	2.347624	0.0118
y_1	ARCH (1)	0.040982**	2.781785	0.0054
y_2	GARCH (1)	0.909369*	28.45292	0.0000\

* Statistically significant at 1% level

** Statistically significant at 5% level

It is observed from the aboveTtable 7 that Lag Nifty effect has vanished after index futures. In the post-index futures period, the Monday effect has disappeared and coefficient sign has also changed from negative to positive. The Friday coefficient is statistically significant at 5% level. The conditional variance equation output y_0, y_1 and y_2 coefficients are statistically significant. Hence, it can be inferred that there is an impact of old and latest news effect in the market. A close look at the signals indicating the market efficiency as measured by y_1+y_2, signify the persistence of shocks in the market. In the pre-index futures period (y_1+y_2), value was 0.98196 and the same has declined to 0.950351 in the post-index futures period. This clearly indicates that there is a substantial reduction in persistence of volatility from pre-index futures period to post index futures period. This reveals that market efficiency has increased after the introduction of index futures.

Table 8

Estimates of the GARCH (1, 1) Model before Introduction of Index Options

	Particulars	*Coefficient*	*t-Statistic*	*Prob.*
α_0	Intercept	–0.022173	-0.446837	0.655
α_1	Lagged Nifty Return	–0.029525**	-2.12089	0.0339
α_2	Nifty Junior Return	0.786389*	73.24276	0.0000
α_3	Lagged S&P 500 Return	0.100516*	5.713709	0.0000
α_4	Dummy-Monday	–0.124197***	-1.759886	0.0784
α_5	Dummy-Tuesday	0.019548	0.529053	0.5968
α_6	Dummy-Wednesday	–0.011454	-0.517595	0.6047
α_7	Dummy-Friday	0.022725	1.520238	0.1285

y_0	ARCH (0)	0.020789*	3.828287	0.0001
y_1	ARCH (1)	0.056676*	5.176842	0.0000
y_2	GARCH (1)	0.920994*	65.8113	0.0000

* Statistically significant at 1% level

** Statistically significant at 5% level

*** Statistically significant at 10% level

Table 8 depicts the GARCH analysis of before introduction of index options explains that there is an impact of Lag Nifty returns, Nifty Junior, and Lag S&P 500 on Nifty. It is observed that there is a Monday effect in the market as its coefficient is significant before the introduction of index options. The output of conditional variance equation y_1 and y_2 are related to efficiency of news. y_1 relates to the impact of yesterday's market specific changes today. It is observed that recent news has an impact on price changes. y_2 coefficient reflects the impact of old news on yesterday's variance and as such it indicates the level of persistence in the information effect on volatility.

Table 9

Estimates of the GARCH (1, 1) Model after Introduction of Index Options

	Particulars	*Coefficient*	*t-Statistic*	*Prob.*
α_0	Intercept	-0.047709	-0.859812	0.3899
α_1	Lagged Nifty Return	-0.021352	-1.192609	0.2330
α_2	Nifty Junior Return	0.717164*	61.39636	0.0000
α_3	Lagged S&P 500 Return	0.070346*	3.375954	0.0007
α_4	Dummy-Monday	0.028089	0.36258	0.7169
α_5	Dummy-Tuesday	0.039948	0.937569	0.3485
α_6	Dummy-Wednesday	-0.017907	-0.626009	0.5313
α_7	Dummy-Friday	0.026069***	1.658368	0.0972
y_0	ARCH(0)	0.038553**	2.096763	0.036
y_1	ARCH (1)	0.04142**	2.12461	0.0336
y_2	GARCH (1)	0.896665*	20.80725	0.0000

* Statistically significant at 1% level

** Statistically significant at 5% level

*** Statistically significant at 10% level

Table 9 exhibited that Lag Nifty effect has vanished after index options. In the post-index options period, Monday effect has disappeared. The Friday coefficient is statistically significant at 5% level. The conditional variance equation output y_0, y_1 and y_2 coefficients are statistically significant. Hence, it can be concluded that there is an impact of old and latest news effect in the market. The market efficiency, which is measured by y_1+y_2, signifies the persistence of shocks in the market coefficient, shows negative sign. But however, it has become positive in the post-index options period but not statistically significant. The y_1 and y_2 coefficients relate to latest and old news respectively.

y_1 coefficient is significant hence it can be inferred that recent news has an impact on price changes. Similarly, y_2 coefficient suggests that the market has been picking up impact of old news. The market efficiency as a measure of (y_1+y_2) indicates that there is a reduction of persistence of volatility in the post-index options period because the value of (y_1+y_2) has come down from 0.97767 to 0.938085. It indicates that the market efficiency has improved after the introduction of index options.

EFFICIENCY

The efficiency of the derivatives market has increased significantly in recent years. This is true both in terms of cost efficiency and price efficiency. The exchange segment has proven particularly efficient due to the standardization of exchange-traded derivatives, available economies of scale and its complete automation.

CONCLUDING OBSERVATION

The relationship between financial derivatives such as index futures, index options and corresponding spot market volatility of Nifty has been analyzed by using the GARCH (1, 1) model. The GARCH (1, 1) model included the variables of the day of week effect, domestic market factors, previous day's Nifty effect and worldwide market factors. The analysis of information efficiency through a separate GARCH model for pre- and post-derivatives period showed that there is a shift in market efficiency due to information flow. There is a Friday effect in the market after introduction of derivative products into the Indian capital market. Apart from this, the result shows that the spot market volatility has not been affected by the introduction of financial derivatives since the dummy coefficients for index futures and index options are not statistically significant. But the findings indicate that the market has become more efficient after introduction of derivative products. However, it concludes that financial derivative products are not responsible for increase or decrease in spot market volatility, there could be other market factors which influenced the Nifty volatility. The reasons for increase in volatility could be the enhancement of Foreign Institutional Investors participation in the equity market. Another reason could be the turnover of NSE grew by 69% and also the retail investors' participation in securities markets has increased in the recent years.

Disasters prove that derivatives are very risky and highly leveraged instruments. Disasters can take place in any system. Disasters are not necessarily due to dealing in derivatives, but derivatives make headlines. Some of the reasons behind disasters related to derivatives are: lack of independent risk management, improper internal control mechanisms, problems in external monitoring done by exchanges and regulators, trader taking unauthorized positions and lack of transparency in the entire process.

REVIEW QUESTIONS

1. Briefly discuss the events that led to the introduction of derivatives trading in Indian stock markets.
2. Though trading in derivatives has been introduced in India, analysts feel that there is still a long way to go before we realize their full potential. What issues need to be addressed to accelerate the growth of derivatives market?

3. Do you think the recent measures taken by SEBI, RBI and the stock exchanges are adequate?
4. Critically comment on the views on introduction of derivatives. Do you think derivatives should have been introduced? Take a stand and justify it.
5. Which of the following best describes options on futures?
   (a) the right to buy or sell a futures contract
   (b) the right to take delivery of a cash commodity
   (c) the right to assign a futures contract
6. A put option is:
   (a) the other side of a call option position
   (b) the right to buy a futures contract
   (c) the right to sell a futures contract
7. A call option is:
   (a) the other side of a put option transaction
   (b) the same as a short futures position
   (c) the right to go long a futures contract
8. Options on futures are:
   (a) usually offset before expiration
   (b) wasting assets
   (c) traded on regulated commodity exchanges
9. The premium of an option is:
   (a) set by the exchange staff
   (b) unaffected by futures prices
   (c) determined by buyers and sellers reflecting supply and demand
10. Quiz
   (a) Financial derivatives first emerge in the ___ in the early ____.
   (b) OTC contracts, such as _____ and _____ is bilaterally negotiated between two parties.
   (c) The difference between the spot price and the futures price is called the ——.
   (d) Which month and year the Bombay Stock Exchange (BSE) introduced India's first derivative instrument — the BSE-30(Sensex) index futures?
   (e) Which price is the price at which the option buyer may buy or sell the underlying futures contracts?

3

Expiration and Week Effect on Indian Derivative Market

This chapter investigates the expiration day and week effects for nifty futures and day-of-the-week effect in Bearish phase and Bullish phase to see to what extent the day-of-the-week effect is visible in these specific market phases. This chapter concludes that the day-of-the-week effect is not persistent in either the derivatives or the cash markets in India.

INTRODUCTION

Stock prices change every day by market forces. Share prices change because of supply and demand. If more people want to buy a stock (demand) than sell it (supply), then the price moves up. Conversely, if more people wanted to sell a stock than buy it, there would be greater supply than demand, and the price would fall. Understanding supply and demand is easy. What is difficult to comprehend is what makes people like a particular stock and dislike another stock. This comes down to figuring out what news is positive for a company and what news is negative. Share prices and the stock market, are affected by a wide range of factors (e.g., interest rates, social unrest, changes in government policy), some of which defy prediction. Mathematicians, traders and financiers have studied the stock markets several hundred years ago, but no one has yet managed to devise a foolproof system for working out what will happen next. But financial analysts can use historical data and mathematical calculations, such as moving averages, on balance volume and the stochastic oscillator, to try to predict future changes in the stock market.

Volatility is a key input for market risk evaluation. The high-frequency prices in financial assets provide us price reactions to information and the evaluation of intraday market risk. This knowledge is of particular benefit to market participants who are involved in intraday trading, such as day traders, high-frequency portfolio managers, and program traders. Various explanations for large price movements have been promulgated. For instance, some research has shown that changes in estimated risk, and the use of certain strategies, such as stop-loss limits and Value at Risk limits, theoretically could cause financial markets to overreact. Other research has shown that psychological factors may result in exaggerated stock price movements. Psychological research has demonstrated that people are predisposed to 'seeing' patterns, and often perceive a pattern in what is, in fact, just *noise*. In the present context, this means that a succession of good news items about a company may lead investors to overreact positively (unjustifiably driving the price up). A period of good returns also boosts the investor's self-confidence, reducing his (psychological) risk threshold. The theory behind the base-broadening hypothesis suggests that the expansion of investor base to include foreign investors leads to increased diversification followed by reduced risk and consequently lowering the required risk premium. Thus, there is a permanent increase in the equity share price through risk pooling (Merton, 1987).

An efficient market should not react to anticipated flows. It is the shock brought in by the surprise of the unanticipated flows to which the market reacts. To investigate the positive correlation between returns and flows further, we consider the feedback trader hypothesis and price pressure hypothesis. Investors who base their portfolio decisions on the expectations, which are in turn based on past returns, are termed as feedback or momentum traders. The positive feedback-trader hypothesis posits that FIIs move money into the market in response to the increasing returns at the market, that is, the flow must lag returns. On the other hand, negative feedback trading suggests that investors buy when prices are low and sell after prices increase. The rationale behind this hypothesis is that the shocks from increased flows generate expectations of additional future flows. This expectation is reflected by the current price increase followed by increase in expected future flows. When the expected flows do not materialize in the future, the prices fall. The theory of price pressure hypothesis suggests that the rise in prices is associated with increased inflows; based on this it is expected to look the prices return to the fundamental when the actual flows do not match the expected flows. Warther (1995) posits that the rise in prices caused by inflow surges are due to temporary illiquidity and such a theory predicts that the prices would return to fundamentals.

Stock index future contracts are the most successful financial innovation during 1980s. The main reason for the success of this instrument is that index futures provide a fast and inexpensive means of changing stock market risk exposures internationally. All stock index future contracts call for cash settlement on the expiration day. The day-of-the-week effect has been one of the widely studied market anomalies (See Pettengill, 2003 and Bildik, 2004 for survey), but researchers are still not unanimous about its exact source and implication. However, most of the published research work in the past has focused on developed market. Over the last two decades, the emerging markets, with their liberalization policies have gained the significance both for researchers and investors world over (See for example, Bekaert *et al.*, 2003, 2007; Bekaert and Harvey, 2003, Phylaktis and Ravazzolo, 2005). Since these markets have gone through many changes in their macro and micro structure; they provide us a good opportunity to understand the importance of market structure, practices and policies in price discovery process.

WHAT IS CALENDAR ANOMALIES?

One of the implications of the efficient market hypothesis (EMH) is that the expected returns on assets should be evenly distributed across the days, weeks, months, years or any other unit of time. But the empirical studies on the behaviour of stock returns have disclosed certain anomalies where variances in asset returns are found to be associated with the unit of time. These are called calendar anomalies. The day-of-the-week effect, the turn-of-the-month effect, the month-of-the-year effect etc. are some of the examples of the calendar anomalies reported in the literature. However among them, the day-of-the-week effect is the most widely reported calendar anomaly across the countries and financial markets. As far as the stock returns are concerned, generally the average Monday-returns have been found significantly negative and lower than average returns on other weekdays.

WHAT IS EXPIRATION DAY EFFECT?

However, certain other versions of this anomaly have also been reported from different countries where the abnormal behaviour of average returns was found to be associated with days of the week other than Monday. Index derivatives are frequently accused of creating "undesirable" effects on the market for the underlying securities. One of these effects is the expiration day effect. Expiration day effects may arise from stock index arbitrageurs unwinding of arbitrage positions in the stock market. If many arbitrageurs liquidate at the same time and in the same direction, price effects are possible. Another possible explanation for expiration day price effects is deliberate attempts to manipulate prices. A speculator with a naked position in an expiring contract may have a significant financial interest in the contract's settlement price and may be willing to put through small cash market trades at non-equilibrium prices to manipulate the index in a favorable direction.

WHAT IS EXPIRATION DATE/LAST TRADING DAY?

This is the last day on which an option can be exercised into the underlying futures contract. After this point the option will cease to exist; the buyer cannot exercise and the seller has no obligation. Note that some options expire prior to the final settlement or expiration of the underlying futures contract. For example, a Sep 2005 CME British pound 2000 call option will expire September 9, 2005. However, the underlying futures will expire on September 19, 2005. The last trading day is the last day on which an option can be offset. Before proceeding further, we would like to formally clarify our usage of the terms "expiration day" and "expiration hour". Expiration day refers to the last Thursday, when all contracts (index futures, index options, stock futures, stock options) expire; expiration hour refers to the last *half-hour* of the expiration day. *Friday Effect* is argued that as the Friday is the last trading day of the week and most of the results of the companies are made public on this day, it brings enthusiasm in the market resulting in a bulk buying by the investors. Hence, the mean return on Friday will be higher than the other days of the week [Cross (1973), Gibbons and Hess (1981), Harris (1986), Board and Stucliffe (1988) etc]. The research study by Gibbons and Hess (1981) has shown that the return of Monday is significantly different from the return of other days and it is usually negative. The same is concluded by Harris (1986). The most satisfactory explanation given for the negative return is that usually most unfavorable news appears during weekends. This unfavorable news disappoints the market resulting in a distress selling on the following Monday. When the return in any of the month is higher than the return in other months, this anomaly is called as month effect.

WHAT ARE SOURCES OF EXPIRATION DAY EFFECTS?

Expiration day price effects may arise from a combination of factors including the existence of arbitrage opportunities, the cash settlement feature of options, the stock market procedures for accommodating the unwinding of arbitrage positions in the stocks, and attempts to purposely manipulate prices. This section discusses these possibilities.

Cash Settlement

Arbitrage positions are frequently unwound at the expiration of the options contract. If a stock option expires at the close, the option self-liquidates through cash settlement at the closing price level. The stock position, on the other hand, must be liquidated through trades in the marketplace. An arbitrageur who is long the underlying stocks and short the option contract must sell the underlying stocks at their closing prices. If many arbitrageurs liquidate positions at the same time and in the same direction, price effects are possible.

Stock Market Procedures

The strictness of price effects on expiration day depends in part on the stock market procedures for accommodating order imbalances that may arise when arbitrage positions are unwound. If the underlying market for the stocks is deep and if suppliers of liquidity are quick to respond to selling or buying pressure, the price effects of large arbitrage unwinding will be small. If unjustified price effects were known to occur, knowledgeable investors would stand ready to buy underpriced stocks and sell overpriced stocks—actions that would normally limit price effects to fall within the bounds of transaction costs. If market mechanisms are not well designed to offset sudden imbalances, however, the price effects may be substantial. In the case of stock options contracts that settle at the close, arbitrage positions must be unwound at closing prices. In the US, arbitrageurs place market-on-close (MOC) orders, indicating their desire to trade at the closing price, whatever it may be. If large MOC orders are received late in the day and investors to take the other side are difficult to locate, price effects are possible. Modifications in trading mechanisms such as requiring early placement of MOC orders can reduce the risk of unexpected imbalances at the close.

Manipulation

Expiration-day stock price effects may also arise from attempts to manipulate stock prices. Such attempts may occur directly in the way an arbitrage position is unwound or indirectly through arbitrage unwinding that benefit other positions. An arbitrageur might engage in indirect manipulation, not to benefit the arbitrage account but to benefit another account. The manipulation effort will fail and the effect on stock prices will be limited, however, if other knowledgeable investors are standing ready to buy at bargain prices and thereby keep prices from falling.

Previous research on expiration day effects on Index futures has generally found that spot trading volume is abnormally high at expiration and that the volatility increases as the expiration date comes nearer. Others studies have found no significant affect on volatility. Keeping in view, the present chapter explicitly addresses the effect of changing expiration day effects of the index futures on their volatility on the intra-week behaviour of the stock returns.

LITERATURE REVIEW

Among all the stock market anomalies the day-of-the-week effect, without any doubt, has attracted high attraction in the literature. Early research on this topic was conducted by Cross (1973), French (1980), Gibbons and Hess (1981). Chang *et al.* (1993), Agrawal and Tandon (1994), Maberly (1995) and Bildik (2004) provide comprehensive account of research on this issue. The studies generally conclude that the stock returns on Monday, all in average, are negative and they are significantly lower than the returns on other days of the week. However certain variations in the intra-week behaviour of stock returns were also observed across the countries, which are found to be associated with market microstructures and practices.

Several hypotheses have been suggested to explain the day-of-the-week effect; the most prominent among them are the information release hypothesis, the information-processing hypothesis and the settlement regime hypothesis (Keef and Roush, 2005). *The information release hypothesis* (French, 1980; Rogalski, 1984; Penman, 1987; Damodaran, 1989; DeFusco *et al.*, 1993) suggests that business leaders delay in release of negative information until after the closure of stock exchange on Friday. Clustering of negative information release at weekends is responsible for bearish environment in the stock market on its reopening on Monday.

The information-processing hypothesis (Miller, 1988; Lakonishok and Maberly, 1990; Abraham and Ikenberry, 1994; Sias and Stark, 1995) argues that the behavior of individual investors is responsible for observed Monday-effect. It is argued that gathering information during weekdays trading hours is particularly costly for individual investors as most of them are employed with other activities during that period. For them, weekend provide a convenient opportunity to gather and process the information and to reach at an investment decision. They may put some buying orders on weekdays also based on their brokers' recommendations. It has been observed that the broker community produces more buying recommendations than the selling recommendations; hence, for selling decisions the individual investors have to be based predominantly on their own information processing. Therefore, there is a clustering of selling orders from individuals on Monday. On the other hand, the institutional investors use Monday morning to frame the trading strategy for the coming week (Osborne, 1962), therefore there is less trading from institutional traders on Monday. This situation produces a downward pressure on prices on that day.

The settlement regime hypothesis (Gibbons and Hess, 1981; Lakonishok and Levi, 1982; Solnik and Bousquet, 1990, Agrawal and Tandon, 1994) suggests that the delay in cash payment for the security can lead to escalation of rate of returns on specific days due to extra credit period availability. The exact nature of this effect depends on our assumptions regarding the determination of the credit period in presence of holidays and the settlement system in practice. We may have two alternative hypotheses regarding determination of the credit period — the calendar time hypothesis and the trading time hypothesis[1]. Under the calendar-period hypothesis, if the settlement of a transaction is delayed because of holidays, the market will expect extra interest for this extended credit period and the prices will get adjusted accordingly to accommodate for this interest cost. On the other hand, the trading time hypothesis postulates that market considers only the trading time while determining the period of credit available for settlement and does not expect any interest for the delay in settlement because of holidays. The applicability of either of these two alternative hypotheses must depend on cost of capital involved in transition. If the monetary and the opportunity cost of capital during the holiday period is zero, the trading time hypothesis bears more economic sense. However, on the other hand, if the cost of capital during holidays is not zero, the market will adjust the prices around holidays to compensate for this cost.

The settlement procedures vary considerably across the stock markets. Solnik (1990) classifies them into two categories — the fixed settlement-lag system and the fixed settlement date system. Under the fixed settlement-lag system (we will use the term more popular in India – the 'rolling settlement system'), the settlements take place a fixed number of business days after the transaction. The settlement-lag may differ from country to country. If the trading time hypothesis is correct, the returns must be identically distributed across the weekdays under this system. However, under the calendar time hypothesis this system is expected to produce typical day-of-the-week effect around the holidays (Lakonishok and Levi, 1982; Jaffe and Westerfield, 1985). For example, if the transactions are settled after one day (i.e., on T+1 basis) and Saturday and Sunday are the weekly holidays, the extra two days credit period will be available for the transaction taken place on Friday. The interest cost for this extended credit period will push up the prices on Friday and will lead to higher daily return on Friday and lower returns on Monday, when returns are measured on the basis of daily closing prices. This argument can be extended for other holidays besides the weekly holidays. The empirical studies have also supported the postulation that pre-holiday returns should be higher than the returns on other trading days (Arial, 1990; Kim and Park, 1994; Keef and Roush, 2005).

However, the empirical studies of intraweek behaviour of stock returns in the market with rolling settlement system do not completely reconcile with expectations formed on the basis of above analysis. In US, the negative Monday-effect has been found much larger than the positive Friday-effect and the settlement procedure is unable to explain it completely (Gibbons and Hess, 1981; Dyl and Martin, 1985). In some other markets, the day-of-the-week effect has been found to take place on the days other than the days which are expected to produce higher or lower returns on the basis of settlement system (Lakonishok and Levi, 1982; Jaffe and Westerfield, 1985, Choudhry, 2000). There is extensive empirical evidence on the expiration day effects of US derivatives markets, where the *triple witching hour* has encouraged specific studies (Feinstein and Goetzmann 1988, Herbst and Maberly, 1990, Hancock, 1993). Empirical results generally report abnormally high trading volume and lower average returns on expiration days. However, the downward pressure on the underlying stock market does not tend to reverse at the next opening, suggesting that expiration should not be associated with this price pattern.

Under the fixed settlement date system (in this study we will use the term 'fixed-day weekly settlement system', as at NSE the settlement used to take place on Wednesday on weekly basis), settlement takes place periodically on fixed date and all the transactions performed before this date are settled then. While the expected influence of settlement procedure on distribution of daily returns is quite small for countries with fixed settlement-lag or rolling settlement system, it is usually much stronger for countries with fixed settlement dates such as UK (Draper and Paudyal, 1997; Board and Sutecliffe, 1988), France (Solnik, 1990; Solnik and Bousquet, 1990, Crouhy and

Galai, 1992) and other European countries. Under this settlement system, market behaves like a typical forward market where taking arbitrage position is possible and that can be squared-off before the settlement date. In theory, the forward stock price converse to the implicit (unobserved) spot price on the last day of the settlement cycle and moves up from the sport price on the first day of the cycle by an amount equal to the basis (cost of carry or interest cost) for the period of settlement in absence of any dividend and transaction cost (Solnik, 1990). This leads to higher daily returns on the first day of the settlement cycle. If the length of the settlement cycle is one week (as it used to be at NSE), it is likely to produce typical day-of-the-week effect. Obviously, different settlement systems produce different patterns of behaviour of stock returns under the different time frames and a change in settlement system is likely to change this behaviour also. Studies has also recorded shift in the day-of-the-week effect with changes in settlement regimes in some stock exchanges, e.g., in Kuala Lumpur (Clare *et al.*, 1998), New Zealand (Keef and McGuinness, 2001) etc. Fung, Joseph K.W. and Yung, Haynes (2007) does not find significant price reversal and price compression patterns but order imbalance pattern is found on some expiration days. The results show no association between order imbalance pattern and the next-day return also. No price reversal pattern can be found on the next day.

The day of the week effect in Indian market was examined by many researchers in the Indian context as well. Bhattacharya *et al.* (2003) used GARCH framework by incorporating the lagged returns (BSE 1001) as explanatory variables in the conditional mean. They have used reporting and non-reporting weeks[2] to study the day-of-the-week effect. Goswami and Angshuman (2000) examined the prices of seventy individual securities at BSE from 1991 to 1996 and found a significant positive Friday-effect which was correlated with the firm size. A more recent study by Nath and Dalvi (2004) examines the impact of the introduction of rolling settlement. They use high frequency data for the period of 1999 to 2003 and analyse them using robust regression technique. They conclude that there were Monday and Friday-effects before introduction of rolling settlement; however, after the introduction of rolling settlement only Friday-effect is surviving. Arora, Varun and Das, Sromon (2007) investigates the existence of seasonality in India's stock market, primarily trying to detect the day-of-the-week effect in the Stocks listed on the National Stock Exchange for the period from November 1994 to September 2007. The results confirm the existence of seasonality (in the form of Day-of-the-Week Effect) stock returns in India for 66 Stocks spanning across various sectors. The results of the study imply that the stock market in India is inefficient, and hence, investors can time their share investments to improve returns and make abnormal profits. However, the day-of-the-week effect was found to be absent in the Bullish as well as the Bearish phase. No Indian study so far explicitly addresses the effect of changing settlement system on the intra-week behaviour of the stock returns. This study will make an attempt to fill this gap.

LET TAKE THE CASE OF INDEX FUTURES TO DETERMINE EXPIRATION DAY EFFECTS AND VOLATILITY ON THE INTRA-WEEK BEHAVIOUR OF THE STOCK RETURNS

The required time series data which we have chosen consist of index futures having 25 different expiration dates. For convenience, we treat all those index futures differently. The expiration dates are 29-Nov-07, 27-Dec-07, 31-Jan-08, 28-Feb-08, 27-Mar-08, 24-Apr-08, 29-May-08,

26-Jun-08, 31-Jul-08, 28-Aug-08, 25-Sep-08, 29-Oct-08, 27-Nov-08, 25-Dec-08, 29-Jan-09, 26-Feb-09, 26-Mar-09, 30-Apr-09, 28-May-09, 25-Jun-09, 30-Jul-09, 27-Aug-09, 24-Sep-09, 29-Oct-09, and 26-Nov-09. Returns are proxied by the log difference change in the price index. The index return is calculated as the continuously-compounded return using the closing price:

$$R_t = \ln(\frac{P_t}{P_{t-1}}) * 100\%$$

Now, the study is divided into two parts. First is to determine the expiration day effects on the price volatility and volume for NIFTY Index futures. For determining the expiration day effect on volatility, we took the 30 day moving standard deviation of the returns multiplied by the square root of the no. of trading days which would be 252 in our case:

$$\text{Volatility per annum} = \text{Volatility per trading day} \times \sqrt{\text{No. of trading days per annum}}$$

Both t-test and F-test are applied on the data to find whether the trading volume, volatility and returns change significantly on the expiration day and expiration week effect on volatility of NIFTY futures index.

The effect on trading volume is found out by looking at the absolute volume figures and by analysing graphs. Both t-test and F-test are applied on the data to find whether the trading volume, volatility and returns change significantly on the expiration day. For the expiration week effect on volatility of NIFTY futures index, the data is divided into two groups: the comparison group (having all the returns except that of expiration week) and the expiration group (having the returns of the expiration week). The mean and standard deviation are calculated for both comparison and expiration groups. And then, two-sided t-test is applied to find out whether or not the mean return at expiration is different than the mean return of the data comprising the comparison group. Also, F-test is applied to find out whether or not the volatility at expiration is same or different than the volatility during the comparison weeks. The t-test and F-test is also applied to all data (irrespective of the expiration dates) to find out the expiration week effect on volatility of NIFTY futures index. For the expiration effect on trading volume of NIFTY futures index, the data is again divided into two groups: the comparison group and expiration group and the mean and standard deviation are found out for the two groups. The two-sided t-test is applied to find out whether or not the trading volume at expiration week is different than the trading volume during comparison weeks.

The F-test is used for testing the equality of the variances of two populations. If we let σ_1^2 and σ_2^2 be the variances of two normally distributed populations 1 and 2 respectively, the hypothesis of the two-tailed F-test of differences in the variances can be structured as:

$$H_0 : \sigma_1^2 = \sigma_2^2 \text{ versus } H_a : \sigma_1^2 \neq \sigma_2^2$$

The test-statistic for the F-test is the ratio of sample variances. The F-statistic is computed as:

$$F = \frac{s_1^2}{s_2^2}$$

Where,

s_1^2 = variance of the sample of n_1 observations drawn from population 1

s_2^2 = variance of the sample of n_2 observations drawn from population 2

(n_1-1) and (n_2-1) are the degrees of freedom used along with the significance level to identify the appropriate critical-value from the F-table.

The t-test is used for hypothesis tests concerning the equality of the population means of two populations, based on independent random samples with equal assumed variances. When testing differences between the mean of Population 1, μ_1, and mean of Population 2, μ_2, we may be interested in knowing if the two means are equal (i.e., $\mu_1 = \mu_2$). The hypothesis is structured as:

$$H_0 : \mu_1 - \mu_2 = 0 \text{ versus } H_a : \mu_1 - \mu_2 \neq 0$$

Assuming independent samples, the t-statistic is computed as:

$$t = \frac{(x_1 - x_2) - (\mu_1 - \mu_2)}{\text{sqrt}\left(\frac{s_p^2}{n_1} + \frac{s_p^2}{n_2}\right)}$$

Where,

$$s_p^2 = \frac{(n_1 - 1)s_1^2 + (n_2 - 1)s_2^2}{n_1 + n_2 - 2}$$

s_1^2= variance of the first sample

s_2^2= variance of the second sample

n_1= number of observations in the first sample

n_2=number of observations in the second sample

The degrees of freedom, df, is ($n_1 + n_2 - 2$), and for a test of equality of means, μ_1-μ_2=0

When testing the hypothesis of equality, $\mu_1 - \mu_2$=0, so that the numerator is just the difference between the sample means, $x_1 - x_2$. Since it is assumed that the variances are equal, the variances of the two sample means are just added in order to calculate the standard error in the denominator.

For day of the week effect, we use the Kruskal-Wallis test. The Kruskal-Wallis one way analysis of variance by ranks is a non-parametric method for testing equality of means across groups. It is similar to a one way analysis of variance with the data replaced by their ranks. The reason why we chose this test is that it is non-parametric in nature, and thus does not compel us to assume a normal population. For this purpose, our null hypothesis is that the mean returns across all the trading days are equal. If the Kruskal-Wallis statistic is less than the critical chi-square value, it implies that the null hypothesis should not be rejected, and that mean returns across the week-days are not significantly different from each other. The opposite reasoning holds when the K-W statistic is more than the critical value.

The formula for calculating the K-W statistic is:

$$K - W = \frac{12}{N(N+1)} \sum_{i=1}^{k} R_i^2 - 3(N+1)$$

ANALYSIS

The trading volume for the NIFTY future index increased as the expiration date came nearer. It is maximum around 10-15 days prior to expiration and decreased as the expiration approached. This can be attributed to the fact that the strike price equals the spot price on the expiration date. As far as the price volatility is concerned, it is observed that for some index futures, the volatility increased as expiration date came nearer, for some it decreased and for some it had an irregular pattern. The above Table 1 shows that the daily returns and volatility on the expiration day is not significantly different from the returns and volatilities on other days.

Table 1
Expiration Day Effect on Volatility
Daily returns and standard deviation for the NIFTY future index

Expiry Date	*Statistics*	*Comparison Group*	*Expiration Group*	*t-test*	*Critical t-value (5%)*	*F-test*
Common	Mean	–0.000729	0.00148			
	Standard Deviation	0.027887	0.01476	0.3788	1.96	0.2801

Table 2
Expiration Day Effect on Trading Volume
Daily adjusted trading volume for the NIFTY Future index

Expiry Date	*Statistics*	*Comparison Group*	*Expiration Group*	*t-test*	*Critical t-value (5%)*
Common	Mean	245533.47	485576		
	Standard Deviation	315497.57	114912	3.6433*	1.96

The Table 2 output shows that the trading volume on the expiration day is significantly different than the trading volume on other days at 95% confidence level.

Table 3
Expiration Week Effect on Volatility
Daily returns and standard deviation for the NIFTY future index

Expiry Date	*Statistics*	*Comparison Group*	*Expiration Group*	*t-test*	*F-test*	*Critical t-value*	*Critical F-Value*
29-Nov-07	Mean	–0.0085594	0.00135				
	Standard Deviation	0.02106965	0.017146	–0.78	0.662	2.306	5.41

	Number of Days	6	4				
27-Dec-07	Mean	–0.0007688	0.016303				
	Standard Deviation	0.01829414	0.016303	–1.54	0.794	2.056	3.4
	Number of Days	25	3				
31-Jan-08	Mean	-0.0017997	-0.0122				
	Standard Deviation	0.02696625	0.008383	0.762	0.097	2.01	2.84
	Number of Days	49	4				
28-Feb-08	Mean	-0.0017832	0.5816				
	Standard Deviation	0.02831797	0.00111	40.9*	0.002	2	2.76
	Number of Days	59	4				
27-Mar-08	Mean	-0.0050577	0.45272				
	Standard Deviation	0.03067275	0.015469	29.4*	0.254	2	2.76
	Number of Days	57	4				
24-Apr-08	Mean	-0.0013157	0.00209				
	Standard Deviation	0.02657617	0.009943	-0.25	0.14	2.01	2.8
	Number of Days	50	4				
29-May-08	Mean	-0.0008189	-0.00514				
	Standard Deviation	0.02210138	0.016249	0.382	0.541	2.005	2.8
	Number of Days	53	4				
26-Jun-08	Mean	-0.0023319	-0.00155				
	Standard Deviation	0.01636826	0.020603	-0.09	1.584	2	2.82
	Number of Days	56	4				
31-Jul-08	Mean	-0.0026535	0.000139				
	Standard Deviation	0.02332009	0.025488	-0.23	1.195	2	2.76

	Number of Days	63	4				
28-Aug-08	Mean	-0.0019422	-0.0062				
	Standard Deviation	0.02523011	0.010727	0.333	0.181	2	2.76
	Number of Days	59	4				
25-Sep-08	Mean	0.00084831	-0.0094				
	Standard Deviation	0.02620213	0.013301	0.771	0.258	2	2.82
	Number of Days	58	4				
29-Oct-08	Mean	-0.009766	0.016489				
	Standard Deviation	0.03316047	0.043853	-1.32	1.749	2.0025	3.17
	Number of Days	56	3				
27-Nov-08	Mean	-0.0084689	0.00483				
	Standard Deviation	0.04120625	0.032601	-0.55	0.626	2	3.17
	Number of Days	56	3				
25-Dec-08	Mean	-0.0048474	-0.0188				
	Standard Deviation	0.04293966	0.004211	0.558	0.01	2.005	3.175
	Number of Days	54	3				
29-Jan-09	Mean	-0.0015456	0.020497				
	Standard Deviation	0.03237503	0.025584	-1.15	0.624	2.003	3.17
	Number of Days	55	3				
26-Feb-09	Mean	0.00028159	0.007564				
	Standard Deviation	0.0136065	0.005795	-0.92	0.181	2.0025	3.17
	Number of Days	55	3				
26-Mar-09	Mean	-0.0005554	0.023899				
	Standard Deviation	0.02405466	0.020811	-1.98	0.748	2.0025	2.8

	Number of Days	55	4				
30-Apr-09	Mean	0.00365162	-0.00078				
	Standard Deviation	0.02268042	0.033884	0.322	2.232	2.005	3.16
	Number of Days	53	3				
28-May-09	Mean	0.00857163	0.00496				
	Standard Deviation	0.03150738	0.029598	0.222	0.882	2.005	2.8
	Number of Days	52	4				
25-Jun-09	Mean	0.00599638	-0.00479				
	Standard Deviation	0.00825194	0.015665	2.36*	3.60*	2.005	2.8
	Number of Days	54	4				
30-Jul-09	Mean	0.0037833	-0.00024				
	Standard Deviation	0.09824903	0.010254	0.081	0.011	2	2.76
	Number of Days	59	4				
27-Aug-09	Mean	0.00031302	0.008229				
	Standard Deviation	0.02090352	0.011354	-0.75	0.295	2	2.76
	Number of Days	60	4				
24-Sep-09	Mean	0.00178311	0.005969				
	Standard Deviation	0.01930809	0.014237	-0.3	0.544	2.005	2.8
	Number of Days	55	2				
Common	Mean	-0.0009452	0.002901				
	Standard Deviation	0.02814569	0.020306	7.51*	1.521	1.96	1.39
	Number of Days	1199	83				

It is seen from the Table 3 that the returns in the expiration week are significantly different than the returns in other comparison weeks for 3 out of 25 NIFTY futures index (with different expiration dates). Also, the volatility of the futures in the expiration week is significantly different than that of comparison week in one case only. Effectively, the weekly returns and volatilities of NIFTY futures during the expiration week are not significantly different from the returns and volatilities during other comparison weeks. The evidence indicates that the trading volume on expiration days and in expiration weeks is significantly larger than on comparison days and during comparison weeks. So, it suggests that there are no price distortions on the expiration day or during the expiration week for the complete sample period.

Table 4
Expiration Week Effect on Trading Volume
Daily adjusted trading volume for the NIFTY Future index

Expiry Date	*Statistics*	*Comparison Group*	*Expiration Group*	*t-test*	*Critical t-value*
29-Nov-07	Mean	529493.6	461408		
	Standard Deviation	174767.5	42593.7	0.75	2.262
	Number of Days	7	4		
27-Dec-07	Mean	317851.9	359967		
	Standard Deviation	212112.7	91027.7	-0.34	2.053
	Number of Days	26	3		
31-Jan-08	Mean	271830.1	499531		
	Standard Deviation	303361.7	33366.3	-1.49	2.01
	Number of Days	50	4		
28-Feb-08	Mean	179746.3	543853		
	Standard Deviation	244885.6	83282	2.94*	2
	Number of Days	60	4		
27-Mar-08	Mean	187810.2	686649		
	Standard Deviation	300942.2	150929	3.27*	2
	Number of Days	58	4		
24-Apr-08	Mean	199821.9	349031		
	Standard Deviation	286414.5	74333	-1.03	2.01

	Number of Days	51	4		
29-May-08	Mean	170000.1	446572		
	Standard Deviation	197514.5	57687.3	2.77*	2.005
	Number of Days	54	4		
26-Jun-08	Mean	207278.2	781859		
	Standard Deviation	291605.4	97260.5	-3.9*	2
	Number of Days	57	4		
31-Jul-08	Mean	283721.7	534744		
	Standard Deviation	359965.5	124235	-1.38	2
	Number of Days	64	4		
28-Aug-08	Mean	176875.4	461116		
	Standard Deviation	258568.4	27013.7	2.18*	2
	Number of Days	60	4		
25-Sep-08	Mean	206167.2	653822		
	Standard Deviation	320744.8	75152.6	2.77*	2
	Number of Days	59	4		
29-Oct-08	Mean	312692.1	648657		
	Standard Deviation	404711.2	425071	-1.4	2.003
	Number of Days	57	3		
27-Nov-08	Mean	285067.4	712969		
	Standard Deviation	391268.2	148140	-1.87	2
	Number of Days	57	4		
25-Dec-08	Mean	239408.1	611645		
	Standard Deviation	347102.2	134511	-1.84	2.003

	Number of Days	55	3		
29-Jan-09	Mean	271794.4	533759		
	Standard Deviation	332775.2	96976.2	-1.35	2.001
	Number of Days	56	3		
26-Feb-09	Mean	210350.1	542620		
	Standard Deviation	286168.4	145651	-1.99	2.001
	Number of Days	56	3		
26-Mar-09	Mean	213443.6	812752		
	Standard Deviation	320441.3	120205	-3.7*	2.001
	Number of Days	56	4		
30-Apr-09	Mean	297786.4	742186		
	Standard Deviation	380553.1	99586.7	-2*	2.005
	Number of Days	54	3		
28-May-09	Mean	226511.8	552379		
	Standard Deviation	319794.2	68401	2.02*	2.005
	Number of Days	53	4		
25-Jun-09	Mean	194571.3	587845		
	Standard Deviation	261768.1	70632.9	2.97*	2.001
	Number of Days	55	4		
30-Jul-09	Mean	242088.9	539921		
	Standard Deviation	307691.6	227502	-1.9	2
	Number of Days	60	4		
27-Aug-09	Mean	197071.2	501592		
	Standard Deviation	294255.2	93233.1	2.05*	2

	Number of Days	61	4		
24-Sep-09	Mean	134080.1	441955		
	Standard Deviation	230090.5	34567.6	-1.88	2.001
	Number of Days	56	2		
Common	Mean	216957.7	566164		
	Standard Deviation	306701.4	165922	10.3*	1.96
	Number of Days	1222	83		

* Null hypothesis rejected at 5% significance level

It is seen from the Table 4 that the trading volume during the expiration week is significantly different than that of other comparison weeks for 9 out of 25 cases. Also, when all the NIFTY futures indices are taken as one irrespective of their expiration dates, it is found that the trading volume during expiration week is found to be significantly different than that of other comparison weeks at 5% significance level. The significantly higher trading volumes on the expiration day and during the expiration week suggest that arbitrage activity took place and that positions are unwound at and before the actual expiration.

Table 5
Day-of-the-Week Effect: NIFTY Futures
Kruskal-Wallis Test

Day	*N*	*Mean Rank*
Monday	13	31.92
Tuesday	13	40.38
Wednesday	12	28.17
Thursday	10	22.70
Friday	11	24.09
Total	59	

Test Statistics

Chi-square	8.160*
df	4
Asymp.sig	0.086

The null hypothesis states that the mean rank of the returns in the given period is equal for all weekdays. The probability of the Kruskal-Wallis is 0.086, which is less than or equal to the level of significance of 10%. We reject the null hypothesis that the mean rank of the returns in the given time horizon are different for one or more weekdays.

Table 6
Day-of-Week Effect

Expiry Date	*Chi-square Value*	*Asymp. Sig.*
29-Nov-07	7.091	0.131
27-Dec-07	2.117	0.714
31-Jan-08	5.043	0.283
28-Feb-08	2.178	0.703
27-Mar-08	2.846	0.584
24-Apr-08	1.312	0.859
29-May-08	2.161	0.706
26-Jun-08	2.258	0.668
31-Jul-08	7.795*	0.093
28-Aug-08	4.281	0.369
25-Sep-08	6.389	0.172
29-Oct-08	8.16*	0.086
27-Nov-08	4.445	0.349
25-Dec-08	2.121	0.714
29-Jan-09	2.618	0.624
26-Feb-09	0.453	0.978
26-Mar-09	1.681	0.794
30-Apr-09	7.562*	0.109
28-May-09	3.576	0.466
25-Jun-09	2.173	0.704
30-Jul-09	3.482	0.481
27-Aug-09	2.824	0.588
24-Sep-09	3.047	0.555
29-Oct-09	1.26	0.868
26-Nov-09	3.436	0.488

* Null hypothesis rejected at 10% significance level

K-W statistics gives us a basic idea of non-existence of the market anomalies in the Indian market. It is clearly visible from Table 6 that day-of-the-week effect is observed in only three out of twenty-five futures indices expiration dates. This indicates that day-of-the-week effect is not present in almost all of the NIFTY futures indices. This could be attributed to the fact that the data we have taken is primarily of the bearish phase. However, one needs to discount these findings in light of the fact that the K-W test is after all a non-parametric test, and its results are not conclusive.

Table 7
Day-of-the-week effect: 50 stocks constituting the NIFTY

Name of Stock	*Bullish*	*Weekday Effect Observed for Bullish Market*	*Bearish*	*Weekday Effect Observed for Bearish Market*
ABB Ltd.	35.994	Y	42.217	Y
ACC Ltd.	48.077	Y	5.822	N
Ambuja Cements Ltd.	3.984	N	11.322	Y
Axis Bank Ltd.	1.95	N	599.19	Y
Bharat Heavy Electricals Ltd.	43.76	Y	11.544	Y
Bharat Petroleum Corporation Ltd.	15.276	Y	9.69	Y
Bharti Airtel Ltd.	16.34	Y	6.392	N
Cairn India Ltd.	3.151	N	6.69	N
Cipla Ltd.	40.17	Y	1.352	N
DLF Ltd.	3.213	N	1.84	N
GAIL (India) Ltd.	35.374	Y	-189.327	N
Grasim Industries Ltd.	41.449	Y	2.752	N
HCL Technologies Ltd.	51.9	Y	2.998	N
HDFC Bank Ltd.	60.01	Y	1.424	N
Hero Honda Motors Ltd.	52.758	Y	3.925	N
Hindalco Industries Ltd.	4.34	N	3.222	N
Hindustan Unilever Ltd.	8.04	N	-59.7	N
Housing Development Finance Corporation Ltd.	45.397	Y	0.8679	N
I T C Ltd.	41.01	Y	1.688	N
ICICI Bank Ltd.	42.62	Y	1.171	N
Idea Cellular Ltd.	2.98	N	6.91	N
Infosys Technologies Ltd.	43.49	Y	4.32	N
Jindal Steel & Power Ltd.	33.4	Y	2.176	N
Larsen & Toubro Ltd.	-9.43	N	3.177	N
Mahindra & Mahindra Ltd.	41.95	Y	2.002	N
Maruti Suzuki India Ltd.	48.51	Y	1.698	N
NTPC Ltd.	30.004	Y	1.129	N
National Aluminium Co. Ltd.	38.59	Y	2.29	N
Oil & Natural Gas Corporation Ltd.	42.89	Y	1.482	N
Power Grid Corporation of India	3.551	N	1.636	N

Punjab National Bank	45.8	Y	-5.44	N
Ranbaxy Laboratories Ltd.	44.174	Y	4.977	N
Reliance Capital Ltd.	42.62	Y	2.8	N
Reliance Communications Ltd.	11.18	Y	2.04	N
Reliance Industries Ltd.	43.88	Y	2.66	N
Reliance Infrastructure Ltd.			1.334	N
Reliance Power Ltd.			1.504	N
Siemens Ltd.	39.45	Y	2.508	N
State Bank of India	42.3	Y	2.384	N
Steel Authority of India Ltd.	35.875	Y	1.535	N
Sterlite Industries (India) Ltd.	26.33	Y	2.695	N
Sun Pharmaceutical Industries	40.77	Y	2.021	N
Suzlon Energy Ltd.	20.736	Y	7.827	N
Tata Communications Ltd.			4.076	N
Tata Consultancy Services Ltd.	39.89	Y	4.79	N
Tata Motors Ltd.	49.88	Y	4.688	N
Tata Power Co. Ltd.	37.58	Y	3.814	N
Tata Steel Ltd.	13.64	Y	1.66	N
Unitech Ltd.	38.588	Y	1.03	N
Wipro Ltd.	50.83	Y	-8.5	N

It is observed from the Table 7 that three stocks — Tata Communications Ltd., Reliance Power Ltd. and Reliance Infrastructure Ltd. are listed at the beginning of the bearish phase, hence the k-values for the bullish phase are absent for these stocks. It is also evident that in the bullish phase (1st January 2005 to 18th January 2008), 38 stocks exhibit the weekday effect and 9 stocks don't exhibit the weekday effect. In the bearish phase (21st January, 2008 to 6th August, 2009), 5 stocks exhibit the weekday effect and 45 stocks don't exhibit the weekday effect.

CONCLUDING OBSERVATION

This chapter examined potential expiration effects on the nifty index by comparing the trading volume and return process on expiration days and during expiration weeks with a set of comparison days and comparison weeks. On the basis of our analysis, it is found that the daily returns and volatility on the expiration day is not significantly different from the returns and volatilities on other days. But the trading volume on the expiration day is significantly different than the trading volume on other days at 95% confidence level. It is also observed from the expiration week effects on volatility and trading volume and found that the weekly returns and volatilities of NIFTY futures during the expiration week are not significantly different from the returns and volatilities during other comparison weeks. The results suggest that there are no price distortions on the expiration day or during the expiration week for the complete sample period. The study also found that day-of-the-week effect is not present in almost all of the NIFTY futures indices. While looking for day-of-the-week effect for the fifty stocks constituting the NIFTY, it is found that in the bullish phase thirty-eight stocks exhibit the weekday effect and nine stocks don't exhibit the weekday effect. In the bearish phase five stocks exhibit the weekday effect and forty stocks don't exhibit the weekday effect. One of the limitations of study is that we have used the K-W test which only gives us an indicative answer, and not a conclusive one. Secondly, we have taken data for a period of two years. This period is mainly turmoil phase of world financial market. So, the day-of-the-week effect in case of derivatives and stocks have shown similar results because of the common time period chosen in the stock market. This can be attributed to the fact that all investors think in same way and are driven by the same instincts during these phases of the market.

REVIEW QUESTIONS

1. How do the Expiration day price effects take place?
2. What is the significance of calendar anomalies?
3. How many hypotheses have been suggested to explain the day-of-the-week effect? Justify it relevance to stock market?
4. How do you resolve the expiration day effects and volatility in stock market?
5. Quiz
   (a) _____ Hypothesis suggests that investors buy when prices are low and sell after prices increase.
   (b) _____ effects may arise from stock index arbitrageurs unwinding of arbitrage positions in the stock market.
   (c) Expiration day refers to the last _____ when all contracts expire; expiration hour refers to the last _____ of the expiration day.
   (d) Which hypothesis suggests that the delay in cash payment for the security can lead to escalation of rate of returns on specific days due to extra credit period availability?

4

Currency Derivatives in Indian Stock Market

As the process of deregulation moves on, the need for various derivative instruments for covering foreign exchange risk is felt more and more. Thus, in this context, priorities preferences and perception of derivative products has become essential for corporate firm and stock market as well. This chapter also highlights the issues that need to be addressed to increase the pace of development of this segment of the financial sector.

INTRODUCTION

Foreign exchange market in India has made significant strides in the recent years. To facilitate the increased cross-border transfer of funds, the RBI has permitted exchange trade of currency futures in 2008. Consequently, currency futures contracts were introduced for trading on the National Stock Exchange Ltd. (NSE) with effect from Aug 29, 2008. Following this, two more exchanges, Bombay Stock Exchange (BSE) and Multi-Commodity Exchange-Stock Exchange (MCX-SX), also started offering currency futures trade in Sept and Oct respectively, in 2008. Soon after their introduction, trading in currency futures picked up momentum quickly and the total volumes reached ₹ 5.14 lakh crore by the end of May 2009. Currency Option has been the recent introduction, introduced on October 29, 2010 only. Underlying currency pairs for currency futures are USD-INR, EUR-INR, GBP-INR and JPY-INR. In case of currency options underlying currency pair is only USD-INR, while currency forwards are available for all currency pairs. However, futures' trading also involves speculators and arbitrageurs who don't have any underlying physical exposure but participate in trading with profit motive. As a result, there are apprehensions that the excessive speculation may adversely affect both futures as well as the underlying spot markets. Derivatives are widely used worldwide for hedging risk.

The objective of this chapter is to examine the perception of corporate executive towards derivative products through marketing variables. Further, this chapter studies the trends of trading in the Currency Derivatives market to understand the comparative economics driving currency derivatives in India.

WHAT ARE ADVANTAGES OF CURRENCY DERIVATIVES?

The main advantage of currency futures is its closest substitute product, viz., forwards which is traded over-the-counter (OTC) exchange. At present, various banks are providing the hedging of foreign exchange exposure through options to its clients. As the FX market is developing in India and foreign trade is increasing on a very fast pace so the opportunities are just started coming. Currency Option Pricing in banks is done through software called Super Derivative (SD) Software. Also due to flooding of foreign currency in India and the frequent interest rate changes taking place in the economy, the exchange rate fluctuation has become very pronounced. So in order to hedge them from the foreign currency fluctuation Indian corporate are using these non-linear hedge instruments options in order to hedge their risk. Currency options are primarily traded in the over-the-counter market. The advantage of this market is that large trades are possible with strike prices, expiration dates, and other features tailored to meet the needs of corporate treasurers.

LET'S TAKE THE SURVEY OF CORPORATE EXECUTIVES TO KNOW THE PERCEPTION OF CURRENCY FUTURES MARKETS IN INDIA:

This chapter has been based in a questioner survey of 200 corporate executives, which cover the companies randomly selected from those having foreign business operations mainly in Delhi and Bombay. Simple techniques like percentage, weighted average score, standard deviation and ranking method have been used to determine the perception of corporate executive towards derivative products. For further analysis to know the impact of currency futures market on trading volume, data for the Spot rate and forwards rate is taken from RBI, while data on Futures rate is taken from nseindia.com. In order to bring compatibility, the data is collated into different term structures like 1-month, 3-month, 6 month and one-year. Data corresponding to only 1-month contracts is used for the subsequent tests. One-month contract offers the maximum liquidity as has been observed in trend analysis and to keep the complexity of the analysis to the minimum.

ANALYSIS

One of the important determinants of the value of the rupee is India's trading position with our major export markets, as well as generally commodity price levels. Long-run real interest rate differentials, relative money supplies as well as the level of GDP also influence exchange rates. A foreign exchange risk exposure exists whenever the receipts or payments are denominated in foreign currency. The firms operation is relate to trade transaction or financial transaction. The exchange rate risk is cause due to this operation. The Table 1 presents the opinion of corporate executive regarding the transaction specifically, which create exchange risk for the company.

Table 1
Operation Causing Exchange Rate Risk

Operations	*Response*	*Percentage*
Exports	80	40
Imports	70	35
Borrowings	40	20
Lending	10	5

It is observed from the table 1 that 40 per cent corporate executive have opined that majority of operations are limited to trade activities, which exposes the corporate firm to exchange risk. Twenty-five per cent expressed that the firm is also exposed to risk due to borrowings and lending. Indian firms are having little scope for lending foreign currency but they frequently borrowed more in foreign currency.

Table 2
Yearly Foreign Exchange Transaction

Size of transaction (Million)	*Response*	*Percentage*
Less than <10 million	36	18
10-50	40	20
50-100	20	10
100-500	50	25
500-1 billion	30	15
> 1 billion	26	13

The corporate were asked to specify their size of foreign exchange transaction made in the firms. It is evident from the table 2 that 25 per cent corporate executive have opinion that most of the companies have a foreign transaction in the range of 100-500 million. About 18 per cent companies have their foreign exchange transaction at less than 10 million. Only 13 per cent of companies have more than ₹ 1 billion of foreign exchange.

Table 3
Foreign Exchange Exposure Covered

Extent of coverage	*Response*	*Percentage*	*Cumulative*
100 per cent	70	35	35
90 per cent	20	10	45
80 per cent	21	10.5	55.5
70 per cent	22	11	66.5
60 per cent	15	7.5	74
50 per cent	32	16	100

It is inferred from the Table 3 that only 30 per cent of companies cover their exposure fully. About half of the companies cover their exposure upto 80 per cent. Still it is required to opt for active exchange exposure management.

Table 4
Hedging Strategy Applied to Control Depreciation of Local Currency

Strategies	*Response*	*Percentage*
Sell local currency forward	60	30
Reduce local currency receivables	20	10
Reduce local currency cash and MKT Securities	22	11
Delay collection hard currency	30	15
Borrow locally	12	6
Delay payments of accounts payable	10	5
Speed up dividend and other remittances to parent	8	4
Invoice exports in foreign currency and imports in local currency	38	19

The Table 4 depicts that 30 per cent corporate executives gave their opinion that selling of local currency forward is the most popular strategy. 19 per cent opinion that the next strategy responding to anticipated depreciation of local currency are invoice exports in foreign currency and imports in local currency 16 per cent focused delay collection hard currency is also equal techniques to anticipated depreciation of local currency.

Table 5
Hedging Strategies against Anticipated Appreciation of Local Currency

Strategy	*Response*	*Percentage*
Buy local currency forward	60	30
Increase levels of local currency cash and marketable securities	28	14
Relax local currency credit terms	20	10
Speed up collection of soft-currency	22	11
Reduce local borrowing	24	12
Speed up payments of accounts payable	16	8
Delay dividend and other remittances to parent	4	2
Invoice exports in local currency and imports in foreign currency	26	13

It is inferred from the Table 5 that 30 per cent have gave their opinion that buying local currency forward is the most popular method to hedge the anticipated appreciation of local currency. 13 per cent gave their view that invoicing exports in local currency is the next popular method to hedge the appreciation of local currency. It is interesting to note here that in case of anticipated depreciation, invoicing in a currency of one's choice has greater relative popularity than in the case of anticipated appreciation of local currency.

Table 6
Preference for Derivative Instruments

	Ranking Response				***Score***	***Total Score***	***Mean S.D***	***Rank***
Instrument	1	2	3	4			.	
Currency forward contracts	9	45	0	29	186	2.26	.26	1
Currency options	15	39	30	0	180	2.14	.25	2
Currency swaps	3	12	57	0	141	2	.28	3
Currency futures	48	20	8	0	104	1.36	.36	4

It is observed from the Table 6 that currency forward contract is the most preferred instrument, followed by currency options, currency swaps and currency futures. Surprisingly, currency futures contracts are perceived to be the least preferred instrument among the companies as the standard deviation is more in currency features.

Table 7
Popularity of Derivative Instrument Hedging Foreign Exchange Risk

	Ranking Response				***Score***	***Total Score***	***Mean S.D***	***Rank***
Instrument	1	2	3	4				
Currency forward	10	42	35	0	199	2.3	.24	1
Currency options	20	35	32	0	186	2.13	.25	2
Currency swaps	8	12	45	15	152	1.9	.28	3
Currency futures	40	10	4	6	96	1.6	.37	4

The able 7 exhibits that currency forward contracts is the most popular instrument, because of familiarity about it. It is already used by the most of the companies. The least popularity instrument is the currency feature. The S.D. is also high indicating 0.37.

Table 8
Use of Derivative instrument

	Response	***Percentage***
Slowly	90	45
Very Slowly	12	6
Speedily	80	40
Very Speedily	18	9

The Table 8 exhibits the use of derivative instruments in the Indian Stock Market. It becomes clear from the table that majority of responses are in the middle, meaning thereby, speedily (forty per cent), or slowly (forty-five per cent). The extreme responses such as very speedily (nine per cent) and very slowly (six per cent) both accounting for fifteen per cent response. About 45 per cent are in favour of slowly is in tune with general reluctance seen in the use of currency options. Though this instrument has launched in much earlier but only few deals have been made so far. However, 40 per cent are in favour of speedily may be indicative of the momentum that the use of this instrument may gather in the coming future.

Table 9

Preference for the Maturity Period of Derivative Instrument

Maturity period	*Ranking Response*							*Total Score*	*Mean Score*
	1	2	3	4	5	6	7		
One month	0	50	0	0	0	0	150	1150	5.75
Two months	0	0	40	0	0	40	120	1200	6.00
Three months	0	0	0	0	16.6	33.4	150	1250.4	6.67
Six months	0	0	0	16.6	0	16.6	166.6	1342.2	6.71
Nine months	0	0	100	0	100	0	0	800	4.00
Twelve months	0	66.6	0	66.6	0	0	66.6	599.4	4.32

It is evident from the Table 9 that generally the corporate management practitioners followed by six months, two months, one month, and 1 year and nine months prefer the maturity period of three months.

It is to be noted here that neither two long periods nor too short period is preferred by the corporate world. The reason is that maturity for setting the underlying transaction match exactly with the maturity of the derivative instrument used for hedging.

Table 10

Foreign Exchange Risk Management

Advisor	*Response*	*Percentage*
Outside individual consultant	30	15
Outside Institutional consultancy services	48	24
Internal teams	80	40
Any other	42	21

It is inferred from the Table 10 that majority of the firms (40 per cent) depend on their internal teams to take advice on exchange risk management followed by outside institutional. Only 15 per cent consultancy services firms are seeking advice of outside individual consultant. Also 21 per cent used other source but they have not specified the exact source, which they are using. It is apparent that corporate firms are developing expertise of their own to take decision on foreign exchange risk management.

Further an analysis has been made to determine the trends in the trade of Currency forwards in Indian market. It is found from the Fig. 1 that majority of the trades are concentrated in the tenor of 6 months to one year followed by less than 30 days and 30-90 days tenor. The shares of less than 30 days and 30-90 days were almost equal during most of the time though, the trade concentration in the shortest tenor (<30 days) has increased significantly during 2008-09 and 2009-10. On the other hand, the share of 90-180 days tenor has steadily declined through the past 7 years. The Fig. 1 shown below also depicts the same.

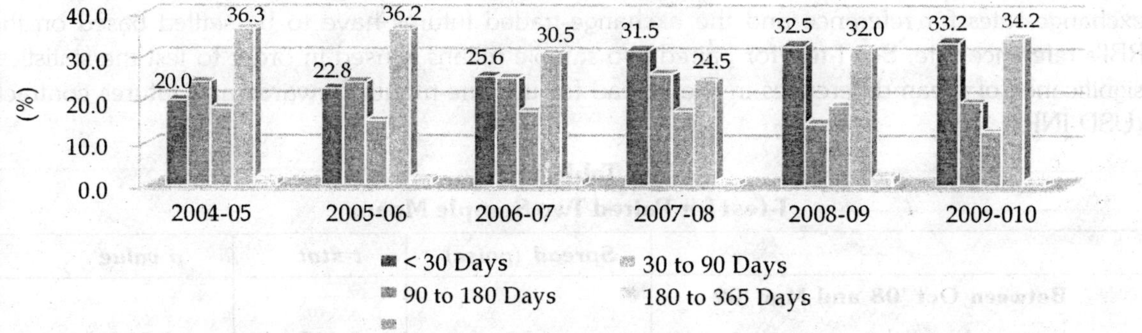

Fig. 1: Currency Forwards: tenor Analysis

The Fig. 2 indicated that currency futures gained significant volumes soon after their introduction on domestic exchanges and have grown many folds, from about ₹ 5 thousand crore in September 2008 to ₹124 thousand crore in May 2009. Unlike the case of OTC forward market, where trading is well diversified across different tenors and the long tenors are relatively more active, futures volumes have largely been confined to near-month contracts accounting for about 90%. Although three trading platforms are available for trading, the BSE could not gain much volume while the MCX-SX and NSE have been contributing nearly equal share to the total traded volumes of currency futures market depicted in Fig. 2.

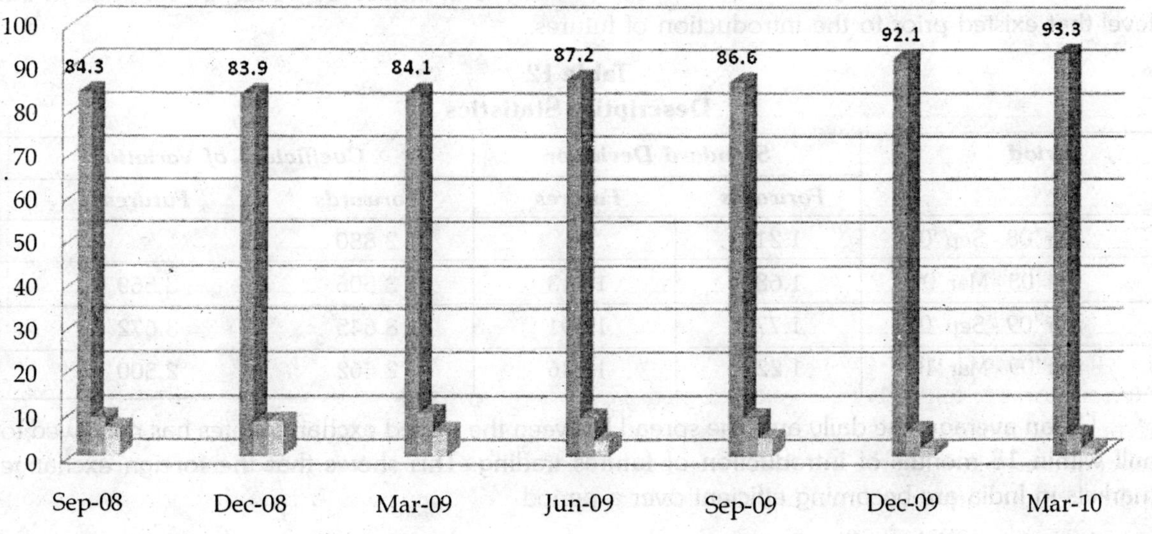

Fig. 2: Currency Futures: Tenor Analysis

Simultaneous trade of foreign exchange on different platforms as well as in the OTC market provides arbitrage opportunity if there is any significant difference in the rates traded across different platforms. *Lesser the spread, efficient are the markets.* Spread between the exchange traded futures and OTC forwards is calculated and tested for its statistical significance. RBI also fixes daily exchange rates for reference and the exchange-traded futures have to be settled based on the RBI's reference rate. So, T-test for paired two sample means is used in order to test the statistical significance of mean differences in the spread for the one-month forwards and futures contracts (USD-INR).

Table 11

T-test for Paired Two Sample Means

	Spread (paise)	*t-stat*	*p value*
Between Oct '08 and Mar '09			
Futures - Forwards	6.33	2.465	0.037
Between Apr '09 and Sep '09			
Futures - Forwards	3.09	2.591	0.053
Between Oct '09 and Mar '10			
Futures - Forwards	2.99	2.602	0.082

Volatility in the three exchange rates is measured by using the standard deviation and coefficient of variation. The results indicated in the Table 12 that the volatility is relatively lower in the case of forwards prior to introduction of futures. Although the increase in volatility during Oct '08 - Sep'09 coincided with the introduction of futures, the volatility level in Oct '09 - Mar '10 returned to the level that existed prior to the introduction of futures.

Table 12

Descriptive Statistics

Period	*Standard Deviation*		*Coefficient of Variation*	
	Forwards	*Futures*	*Forwards*	*Futures*
Apr '08 - Sep '08	1.216	-	2.880	-
Oct '08 - Mar '09	1.680	1.713	3.506	3.569
Apr '09 - Sep '09	1.776	1.791	3.645	3.672
Oct '09 - Mar '10	1.227	1.246	2.462	2.500

On an average, the daily average spread between the traded exchange rates has narrowed to half within 18 months of introduction of futures trading. This shows that the foreign exchange markets in India are becoming efficient over a period

It is observed from Fig. 3 that there is no perceptible impact of futures trading on forward trade volumes is found. Trade volumes in forwards declined during Dec '08 quarter coinciding with the initiation of currency futures trade. But the period also coincided with the deepening of global financial crisis that led to less activity in financial markets in general. Barring last quarter of 2008 and beginning few months of 2009, the activity in the currency forwards returned to its previous growth levels is exhibited in Fig. 3.

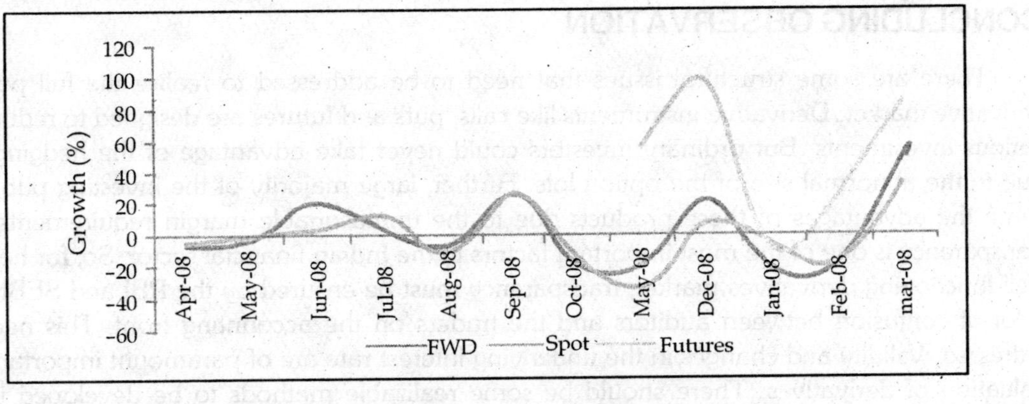

Fig. 3: Growth Trends in Foreign Exchange Volumes

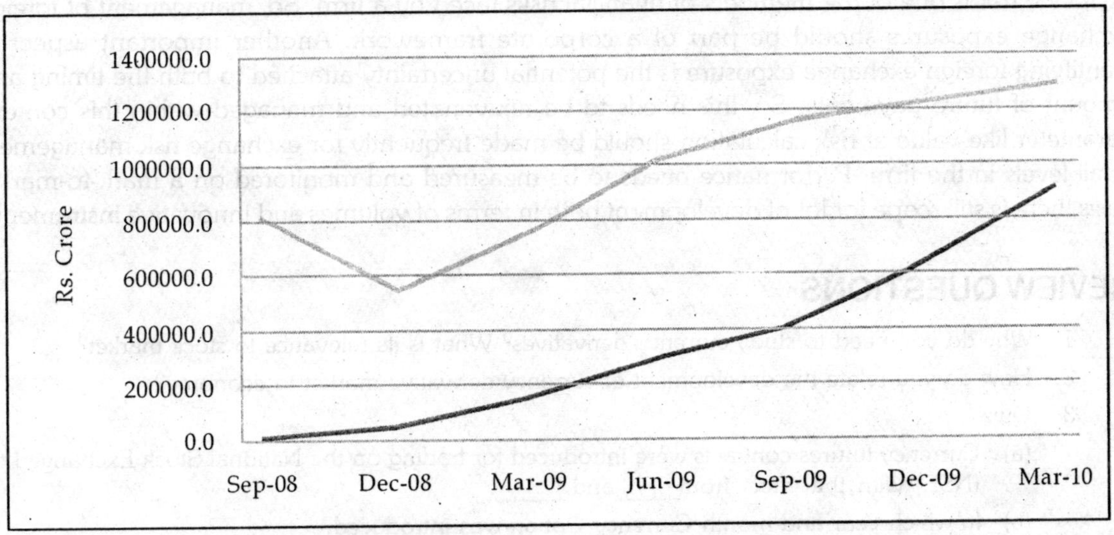

Fig. 4: Growth Trends from Dec '08 to Mar '10

No notable shift in volumes from forwards to futures, despite the rapid and significant increase in futures volumes. The existing trends so far suggest that despite the significant rise in futures volumes, there was no notable shift in volumes from forwards to futures market. The fee structure and near-month liquidity in currency futures possibly attracted the participation of arbitrageurs and speculators, while the hedgers continued to prefer OTC forward contracts due to the flexibility and customization particularly in case of long-term requirements. Thus, the remarkable growth in futures could not bring any notable changes in forward markets so far since the purpose as well as nature of participation in futures was different from that of the forwards market.

CONCLUDING OBSERVATION

There are some structural issues that need to be addressed to realize the full potential of derivative market. Derivative instruments like calls, puts and futures are designed to reduce risks in various investments. But ordinary investors could never take advantage of the hedging facilities due to the abnormal size of the option lots. Further, large majority of the investing public do not share the advantages of these products due to the unreasonable margin requirements. Lack of transparency is one of the most important factors in the Indian financial sector. So, for healthy and well-functioning derivatives market, transparency must be ensured by the RBI and SEBI. There is a lot of confusion between auditors and the traders on the accounting front. This needs to be redressed. Validity and changes in the underlying interest rate are of paramount importance to the valuation of derivatives. There should be some realizable methods to be developed to predict these parameters. There is a lack of awareness of the derivatives product. So, corporate sector units are needed to be educated about their use of derivatives, advantages as well as risks. Foreign exchange risk is one of the members of financial risks faced by a firm. So, management of foreign exchange exposures should be part of a corporate framework. Another important aspect of identifying foreign exchange exposure is the potential uncertainty attached to both the timing and amount of future payments. So, this needs to be rejuvenated and managed within this context. Parameter like value at risk calculation should be made frequently for exchange risk management at all levels in the firm. Performance needs to be measured and monitored on a mark-to-market basis there is still scope for lot of development both in terms of volumes and innovative instruments.

REVIEW QUESTIONS

1. Why do you need to study currency derivatives? What is its relevance to stock market?
2. How do you relate the development of currency derivative market to economy?
3. Quiz
   (a) Currency futures contracts were introduced for trading on the National Stock Exchange Ltd. (NSE) with the effect from_____and _____.
   (b) In which year and month Currency Option was introduced?
   (c) Currency Option pricing in banks is done through software called _____.

5

A Study on Commodity Market in India

The present chapter has been undertaken to study the effect of global financial crisis on Commodity Market in India. This chapter also discuss the effect of global financial crisis on spot prices and future price of select agricultural commodities in India and compare the performance of Indian stock market and commodities market during the meltdown period.

INTRODUCTION

The stock markets, financial markets, export of goods and services and corporate profits have witnessed negative growth during global financial crisis period and its effects had been well studied and widely reported in media, business magazines and academic journals. However, no research is made so far to study the effect of global financial crisis/meltdown effects on agricultural commodities markets in the Indian context. The commodity markets in India are social institutions that facilitate exchange of goods for money. The cost of goods is estimated in terms of domestic currency.

Indian Commodity Market is subdivided into the following two categories: Wholesale Market and Retail Market. The traditional wholesale market in India dealt with wholesalers who bought goods from the farmers and manufacturers and then sold them to the retailers after making a profit in the process. It is the retailers who finally sold the goods to the consumers. With the passage of time, the importance of wholesalers began to vanish due to the improvement in transport facilities which made the retailers easy to directly interact with the producers. In recent years, the extent of the retail market (both organized and unorganized) has evolved in leaps and bounds. In fact, the success stories of the commodity market of India in recent years have mainly centred on the growth generated by the Retail Sector. Almost every commodity under both agricultural and industrial is now being provided at well distributed retail outlets throughout the country. Moreover, the retail outlets belong to both the organized as well as the unorganized sector. The unorganized retail outlets consist of small shopowners who are price takers where consumers face a highly competitive price structure. The organized sectors on the other hand are owned by various business houses like Pantaloons, Reliance, Tata and others. Such markets are usually selling a wide range of articles — agricultural and manufactured, edible and inedible, perishable and durable. Modern marketing strategies and other techniques of sales promotion enable such markets to draw customers from every section of the society. However, the growth of such markets has still centred on the urban areas primarily due to infrastructural limitations. Considering the present growth rate, the total valuation of the Indian Retail Market is estimated to cross ₹ 10,000 billion by the year 2010. Demand for commodities is likely to become four times by 2010 than what it presently is.

WHAT IS COMMODITY MARKET?

A commodity may be defined as an article, a product or material that is bought and sold. It is classified as every kind of movable property, except Actionable Claims, Money and Securities. Commodities actually offer immense potential to become a separate asset class for market-savvy investors, arbitrageurs and speculators. Retail investors, who claim to understand the equity markets, may find commodities an unsounded market. But commodities are easy to understand as far as fundamentals of demand and supply are concerned. Retail investors should understand the risks and advantages of trading in commodities futures before taking a leap. Historically, pricing in commodities futures has been less volatile compared with equity and bonds, thus providing an efficient portfolio diversification option. In fact, the size of the commodities markets in India is also quite significant. Of the country's GDP of ₹ 13, 20,730 crore (₹ 13,207.3 billion), commodities related (and dependent) industries constitute about 58 per cent. Currently, the various commodities across the country monitor an annual turnover of ₹ 1, 40,000 crore (₹ 1,400 billion). With the introduction of futures trading, the size of the commodities market grows many folds hereon.

HISTORY OF COMMODITY MARKETS

Commodities future trading was evolved from need of assured continuous supply of seasonal agricultural crops. The concept of organized trading in commodities evolved in Chicago, in 1848. But one can trace its roots in Japan. In 19th century, Chicago in United States had emerged as a major commercial hub. So that wheat producers from Mid-west attracted here to sell their produce to dealers and distributors. Due to lack of organized storage facilities, absence of uniform weighing and grading mechanisms, producers often confined to the mercy of dealers discretion. These situations lead to need of establishing a common meeting place for farmers and dealers to transact in spot grain to deliver wheat and receive cash in return.

Gradually, sellers and buyers started making commitments to exchange the produce for cash in future and thus contract for "futures trading" evolved; whereby the producer would agree to sell his produce to the buyer at a future delivery date at an agreed upon price. Trading of wheat in futures became very profitable which encouraged the entry of other commodities in futures market. This created a platform for establishment of a body to regulate and supervise these contracts. That's why Chicago Board of Trade (CBOT) was established in 1848. In 1870 and 1880s, the New York Coffee, Cotton and Produce Exchanges were born. Agricultural commodities were mostly traded but as long as there are buyers and sellers, any commodity can be traded. In 1872, a group of Manhattan dairy merchants got together to bring chaotic condition in New York market to a system in terms of storage, pricing, and transfer of agricultural products. The largest commodity exchange in USA is Chicago Board of Trade, The Chicago Mercantile Exchange, the New York Mercantile Exchange, the New York Commodity Exchange and New York Coffee, Sugar and Cocoa Exchange. Worldwide, there are major futures trading exchanges in over twenty countries including Canada, England, India, France, Singapore, Japan, Australia and New Zealand.

Some of the Commodity Exchanges of the World are:

Table 1

S. No.	*Global Commodity Exchanges*
1	New York Mercantile Exchange (NYMEX)
2	London Metal Exchange (LME)
3	Chicago Board of Trade (CBOT)
4	New York Board of Trade (NYBOT)
5	Kansas Board of Trade
6	Winnipeg Commodity Exchange, Manitoba
7	Dalian Commodity Exchange, China
8	Bursa Malaysia Derivatives exchange
9	Singapore Commodity Exchange (SICOM)
10	Chicago Mercantile Exchange (CME), US
11	London Metal Exchange
12	Tokyo Commodity Exchange (TOCOM)
13	Shangai Future Exchange
14	Sudney Future Exchange
15	London International Financial Futures and Options Exchange (LIFFE)
16	National Multi-Commodity Exchange in India (NMCE), India
17	National Commodity and Derivatives Exchange (NCDEX), India
18	Multi Commodity Exchange of India Limited (MCX), India
19	Dubai Gold & Commodity Exchange (DGCX)
20	Dubai Mercantile Exchange (DME), (joint venture between Dubai holding and the New York Mercantile Exchange (NYMEX))

India being predominantly an agricultural economy, contributing 20% to the GDP, with more than 57% of the total population engaged in agricultural activities. So the importance of the commodities market cannot be emphasized more. The history of organized commodity derivatives in India goes back to the nineteenth century when Cotton Trade Association started futures trading in 1875, about a decade after they started in Chicago. Over the time, derivatives market developed in several commodities in India. Following Cotton derivatives trading started in oilseed in Bombay (1900), raw jute and jute goods in Calcutta (1912), Wheat in Hapur (1913) and Bullion in Bombay

(1920). However, many feared that derivatives fuelled unnecessary speculation and were detrimental to the healthy functioning of the market. The parliament passed the Forward Contracts (Regulation) Act, 1952, which regulated contracts in Commodities all over the India. The act prohibited options trading in goods along with cash settlement of forward trades, rendering a crushing blow to the commodity derivatives market. Under the actg only those associations/exchanges, which are granted reorganization from the Government, are allowed to organize forward trading in regulated commodities.

The act envisages three-tier regulations: (i) Exchange which organizes forward trading in commodities can regulate trading on day-to-day basis; (ii) Forward Markets Commission provides regulatory oversight under the powers delegated to it by the Central Government and (iii) The Central Government — Department of Consumer Affairs, Ministry of Consumer Affairs, Food and Public Distribution — is the ultimate regulatory authority.

After liberalization and globalization in 1990, the Government set up a committee (1993) headed by Prof. K.N. Kabra to examine the role of futures trading. The Committee allowed futures trading in 17 commodity groups. The Government also accepted most of the recommendations and futures trading were permitted in all recommended commodities. Commodity exchange in India plays an important role where the prices of any commodity are not fixed; in an organized way. Commodity market is an important constituent of the financial markets of any country. It is the market where a wide range of products, viz., precious metals, base metals, crude oil, energy and soft commodities like palm oil, coffee etc. are traded. The structure of Indian commodity market is exhibited in Fig. 1.

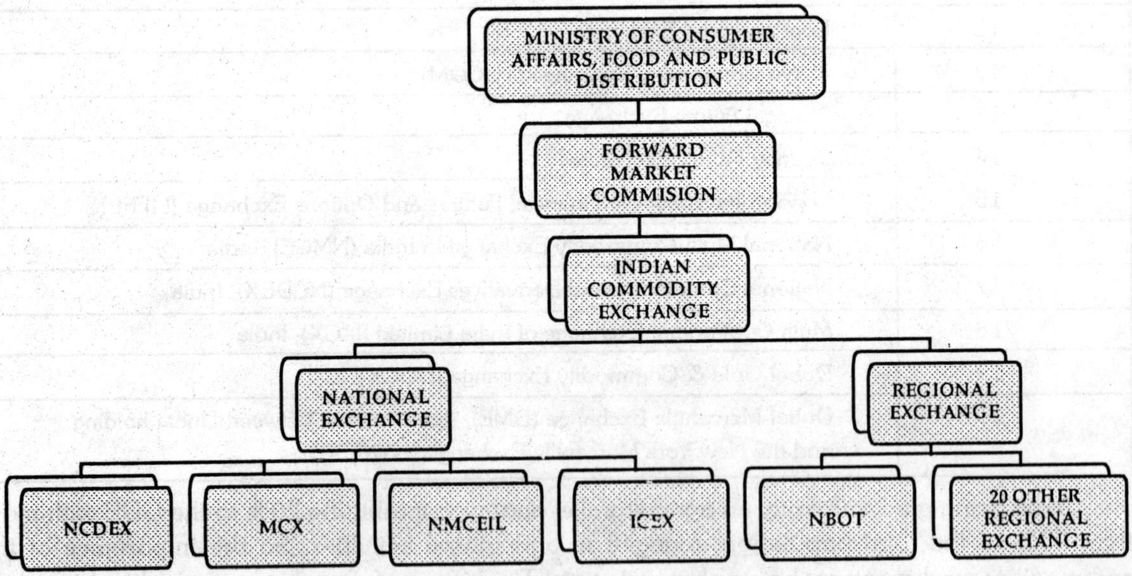

Fig. 1: Structure of Indian Commodity Market

Different Types of Commodities Traded:

These commodities can be broadly classified into the following:

Table 2

METAL	Aluminium, Copper, Lead, Nickel, Sponge, Iron, Steel Lobg (Bhavnagar) Steel Long (Govindgarh), Steel Flat, Tin, Zinc
BULLION	Gold, Gold IINI, Gold M, i-gold, Silver, Silver IINI, Silver M
FIBER	Cotton L Staple, Cotton M Staple, Cotton S Staple, Cotton Yarn, Kapas
ENERGY	Brent Crude Oil, Crude Oil, Furance Oil, Natural Gas, M. E. Sour Crude Oil
SPICES	Cardamorn, Jeera, Pepper, Red Chilli
PLANTATIONS	Arecanut, Cashew Kernel, Coffee (Robusta), Rubber
PULSES	Chana, Masur, Yellow Peas
PETROCHEMICALS	HDPE, Polypropylene(pp), PVC
OIL & OIL SEEDS	Castor Oil, Castor Seeds, Coconut Cake, Coconut Oil, Cotton Seed, Crude Palm Oil, Groundnut Oil, Kapasia Khalli, Mustard Oil, Mustard Seed (Jaipur), Mustard Seed (Sirsa), RBD palmolein, Refined Soy Oil, Refined Sunflower Oil, Rice Bran DOC, Rice Bran Refined Oil, Sesame Seed, Soymeal, Soy Nean, Soy Seeds
CEREALS	Maize
OTHERS	Guargum, Guar Seed, Gurchaku, Mentha Oil, Pototo (Agra), pototo (Tarkeshwar), Sugar M-30, Sugar S-30

These different types of commodities are revealed in Fig. 2.

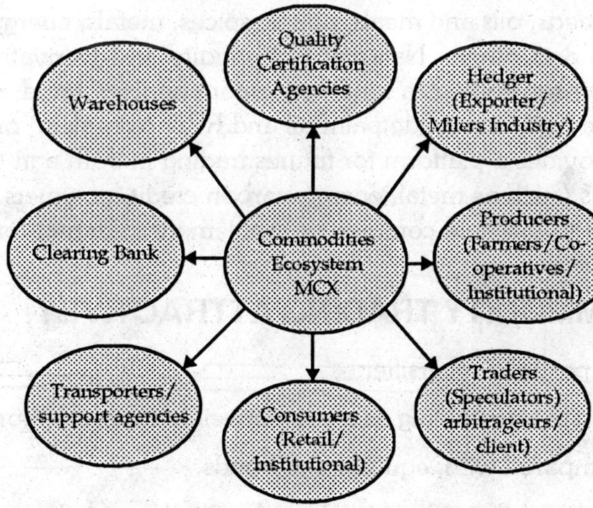

Fig. 2

The most popular physical commodities contracts are metals, energy, grains, livestock, and food and fibre. Commodities are mainly subject to price fluctuations based on supply and demand factors in consuming and producing countries. The major metals futures contracts include copper, gold and silver. Their uses include industrial purposes, in construction, and for jewelelry. Copper is also used for electrical and electronic products, transportation and industrial machinery manufacturing. The price of copper is therefore sensitive to statistics related to economic growth, particularly reports such as housing starts. For that reason, participants in financial markets often also look to price action in copper futures as a gauge of general economic trends. In another example, gold has long been used as a hedge against political and economic uncertainties, and many central banks back their currency with gold reserves.

The most popular energy futures contracts are crude oil, heating oil and natural gas. These natural resource markets have become one of the most important gauges of world economic and political developments, and are therefore heavily influenced by disruptions in producing nations. The value of the US dollar is significant because much of the world's crude oil is priced in dollars. US energy prices are quite sensitive to statistical reports detailing production, imports and especially stocks. All energy futures markets are subject to seasonal fluctuations.

Grains and soybeans are essential to food and feed supplies, and prices are especially sensitive to weather conditions in growing areas at key times. The major futures contracts in this category are soybeans, crude soy oil, and wheat. Each product has its own unique fundamental factors, depending on their use for human or animal consumption, or for industrial and energy needs.

Fiber crops category for futures trading includes coffee, cotton. In addition to global consumer demand, the usual growing factors such as disease, insects and drought affect prices for all of these commodities.

Commodities have been defined by the Forward Contracts (Regulation) Act 1952 as "Every kind of movable property other than actionable claims, money and securities."

The commodities tradable on commodity exchanges in India are classified into following categories: vegetable oil seeds, oils and meals, pulses, spices, metals, energy products, vegetables, Fibres and manufactures and others. National Commodity and Derivatives Exchange Limited (NCDEX) commenced futures trading in nine major commodities (gold, silver, cotton, soybean oil, mustard seed, rapeseed oil, and crude palm oil and RBD palmolein) on December 15, 2003. Currently, the NCDEX provides a platform for futures trading in both agri (such as pulses, spices) and non-agri commodities (such as metal, energy, carbon credit, polymers etc.). NCDEX was the first commodity exchange to facilitate commodities settlement in demat form.

WHAT MAKES COMMODITY TRADING ATTRACTIVE?

- A good low-risk portfolio diversifier.
- A highly liquid asset class, acting as a counterweight to stocks, bonds and real estate.
- Less volatile, compared with, equities and bonds.
- Investors can leverage their investments and multiply potential earnings.
- Better risk-adjusted returns.
- A good hedge against any downturn in equities or bonds as there is little correlation with equity and bond markets.

- High co-rrelation with changes in inflation.
- No securities transaction tax levied.

COMMODITIES TRADED ON NCDEX

NCDEX gives priority to commodities that are most relevant to India, and where the price discovery process takes place domestically. The products chosen are based on certain criteria such as price volatility, share in GDP, correlation with global markets, share in external trade, warehousing facilities, traders' distribution, geographical spread, varieties etc. List of commodities offered for futures trading on NCDEX are given in Table 3.

Table 3

Almond	Polyvinyl Chloride	Raw Jute
Gur	Linear Low Density Polyethylene	Kapas
CER	Polypropylene	Medium Staple Cotton
Guar	Gum Polymers	V -797 Kapas
Mentha Oil	Cashew	Indian 28.5 mm Cotton
Potato	Coffee-Robusta Cherry	AB Fibres
Guar Seeds	Rubber	Natural Gas
Others	Plantation Products	Brent Crude Oil
Yellow Peas	Groundnut Expeller Oil	Thermal Coal
Spices	Oil and Oilseeds	Precious Metals
Pepper	Castor Seed	Gold
Chilli	Sesame Seeds	Silver
Jeera	Cotton Seed	Oilcake Platinum
Turmeric	Soy Bean	Metals
Coriander	Refined Soy	Oil Steel
Cereals	Soybean Meal (local & export)	Copper
Wheat	Mustard Seed	Zinc
Barley	Kachhi Ghani Mustard Oil	Aluminium
Maize	(Yellow/Red) Rapeseed — Mustard Seed Oil Cake	Nickel
Pulses	Crude	Palm Oil
Chana	RBD Palmolein	Crude Oil
Masoor	Groundnut in Shell	Furnace Oil

Source: NCDEX

RECENT DEVELOPMENTS

Currently, all agricultural commodities are traded in the physical markets or mandis. The regular practice followed is that on harvest time the farmers bring their produce to these mandis and dispose of the same through either bilateral negotiations or through an auction process. The farmer gets only a small fraction of what ultimate consumer pays for agricultural commodities. But a significant part of their income is consumed in servicing intermediaries in the form of commission, interest burden, transportation and warehousing charges etc. A major portion of the loss in value of commodities due to wastages, pest attack, transportation, storage, handling etc. is again borne by the farmer. Therefore, the NCDEX has taken up an initiative to launch NCDEX Spot Exchange (NSPOT) at the national level. Electronic spot exchanges are an emerging phenomenon in the country. These spot exchanges provide real time, online, transparent and vibrant spot platform for commodities. The contracts allow participants from all over the country to buy and sell, thereby enabling producers and users to find out best price. During 2009, there was significant expansion of spot exchanges' trading facilities in India. These spot exchanges have created an avenue for direct market linkage among farmers, processors, exporters and end-users with a view to reducing the cost of intermediation and enhancing price realization by farmers. They are also providing the most efficient spot price inputs to the futures exchanges. The spot exchanges are encompassing the entire spectrum of commodities across the country and are bringing home the advantages of an electronic spot trading platform to all market participants in the agricultural and non-agricultural segments. The Government has allowed the National Commodity Exchanges to set up three spot exchanges in the country, namely the National Spot Exchange Ltd. (NSEL), NCDEX Spot Exchange Ltd. (NSPOT) and National Agriculture Produce Marketing Company of India Ltd. (NAPMC). The online, electronic spot market NSPOT is bringing the buyers and sellers (traders and farmers) closer to each other and help in actual price discovery between the buyer and seller directly. NSPOT is also facilitating wider reach, liquidity, counterparty guarantee-risk protection, timely settlement. Agriculture commodity futures staged a remarkable recovery after steady decline over the last two years, recording a trading value of ₹ 10.88 lakh crore in 2009, signifying growth of 48 per cent over the previous year. During the year 2009, a new National Commodity Exchange called Indian Commodity Exchange (ICEX) became operational. Besides, a scheme of upgradation of Ahmedabad Commodity Exchange to National Commodity Exchange status has been approved.

PRICING COMMODITY FUTURES

The process of determining a price at which a person buys and another sells a futures contract for a specific expiration date, through basic supply and demand factors related to the market, is called price discovery. The prices are freely and competitively derived. Historically, pricing in commodities futures has been less volatile compared to equity and bonds, thus providing an efficient portfolio diversification option. In an active futures market, the free flow of information is very important, which is facilitated by price discovery. The market determines the best estimate of today and tomorrow's prices and it is considered to be the reflection of the supply and demand for the underlying commodity. For pricing purposes, both forward and the futures market is one and same for investment asset (stocks, bonds, gold and silver are examples) and consumption asset (Commodities like copper and oil are examples). A futures contract is a forward contract that is exchange-traded and settled at the end of each day. The buyer who needs an asset in the future has the choice between buying the asset today in the spot market and holding it; or buying it in the forward market, in which case the seller of the forward contract incurs the costs of holding the assets, and hence charges the buyer a higher price. In the case of commodity futures, the holding cost is the cost of financing plus cost of storage and insurance purchased.

The Futures price **$F = S + C$**, where: S = Spot price, C = Holding costs or carry costs

The fair value of a futures contract can be expressed as:

$F = S(1 + r)^T$, where: r = Per cent cost of financing, T = Time till expiration

In the case of continuous compounding, **$F = Se^{rT}$**, in the absence of storage costs

For Investment commodities, if U is the present value of all the storage costs that will be incurred during the life of a futures contract, **$F = (S + U)e^{rT}$.**

Warehouse charges include a fixed charge per deposit of commodity into the warehouse, and per unit per week charge. The per unit charges include storage costs and insurance charges. The Table 4 lists the warehouse charges for accredited warehouses/vaults that function as delivery centers for contracts that trade on the NCDEX.

Table 4

Commodity	***Fixed Charges per lot at the time of deposit***	***Warehouse Charges for a day per delivery units (₹)***
Gold	310	7.5 per Kg
Silver	310	0.35 per Kg
Groundnut (in Shell) — Bikaner	310	4.75 per MT
Potatoes	310	1.5 per MT
Copper Cathode	310	5 per MT

Suppose **$F > (S + U)e^{rT}$**,

To take advantage of this opportunity, an arbitrageur can implement the following strategy:

1. Borrow an amount S+U at the risk-free interest rate and use it to purchase one unit of the commodity and pay storage costs.
2. Short a forward contract on one unit of the commodity.

This strategy leads to a profit of **$F - (S+U)e^{rT}$** at the expiration of the futures contract. As arbitragers exploit this opportunity, the spot price will increase and the futures price will decrease until the equation holds good. Suppose **$F < (S + U)e^{rT}$**,

In case of investment assets such as gold and silver, where investors hold the commodity purely for investment, they will find it profitable to trade in the following manner:

1. Sell the commodity, save the storage costs, and invest the proceeds at the risk-free interest rate.
2. Take a long position in a forward contract.

This would result in a profit at maturity of $(S + U)e^{rT} - F$ relative to the position that the investors would have been in had they held the underlying commodity. As arbitrageurs exploit this opportunity, the spot price will decrease and the futures price will increase until the equation holds good.

However, in the case of consumption commodities, individuals and companies, keep them in inventory because of its consumption value — not because of its value as an investment. They are reluctant to sell these commodities and buy forward or futures contracts because these contracts cannot be consumed. Therefore, there is unlikely to be arbitrage in this case.

Therefore, for a consumption commodity, **F d" (S + U)e^rT^**

PARTICIPANTS IN COMMODITY FUTURES

For a market to succeed, it must have all three kinds of participants — hedgers, speculators and arbitrageurs. This ensures liquidity and efficient price discovery in the market. Commodity markets give opportunity for all three kinds of participants.

Hedging

Many participants in the commodity futures market are hedgers. They use the futures market to reduce a particular risk that they face. This risk might relate to the price of any commodity that they deal in. Hedging does not necessarily improve the financial outcome but makes the outcome more certain. When an individual or a company decides to use the futures markets to hedge a risk, the objective is to take a position that neutralizes the risk as much as possible. There are basically two kinds of hedges that can be taken. A company that wants to sell an asset at a particular time in the future can hedge by taking short futures position. This is called a short hedge. Similarly, a company that knows that it is due to buy an asset in the future can hedge by taking long futures position. This is known as long hedge.

Hedge Ratio

Hedge ratio is the ratio of the size of position taken in the futures contracts to the size of the exposure in the underlying asset.

The optimal hedge ratio, the one that minimizes the variance of the hedger's position:

$h = \rho\sigma_S / \sigma_F$, where

- σ_S: Standard deviation of ΔS
- σ_F: Standard deviation of ΔF
- ρ: Coefficient of correlation between DS and DF
- h: Hedge ratio
- ΔS: Change in spot price, S, during a period of time equal to the life of the hedge
- ΔF: Change in futures price, F, during a period of time equal to the life of the hedge

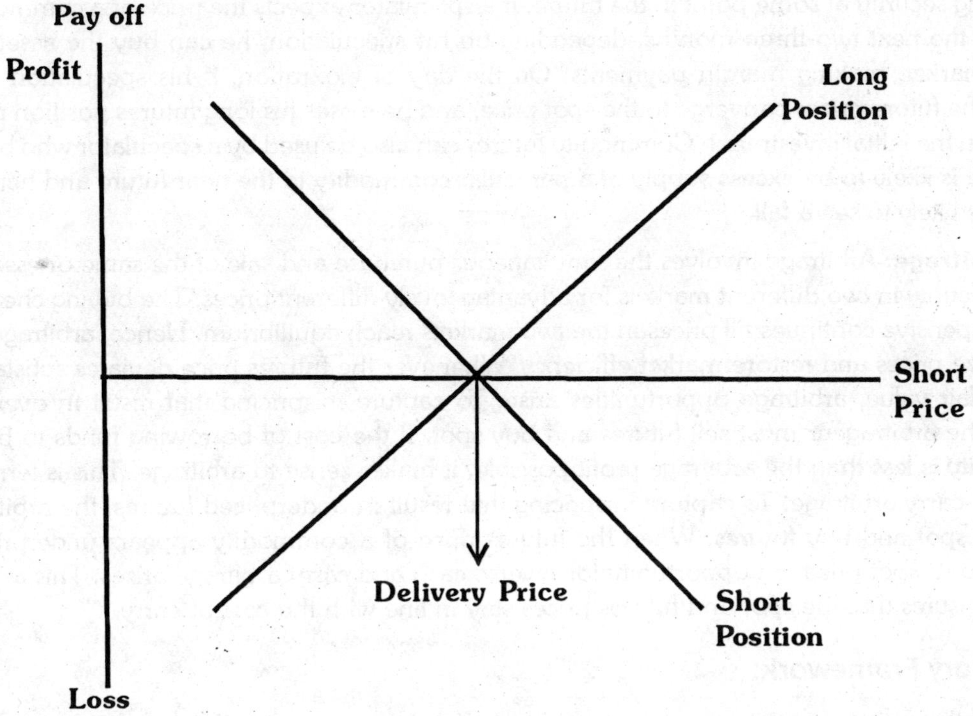

Fig. 3

Advantages of hedging are Hedging stretches the marketing period, Hedging protects inventory values, Hedging permits forward pricing of products. However, hedging can only minimize the risk but cannot fully eliminate it. The loss made during selling of an asset may not always be equal to the profits made by taking a short futures position. This is because the value of the asset sold in the spot market and the value of the asset underlying the future contract may not be the same. This is called the basis risk. The hedger may not be able to identify the precise date in the future when an asset would be bought or sold, for various reasons: Firstly, the asset whose price is to be hedged may not be exactly the same as the asset underlying the futures contract. Secondly, the hedger may be uncertain as to the exact date when the asset will be bought or sold. Often the hedge may require the futures contract to be closed out well before its expiration date. This could result in an imperfect hedge. Thirdly, the expiration date of the hedge may be later than the delivery date of the futures contract. In such circumstances, the hedger is required to close out the futures contracts entered into and take the same position in futures contracts with a later delivery date. This is called a rollover. Hedges can be rolled forward many times. However, multiple rollovers could lead to short-term cash flow problems.

Speculation: The commodities futures markets provide speculators with an easy mechanism to speculate on the price of underlying commodities. To trade commodity futures on the NCDEX, a customer must open a futures trading account with a commodity derivatives broker with simply putting the margin money. This enables futures traders to take a position in the underlying commodity without having actually held that commodity. With the purchase of futures contract on a commodity, the holder essentially makes a legally binding promise or obligation to buy the underlying security at some point in the future. If a speculator expects the price of a commodity to go up in the next two-three months, depending on his speculation, he can buy the asset in the futures market, making margin payments. On the day of expiration, if his speculation proves correct, the future prices converge to the spot price, and he closes his long futures position making a profit on the initial investment. Commodity futures can also be used by a speculator who believes that there is likely to be excess supply of a particular commodity in the near future and hence the prices are likely to see a fall.

Arbitrage: Arbitrage involves the simultaneous purchase and sale of the same or essentially similar security in two different markets for advantageously different prices. The buying cheap and selling expensive continues till prices in the two markets reach equilibrium. Hence, arbitrage helps to equalize prices and restore market efficiency. Whenever the futures price deviates substantially from its fair value, arbitrage opportunities arise. To capture mispricing that result in overpriced futures, the arbitrageur must sell futures and buy spot. If the cost of borrowing funds to buy the commodity is less than the arbitrage profit possible, it makes sense to arbitrage. This is termed as cash-and-carry arbitrage. To capture mispricing that result in underpriced futures, the arbitrageur must sell spot and buy futures. When the futures price of a commodity appears underpriced in relation to its spot price, an opportunity for reverse cash and carry arbitrage arises. This arbitrage activity ensures that the spot and futures prices stay in line with the cost-of-carry.

Regulatory Framework:

The three tiers regulations of forward/futures trading system in India are Government of India, Forward Markets Commission (FMC) and Commodity Exchanges. Regulation is needed to avoid the use of the leveraged contracts for the manipulation of prices by the unscrupulous participants, to create competitive conditions, to ensure that the market has appropriate risk management system and to ensure fairness and transparency in trading, clearing, settlement and management of the Exchange so as to protect and promote the interest of various stakeholders, particularly non-member users of the market.

Table 5

Country	*Regulatory Agency*
Australia	Australian Securities and Investments Commission
Chinese Mainland	China Securities Regulatory Commission
Hong King	Securities and Future Commission
India	Securities and Exchange Board of India and Forward
Pakistan	Securities and Exchange Commission of Pakistan
Singapore	Monetary Authority of Singapore
UK	Financial Services Authority
USA	Commodity Futures Trading Commission
Malaysia	Securities Commission

Forward Markets Commission provides regulatory oversight in order to ensure financial integrity, market integrity and to protect and promote interest of customers/non-members. Some of the regulatory measures by Forward Markets Commission include:

1. Limit on net open position as on the close of the trading hours. Sometimes, limit is also imposed on intra-day net open position, member-wise and client-wise.
2. Circuit-filters or limit on price fluctuations to allow cooling of market in the event of abrupt upswing or downswing in prices.
3. Special margin deposit to be collected on outstanding purchases or sales when price moves up or down sharply above or below the previous day closing price.
4. Circuit breakers or minimum/maximum prices: prescribed to prevent futures prices from falling below as rising above not warranted by prospective supply and demand factors.
5. Stopping trading in certain derivatives of the contract, closing the market for a specified period and even closing out the contract.

Rules Governing Trading on Exchange:

Important regulations that govern NCDEX (Exchange) have been divided into two main divisions pertaining to trading and clearing.

TRADING

Most futures contracts do not lead to the actual physical delivery of the underlying asset. The settlement is done by closing out open positions, physical delivery or cash settlement. All these settlement functions are taken care of by an entity called clearing house or clearing corporation. National Commodity Clearing Limited (NCCL) undertakes clearing of trades executed on the NCDEX. The Exchange from time to time specifies various trading parameters relating to the trading system. A clearing house is a system by which Exchanges guarantee the faithful compliance of all trade commitments undertaken on the trading floor or electronically over the electronic trading systems. Only clearing members including professional clearing members (PCMs) are entitled to clear and settle contracts through the clearing house. The clearing mechanism essentially involves working out open positions and obligations of clearing members. This position is considered for exposure and daily margin purposes. Every clearing member has to deposit a margin with the Exchange in respect of the trades to which he is party. Every trading member is required to specify the buy or sell orders as either an open order or a close order for derivatives contracts. Trading members have to ensure that appropriate confirmed order instructions are obtained from the constituents before placement of an order on the system. A Trading-cum-Clearing Member's (TCM) open position is arrived at by the summation of his clients' open positions, in the contracts in which they have traded. At NCDEX, after the trading hours on the expiry date, based on the available information, the matching for deliveries takes place firstly, on the basis of locations and then randomly, keeping in view the factors such as available capacity of the vault/warehouse, commodities already deposited and dematerialized and offered for delivery etc. Matching done by this process is binding on the clearing members.

National Commodity Clearing Limited (NCCL) as the clearing house undertakes clearing of trades executed on the NCDEX platform. During the specified period as per settlement calendar, the Exchange provides a window on the trading system to submit delivery information for all open positions for contracts having sellers' option and intention matching contract. For contracts having compulsory delivery, all the members having open positions at the end of trading hours on the expiry date of the contracts, will have to give or take delivery as the case may be. Trading-cum-Clearing Members can carry out the transactions (trading, clearing and settling) on their own account and also on their clients' accounts. The Exchange assigns a unique ID to each TCM. Each TCM can have more than one user. It is the responsibility of the TCM to maintain adequate control over persons having access to the firm's User IDs. Member who only trade through their account or on account of their clients and will however have to clear their trade through PCMs/STCMs. Such member can trade on their own account, also on account of their clients. They can clear and settle these trades and also clear and settle trades of other trading members who are only allowed to trade and are not allowed to settle and clear.

STRUCTURE

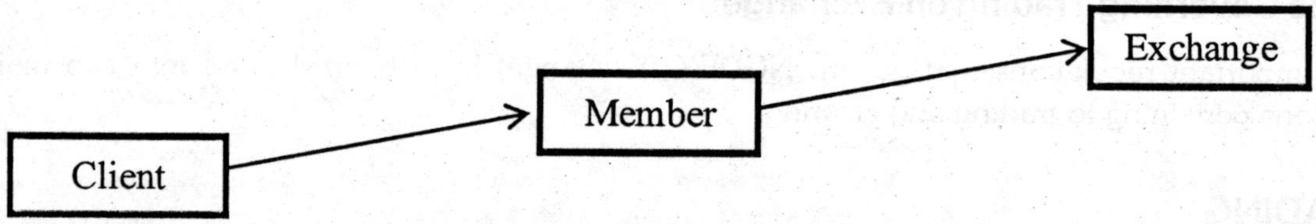

Fig. 4

NCDEX has designated clearing banks through who funds to be paid and/or to be received must be settled. Every clearing member is required to maintain and operate a clearing account with any one of the designated clearing bank branches. The clearing bank will debit/credit the clearing account of clearing members as per instructions received from NCDEX.

- Bank of India
- Canara Bank
- HDFC Bank Ltd.
- ICICI Bank Ltd.
- Punjab National Bank
- Axis Bank Ltd.
- IndusInd Bank Ltd.
- Kotak Mahindra Bank Ltd.
- Tamilnad Mercantile Bank Ltd..
- Union Bank of India
- YES Bank Ltd.
- Standard Chartered Bank Ltd.
- State Bank of India

Every clearing member is required to maintain and operate two CM pool account each at NSDL and CDSL through any one of the empanelled depository participants. The CM pool account is to be used exclusively for clearing operations, i.e., for effecting and receiving deliveries from NCDEX. Futures contracts have two types of settlements, the Mark-to-Market (MTM) settlement which happens on a continuous basis at the end of each day, and the final settlement which happens on the last trading day of the futures contract. Daily settlement price is the consensus closing price as arrived after closing session of the relevant futures contract for the trading day. However, in the absence of trading for a contract during closing session, daily settlement price is computed as per the methods prescribed by the exchange from time to time. Final settlement price is the polled spot price of the underlying commodity in the spot market on the last trading day of the futures contract. All open positions in a futures contract cease to exist after its expiration day. The Exchange prescribes the procedure for sales tax/VAT settlement applicable to the deals culminating into sale with physical delivery of commodities. In the event of a default by the seller in delivery of commodities, the Exchange closes out the derivatives contracts and imposes penalties on the defaulting seller. Any person seeking to dematerialize a commodity has to open a demat account with an approved Depository Participant (DP).

All the commodities deposited in the warehouse are given a Fixed Expiry Date (FED). The commodities cannot be revalidated after the FED. The relevant authority from time to time fixes the various clearing days, the pay-in and payout days and the scheduled time to be observed in connection with the clearing and settlement operations of deals in commodities futures contracts. Based on the settlement obligations statements, the Exchange generates delivery statement and receipt statement for each clearing member. The delivery and receipt statement contains details of commodities to be delivered to and received from other clearing members, the details of the corresponding buying/selling constituent and such other details. Clearing members are required to authorize the specified depositories and DP with whom they have a clearing account to access their clearing account for debiting and crediting their accounts as per instructions received from the Exchange and to report balances and other credit information to the Exchange. TCM has to have pool accounts with both the depositories (NSDL and CDSL).

ORDER TYPES AND TRADING PARAMETERS

An electronic trading system allows the trading members to enter orders with various conditions attached to them as per their requirements. These conditions are broadly divided into three categories — namely time conditions, price conditions and other conditions.

1. Time conditions:

(a) **Good till day order:** A day order is an order which is valid for the day on which it is entered. If the order is not executed during the day, the system cancels the order automatically at the end of the day. Example: A trader wants to go long on February 1, 2010 in refined soy oil on the commodity exchange. A day order is placed at ₹ 660/ 10 kg. If the market does not reach this price, the order does not get filled even if the market touches ₹ 661 and closes. In other words, day order is for a specific price and if the order does not get filled that day, one has to place the order again the next day.

(b) Good till cancelled (GTC): A GTC order remains in the system until the user cancels it. Consequently, it spans trading days, if not traded on the day the order is entered. Example: A trader wants to go long on refined soy oil when the market touches ₹ 650/ 10kg. Theoretically, the order exists until it is filled up, even if it takes months for it to happen.

(c) Good till date (GTD): A GTD order allows the user to specify the date till which the order should remain in the system if not executed. The maximum days allowed by the system are the same as in GTC order. At the end of this day/date, the order is cancelled from the system.

(d) Immediate or Cancel (IOC)/Fill or kill order: An IOC order allows the user to buy or sell a contract as soon as the order is released into the system, failing which the order is cancelled from the system.

(e) All or none order: All or none order (AON) is a limit order, which is to be executed in its entirety, or not at all.

2. Price conditions:

(a) Limit order: An order to buy or sell a stated amount of a commodity at a specified price, or at a better price, if obtainable at the time of execution. The disadvantage is that the order may not get filled at all if the price for that day does not reach the specified price.

(b) Stop-loss: A stop-loss order is an order, placed with the broker, to buy or sell a particular futures contract at the market price if and when the price reaches a specified level. Most of the time, stop orders are used to exit a trade.

3. Other conditions:

(a) Market price: Market orders are orders for which no price is specified at the time the order is entered (i.e., price is market price). For such orders, the system determines the price. Only the position to be taken long/short is stated.

(b) Trigger price: Price at which an order gets triggered from the stop-loss book.

(c) Spread order: A simple spread order involves two positions, one long and one short. They are taken in the same commodity with different months (calendar spread) or in closely related commodities. Prices of the two futures contract therefore tend to go up and down together, and gains on one side of the spread are offset by losses on the other. The spreader's goal is to profit from a change in the difference between the two futures prices.

BENEFITS OF COMMODITY FUTURES MARKETS

The primary objectives of any futures exchange are authentic price discovery and an efficient price risk management to function smoothly.

- **Price Discovery:** Based on inputs regarding specific market information, the demand and supply equilibrium, weather forecasts, expert views and comments, inflation rates, government policies, market dynamics, hopes and fears, buyers and sellers conduct trading at futures exchanges. This transforms into continuous price discovery mechanism. The execution of trade between buyers and sellers leads to assessment of fair value of a particular commodity that is immediately disseminated on the trading terminal.

- **Price Risk Management:** Hedging is the most common method of price risk management. It is strategy of offering price risk that is inherent in spot market by taking an equal but opposite position in the futures market. Futures markets are used as a mode by hedgers to protect their business from adverse price change. This may depression the profitability of their business. Farmers, processors, merchandisers, manufacturers, exporters, importers etc. are involved in trading of commodities for hedging benefits.
- **Import-Export competitiveness:** The exporters can hedge their price risk and improve their competitiveness by making use of futures market. A majority of traders which are involved in physical trade internationally intend to buy forwards. The purchases made from the physical market might expose them to the risk of price risk resulting to losses. The existence of futures market are allowed the exporters to hedge their proposed purchase by temporarily substituting for actual purchase till the time is mature to buy in physical market. In the absence of futures market, it is meticulous, time-consuming and costly physical transactions.
- **Predictable Pricing:** The demand for certain commodities is highly price elastic. The manufacturers have to ensure that the prices should be stable in order to protect their market share with the free entry of imports. Futures contracts will enable predictability in domestic prices. The manufacturers can, as a result, flat out the influence of changes in their input prices very easily. With no futures market, the manufacturer can be caught between severe short-term price movements.

BENEFITS FOR FARMERS/AGRICULTURALISTS

Price instability has a direct bearing on farmers in the absence of futures market. There is no need to have large reserves to cover against unfavorable price fluctuations. This will reduce the risk premiums associated with the marketing or processing margins enabling more returns on produce. The price information accessible to the farmers determines the extent to which traders/processors increase price to them. Since one of the objectives of futures exchange is to make available these prices as far as possible, it is very likely to benefit the farmers. Also, due to the time lag between planning and production, the market-determined price information disseminated by futures exchanges would be crucial for their production decisions.

- **Credit accessibility:** The absence of proper risk management tools attracts the marketing and processing of commodities to high-risk exposure. Even a small movement in prices can consume huge proportion of capital owned by traders, at times making it virtually impossible to pay back the loan. There is a high degree of reluctance among banks to fund commodity traders, especially those who do not manage price risks. If in case they do, the interest rate is likely to be high and terms and conditions very stringent. This possesses a huge obstacle in the smooth functioning and competition of commodities market.

- **Improved product quality:** The existence of warehouses for facilitating delivery with grading facilities along with other related benefits provides a very strong reason to upgrade and enhance the quality of the commodity. It ensures uniform standardization of commodity trade, including the terms of quality standard: the quality certificates that are issued by the exchange. Only certified warehouses have the potential to become the norm for physical trade.
- **Commodities as an asset class for diversification of portfolio risk:** Commodities have historically an inverse correlation of daily returns as compared to equities. Thus, an investor can effectively minimize the portfolio risk arising due to price fluctuations in other asset classes by including commodities in the portfolio.
- **Commodity derivatives markets are extremely transparent** in the sense that the manipulation of prices of a commodity is extremely difficult due to globalization of economies, thereby providing for prices benchmarked across different countries and continents. For example, gold, silver, crude oil, natural gas, etc. are international commodities, whose prices in India are indicative of the global situation.
- **In option for high net worth investors:** With the rapid spread of derivatives trading in commodities, the commodities route too has become an option for high net worth and savvy investors to consider in their overall asset allocation.
- **Useful to the producer:** Commodity trade is useful to the producer because it enables to get an idea of the price likely to prevail on a future date and therefore can decide between various competing commodities, the best that suits him.
- **Useful for the consumer:** Commodity trade is useful for the consumer because it facilitates to get an idea of the price at which the commodity would be available at a future point of time. Further, consumer can do proper costing/financial planning and also cover its purchases by making forward contracts.

COMMODITY FUTURES TRADING IN INDIA

Commodities futures, or futures contracts, are agreements to buy or sell a commodity at a specific date in the future at a specific price. The prices of commodities can change on a weekly or even daily basis. If the price goes up, the buyer of the futures contract makes money. If the price goes down, the seller makes money. The NCDEX system supports an order driven market, where orders match automatically. The Exchange specifies the unit of trading and the delivery unit for futures contracts on various commodities. The Exchange notifies the regular lot size and tick size for each of the contracts traded from time to time. When any order enters the trading system, it is an active order. It tries to find a match on the other side of the book. If it finds a match, a trade is generated. If it does not find a match, the order becomes passive and gets queued in the respective outstanding order book in the system. Time stamping is done for each trade and provides the possibility for a complete audit trail, if required.

LITERATURE REVIEW

The efficiency test of agricultural commodity future market was also done in China by Wang and Bingfanke (2005) and the results suggested a long-term equilibrium relationship between the future price and cash price (spot price) for Soya beans and weak short term efficiency in Soya bean future market. The study also highlighted inefficient future market for wheat and suggested that it may have been caused by overspeculation and government intervention. In India, the commodities markets are highly fragmented, which according to Thomas (2003) is a major hindrance in development of the derivative market. Because of fragmentation, prices of major commodities vary widely across the markets. A later research by Bhattacharya (2007) elaborates on this stating that the differences arise because of poor grading, differential rates of taxes and levies and inadequacy of storage facilities. Bose (2007) found that Indian stock markets are more volatile as compared to developed markets. He also noted that the Indian commodity future markets are going through many ups and downs and allegations have been made of speculative activity. Mishra (2008) however pointed out that in the period 2003-08, there has been considerable growth in the Indian Commodity Market. Lokare (2007) found that although Indian commodity market is yet to achieve minimum critical liquidity in some commodities (sugar, pepper, gur and groundnut), almost all the commodities show an evidence of co-integration between spot and future prices revealing the right direction of achieving the improved operational efficiency, though at a slower rate. Further hedging proves to be effective in respect of some commodities. However, for a few commodities, the volatility in future price has been substantially lower than the spot price indicating an inefficient utilization of information. Roy and Kumar (2007) studied hedging effectiveness of wheat futures in India and found that hedging effectiveness provided by futures markets was low. Sandhya (2008) in her study brought out that the extent to which spot and futures markets influence each other depends on the level of integration of the two markets. Nath and Tulsi (2008) studied whether the seasonal/cyclical fluctuations in commodities prices have been affected by the introduction of futures in those commodities. Gurbandini and Rao (2009) empirically researched the correlation between spot and future prices to ascertain the extent to which spot prices impact the prices of future contracts for select two agricultural commodities, namely, Chilli, and Mustard seed. This paper tries to identify the gap in researches done in the Indian context by studying the relation between spot price and future price and how far the future contracts are fairly priced in the context of agricultural products.

LET TAKE CASE OF AGRICULTURAL COMMODITIES, I.E., CHILLI AND MUSTRAD SEED TO KNOW THE RELATION BETWEEN SPOT PRICE AND FUTURE PRICE:

National Commodities Derivatives Exchange (NCDEX) is chosen as it is India's largest commodities derivative exchange and is considered to be the world's second largest commodities exchange. NCDEX trades 57 agricultural commodities. The total turnover at Exchange level was ₹ 49.15 billion by August 2009 for the financial year 2009-10. The two agricultural commodities, i.e., Chilli and Mustard seed are chosen for study. These two commodities are chosen because of their high volumes (in value) traded on NCDEX during the year 2009. These two commodities together contribute around 20% of the total volume (value). The time frame chosen for the study is three years, that is, 1st August 2006 to 31st July 2009. The reason for choosing this time frame is that the Indian economy did not fare well as compared to that of corresponding period in the previous year due to intense global meltdown. Hence time frame is categorised into three phase: 1st August 2006 to 31st July 2007: period prior to global meltdown (Pre-meltdown) 1st August 2007 to 31st July 2008: period of severe global meltdown (Severe Meltdown) 1st August 2008 to 31st July 2009: period of moderate global meltdown (Moderate Meltdown). Again Stock market performance, SENSEX (BSE-30) is chosen being the barometer of stock markets in India. The metrics chosen for performance analysis are the stock market return (CAGR), risk associated with the return (standard deviation) and the risk per return (coefficient of variation which is computed as standard deviation/stock market return). The SENSEX (BSE-30) values are obtained from Bombay Stock Exchange for the three year period from 1st August 2006 to 31st July 2009. For commodity market performance, NCDEXAGRI and AGRIFUTEX are chosen. The metrics used for performance analysis are the growth of the index (CAGR), volatility associated with the growth (standard deviation) and the volatility per unit growth (coefficient of variation which is computed as standard deviation/ stock market return), slope, skewness and kurtosis of the index. The NCDEXAGRI and AGRIFUTEX values are obtained from NCDEX directly for the two-year period from 1st August 2007 to 31st July 2009. The variables chosen are volumes (both quantity and value), spot prices and futures prices of the select agricultural commodities (Chilli, Mustard seed). The data are obtained from www.ncdex.com for the period from 1st August 2006 to 31st July 2009.

HYPOTHESES TESTING

H_0: The economic meltdown does not affect the volumes (quantities) of the select agricultural commodities traded on NCDEX during the period of study.

H_1: The economic meltdown does affect the volumes (quantities) of the select agricultural commodities traded on NCDEX during the period of study.

H_0: The economic meltdown does not affect the volumes (values) of the select agricultural commodities traded on NCDEX during the period of study.

H_1: The economic meltdown does affect the volumes (values) of the select agricultural commodities traded on NCDEX during the period of study.

H_0: The economic meltdown does not affect the prices of futures contracts of the select agricultural commodities traded on NCDEX during the period of study.

H_1: The economic meltdown does affect the prices of futures contracts of the select agricultural commodities traded on NCDEX during the period of study.

H_0: The economic meltdown does not affect the spot prices of the select agricultural commodities traded on NCDEX during the period of study.

H_1: The economic meltdown does affect the spot prices of the select agricultural commodities traded on NCDEX during the period of study.

ANALYSIS

The growth and volatility of NCDEXAGRI and FUTEXAGRI for 2008-09 had been significantly lower than that of 2007-08, while the coefficient of variance (a measure of dispersion indicating volatility per unit of average quantity traded) have increased significantly for the period. Further, it may be observed that the slope (or gradient) of the index lines and skewness (a measure of degree of asymmetry of a distribution around its mean) have been significantly lower. Positive skewness indicates a distribution with an asymmetric tail extending towards more positive values while Negative skewness indicates a distribution with an asymmetric tail extending towards more negative values. It may be observed that the Kurtosis statistic of NCDEXAGRI turned positive in 2008-09 as compared to that of 2007-08 while the Kurtosis statistic of FUTEXAGRI had increased more on the negative side. Kurtosis characterizes the relative peakedness or flatness of a distribution compared to the normal distribution. Positive kurtosis indicates a relatively peaked distribution. Negative kurtosis indicates a relatively flat distribution.

Table 4
Descriptive Statistics

NCDEXAGRI	*CAGR*	*SD*	*CV*	*Slope*	*Skewness*	*Kurtosis*
2007-08	44.27	0.0094	0.0002	2.0429	0.9765	-0.328
2008-09	3.941	0.0051	0.0013	0.5285	0.2167	1.5532
2007-09	53.8921	0.0076	0.0001	1.0493	–0.2422	1.3074
FUTEXAGRI						
2007-08	50.696	265.6008	5.2391	2.2875	0.8088	–0.6874
2008-09	1.8348	150.8315	82.2064	0.7705	0.0733	–1.4752
2007-09	52.0802	0.0092	0.0002	1.0054	–0.1703	–1.2298

The return (CAGR), risk (SD) and risk per return (coefficient of variance, CV) for the meltdown periods (2007-08 and 2008-09) are significantly lower than pre-meltdown period (2006-07) is exhibited in Table 4.

Table 5
SENSEX

Sensex	*CAGR*	*SD*	*CV*
2006-07	42.9012	0.0477	0.0011
2007-08	-8.3405	0.1046	-0.0125
2008-09	11.5934	0.1352	0.0117
2007-09	-1.2171	0.1179	-0.0968
2006-09	46.1679	0.1004	0.0022

From the Tables 4 and 5, it is observed that the commodities market got more affected due to meltdown than stock market during 2008-09.

Table 6

Descriptive Statistics of Volume Traded (Qty in Mt)

	Mean	*SD*	*CV*	*Skewness*	*Kurtosis*
Chilli					
2006-07	5673689	2224667	0.3921	0.5434	0.0817
2007-08	2418432	1336633	0.5527	0.38	-0.8985
2008-09	1878698	1423451	0.7577	1.6547	3.5544
Mustard Seed					
2006-07	7701362	2699647	0.3505	0.5246	-0.9036
2007-08	5190964	2212776	0.4263	1.1774	0.3564
2008-09	4866876	2391821	0.4915	1.706	3.3023

It is observed from the above Table 6 that the average quantities traded for Chilli, and mustard seed during 2007-08 and 2008-09 have been significantly lower than that of 2006-07 implying that the meltdown have affected the quantum of trading and the number of contracts traded on NCDEX (the standard size of one future contract is 10 MT) for these three commodities while the quantities traded for Mustard seed have increased significantly for meltdown period in comparison to pre-meltdown period.

The standard deviation gives an idea of volatility/variance of quantities traded and it is observed that during the years 2007-08 and 2008-09, it is much lower for Chilli, and Mustard seed implying that these commodities is not experience much volatility as compared to that of 2006-07. The other descriptive statistics (coefficient of variation, skewness and kurtosis) have yielded mixed results.

Table 7

Analysis of Volume Traded (Value in Indian Rupees Lakhs)

	Mean	*SD*	*CV*	*Skewness*	*Kurtosis*
Chilli					
2006-07	1471380	726953.7	0.4941	0.9679	0.5742
2007-08	612518.7	388058	0.6335	0.7105	-0.7011
2008-09	436718.9	350170.8	0.8018	1.7789	3.9667
Mustard Seed					
2006-07	1483399	547315.4	0.36896	0.559454	-0.9771
2007-08	973050.8	450474.3	0.46295	1.1138	0.1134
2008-09	863322.3	505933.5	0.586	1.8879	4.1618

Value traded being derivative of quantity traded, similar trends have been observed for all the descriptive statistics and the analysis for value traded is on the similar lines as presented above for quantity traded.

Table 8 presents the analysis of prices of futures contracted on NCDEX during the period of study. It is observed that the prices of futures contracts for Cotton and Mustard seed have gone up significantly during the meltdown period as compared to that of pre-meltdown period. The other descriptive statistics presented in the Table 8 yielded mixed trends.

Table 8
Descriptive Analysis of Prices of Futures Contracts

Chilli	*CAGR*	*SD*	*CV*	*Slope*	*Skewness*	*Kurtosis*
2006-07	–8.5268	0.1133	–0.0133	–1.891	1.0116	0.2444
2007-08	15.8812	0.1104	0.007	2.0111	1.0802	0.3901
2008-09	15.9801	0.0983	0.0062	–0.1963	0.4124	–2.0119
2006-09	–0.6986	0.1104	–0.1581	–0.3669	1.3439	1.3862
Mustard Seed						
2006-07	–9.2752	0.0777	–0.0084	–0.2425	–0.1906	–1.1893
2007-08	7.9603	0.3427	0.0431	0.0163	–2.7933	8.9276
2008-09	11.2304	0.0885	0.0079	0.4498	1.2624	2.1144
2006-09	8.9512	0.2046	0.0229	–0.1817	–1.6802	6.6412

Table 9
Descriptive Statistics of Spot Prices

Chilli	*CAGR*	*SD*	*CV*	*Slope*	*Skewness*	*Kurtosis*
2006-07	-7.575	0.1113	-0.0147	-1.9161	0.9501	-0.4077
2007-08	18.06	0.0918	0.0051	1.0806	0.7527	-0.1882
2008-09	-9.6941	0.0629	-0.0065	-0.7607	0.9471	0.1221
2006-09	-1.4627	0.0889	-0.0608	-0.4275	1.5055	2.0409
Mustard Seed						
2006-07	-8.935	0.0677	-0.0076	-0.1411	-0.3569	-1.0485
2007-08	7.56	0.0449	0.0059	0.5979	-0.0142	-1.3685
2008-09	13.97	0.0763	0.0055	0.5265	1.3136	2.3186
2006-09	11.62	0.063	0.0054	-0.0607	0.4181	0.2285

The following Table 9 presents the analysis of prices of futures contracted on NCDEX during the period of study. It is experiential that Mustard seed have witnessed growth in spot prices; the other commodity has yielded mixed trends. The other descriptive statistics also present mixed trends.

Hypothesis Testing for Volume Traded (Quantity and Value)

Results of Hypothesis testing for Hypotheses for 1 and 2 are presented in Table 10. The results are statistically significant for Mustard and chilli leading to the rejection of Null Hypothesis (H_0) and acceptance of Alternative Hypothesis (H_1).

Table 10

Results of Hypothesis Testing for Volume Traded(Quantity & Value)

Hypothesis 1			*Hypothesis 2*		
Volume (Quantity)	***2006-07/ 2007-08***	***2006-07/ 2008-09***	***Volume (Value)***	***2006-07/ 2007-08***	***2006-07/ 2008-09***
Chilli	t =4.2341* df = 19P =0.0005 (2-tailed)	t = 4.0488* df = 15P =0.0006 (2-tailed)	***Chilli***	t = 3.5330* df = 17 = 0.0026 (2-tailed)	t = 4.2465* df = 17P = 0.0006 (2-tailed)
Mustard Seed	t =10.5816* df =11P =0.0001 (2-tailed)	t =4.3105* df = 11P =0.0012 (2-tailed)	***Mustard Seed***	t = 9.3317* df = 11P = 0.0005 (2-tailed)	t = 4.8199* df = 11P = 0.0010 (2-tailed)

* 1%, statistically significant

* 5% statistically not significant

HYPOTHESIS TESTING FOR FUTURES AND SPOT PRICES

Results of Hypothesis testing for Hypotheses for 3 and 4 are presented in Table 11. Barring Mustard seed for which the results are statistically significant, the results are mixed in case of chilli. In the case of Mustard seed, the Null Hypothesis is rejected and Alternative Hypothesis is accepted.

Table 11

Results of Hypothesis Testing for Futures an Spot Prices

Hypothesis 3			*Hypothesis 4*		
Futures	***2006-07/ 2007-08***	***2006-07/ 2008-09***	***Spot Prices***	***2006-07/ 2007-08***	***2006-07/ 2008-09***
Chilli	t = 0.9739 df = 19 P = 0.3424 (2-tailed)	t = 2.6359* df = 15 P =0.0187 (2-tailed)	***Chilli***	t = 1.5529 df = 11 P = 0.1487 (2-tailed)	t = 3.0988* df = 11 P = 0.0101 (2-tailed)
Mustard Seed	t = 8.1345* df = 11 P =0.0001 (2-tailed)	t = 6.3535* df = 11 P = 0.0001 (2-tailed)	***Mustard Seed***	t = 7.8813* df = 11 P = 0.0001 (2-tailed)	t = 6.4040* df = 11 P = 0.0001 (2-tailed)

* 1%, statistically significant

* 5% statistically not significant

CONCLUDING OBSERVATION

The stock markets, financial markets, export of goods and services and corporate profits have witnessed negative growth during global financial crisis period. So, the present chapter has undertaken the study from 1st August 2005 to 31st July 2009 to determine the meltdown effects on agricultural commodities markets in the India. This chapter found that the growth and volatility of NCDEXAGRI and FUTEXAGRI for 2008-09 have been significantly lower than that of 2007-08 also commodities market got more affected than stock market due to meltdown/global financial crisis happened in world market. This chapter also found that the trading activity in terms of quantity and value traded for chilli has been significantly lower during meltdown period. The commodities market witnessed lower volatility probably due to weak sentiment that prevailed during the meltdown period. This chapter concludes that the trading activities of (both volume and value) chilli and mustard seed are significantly affected during the meltdown period and the spot and futures prices are closely tracked each other arbitrage opportunities are not found during this period.

REVIEW QUESTIONS

1. Who are the participants in commodity futures?
2. Explain the structure of Indian Commodity market?
3. Explain the history of Commodity market?
4. What are the benefits of commodity future markets?
5. What are the latest developments of commodity market?
6. How do you justify the importance of commodity market in India?
7. Quiz
   (a) Indian Commodity Market is subdivided into ____ and ____ Market.
   (b) The concept of organized trading in commodities evolved in____, in ____.
   (c) Cotton derivatives trading started in oilseed in______, raw jute and jute goods in____, Wheat in ____ and Bullion in ____.
   (d) The most popular energy futures contracts are ____,____ and____.
   (e) Commodities have been defined by——— as "Every kind of movable property other than actionable claims, money and securities."
   (f) Which was the first commodity exchange to facilitate commodities settlement in demat form?
   (g) Who are the participants of commodity markets?

6

Behaviour Dynamics of Indian IPO Market

Pricing of Capital is important in capital market to allocate resources for the productive needs of the society. Also, underpricing is a well-documented phenomenon in the stock market. Here, this chapter indicates that the underpricing in the Indian IPOs in the short run is higher than the experiences of other countries. It emphasizes that IPOs are composed of premium or for issues outperformed the market and market price is found to be higher than the intrinsic value.

INTRODUCTION

Indian Capital Market is one of the oldest and second largest in the world in terms of number of listed companies. Today, the capital market is passing through a phase of structural transformation. The reforms initiated in the financial sector in general and in the capital market in particular may be viewed in concomitance with the general economic reforms, in order to ensure inter-sectoral harmony and speedy development of the economy. Freedom of pricing of security is an important aspect of liberalization programme initiated by the capital market in India. So, the events which led to the introduction of free pricing of equity and emergence of Securities Exchange Board of India as the only regulatory body for the entire capital market has now became the backbone of Indian Capital Market.

WHY DO COMPANIES OFFER IPO?

In general, companies offer IPOs in order to raise money that they need for business expansion and new business opportunities. By offering shares to investors, a company stands to bring in a lot of money that can be used to grow their business. The more their business grows, the higher the share prices grow and the more money is generated by investors purchasing shares. If the company loses money, they will not need to repay their investors, although investors in general demand high accountability from a company they are buying stocks from. There are three main reasons behind the offering of IPOs:

- Provide liquidity to securities;
- Mobilize savings for economic development;
- Protect interest of investors by ensuring full disclosures.

TYPES OF IPO

There are many types of IPO, illustrating the different management and owner compensation contracts in firms.

- The **plain vanilla** IPO is undertaken by a privately held company, mostly owned by management, who want to secure additional funding and determine the company's fair market value.
- A **venture capital-backed** IPO refers to a company in which management has sold its shares to one or more groups of private investors in return for funding and advice. This provides an effective incentive scheme for venture capitalists to implement their exit strategy after they have successfully transformed a firm in which they invested so that it is financially viable in the market.
- In a **reverse-leveraged** buyout, the proceeds of the IPO are used to pay off the debt accumulated when a company was privatized after a previous listing on an exchange. This process enables owners who own majority shares to privatize their publicly trading firms, which are undervalued in the market, thus realizing financial gains after the public was informed of the high intrinsic value of the private firm.
- A **spin-off** IPO denotes the process whereby a large company carves out a stand-alone subsidiary and sells it to the public. A spin-off may also offer owners of the parent firm and hedge funds the opportunity to capitalize mispricing in both the subsidiary and parent if the market is not efficient enough.

Table 1
Showing Indian IPOs in 2009

IPO	***Issue Open***	***Issue Close***	***Listing At***	***Price Range***
D B Corp Limited IPO	Dec 11, 2009	Dec 15, 2009	BSE, NSE	₹ */- to ₹ */-
Godrej Properties Ltd. IPO	Dec 09, 2009	Dec 11, 2009	BSE, NSE	₹ 490/- to ₹ 530/-
JSW Energy Limited IPO	Dec 07, 2009	Dec 09, 2009	BSE, NSE	₹ 100/- to ₹ 115/-
MBI infrastructures Ltd. IPO	Nov 27, 2009	Dec 01, 2009	BSE, NSE	₹ 165/- to ₹ 180/-
Cox and Kings (India) Ltd. IPO	Nov 18, 2009	NOv 20, 2009	BSE, NSE	₹ 316/- to ₹ 330/-
Astec Life Sciences Ltd. IPO	Oct 29, 2009	Nov 04, 2009	BSE, NSE	₹ 77/- to ₹ 82/-
Den Networks Ltd. IPO	Oct 28, 2009	Oct 30, 2009	BSE, NSE	₹ 195/- to ₹ 205/-

Indiabulls Power Ltd. IPO	Oct 12, 2009	Oct 15, 2009	BSE, NSE	₹ 40/- to ₹ 45/-
Thinksoft Global Services Ltd. IPO	Sept 22, 2009	Sept 24, 2009	BSE, NSE	₹ 120/- to ₹ 130/-
Euro multivision Ltd. IPO	Sept 22, 2009	Sept 24, 2009	BSE, NSE	₹ 70/- to ₹ 75/-
Pipavav Shipyard Ltd. IPO	Sept 16, 2009	Sept 18, 2009	BSE, NSE	₹ 55/- to ₹ 60/-
Oil India Ltd. IPO	Sept 7, 2009	Sept 10, 2009	BSE, NSE	₹ 950/- to ₹ 1050
Globus Spirits Ltd. IPO	Aug 31, 2009	Sep 02, 2009	BSE, NSE	₹ 90/- to ₹ 100/-
Jindal Cotex Limited IPO	Aug 27, 2009	Sep 01, 2009	BSE, NSE	₹ 70/- to ₹ 75/-
NHPC Limited IPO	Aug 7, 2009	Aug 12,2009	BSE, NSE	₹ 30 to ₹ 36/-
Adani Power Limited IPO	July 28, 2009	July 31, 2009	BSE, NSE	₹ 90/- to ₹ 100/-
Raj Oil Mills Ltd. IPO	July 20, 2009	July 23, 2009	BSE, NSE	₹ 100/- to ₹ 120/-
Mahindra Holidays and Reorts India Ltd. IPO	June 23, 2009	June 26, 2009	BSE, NSE	₹ 275/- to ₹ 325/-
Rishabhdev Technocable Ltd. IPO	June 4, 2009	June 09, 2009	BSE, PSE, JSE	₹ 29/- to ₹ 33/-
Edserv Softsystems Ltd. IPO	Feb 05, 2009	Feb 09, 2009	BSE, NSE	₹ 55/- to ₹ 60/-
Gemini Engi-Fab Ltd. IPO	Feb 03, 2009	Feb 06, 2009	BSE, NSE	₹ 75/- to ₹ 80/-

Source: BSE, NSE

PROCEDURE OF GOING – PUBLIC IN INDIA

The following steps are involved in the process:

- The firm and the investment banker decide upon an offer price (also called issue price) and prepare a prospectus. This takes place roughly 5 months before the issue date. The face value of all shares in India is usually ₹ 10. The difference between the face value and the offer price is called 'premium'. Pricing of equity is allowed only when the company has made profits for the last three years. After this criterion is satisfied, there is no further restriction on deciding the price of the offer by the firm from the regulatory bodies.
- The prospectus is submitted to SEBI for approval. It is not necessary for the firm to declare the exact offer price to SEBI during the submission of the prospectus. If the company specifies an offer price of x, then the actual offer price could be anywhere in between x and 1.2x, i.e., a margin of 20% is allowed.
- Roughly before a month of the issue, a massive campaign is organized to capture the attention of the investors.
- The issue closes for four to ten days after it opens. Subscription takes place in this window, i.e., investors apply for shares and pay an amount that is less than the offer price. If there is oversubscription, then the money paid at the time of application is returned after a few months.
- After the issue closes, allotment of shares takes place. In case of an oversubscription, the allotment of shares is delayed. Then the investors receive their shares if they are allotted some, or the cheques if they have been denied shares due to a heavy oversubscription.
- The first day of trading takes place after a considerable time of the issue date.

ELIGIBILITY CRITERIA FOR PRIMARY ISSUANCE (IPO OR OFFER FOR SALE):

The following eligibility criteria have been prescribed effective August 1, 2006 for listing of companies on BSE, through Initial Public Offerings (IPOs):

1. Companies have been classified as large cap companies and small cap companies. A large cap company is a company with a minimum issue size of ₹ 10 crore and market capitalization of not less than ₹ 25 crore. A small cap company is a company other than a large cap company.

   (a) In respect of Large Cap Companies

      (i) The minimum post-issue paid-up capital of the applicant company (hereinafter referred to as "the Company") shall be ₹ 3 crore; and

      (ii) The minimum issue size shall be ₹ 10 crore; and

      (iii) The minimum market capitalization of the company shall be ₹ 25 crore (market capitalization shall be calculated by multiplying the post-issue paid-up number of equity shares with the issue price).

   (b) In respect of Small Cap Companies

      (i) The minimum post-issue paid-up capital of the Company shall be ₹ 3 crore; and

      (ii) The minimum issue size shall be ₹ 3 crore; and

      (iii) The minimum market capitalization of the company shall be ₹ 5 crore (market capitalization shall be calculated by multiplying the post-issue paid-up number of equity shares with the issue price); and

      (iv) The minimum income/turnover of the company shall be ₹ 3 crore in each of the preceding three 12-month period; and

      (v) The minimum number of public shareholders after the issue shall be 1000.

      (vi) A due diligence study may be conducted by an independent team of Chartered Accountants or Merchant Bankers appointed by BSE, the cost of which will be borne by the company. The requirement of a due diligence study may be waived if a financial institution or a scheduled commercial bank has appraised the project in the preceding 12 months.

2. For all companies:

   (a) In respect of the requirement of paid-up capital and market capitalization, the issuers shall be required to include in the disclaimer clause forming a part of the offer document that in the event of the market capitalization (product of issue price and the post issue number of shares) requirement of BSE not being met, the securities of the issuer would not be listed on BSE.

   (b) The applicant, promoters and/or group companies, shall not be in default in compliance of the listing agreement.

(c) The above eligibility criteria would be in addition to the conditions prescribed under SEBI (Disclosure and Investor Protection) Guidelines, 2000.

EFFECT OF RECESSION ON IPO MARKET

The liquidity crunch has had an adverse impact on global IPO market with firms and financial institutions running low on cash. Widespread pessimism has also had a negative impact on the launching of new IPOs which have sufficiently decreased in number since the economic meltdown.

The recession and shuttered IPO market have placed tremendous pressure on portfolio companies to restructure and plan the future course of action. A marked slowdown of new investments is seen, as venture capitalists have turned their attention to supporting these existing companies. However, most venture capitalists feel that a down market is the best time to invest when valuations and competition are lower. The following section analyses effect of recession on IPOs in various countries.

Russia:

The current global trend is such that regional companies prefer to choose local floors. In Russia, in 2007, about 38% of the total volume of placements (about 11.7 billion dollars) was accounted for by Russian floors. This figure considerably exceeds the results of 2006, when the volume of placements in the domestic market reached only 1.2 billion dollars. There were quite a few so-called dual IPOs, when companies make their placements on both Russian and Western floors. In 2007, the volume of dual IPOs reached about 16.2 billion dollars.

The aftermath of the mortgage crisis in the United States and the destabilization of the global financial market resulted in the decline of the value of various companies' stocks. As far as Russia is concerned, on the one hand, it is in a somewhat privileged position, because Russia has all prerequisites for further stable economic growth, and the stock market mirrors the state the economy. On the other hand, as a part of the global financial market and we are influenced by events occurring in the world. Issuers who counted on certain price levels have to put up with the ongoing price drop. The speed at which the population is getting involved in the stock market is very high. Despite today's increased volatility of the stock market, about 2500 individuals begin to participate in trading on the MICEX Stock Exchange each week. Thus, the size of the investment base doubles in one year. This year, jointly with Public Opinion Foundation, we have conducted a study which showed that in the near future up to 5 million individual Russian investors can enter the stock market. Domestic investors will be investing primarily in the Russian market, where they are protected by the law and the regulator against all kinds of legal risks and where they know the companies in which they decide to invest. This means Russian issuers have a very powerful incentive to make their placements in the domestic market.

USA

US economy relies on a steady stream of venture-backed companies, whc collectively produce more than one-fifth of the US gross domestic product. In fact, public companies that were VC-funded currently account for more than 12 million US jobs and $2.9 trillion in revenues.

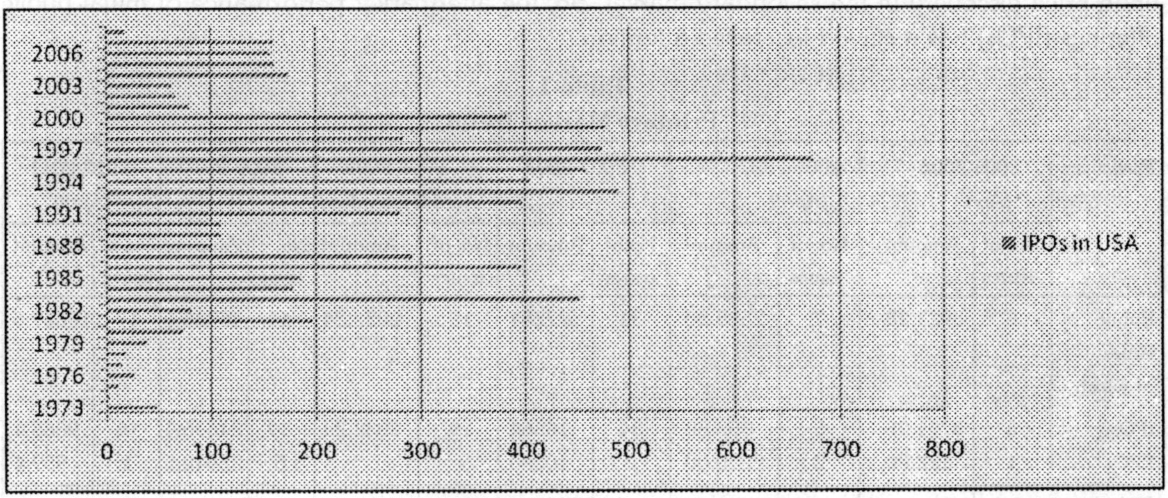

Fig. 1: IPOs in USA

Research firm Global Insight estimates that 92 per cent of job growth at these companies occurs once the company enters the public market. However, economic uncertainty, and an adversity to risk has substantially reduced the IPO pipeline, and broken this cycle. Instead, VC-backed companies today are currently struggling to maintain cash sufficiency, which leaves investors holding the bag. The problem is investors have abandoned long-term strategies in favor of short-term returns, and this shift to much more conservative investing is stifling innovation. As a result, investors may well be passing up on what could be the next Google or Face book. In order to survive, VCs need to re-think how and where they can help their portfolio companies remain innovative and profitable in the current economy.

INDIAN IPO MARKET

During the past few years, the Indian stock market has been passing through a tremendous qualitative and quantitative change. During April 2006, ₹ 8990 crore was raised from the primary market through 9 issues. There were 6 public issues, which raised ₹ 8923 crore. Of the 6 public issues, 5 were initial public offerings (IPOs), which raised ₹ 8,791 crore. There is again one public offerings (FPO) which mobilized ₹ 132 crore, which is depicted in the Table 1. Fair pricing of initial public offerings (IPO) is a pre-condition for overall allocation efficiency of the financial system. So, the companies which have a three-year dividend track record during the preceding five years, will be eligible to tap the capital market. Once the company and merchant bankers fix an offer price, they only need to submit a copy of the prospectus to SEBI. Some of the features of Indian IPO markets are unique in comparison to the world standards. In contrast to most of the developed markets, there is no mechanism by which the offer price of an Indian issue can be changed according to the demand for the issue.

In an efficient market if the prices of IPO are set at their intrinsic values, then the firm should be able to raise the quantum of funds while underpricing would result in flow of too little capital into the firm, this would be reflected in high after market returns for the IPO investor consequent upon price discovery in the secondary market. So, the aftermarket performance of initial public offerings (IPOs) has received increased attention.

Table 1
Primary Market Trend

Particulars	*2005-2006 (April)*		*2006-2007 (April)*		*2007-2008*		*2008-2009 (April-September)*		*2009-2010*		*2010-2011 (April)*	
	No. of issues	Amount	No. of issues	Amount	No.of issues	Amount	No. of issues	Amount	No. of issues	Amount	No. of issues	Amount
Public issues of which	6	8923.28	7	2625.50	36	27254	19	2032.24	44	46736.6	17	10627.8
IPOs	5	8791.28	5	355.50	34	16664	19	2032.24	39	24696.1	16	9668.4
FPOs	1	132.00	2	2270.00	2	10590	-	-	5	22040.5	1	959.4
Rights issues	3	66.57	1	11.75	4	357	14	10377.48	29	8318.6	8	2811
Total	9	8989.85	8	2637.25	40	27611	33	12409.72	73	55055.2	25	134388

Source: SEBI Bulletin, August 2008, Ocotober 2009, September 2010

India has too suffered a drastic decrease in the number of IPOs due to recession with few companies going public. Even the existing companies have been cutting down on costs to generate the necessary working capital to see through the bad economic climate. The meltdown has decreased the number of IPO launches significantly in India with both the companies and the investors being more cautious.

BEHAVIORAL DYNAMICS OF THE INDIAN IPO MARKET

IPO is a very significant moment for all the stakeholders of the company, which included the management, the VCs with a holding and the underwriters.

- **Stake of the Managers:** In the case of a small start-up, the manager is often the promoter of the company and has a long term stake in the company. So, the managers are going to stay for a long time and are not interested in any short-term gains.
- **Stake of the VCs:** The Venture Capitalists are organizations that have provided the necessary capital to the fledging firm to grow in its time of need. Their stake is a short-term one and they are eager to reap quick profits. Their main aim is to make the company go public and exit soon after its ownership.
- **Underwriter:** The underwriter is the Investment Banker who has been hired to carry out the Initial Public Offering on behalf of the firm. It is the onus of the underwriter to see that the IPO is oversubscribed by a wide margin and that it succeeds. If the IPO fails, the reputation of the underwriter is invariably tarnished. If the IPO succeeds on the other hand, the underwriter enhances its chances of attracting more prospective clients. Hence, the underwriter would do anything for the success of the IPO and has short-term interests with the company.

UNDER PRICING OF IPOS

An IPO is a risky proposition for a company. For the individual investor, it is tough to predict what the stock or shares will do on its initial day of trading and in the near future. Also, most IPOs are of companies going through a transitory growth period, and they are therefore subject to additional uncertainty regarding their future value. This leads to under pricing of IPOs. On an average, IPOs are (15%) underpriced, so at the end of the first day of trading, the price is (15%) higher than the price set by the underwriter. This widespread phenomenon has received a lot of attention from researchers in the past few decades.

Theories behind under pricing of IPOs:

- **Information Asymmetry:** Investors do not know the firm well enough to invest their money in it. And information doesn't come free of cost. Information analysis is costly and hence it is optimal for investors not to learn about the company that well. So, the investor will be suspicious of the firm and hence this will lead to under pricing by the underwriter.
- **Fixing the Offer Price early:** Firms fix their offer price sufficiently before the issue happens. Firms are likely to be risk-averse with respect to the prospect of issues failing. Even if the firm has an exact idea of the price at the time of fixing the offer price, it would fix it lower than the correct estimate because it would fear that the stock prices will fall by the time of the issue, rendering the offer unattractive.
- **Liquidity Premium:** It is a premium that investors will demand when any given security cannot be easily converted into cash, and converted at the fair market value. When the liquidity premium is high, then the asset is said to be illiquid, which will cause prices to fall, and interest rates to rise. So when investors who apply for public issues, they lose liquidity on the amount paid at the issue date. Hence, the underpricing.
- **Building loyal Shareholders:** Firms underpriced their issues when they expect to return to the capital market to raise further resources at a further date. This could maintain a good impression in the eyes of the investors.
- **Merchant Banker rewarding favoured clients:** The relationship between the firm and the merchant banker is a one time. The underwriter hence under prices to favour these big clients.

LITERATURE REVIEW

Over the past three decades, several empirical studies have reported that IPOs achieve sizeable average returns over very short periods, suggesting that these offerings might be underpriced. McDonald and Fisher (1972) reported an average excess return of 28.5% for a sample of 142 issues in 1969. Ibbotson (1975), using risk-adjusted returns, finds average excess returns of a sample of IPOs occurring during the1960s to be 11.4%. Using a simpler model and a larger sample, Ibbotson and Jaffe (1975) reported average excess returns of 16.8%. For over 5000 IPOs occurring from 1960 to 1982, Ritter (1984) reported the initial average return to be 18.8%. Other early studies of IPOs like Block and Stanley (1980), Brown (1970), Logue (1973a, 1973b), Neuberger and LaChapelle (1983), Reilley (1973, 1977), Reilley and Hatfield (1969), Stoll and

Curley (1970) etc. were primarily concerned with examining the profit potential for investors in these issues. The results of these studies consistently indicated that, on an average, IPOs offered significant positive excess returns in the short run, and it was generally agreed that this was attributable to the under pricing of these new issues by the underwriters. Many of these studies also explored the implications of these findings for efficient market hypotheses (EMH). The general conclusion has been that prices of the newly issued securities adjust very rapidly to the underpricing, if any, and investors who purchase the new issues in the aftermarket (i.e., a week or a month after the initial issue) cannot have excess returns on the average. Some other works like Beatty and Ritter (1986), Ritter (1984), Rock (1986) etc. in the subsequent years explored beyond the empirical evidence of underpricing and set forth theoretical arguments that explain the underpricing in terms of information asymmetry among investors. They argue that the investor in the IPO is either 'informed' ex-ante about the aftermarket price or is 'uninformed' about the price. If the IPO is actually underpriced, then the informed investors will enter orders for the issue causing the issue to be oversubscribed, thereby leading to a rationing of the issue. Uninformed investors will thus receive some rationed amount against their bids.

On the other hand if an issue is overpriced, informed investors stay out of the offering, leaving only uninformed investors to absorb the overpricing. Thus, for profitable issues informed investors' crowd out the uninformed investors while for less/ non-profitable issues the uninformed investors suffer from a 'winner's curse' problem having received the bulk of the allocation. Therefore, the average underpricing is considered to be the compensation required to induce the uninformed investors to participate in the IPO market. Of course, this argument is difficult to reconcile with the preferences of issuers, assuming rationality on their part. The motivation for issuers to underprice to attract uninformed investors is not obvious. The extensive oversubscription reported in several studies (Benveniste and Spindt-1989, Ibbotson and Jaffe-1975, Koh and Walter-1989) suggestted that underpricing to attract uninformed capital is unnecessary. Even if issuer's desire to attract uninformed participation is taken as given, there is likely to be a 'free rider problem' among issuers; even if they knew that IPOs need to be underpriced on the average, no individual issuer would be willing to underprice the issue. For the developed market, Rock (1986), Benveniste and Spindt (1989) revealed that those investors receiving at the initial allocation of the securities keep the benefit associated with the underpricing. Allen and Faulhaber (1989) showed that underpricing can be a signal favorable prospect for the firm and there is positive relation between the degree of underpricing and subsequent earnings performance and the dividend policy of the firm. Beauty and Riffer (1986) assertrd that underpricing should be related to the ex-ante uncertainty surrounding the value of an issue. The greater the degree of uncertainty, the higher the extent of underpricing likely to be. Jegadeesh *et al.* (1993) found a positive relation between IPO underpricing and the likelihood of a subsequent seasoned equity offering. In contrast, Carter (1992) found that higher reputation for the IPO underwriter is associated with less underpricing at the IPO and with a greater likelihood of a subsequent offering of either debt or common equity. Very little work has been done on the performance of IPOs in India. Aggarwal (1994), Krishnamurthi and Kumar (1994), Narasimhan and Ramana (1995) and Shah (1995) have done an analysis of IPOs and almost all these studies have analysed the short-run performance of new issues, i.e., the return in the first day of trading. Again these studies suggest that IPOs are under priced in the short run while in the long run, the evidence, i.e., that of underperformance, i.e., negative returns accrue to the investors holding these IPOs. The focus of this chapter is to find out whether a stock has been priced at its intrinsic worth or not. Secondly to determine the magnitude and degree of the deviations of the market price of the stock from its offer price, and thirdly to know whether it is underpricing or overpricing.

LET'S TAKE CASE OF THIRTY-THREE COMPANIES LISTED IN THE BOMABAY STOCK EXCHANDE TO DETERMINE STOCK IS OVER PRICED/ UNDERPRICED:

The present chapter undertakes an evaluation of returns for thirty-three companies listed in the Bombay Stock Exchange. The return on a stock is calculated by using the standard formula.

$$R_{it} = \frac{P_{it} - P_{io}}{P_{io}} \times 100$$

Where P_{it} is the price of the stock i in period t.

P_{to} is the offer price of stock I

Sometimes the return of the market index during the period is finding out by using the following formula:

$$R_{mt} = \frac{P_{mt} - P_{mo}}{P_{mo}} \times 100$$

Where P_{mt} is the market index at time t

P_{mo} is the market index on the offer day

Further market adjusted excess return is calculated by the following method:

Market adjusted excess return $= R_{it} - R_{mt}$

Again to determine the performance of the IPOs *vis-à-vis* the market, a wealth relative measure has been calculated. Wealth relative measure is below 1 indicates underperformance and greater than 1 implies outperformed the market in that period. So, it is calculated by using the following formula:

$$WR_{it} = \frac{1 + \frac{1}{N}\sum_{i=1}^{n} r_{it}}{1 + \frac{1}{N}\sum_{i=1}^{n} r_{mt}}$$

Where N is the total number of IPO in the sample

$R_n = R_{it} / 100$ and $r_{mt} = R_n / 100$

Trend Forecasts

Time series forecasting is the use of a model to forecast future events based on known past events: to predict data points before they are measured. Time series data have a natural temporal ordering. This makes time series analysis distinct from other common data analysis problems, in which there is no natural ordering of the observations (e.g., explaining people's wages by reference to their education level, where the individuals' data could be entered in any order). Time series analysis is also distinct from spatial data analysis where the observations typically relate to geographical locations (e.g., accounting for house prices by the location as well as the intrinsic characteristics of the houses). A time series model will generally reflect the fact that observations close together in time will be more closely related than observations further apart. In addition, time series models will often make use of the natural one-way ordering of time so that values for a given period will be expressed as deriving in some way from past values, rather than from future values.

ANALYSIS

The results clearly show that in the Indian IPO market issue price is usually undervalued and thus it witnesses oversubscription which usually happens in an efficient market. Return achieved as compared to market across the 33 companies is coming around 16.81%. This implies that investors putting on money into IPO's as general investors usually get a below market return.

Table 2
Descriptive Statistics

Company	*Mean*	*Standard Deviation*	*Minimum*	*Maximum*	*Median*	*Skew ness*	*Mean Market Adjusted Return*	*Wealth Relative*	*Mean Market Adjusted Return for 2 weeks*
Sita Shree Food Products Ltd.	-2.78	12.37	-25.41	43.67	-3.20	1.02	-1.60	-10.25	13.39
Gammon Infrastructure Projects Ltd.	-3.49	15.70	-80.48	35.38	-2.50	-2.08	-2.45	-63.75	-22.47
Rural Electrification Corporation Ltd.	-0.19	7.33	-22.28	20.07	-0.55	-0.03	1.04	3.62	-0.23
V-Guard Industries Ltd.	-1.15	4.52	-15.79	5.54	-1.18	-1.01	-0.02	-1.12	-0.77
GSS America Infotech Ltd.	-1.68	13.40	-30.65	38.94	-2.28	0.63	-0.49	-3.62	15.35

Tulsi Extrusions Ltd.	-3.15	11.63	-28.35	27.71	-3.80	0.19	-1.85	-7.24	2.36
IRB Infrastructure Developers Ltd.	-0.67	9.66	-25.07	28.56	-1.64	0.67	0.63	1.12	2.91
Shriram Epc Ltd.	-1.57	12.43	-28.00	38.07	-2.31	1.01	-0.33	-2.39	-2.65
Bang Overseas Ltd.	-0.62	10.17	-25.83	28.32	0.88	-0.11	0.62	1.57	-11.31
KNR Constructions Ltd.	-2.30	11.99	-30.10	26.80	-2.41	0.04	-1.06	-5.42	-7.71
Onmobile Global Ltd.	-0.83	9.17	-30.37	24.33	-1.22	-0.22	0.41	0.73	8.45
Cords Cable Industries Ltd.	-2.13	11.38	-35.95	32.51	-1.27	0.17	-0.89	-4.78	-5.86
J.Kumar Infraprojects Ltd.	-1.11	7.08	-19.09	17.00	-1.48	0.10	0.13	-0.46	-3.08
Reliance Power Ltd.	-2.22	11.36	-46.57	27.77	-1.48	-1.02	-0.91	-3.97	-9.90
Future Capital Holdings Ltd.	-0.43	16.15	-85.42	48.74	0.00	-2.48	-0.60	0.49	-7.24
Manaksia Ltd.	-2.84	8.90	-25.78	21.18	-3.99	0.32	-1.45	-4.72	-11.46
Porwal Auto Components Ltd.	-3.95	10.09	-39.10	23.22	-2.11	-0.71	-2.71	-12.29	-12.51
Mahindra Holidays & Resorts India Ltd.	1.16	4.48	-6.44	16.48	0.36	1.03	0.83	1.62	3.03
Edserv Softsystems Ltd.	4.37	14.51	-30.50	36.36	4.30	-0.22	3.09	2.36	-23.40
Alkali Metals Ltd.	2.98	17.46	-23.21	88.64	-0.97	2.73	1.78	1.81	21.55
Resurgere Mines & Minerals India Ltd.	1.86	23.29	-44.86	111.22	0.07	2.23	1.58	2.23	-6.26
Nu Tek India Ltd.	-1.74	15.00	-30.67	41.25	-3.20	0.48	-1.95	-0.62	-8.77
Birla Cotsyn (India) Ltd.	-2.79	17.25	-92.00	26.67	-2.56	-2.77	-3.13	-1.33	-29.02
KSK Energy Ventures Ltd.	0.46	10.81	-26.72	27.01	0.00	0.29	0.08	1.06	-10.35
Lotus Eye Care Hospital Ltd.	0.60	11.15	-27.70	40.79	0.00	0.56	0.40	1.34	1.76
Archidply Industries Ltd.	-1.44	10.66	-31.82	35.82	-0.53	0.86	-1.52	-0.40	-14.68

First Winner Industries Ltd.	-2.29	14.21	-23.56	27.46	-2.90	0.37	-2.49	-1.08	2.98
Niraj Cement Structurals Ltd.	-1.25	12.32	-55.47	27.34	-0.58	-1.52	-1.46	-0.21	-19.67
Anu's Laboratories Ltd.	-0.83	16.61	-93.71	28.79	-0.13	-3.63	-0.12	0.58	-7.93
Gokul Refoils & Solvent Ltd.	-1.54	15.69	-95.80	23.58	0.58	-4.71	-0.83	-1.84	-18.68
Aishwarya Telecom Ltd.	-0.69	24.69	-25.43	146.57	-3.80	4.72	0.11	1.55	40.84
Kiri Dyes And Chemicals Ltd.	-0.40	10.21	-21.74	34.74	-1.25	1.13	0.55	12.05	-3.37
Titagarh Wagons Ltd.	-2.19	12.40	-31.33	29.79	-2.32	0.38	-1.09	-12.38	8.37

Table 3

Wealth Relative Measure for 48 Weeks

Week 1	-2.44	Week 13	-1.43	Week 25	-0.91	Week 37	0.60
Week 2	0.65	Week 14	1.72	Week 26	-16.48	Week 38	0.67
Week 3	-278.32	Week 15	0.91	Week 27	-0.21	Week 39	0.54
Week 4	-13.43	Week 16	-5.36	Week 28	-2.01	Week 40	5.42
Week 5	-8.50	Week 17	-12.14	Week 29	1.28	Week 41	2.39
Week 6	-5.41	Week 18	-5.34	Week 30	-11.23	Week 42	-0.33
Week 7	1.28	Week 19	0.89	Week 31	-0.35	Week 43	0.98
Week 8	-13.85	Week 20	-3.73	Week 32	-1.36	Week 44	0.91
Week 9	0.52	Week 21	-6.16	Week 33	-0.48	Week 45	1.35
Week 10	1.53	Week 22	0.93	Week 34	-0.37	Week 46	4.85
Week 11	1.17	Week 23	2.66	Week 35	2.16	Week 47	0.73
Week 12	-0.93	Week 24	5.48	Week 36	-4.35	Week 48	0.70

It is also inferred from the Table 2 that skewness shows positive values. So, the median returns are less than the mean returns. This is consistent with almost prior research, which has been studied. It is also observed from wealth relative measures over a time frame of 48 weeks and it is seen that initially it increases and finally it stabilizes according to the market. When linear trend forecasting has been used, it cannot witness any definite trend depicted in Fig. 2 which clearly shows IPO returns are very company specific. The study examined the under pricing in Indian IPOs during the year 2008. Using a sample of 33 IPOs, the results indicate evidence of under pricing on the average in Indian IPOs during this period. However, some evidence towards overpricing of a lesser fraction of the issues is also found. One interesting observation from the analysis is that the mispricing adjusts very quickly (within the first day itself in most cases) and no excess returns are available to investors in the aftermarket in the short run which is consistent with the notion of EMH. A strong positive relationship was found between under pricing and exante as well as ex-post measures of uncertainty. The level of activity in the issues measured by the daily trading volume is also found to have strong correlation with underpricing. Overall, the results of the study enhance the findings of some earlier works on underpricing and speed of adjustment in the aftermarket for IPOs in the Indian context. The study also provides empirical evidence relating underpricing to uncertainty.

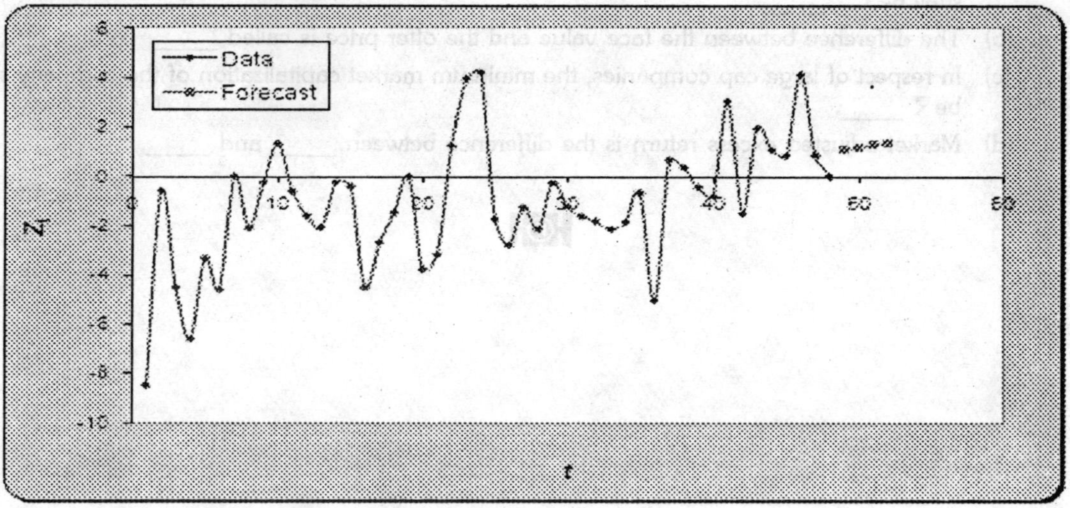

Fig. 2: Trend Analysis

CONCLUDING OBSERVATION

This chapter has made the analysis during the recession period which gives a consistent negative return as compared to the market. Similarly, wealth relative return over the period is negative which signifies that the IPO underperformed during that period. IPO returns are dependent on market conditions. IPOs outperform markets in short term – but recessionary period is an exception. Returns on an IPO do not follow a definite trend and cannot be forecasted. Thus, it can conclude that during a downturn it should be advisable to go for public listing. Indian investors get very good returns from the initial public offerings only after some time in the market. General market condition is very important variable for the better performance of the new issues. This study analyses that market value of these issues is at much higher level than the price at which they were issued. So, it indicates that the issuers could have got better price and merchant bankers are actually not taken care of their interests. However, more underpricing at the IPO does not result in more favorable treatment at the seasonal offering.

REVIEW QUESTIONS

1. How do you measure the efficiency of Indian IPO market?
2. What are the eligibility criteria for issuing IPOs?
3. What is the underlying dimension of underpricing?
4. How do you determine the underpricing/overpricing?
5. Quiz
   (a) In respect of small cap companies, The minimum post-issue paid-up capital of the company shall be ₹ ______.
   (b) The difference between the face value and the offer price is called ______.
   (c) In respect of large cap companies, the minimum market capitalization of the company shall be ₹ ______.
   (d) Market adjusted excess return is the difference between ______ and ______.

7

Stock Market, Market Capitalization and Net FII Investments in India

This chapter examines the dynamic relationship between stock market, market capitalization and net FII investment in India. This chapter explains that stock return and market capitalization have an impact over net FII investment in the expected direction over a short horizon.

INTRODUCTION

Since capital formation plays an important role in the development process, new products have emerged in the market. India has emerged as an important destination for global investment. This is reflected in the number of FIIs registered with Securities and Exchange Board of India (SEBI). The liberalization process of the Indian economy has been a contributing factor for the increase in financial flows. India, in the last ten years, has improved its macroeconomic performance with a shift towards more market discipline and increased capital movements. The liberalization process has given the foreign portfolio management a strategy for international diversification of portfolios to hedge risk. Also it calls for a reexamination of relationship between stock market with foreign sector in the economy. It analyses the relationship between their stock price, market capitalization and FII investment. It is generally believed that FII investment broadens the base of portfolio diversification and causes a long-term increase in the stock prices by reducing the equilibrium rate of return. So, the role of FII investment on the host country stock market has been a subject of interest to academicians and policy makers.

WHAT IS MARKET CAPITALIZATION?

Market cap or market capitalization is simply the worth of a company in terms of its shares. Market cap is a measurement of size of a business enterprise equal to the share price times the number of shares outstanding of a public company. Market capitalization represents aggregate value of a company or stock. An entirely public corporation, including all of its assets, may be freely bought and sold through purchases and sales of stock, which will determine the price of the company's shares. It is obtained by multiplying the "current share price" by the "number of shares issued by the company". Depending on the value of the market cap, the company will either be a "mid cap" or "large cap" or "small cap" company. With over 20 million shareholders, India has the third largest investor base in the world after the USA and Japan. Over 9,000 companies are listed on the stock exchanges, which are serviced by approximately 7,500 stock brokers. The Indian capital market is significant in terms of the degree of development, volume of trading and its tremendous growth potential. India's market capitalization was the highest amongst the emerging markets. Total market capitalization of the BSE as on July 31, 1997 was ₹ 5,573.07 billion growing by 18 per cent over a period of twelve months and as of August 2007 was over $1090 billion (over ₹ 43 lakh crore) (Source: BSE).

The total wealth, measured in terms of cumulative market capitalization of all the listed companies on the Bombay Stock Exchange, has surged to a record high of ₹ 70,38,538 crore (over $1.7 trillion). This marks a tenfold surge in the total market value in just about four-and-a-half years. It stood at about ₹ 7, 00,000 crore in May 2003. The investors' wealth has grown by ₹ 34, 14,181 crore, or about $ 970 billion, since the beginning of 2007. At the end of 2006, the total market capitalization stood at ₹ 36,24,357 crore ($812 billion). The surge of 94.2 per cent in the market cap during 2007 is more than double of the rise in the Sensex, as close to 100 new companies got listed on the bourses in the year. (*Economic Times*, 30th December, 2007). The market capitalization of BSE increased by 0.8 per cent from ₹ 65,10,777 crore as on July 30, 2010 to ₹ 65,62,025 crore as on August 31, 2010. The market capitalization of NSE stood at ₹ 63,93,418 crore on August 31, 2010 as compared to ₹ 63,40,120 crore on July 30, 2010. (SEBI Bulletin, September 2010)

Table 1
Market Capitalization

Market Capitalization* (₹ crore)	***2005-06***	***2006-07***	***2007-08***	***2008-09***	***2009-10***	***2010-11***
BSE	30,22,189	35,45,041	51,38,014.13	30,86,075.17	61,65,619	65,62,025
NSE	28,13,201	33,67,350	48,58,121.72	28,96,194.22	6009173	63,93,418

Source: SEBI Bulletin, Feb 2009, September 2010.

Today, BSE is in the top ten of global exchanges in terms of the market capitalization of its listed companies (as of December 31, 2009). The companies listed on BSE command a total market capitalization of USD 1.28 trillion as of Feb, 2010.

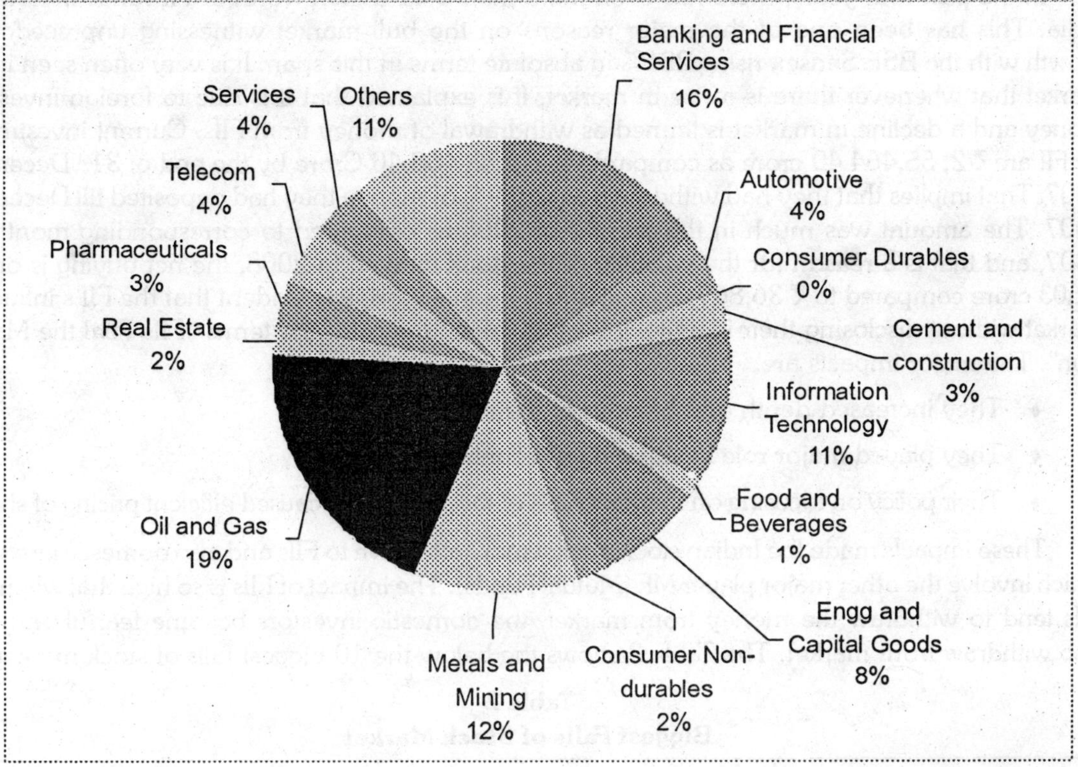

Fig. 1: Market Cap of Various Sectors as on 7th December, 2009

What does FII means?

It is the abbreviation of Foreign Institutional Investments. The term is used most commonly in India to refer to outside companies investing in the financial markets of India. International institutional investors must register with the Securities and Exchange Board of India to participate in the market. One of the major market regulations pertaining to FIIs involves placing limits on FII ownership in Indian companies. Institutional investors include hedge funds, insurance companies, pension funds and mutual funds. India opened its stock market to foreign investors in September 1992, and in 1993, received portfolio investment from foreigners in the form of foreign institutional investment in equities. This has become one of the main channels of FII in India for foreigners. Initially, there were many terms and conditions which restricted many FIIs to invest in India. But in the course of time, in order to attract more investors, SEBI has simplified many terms such as:

- The ceiling for overall investments of FIIs was increased 24% of the paid-up capital of Indian company.
- Allowed foreign individuals and hedge funds to directly register as FIIs.
- Investment in government securities was increased to US $ 5 billion.
- Simplified registration norms.

In the past four years, there has been more than $ 41 trillion worth of FII funds invested in India. This has been one of the major reasons on the bull market witnessing unprecedented growth with the BSE Sensex rising 221% in absolute terms in this span. It is very often seen in the market that whenever there is a rise in market, it is explained that it is due to foreign investors' money and a decline in market is termed as withdrawal of money from FIIs. Current investments by FII are ₹ 2, 55,464.40 crore as compared to ₹ 2,83,468.40 Crore by the end of 31st December 2007. That implies that they had withdrawn almost 9% of money they had deposited till December 2007. The amount was much in the months of 2008 as compared to corresponding months of 2007, and that is a reason for the volatility of the stock market. In 2008, the net buying is only ₹ 5,603 crore compared to ₹ 36,869 crore in 2007. From all this, it is evident that the FII's influence market without disclosing their identity. It is often taking notice of the terms "FIIs Fuel the Market Run". The major impacts are:

- They increased depth and breadth of the market.
- They played major role in expanding securities business.
- Their policy on focusing on fundamentals of the shares had caused efficient pricing of shares.

These impacts made the Indian stock market more attractive to FIIs and also domestic investors, which involve the other major player MF (Mutual Funds). The impact of FIIs is so high that whenever FIIs tend to withdraw the money from market, the domestic investors become fearful and they also withdraw from market. The Table 2 shows the below the 10 biggest falls of stock market:

Table 2
Biggest Falls of Stock Market

Day (Points Loss in Sensex)	***Gross Purchases (₹ crore)***	***Gross Sales (₹ crore)***	***Net Investments (₹ crore)***
01/08/2007 (615)	809.40	956.90	-147.50
02/08/2007 (617)	534.50	542.00	-7.50
16/08/2007 (643)	989.50	750.30	239.20
18/01/2008 (687)	1077.20	1348.40	-271.20
18/10/2007 (717)	1107.00	1372.50	-265.50
17/12/2007 (826)	670.00	869.00	-199.00
18/05/2006 (856)	761.80	527.40	234.40
21/01/2008 (1408)	3062.00	1060.30	2001.80
22/01/2008 (875)	2813.30	1618.20	1195.10

Source: Different SEBI Reports

Table 2 depicts that the major falls are going together with the withdrawal of investments by FIIs.

REVIEW OF LITERATURE

Dornbusch and Fischer (1980) in their 'good market approach' suggested that the change in exchange rate affect a firm's operational exposure and its competitiveness in the international market, and consequently its share prices. At macro level, the impact of exchange rate fluctuations on stock market depends on the relative importance of international trade on the economy and nature of trade imbalances of the country. Merton (1987) showed that the expected return in the market with unrestricted investor base is higher than restricted investor base. Entry of foreign investors in the stock market broadens the investor base, which increases diversification and risk sharing, lowering the risk premium for country-specific volatility. Ma and Kao (1990) found that the currency appreciation negativity affects the domestic stock market for an export-dominant country and positively affects the domestic stock market for an import-dominant country. While the portfolio balancing hypothesis postulates a causality running from stock market to exchange rate, the causality running from exchange rate to stock prices is implied in the good market approach. Warther (1995) in his 'price pressure hypothesis' suggested that the increase in share prices associated with foreign investment flow is caused by temporary illiquidity and predicts that this change in share price is subsequently reversed. Jay and Mougue (1996) showed that an increase in aggregate domestic stock price has a negative short-run effect on domestic currency value but in long-run increases in stock price have a positive effect on domestic currency value. However, currency depreciation has a negative short-run and long-run effect on the stock market. Abdalla and Murinde (1997) using monthly data for the sample period 1985-1994, found the exchange rate granger cause stock prices. Choe *et al.* (1998) analyzed the influence of FIIs on equity returns in Korea before and during the 1997 Asian crisis and found no evidence that stock price start falling because of a withdrawal of foreign equity investors, or that there was a destabilizing effect on Korea's stock market. Stultz (1997), Bekaert and Harvey (1998b) in their studies analyzed that it is not necessary that inviting FIIs to the stock market, would increase its volatility. Chakraborti (2001) used monthly data to examine the nature and cause of FIIs net inflow to the Indian equity market during 1993 to 1999. He finds that FIIs net inflow are correlated with the returns on the equity market and that FIIs inflows are more likely to be the effect than the cause on the returns. Batra (2003) used daily data on FIIs equity purchases and sales and equity returns between 2000 to 2002 on the BSE Sensex and monthly data between the periods 1994 to 2002. The analyses show evidence of FIIs adapting positive feedback trading at two aggregate levels on the daily returns with no such evidence on the monthly returns. Nath and Samanta (2003) with daily data found weak evidences of causality running from stock prices to exchange rate, particularly in recent years. Bhattacharya and Mukherjee (2003) and Muhammed and Rasheed (2004) in their studies did not found any co-integration between exchange rate and stock price. In an increasingly complex scenario of the financial world, it is of paramount importance for the researchers and policy makers to know the scenario of economic and financial system to achieve the regulatory goals of stability and efficiency of the system. Keeping view, the present chapter examines the dynamic relationship between stock market, market capitalization and net FII investment in India. This chapter also analyses the impact of market capitalization and net FII investment on stock market in India.

TAKE THE CASE OF BOMBAY STOCK EXCHANGE INDEX, MARKET CAPITALIZATION AND NET FII INVESTMENT IN INDIA TO DETERMINE THEIR CO-RRELATION:

With strong preference of FII for holding shares of large firms and more liquid stocks, the BSE sensex appears a more reasonable index. Net FII investments in local currency (rupees) are used in the chapter. The rationale behind choosing market capitalization indices is that returns only incorporate the prices changes, whereas market capitalization takes into consideration not only price data but volume of trading as well. Time series theories starts by considering the generating mechanism, which should be able to generate all the statistical properties of the series, or at least the conditional mean, variance and temporal autocorrelations, i.e., "linear properties" of the series, conditional upon past data.

Vector Autoregressive Analysis:

Vector autoregression (VAR) is an econometric model used to capture the evolution and the interdependencies between multiple time series, generalizing the univariate AR models. All the variables in a VAR are treated symmetrically by including for each variable an equation explaining its evolution based on its own lags and the lags of all the other variables in the model. Based on this feature, Christopher Sims advocated the use of VAR models as a theory-free method to estimate economic relationships, thus being an alternative to the "incredible identification restrictions" in structural models· The vector autoregression (VAR) by Sims (1980) assumed simultaneity among a set of variables. VAR is commonly used for forecasting systems of interrelated time series and for analyzing the dynamic impact of random disturbances on the system of variable. A VAR is an-equation n-variable linear model in which each variable is in turn explained by its own lagged values plus current and past values of remaining n — 1 variables. A VAR system consists of a set of regression equations, each of which has an adjustment mechanism such that even small changes in one variable component in the system may be accounted for automatically by possible adjustments in the rest of the variables in the system. Thus, VAR providès a fairly unrestrictive approximation to reduce from structural model without assuming beforehand any of the variables as exogenous. The standard VAR (P)

Model can be represented as

$$Z_{t = C + \Phi 1\, Zt\text{-}1 + \Phi 2\, Z\, t\text{-}2 + \text{—}} \text{————} + {}_{\Phi p\, Zt\text{-}p + et}$$

Where P is the lag order of the VAR. Zt is a vector of endogenous variables, and it is a vector of innovations that may be contemporaneously correlated but are uncorrelated with their own lagged values and uncorrelated with all of the right hand side variables. Any stable VAR (P) process can be inverted and represented as an infinite vector moving average (VMA) process as:

$$Zt = \mu + et + \Psi et\text{-}1 + \Psi\ et\text{-}2 +$$

Impulse Response Functions (IRFs) to generate allow us to trace the time path of the impact of shocks on the variables contained on the VAR. The matrices that are obtained from the coefficients of the VMA representation give us the impulse responses. However, standard impulse response analyses assume that shocks occur only in one variable at a time. Such an assumption may be valid only if the shocks in different variables are independent. However, there is no *a priori* reason to believe that the error terms are independent of each other.

The orthogonalized impulse response at long S is given by Ψp where p is a K*K. lower triangular matrix with the standard deviations of ε along the main diagonal such that PP'=Ω.

The orthogonalized error equation on the jth variable at horizon N is given by,

$[\varepsilon j_{\Psi N} P\varepsilon i], i, j, =1,2$———n,

Where ε_i is an nx_1 vector with all elements equal to zero except for the ith elements which is equal to unity.

ANALYSIS

It is evident from the table that all the price series at level have a unit root but all not stationary. Their second differences are stationary except FIIs as the other two variables exceed the critical values at 1%, 5% and 10% significance level.

Table 3

Pair-wise Granger Causality Tests between BSE Sensex, Market Capitalization and Net FII Investment

Null Hypothesis	*F-values*	*P-values*
Market capitalization does not Granger cause BSE Sensex	7.28238*	0.00264
BSE Sensex does not Granger Cause market capitalization	1.25949	0.29838
Net FII Investment does not Granger Cause BSE Sensex	2.81156**	.07600
BSE Sensex does not Granger cause Net FII Investment	1.73573	.19351
Net FII Investment does not Granger cause market capitalization	1.06875	.35615
Market capitalization does not Granger cause Net FII Investment	1.83787	.17663

* 5% level of significance

** 10% level of significance

It is essential to find out the impact of net FII Investment on stock market. So, the casual link among various variables needs to be explored. The Table 3 reported pair-wise Granger causality test results with lags 2 as two period lags is an appropriate lag order chooses in terms of the Akaike Information Criteria (AIC) for the full sample period. The reported F-values as well as P-values suggest that there is a unidirectional causality between Market Capitalization and BSE sensex, net FII Investment and BSE Sensex. This implies that BSE Sensex influences the market capitalization and net FII Investment It is observed from the table that there is no clear causality between net FII Investment and market capitalization.

Table 4
Estimated VAR

	BSE Sensex	*Market Capitalization*	*Net FII Investment*
BSE Sensex (-1)	1.018173(3.83699)	-34.20128(-.31966)	1.230109(.33510)
Market Capitalization (-1)	.002137(2.74127)	1.168694(3.71749)	.005038(.46704)
Net FII Investment (-1)	-.015271(-.63852)	-6.667068(-.69138)	.142896(.43190)
Intercept	234.8185(1.02)	71388.17(.77)	-1751.124(-.55)

Figures in parenthesis are t-statistics

Table 5
Impulse Response Analysis of BSE Sensex to Shock in Equation for Market Capitalization

Period	*Impulse Response*
1	0
2	88.30739
3	121.6923
4	161.1648
5	204.9998
6	250.5475
7	293.9325
8	336.2368
9	379.1113
10	423.5638

Table 6
Impulse Response Analysis of BSE Sensex to Shock in Equation for Net FII Investment

Period	*Impulse Response*
1	0
2	-23.22833
3	-71.23669
4	-98.66089
5	-94.87934
6	-83.39987
7	-76.05674
8	-72.78774
9	-71.18688
10	-70.65911

To further investigate the dynamic responses between the variables, the impulse response of the VAR system has been calculated and presented in the Table 6. It is observed from the Table 5 that a one standard error shock in market capitalization affects BSE Sensex positively till around 10 months while a one standard error shock in net FII investment affects stock market negatively till around 10 months. Both impulse responses fall between the respective standard error bands. In fact, the impact of net FII investment on stock market appears to be negative till around 10 months, although the strength of the effect weakens after a first couple of months. On the other hand, the shock in market capitalization has positive impact on stock market which continuous till 10 months even though the strength of the impact weakens after the first couple of months. So, the study revealed that shocks in stock returns and market capitalization impact net FII investment in the expected direction over a short horizon.

CONCLUDING OBSERVATION

This chapter examined the interlink ages among stock market, market capitalization and net FII investment by applying both the Granger Causality and the Vector Autoregression (VAR) tests. The results indicate that there is no significant causality between net FII investment and market capitalization but there is unidirectional causal relationship between market capitalization and stock market, net FII investment and stock market. It is also found from the analysis that by using a VAR model based on stationary time series and impulse response analysis that shocks in stock returns and market capitalization impact net FII investment in the expected direction over a short horizon. So, it suggested that the authorities can focus on domestic economic policies to stabilize the stock market.

REVIEW QUESTIONS

1. How do you determine the impact of FII investment on Indian stock market?
2. Briefly explain the significance of FII investment in stock market.
3. Quiz
   (a) _____ represents aggregate value of a company or stock.
   (b) _____ has the third largest investor base in the world after the USA and Japan.
   (c) The market capitalization of BSE increased by _____ per cent from ₹ _____crore as on July 2010.
   (d) The market capitalization of NSE stood at ₹ _____ crore on August 2010.
   (e) India opened its stock market to foreign investors in_____year, and in____ year received portfolio investment from foreigners in the form of foreign institutional investment in equities.
   (f) Who advocates the use of VAR models as a theory-free method to estimate economic relationships, thus being an alternative to the "incredible identification restrictions" in structural models?

8

Indian Stock Market, Trading Volume, Exchange Rate, and Standard Gold Rate

Among the financial market segments, the linkages among the money, government securities and foreign exchange markets have been established and are growing. In the contemporary scenario, the activities in the financial markets and their relationships with the real sector have assumed significant importance. Keeping in view, this chapter has made an attempt to measure the relationship among trading volume, standard gold rate, exchange rate and sensex in India.

INTRODUCTION

Globalization and financial sector reforms in India have ushered in a sea change in the financial architecture of the economy. With the liberalization of capital markets through bold measures by successive governments, stock markets have shown as unprecedented boom. Apart from this, the advent of floating exchange rate, the development of 24-hour screen-based global trading, the increased use of national currency outside the country and innovations in internationally traded financial products call for a reexamination of the relationship between the stock market and the foreign exchange market of Indian economy. Efficient, stable and healthy financial markets constitute the bedrock for successful conduct of monetary policy. Among the financial market segments, the linkages among the money, government securities and foreign exchange markets have been established and are growing. The rise in geopolitical risk, low interest rates, sagging US dollar and stock market contribute to shift to gold as an alternative investment and useful hedge. The investors have recently renewed their interest in gold. But the weak dollar has been the dominant cause of the yellow metal's rise and is having a positive impact on the demand from industrial users. In the contemporary scenario, the activities in the financial market and their relationships with the real sectors have assumed significant importance. Stock price leads the exchange rates. Improvement in the performance of the stock markets will result in an improvement in the economy measured by positive growth in GNP. In this context, close monitoring of trading volume, exchange rate and gold standard rate is essential for inferring return behavior of Indian Stock Market.

WHAT IS TRADING VOLUME IN STOCK MARKET?

There are number of contract traded into equities during period of specified time such as day, weekly, monthly in the stock market. Normally, this number of selling and buying traded contract are recorded as amount and total amount of transacted side both buy and sell known as Volume. Volume is a fundamental parameter of technical analysis which is used to measure worth of stock market move. A market legend suggests that trading volume is positively related to stock return volatility. It can be argued that an increase in price induce investors to trade more, thereby increasing trading volume. Conversely, we can hypothesize that an increase in trading volume can lead to an increase in price. An understanding of the relationship between stock market and volume is important for the microstructure of financial markets. It helps to understand the role of information in the price formation of stocks, with volume and volatility providing measures of significance of information reflected in the market.

In the literature, the informational content of volume has been analyzed through two main informational hypotheses namely the Mixture of Distributions Hypothesis and the Sequential Arrival of Information Hypothesis. Researchers found relationships running from returns to volume and *vice versa* in stock markets. The MD hypothesis states that price volatility and trading volume should be positively correlated because they jointly depend on a common underlying variable. This variable could be interpreted as the rate of information flow to the market. Rational expectations models show disagreement generated by private information. These models generally involve trading among privately informed traders, uninformed traders, and liquidity or noise traders. Investors trade rationally for both informational and no informational reasons. Wang (1984) asserted that trading is always accompanied by price changes, since investors are risk-averse. For example, when a group of investors sells shares to rebalance their portfolios, to induce other investors to buy, the price of the stock must drop. As information asymmetry increases, the uniformed investors demand higher discounts in when they buy the stock from the informed investors. Thus, these investors are able to cover the risk of trading against private information. Therefore, according to this model, trading volume is always positively correlated with the absolute price changes. The difference of opinion model assumes that traders differ in the way in which they interpret the information and each trader believes in the validity of his interpretation. Recently, much attention has been paid to emerging markets particularly the Asian markets because of their available extra diversification benefits to foreign equity investors despite their much smaller market capitalization and higher volatility.

INDIAN GOLD MARKET

Gold is the oldest precious metal known to everyone and for thousands of years it has been valued as a global currency, a commodity, an investment and simply an object of beauty. Gold is unique as it is both a commodity and a monetary asset. Its stability and high value makes it virtually indestructible and ensures that it is almost always recovered and recycled. There is no true consumption of gold in the economic sense as the stock of gold remains essentially constant while ownership shifts from one party to another. Although gold mine production is relatively inelastic, recycled gold (or scrap) ensures there is a potential source of easily traded supply when needed, and this helps to stabilize gold price. Economic forces that determine the price of gold are different from, and in many cases opposed to the forces that influence most financial asset. India is the world's largest consumer of gold. Indians normally buy about 25 per cent of the world's gold, purchasing around 700-750 tonnes of gold every year. However, the sharp price increase in 2008 and 2009 has impacted demand with total demand in 2008 dipping to 660 tonnes. It is further expected to shrink in 2009 with demand in first three quarters of 2009 totaling only around 265 tonnes against 553.5 tonnes in the same period of the previous year. As India's domestic primary production of gold is very less, at around 2-3 tonnes a year, the country imports most of its domestic requirement. Thus, India is also the largest importer of the yellow metal and has averaged imports of around 600 tonnes a year. However, 2008 imports dipped to around 400 tonnes of gold and it is further expected to dip to around 200-220 tonnes in 2009 owing to high prices. India's gold demand is firmly embedded in cultural and religious traditions. It is also valued in India as a savings and investment vehicle and is the second preferred investment after bank deposits. Gold hoarding tendency is well engrained in the Indian society and unofficial stocks held by Indians is estimated to be well above 15,000 tonnes, which is around 9% of the total global gold stocks. Domestic consumption is dictated by monsoon, harvest and marriage season. Indian jeweler offtake is sensitive to price increases and even more so to volatility. In the cities, gold is facing competition from the stock market and a wide range of consumer goods. Facilities for refining, assaying, making them into standard bars, coins in India, as compared to the rest of the world, are insignificant, both qualitatively and quantitatively. In July 1997, the RBI authorized the commercial banks to import gold for sale or loan to jewelers and exporters. At present, 13 banks are active in the import of gold. This reduced the disparity between international and domestic prices of gold from 57 per cent during 1986 to 1991 to 8.5 per cent in 2001. Indian gold prices are highly correlated with international prices. However, the fluctuations in the INR-US Dollar impact domestic gold prices and have to be closely followed. The global prices are driven by a host of factors with macroeconomic factors like strength of the economy, rising importance of emerging markets, currency movements, interest rates being major influencing factors. Supply-demand is a major influencer, amid rising global investor demand and almost stable supplies. Shifts in official gold reserves, reports of sales/ purchases by central banks act as major price influencing factors, whenever such reports surface. The investment in gold is influenced by comparative returns from other markets like stock markets, real estate other commodities like crude oil. Domestically, demand and consequently prices to some extent are influenced by seasonal factors like marriages. The rural demand is influenced by monsoon, agricultural output and health of the rural economy.

WHAT IS EXCHANGE MARKET?

The foreign exchange market is the largest and most liquid financial market in the world. The average daily volume in the global foreign exchange and related markets is continuously growing. Daily turnover was reported to be over US $ 3.2 trillion in April 2007 by the Bank for International Settlements. Trading in the world's main financial markets accounted for $ 3.21 trillion of this. The foreign exchange market is unique because of trading volume results in market liquidity, geographical dispersion, the use of leverage to enhance profit margins with respect to account size. According to Euro money's annual FX Poll, volumes grew a further 41% between 2007 and 2008. The foreign exchange market is a worldwide decentralized over-the-counter financial market for the trading of currencies. Exchange rates are usually fluctuated by actual monetary flows as well as by expectations of changes in monetary flows caused by changes in gross domestic product (GDP) growth, inflation (purchasing power parity theory), interest rates (interest rate parity, Domestic Fisher effect, International Fisher effect), budget and trade deficits or surpluses, large cross-border M&A deals and other macroeconomic conditions. Main foreign exchange market turnover, 1988-2007, measured in billions of USD presented in Fig. 1.

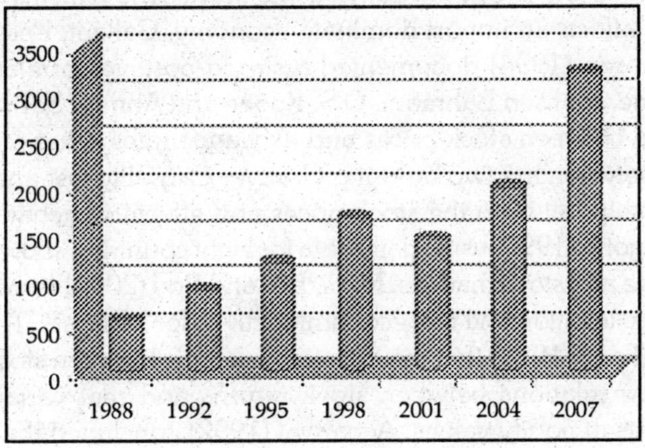

Fig. 1: Foreign Exchange Market Turnover, 1988–2007

REVIEW OF LITERATURE

There is both a theoretical and empirical debate among the researchers to address the question of the relation between stock price and exchange rate changes. Researchers have employed a wide variety of subtle ways to examine the interlink ages between stock market and foreign exchange market. To examine the impact of exchange rate changes on stock markets, Franck and Young (1972) that investigated the relationship between stock prices and exchange rates concluded that there is no relationship between these two variables. Karpoff (1986) attempted to provide a theory that links with returns, volatility and trading volume. Karpoff's model ultimately leads to an asymmetric relationship between volume and price change. Granger and Morgenstern (1963) have included the relation between price indexes and aggregate trading volume. Crouch (1970) studied relation between contemporaneous absolute price change and trading volume while Westerfield (1977), Tauchman and Pitts (1983) and Rogalski (1978) studied relationship between price change and trading volume. Others have studied the relation between variance of price change and trading volume. This includes Epps and Epps (1976) while Harris (1986) and Clarke (1973) who included squared price change in studying the relationship between stock returns and volume. These studies find positive correlation between trading volume and the absolute value of the stock price change and secondly, a positive correlation between trading volume and the stock price change. Chen, Firth and Rui (2001) summarized four theoretical explanations for the positive relation between the absolute price changes and trading volumes. These include a sequential arrival of information (SAI) model, a mixture of distributions (MD) model, a rational expectations asset pricing model, and differences of opinion model. According to SAI model, new information is disseminated sequentially to traders, and traders who are not yet informed cannot perfectly infer the presence of informed trading. Consequently, the sequential arrival of new information to the market generated both trading volume and price movements, both of which increase during periods characterized by numerous information shocks. Solnik (1987) employing regression analysis on monthly data for eight industrialized countries from 1979-83 found a weak but positive relation between real domestic stock returns and real exchange rate movements. Ma and Kao (1990) using monthly data from 1973to 1983 on six major industrialized countries and found that domestic currency appreciation negatively affects the domestic stock price movements for an export dominant economy and positively affects an import dominate economy. Gallant, Rossi and Tauchen (1992) and Jones, Kaul and Lipsen (1994) documented a strong positive correlation between absolute price changes and volume. Mohsen Bahmani, O.S. Kooee and Ahmad Sohrabian (1992) analyzed the long-run relationship between stock prices and exchange rates using co-integration as well as the casual relationship between the two by using Granger Causality test and concluded that there is a dual causal relationship between the stock prices and effective exchange rate, at least in the short run. Ajayi and Mongone (1996) using daily data for eight countries, show significant interactions between foreign exchange and stock markets. Hooi, Lee and Roy (2001) have tested the relationship between real stock returns, inflation and real economic activity for Malaysia. The results are consistent with Fama's hypothesis (Fama 1981) that the negative relations between stock returns and inflation are proxying for positive relations between stock returns and real variables, which are more fundamental determinants of equity values. Aggarwal (1992) concluded that the asset demand for gold is traditionally associated with the view that gold provides an effective hedge against inflation and other forms of uncertainty. Gold may be an inflation hedge in the long run but it is also characterized by significant short-run price volatility. Mittal (1995) investigated that price changes and trading volumes are not significantly correlated, Lead and Lag relationship are also not observed. Yamini Karmarkar and G. Kawadia (2002) tried to investigate the relationship between ₹/$ exchange rate and Indian stock markets. Five composite indices and five sectoral indices were studied over the period of one year: 2000. The results indicated that exchange rate has high correlation with the movement of stock markets. Ghose *et al.* (2002) using monthly gold price data and co integration regression techniques confirmed that gold can be regarded as a long-run inflation hedge. In a study by Nath and Samanta (2003), it was found that the stock market and the exchange rate were not generally co-integrated in India and some amount of causal effect could be noticed only late in 1990s. In another study, he examined the changing pattern in extent of integration between foreign exchange and capital markets in India using daily data and found that in VAR framework empirical results do not point much impressive causal relationship between exchange rate and stock market returns except in some specific years. Indian economy is still passing through a transitional phase. The impact of return measures initiated in different phases during the liberalization era might have reflected fully in the economy. Keeping in view, the present chapter aims at assessing the integration among stock market, trading volume, exchange rate and standard gold rate in Indian financial market.

TAKE THE CASE OF STOCK MARKET, EXCHANGE RATE, TRADING VOLUME AND STANDARD GOLD RATE TO FIND CAUSAL RELATIONSHIP AMONG THEM:

The exchange rate (US $) is the inter-bank rate and standard gold rate (10 gm) is on Mumbai. The selection of scrips has been made on the basis of market activity. All the 25 scripts are actively traded on daily basis. The raw data of all three variables are taking for this investigation.

Granger Causality

Granger causality tests are most useful in situations where one is willing to consider 2-dimensional systems. If the data are reasonably well described by a 2-dimensional system, the Granger causality concept is most straightforward to think about and also to test. It is very often hard to find any clear conclusions unless the data can be described by a simple 2-dimensional" system (since the test may be between 2 vectors, the system may not be 2-dimensional in the usual sense), and another potentially serious problem may be the choice of sampling period: a long sampling period may hide the causality whereas for example VAR systems for monthly data may give serious measurement errors (e.g., due to seasonal adjustment procedures).

The dynamic linkage is also examined by using the concept of Granger's (1969) causality. The Granger type causality procedure (Granger, 1969, 1988) is applied to determine the direction of causation among the variables. The causality procedure is conducted based on bivariate system (x, y). Formally, a time series X_t, Granger causes another time series Y_t if series Y_t can be predicted better by using past values of (X_t, Y_t) than by using only the historical values of Y_t. In other words, X_t fails to Granger cause Y_t if for all M>O the conditional probability distribution of Y_{t+m} given (Y_t, Y_{t-1}) is the same as the conditional probability distribution of Y_{t+m} given both $(Y_t, Y_{t-1}, \ldots)$ and $(X_t, Y_{t-1}, \ldots)$. That is X_t, does not Granger cause Y_t if

$$Pr(Y_{t+m}/\Psi_t)=Pr(Y_{t+m}/\Omega_t)$$

Where Pr denotes conditional probability. Ψ is the information set at time t on past values Y_t, and Ω_t is the information set containing values of both X_t and Y_t up to time point t. Testing causal relations between two stationary series X_t and Y_t can be based on the following bivariate auto regression (Granger, 1969).

$$Y_t=\alpha_0+\sum_{k=1}^{P} akYt\text{-}k+\sum_{k=1}^{P} \beta\ kXt\text{-}k+Ut$$

$$X_t=\varphi_0+\sum_{k=1}^{P} \varphi kYt\text{-}k+\sum_{k=1}^{P} \varphi kXt\text{-}k+Vt$$

Where P is a suitably chosen positive integer; αk's and βk's, $_K$=0,1,——, p are constants; U_t and V_t are usually disturbance terms with zero means and finite variance. The null hypothesis that X_t does not Granger cause Y_t is rejected if the βk's, $_K$> 0 in equation 2 are jointly significantly different from zero using a standard joint test (e.g., an F-test). Similarly, Y_t Granger causes if the φk's, $_K$> 0 are jointly different from zero.

Co-integration Test:

If stationary linear combination exists, the non-stationary time series are said to be co-integrated. The fundamental insight of co-integration is that while economic time series may be individually highly persistent, some linear combinations are much less persistent. Accordingly, a suite of practical methods have been developed for conducting inference about co integrating vectors, the coefficients that lead to this reduction in persistence. In their standard form, these methods assume that the persistence is the result of common 1 (1) stochastic trends, (See, for instance, Johansen (1988), Phillips and Hansen (1990), Saikkonen (1991), Park (1992) and Stock and Watson (1993)) and their statistical properties crucially depend on particular characteristics of 1(1) processes. The stationary linear combination is called the co-integrating equation and is interpreted as a long-run equilibrium relationship among the variables. Since it is possible that co-integrating variables may deviate from their relationship in the short run, but their association would return in the long run. The implication of non-stationary can lead to spurious regression. The test employed for determination of co-integration between the time series is Johansen's test. The Johansen's technique for estimating co-integration is superior because it is based on well-established maximum likelihood procedure that provides test statistics to determine number of co-integration vectors as well as their estimates. The existence of more than one co integrating vector implies higher stability in the system.

The co-integration testing procedure suggested by Johansen (1991, 1995) to test the restrictions imposed by co-integration on the unrestricted VAR involving the series.

Considering a VAR of order ___ :

$$Y_t = A_1 Y_{t-1} + \text{———} ApY_{t-p} + BX_t + \varepsilon_t$$

Where Y_t is a K-vector of non-stationary 1(1) variables, X_t is a d vector of deterministic variables and ε_t is a vector of innovations. It can rewrite the VAR as:

$$\Delta Y_t = \Pi Y_{t-1} + \sum_{i=1}^{P-1} Ti\,\Delta Yt\text{-}1 + BXt + \varepsilon t$$

$$\text{Where } \Pi = \quad Ai\text{-}I,\ Ti = -\sum_{j-i+1}^{P} Aj$$

Granger's representations theorem asserts that if the coefficient matrix Π has reduced rank r<k, then there exist Kr matrixes and α & β each with rank r such that Π = αβ' is stationary, r is the number of co-integrating relations and each column of is the co-integrating rector. The element of are known as the adjustment parameters in the vector error the matrix in an unrestricted form

Johansen's (1995) test the following possibilities:

Series Y have no deterministic trends and the co-integration equations do not have intercepts.

H2(r): $\Pi Yt\text{-}1+BXt=\alpha\beta' Yt\text{-}1$

The likelihood Ratio Test Statistic:

$$Qr=-T\sum_{i-r-1}^{K}\log(1-\lambda)$$

For r=0, 1———— K – 1 where λI is the ith largest Eigen value. Qr is the so-called trace statistics and is the test of H1 (r) against H1 (k).

Johansen also proposes an alternative LR Test Statistic, known as the maximum Eigen value statistics, which tests (r) against (r+1). The maximum Eigen value statistic can be computed from the trace statistics as

$$Qmax=-T\log(1-\lambda_{r+1})=Q_r-Q_{r+1}$$

ANALYSIS:

This chapter here employs unit root test to examine the time series properties of concerned variables. It is evident that all the variables considered are stationary. Hence, the null hypotheses of a unit root are rejected and conclude that all the variables are stationary.

Table 1

Pair-wise Granger Causality Tests among Sensex, Trading Volume, Exchange Rate and Standard Gold Rate

Null Hypothesis	***F-values***	***P-values***
Standard gold rate does not Granger cause sensex	1.66947	.95660
Sensex does not Granger cause standard gold rate	.67751	.51113
Exchange rate does not Granger cause sensex	.86296	.42629
Sensex does not Granger cause exchange rate	3.53680**	.03434
Trading volume does not granger cause sensex	.26872	.76513
Sensex does not granger cause trading volume	2.29765***	.10792
Exchange rate does not Granger cause Standard gold rate	.109759	.89621
Standard gold rate does not Granger cause exchange rate	.69158*	.00019
Trading volume does not Granger cause standard gold rate	2.18076	.12046
Standard gold rate does not Granger cause trading volume	.42002	.65866
Trading volume does not Granger cause exchange rate	.21681	.80561
Exchange rate does not granger cause trading volume	.99584	.37451

* 1% level of significance

** 5% level of significance

*** 10% level of significance

The Table 1 depicts the Granger Causality test results for the concerned variables. It is essential to find out the impact of sensex on trading volume, exchange rate, and Gold standard rate. So, the causal link among various variables needs to be explored. The Table 1 reported pair wise Granger causality test results with lags 2 as two-year period lag is an appropriate lag order chooses in terms of the Akaike Information Criteria (AIC) for the full sample period. The reported F-values as well as P-values suggest that there is a unidirectional causality between sensex and exchange rate, sensex and trading volume, standard gold rate and exchange rate. This implies that sensex influences the trading volume and exchange rate. Similarly, standard gold rate influence the exchange rate. It is apparent that standard gold rate is having short-term relationship with exchange rate during this particular period. It is observed from the Table 1 that there is no clear causality between sensex with standard gold rate, trading volume with standard gold rate and trading volume with exchange rate. The Johansen's co-integration test is revealed in the Table 2.

Table 2
Multivariate Case of Co-integration

Assumptions: No deterministic trend in the series in levels and no intercept in the co integrating equation

Variable	*Eigen-value*	*L. L. Ratio*	*5% C.V*	*1% C.V*	*Hypothesized No. of CE (S)*
Sensex	.226680	35.71012	39.89	45.58	None
Trading volume	.144805	16.17335	24.31	29.75	At most 1
Exchange rate	.054310	4.284954	12.53	16.31	At most 2
Standard gold rate	.000540	.041077	3.84	6.51	At most 3

LR rejects any co-integration at 5% significance level

Normalized co-integrating coefficients (standard error in parenthesis)

Sensex	*Trading Volume*	*Exchange Rate*	*Standard Gold Rate*	*Log Likelihood*
1.0000	-1.011800 (.31753)	13.49128 (42.3266)	-.536842 (.37161)	-1271.562

Table 2a
Co-integration Result

Assumptions: No deterministic trend in the series in levels and no intercept in the co-integrating equation

Variable	*Eigen Value*	*LL Ratio*	*5% CV*	*1% CV*	*Hypothesized No. of CE (s)*
Sensex	.211956	29.09826*	24.31	29.75	None
Trading volume	.127965	10.99499	12.53	16.31	At most 1
Exchange Rate	.007715	.588606	3.84	6.51	At most 2

LR indicates 1 co-integrating equations at 5% significance level

Normalized co-integrating coefficients (standard error in parenthesis)

Sensex	*Trading Volume*	*Exchange Rate*	*Log Likelihood*
1.0000	-1.304152 (.35929)	45.82146 (48.1922)	-837.0223

Table 2b

Co-integration Result

Assumptions: No deterministic trend in the series levels and no intercept in the co-integrating equation

Variable	*Eigen Value*	*LL Ratio*	*5% CV*	*1% CV*	*Hypothesized No. of CE (s)*
Sensex	***.134162***	***14.32965***	***24.31***	***29.75***	**None**
Exchange Rate	.043072	3.381269	12.53	16.31	At most 1
Standard Gold Rate	.000463	.035220	3.84	6.51	At most 2

LR rejects any co-integrating equations at 5% significance level

Normalized co-integrating coefficients (standard error in parenthesis)

Sensex	*Exchange Rate*	*Standard Gold Rate*	*Log Likelihood*
1.0000	-113.8409 (8.31142)	-1.228615 (.65335)	-863.2993

Table 2c

Co-integration Result

Assumptions: No deterministic trend in the series in levels and no intercept in the co-integrating equation

Variable	*Eigen Value*	*LL Ratio*	*5% CV*	*1% CV*	*Hypothesized No. of CE (s)*
Sensex	***.109193***	***14.61261***	***24.31***	***29.75***	**None**
Trading Volume	.049113	5.824923	12.53	16.31	At most 1
Standard Gold Rate	.025942	1.997594	3.84	6.51	At most 2

LR rejects any co integrating equations at 5% significance level

Normalized co-integrating coefficients (standard error in parenthesis)

Sensex	*Exchange Rate*	*Standard Gold Rate*	*Log Likelihood*
1.0000	-.949085 (.06118)	-.033229 (.64690)	-1303.956

The table 2, 2b, 2c, indicated no co-integrating vector at 1% and 5% level of significance. But Table 2a indicated one co-integrating vector at 5% level of significance. So, it clearly rejects the null of no co-integration at the conventional level of significance and fails to reject one co-integrating vector in the case. There is more than one co-integrating equations in case of sensex. Thus, it can be said that sensex is co-integrated with the exchange rate and trading volume in the stock market. So, it has a long-run equilibrium relationship with the exchange rate and trading volume. However, it is possible that co-integrating variables may deviate from their relationship in the short run, but their association would return in the long run.

To enable, interpretation of the results, in economic terms, the normalized co-integrating coefficients with standard errors in parenthesis are reported at the bottom part of Table 2 through Table 2c the estimated co-efficient is generally interpreted as long-run elasticities. However, there is no guidance from theory regarding the acceptable values for these elasticities.

CONCLUDING OBSERVATION

This chapter examined the inter linkages among sensex, trading volume exchange rate and standard gold rate by applying both Granger causality test and Johansen co-integration test. The results indicate that there is no significant causality between standard gold rate with sensex, trading volume with standard gold rate and trading volume with exchange rate. But there is unidirectional causal relationship between sensex and exchange rate, sensex and trading volume, standard gold rate and exchange rate. This study also found that there is no co-integration between any set of variables except one. So, it can be said that the sensex is co-integrated with exchange rate and trading volume indicates the equilibrium long-term relationship. However, the findings of the study are subject to the period of the study selected and the result may change if the study period will change.

REVIEW QUESTIONS

1. What is the rationale behind to find out the linkage between financial market and real sectors?
2. What is Granger Causality test? Explain its significance
3. What is co-integration test? Explain its usefulness.
4. Quiz
   (a) The informational content of volume has been analyzed through two main informational hypotheses namely_____ and _____
   (b) _____ hypothesis states that price volatility and trading volume should be positively correlated because they jointly depend on a common underlying variable.
   (c) Gold is unique as it is both a _____ and a _____ asset.
   (d) The dynamic linkage is examined by using the concept of_____.
   (e) The stationary linear combination is called the _____equation and is interpreted as a long-run equilibrium relationship among the variables.
   (f) The test employed for determination of co-integration between the time series is _____ test.

9

FII Investment and Indian Stock Market Performance

This chapter examines the relationship between FII investment and the Indian stock market performance. This chapter shows that past FII investment have significant impacts on current BSE Sensex and NSE Index; but there is no significant impact of current FII investment on current BSE Sensex and NSE Index.

INTRODUCTION

Though a number of other exchanges exist, NSE and the BSE are the two most significant stock exchanges in India. Between them, they are responsible for the majority of share transactions. This Mumbai-based stock exchange is the largest stock exchange in India in terms of daily turnover and number of trades — for both equities and derivative trading. NSE is expected to become the biggest stock exchange in India in terms of market capitalization by 2009 end. The NSE's key index is the S&P CNX Nifty, popularly known as the Nifty, an index of fifty major stocks which is weighted by market capitalization.

NSE is mutually-owned by a set of leading financial institutions, banks, insurance companies and other financial intermediaries in India. Its ownership and management operate as separate entities. There are at least 2 foreign investors namely NYSE Euro next and Goldman Sachs who have a stake in the NSE. In October 2007, the equity market capitalization of the companies listed on the NSE was US $ 1.46 trillion, which made it the second largest stock exchange in South Asia. It is also the third largest Stock Exchange in the world in terms of the number of trades in equities. Further, it is the second fastest growing stock exchange in the world with a recorded growth of 16.6%. It has consistently remained in the foretront of modernization of India's capital and financial markets. The Bombay Stock Exchange is the oldest stock exchange in Asia and has the greatest number of listed companies in the world. With over 4700 Indian companies list on the stock exchange, it has a significant trading volume. Following are some of the key highlights are given in Table 1:

Table 1
Highlights of Performance of BSE

13,000	October 30, 2006	It took 135 days for the Sensex to move from 12,000 to 13,000.
14,000	December 5, 2006	It took 36 days for the Sensex to move from 13,000 to the 14,000 mark.
15,000	July 6, 2007	
16,000	September 19, 2007	Up by 450 points from the previous close.
17,000	September 26, 2007	
18,000	October 9, 2007	It took just 8 days to cross 18,000 points from the 17,000. The biggest single day gain of 789 points, as well as the largest intra-day gains of 993 points in absolute terms.
19,000	October 15, 2007	Revival of funds-based buying in blue chip stocks in metal, refinery sectors and capital goods.
20,000	October 29, 2007	Aggressive buying ahead of the US Federal Reserve meeting. Larsen and Toubro, Reliance Industries, ICICI Bank, HDFC Bank and SBI were highest gainers.
21,000	January 8, 2008	High market confidence of increased FII investment and strong corporate results for the third quarter resulted in this gain which later fell due to profit booking.
10,527	Oct 10, 2008	Sensex falls continuously following the global meltdown.
14284.21	May 18, 2009	Result of 15th Indian general election resulted in a gain of 2110.79 points, a record one-day gain. In the opening trade itself it evinced a 15% gain over the previous close which led to a two-hour suspension in trading.

Table 2
BSE vis-a-vis NSE

	BSE	NSE
Market capitalization of listed companies:	₹ 5927206.24 Crores	₹ 47,01923 crore.
Number of members:	951 (Oct 2007)	1,009 as on March 2007
Number of listed companies:	4,867 OCT(2007)	1,288 (March 2007)
Geographical spread:	Presence in 417 cities	Presence in 1,486 cities
Website:	www.bseindia.com	www.nse-india.com
Main Index:	BSE Sensex	S&P CNX Nifty
Owner:	Bombay Stock Exchange Limited	National Stock Exchange of India Limited

Key people:	Jagdish Kapoor (Chairman)	R.H. Patil (Founder, MD)
Claim to fame:	Oldest stock exchange in Asia.	Third largest stock exchange in the world in terms of volumes.
What is it?:	Indian Stock exchange	Indian Stock exchange
Location:	Mumbai	Mumbai
Established in:	1875	1993
Index value (2009):	16,960.00	5057
Number of trader workstations:	25,000	
Top trading companies in volumes in main index (Till March 2007):		Reliance Industries Limited, Infosys Technologies Limited,
Top companies in terms of market capitalization in each index (Till March 2007):		Reliance Industries Limited, Oil and Natural Gas Corporation, Bharti Airtel Limited .

With fall in stock prices on news that Lehman Brothers, Merrill Lynch, and many other investment bankers and companies collapsed, Indian stock market has seen its worst time with the global financial crisis. Mostly all the industrial sectors have experienced a consistent low in their stock prices. The Sensex which had reached historically high levels in the beginning of 2008, declined to its levels three years back. Similar trend has also been o.bserved for the S&P CNX Nifty. The movements in Sensex and CNX Nifty between January 2007 and July 2009 are shown in the following figures.

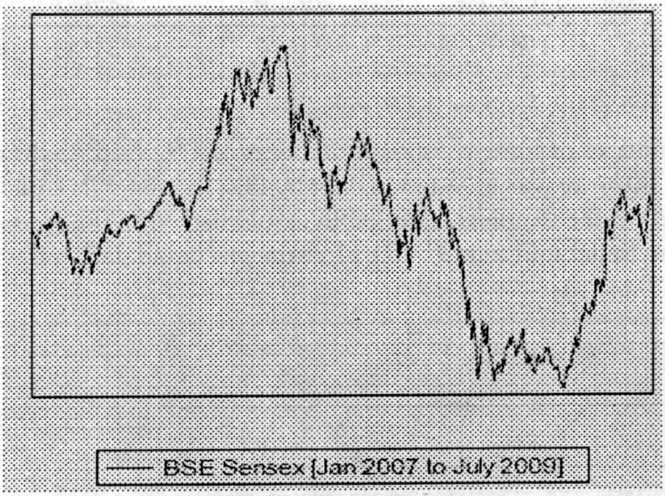

Fig. 1: BSE Sensex

However, Indian stock market showed remarkable resistance to the winds from the international financial implosion. Now, the stock market of India has returned to its previous growth track in spite of a greater degree of volatility. In this context, it is very much essential to know the efficiency of Indian stock market with reference to FIIs behavior in the market.

INFLUENCE OF FIIs ON INDIAN STOCK MARKET

India opened doors to foreign institutional investors in September 1992. This event represents a landmark event since it resulted in effectively globalizing its financial services industry. Though India receives hardly 1 per cent of the FII investments in emerging markets, the portfolio flows to India have been less volatile when compared with that of many other emerging markets. FIIs by adopting a bottom-up approach seem to invest in top-quality, high growth, large cap stocks. Sytse *et al.* (2003) Provide empirical evidence that foreign institutional investors in India, invest in large, liquid companies which enable them to exit their positions quickly at relatively lower cost and also that the foreign institutional owners have a larger impact than foreign corporate owners when performance is measured using stock market valuation criterion.

Table 3
Investment by FIIs

Year	*FII*			
	***Equity* (₹ in crore)**	***Debt* (₹ in crore)**	***Total* (₹ in crore)**	***Net Investment* (US $ Million)**
2004-05	44,123.00	1,759.00	45,882.00	10,172.00
2005-06	48,801.00	-7,334.00	41,467.00	9,332.00
2006-07	25,237.00	5,607.00	30,844.00	6,709.00
2007-08	53,403.30	12,775.90	66,179.20	16,040.20
2008-09	-45,706.20	1895.20	-45811	-9,837.20
2009-10	110220	32438	142658	30252
2010-11	10433	21078	31511	3702

Source: SEBI Bulletin, Feb 2009, October 2009, July 2010

There is a net outflow of foreign funds in January 2009. ₹ 4,245.30 crore is liquidated in equity whereas ₹ 802.30 crore was invested in debt by FIIs. In total, FIIs liquidated ₹ 3,443 crore in the market. During 2008-09 (April-January), FIIs liquidated. 45,706.2 crore in equity whereas invested ₹1895.2 crore in debt. In total ₹ 45,811 crore was liquidated in the market in the current financial year so far. (Table 3).

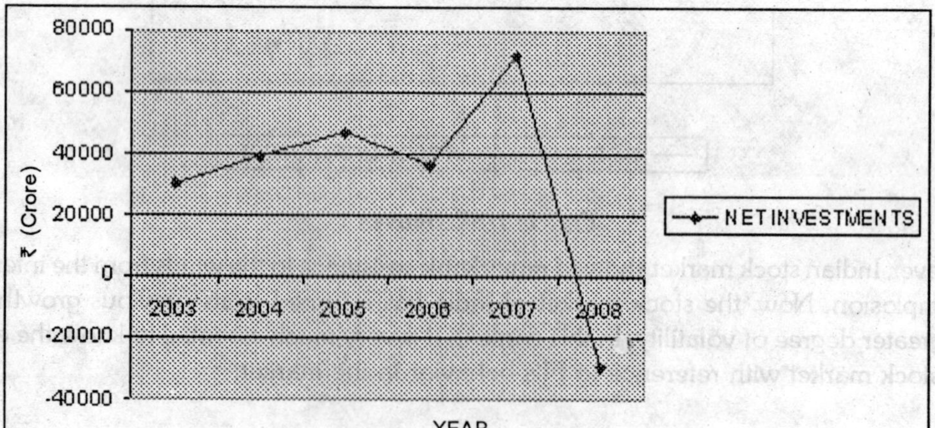

Fig. 3: Net Investments

Fig. 3 depicted that there is an increase in net investments till 2005 and there was small decrease in investments in the year 2006. But there was a vertical increase in the year 2007-08. So, it indicates that stock prices were increased and the market was in good mood during this period in Indian stock market.

Table 4
FIIs Gross Purchases and Sales from 2003-08

Year	*Gross Purchases*	*Gross Sales*
2003	94410.5	63951.8
2004	185671.5	146706.4
2005	286020.5	238839.4
2006	475622.5	439082.8
2007	814877	743390.7
2008 (10/08/08)	560480.9	589650

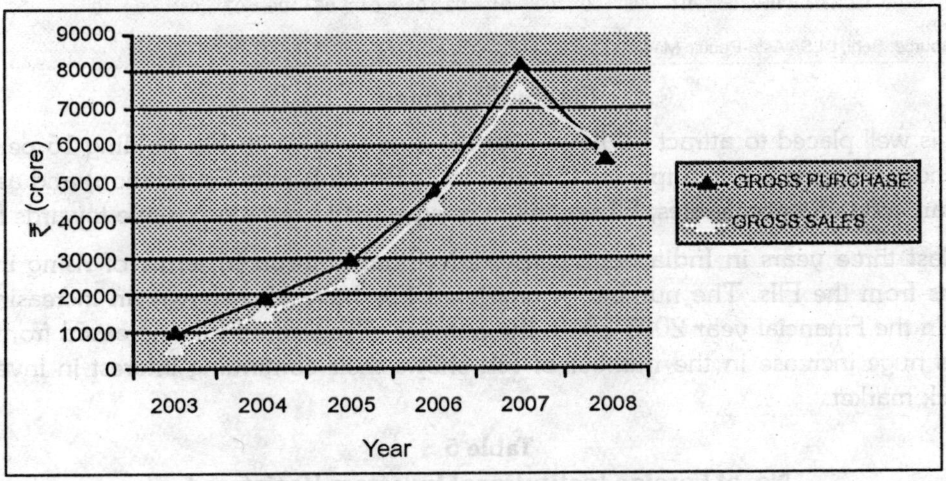

Fig. 4: Gross Purchase and Sells

It is evident from the Fig. 4 that gross purchases are increasing from 2003 to 2007 and gross sales are lower than gross purchases. So, it is concluded that this caused the market to reach the magical figure of 21,000 in Sensex. But the involvement of FIIs is reduced in the year 2008, and it is also seen that during this year the gross sales is higher than gross purchases.

The emerging economies have been witnessing an unprecedented surge in capital inflows, especially short-term investment flows. India, the second fastest growing economy after China, has recently seen positive foreign institutional investor (FII) inflows driven by the sound fundamentals and growth opportunities. FIIs have made net investments of US $ 10 billion in the first six months (April to September) of 2009-10. A major portion of these investments have come through the primary market, than through buying via secondary markets. (Source: India Brand Equity Foundation) With the exception of FY99 and FY09, net flows have been positive. FIIs own a dominant 16% of Indian equities (worth US $ 147 bn) and account for 10-15% of the equity volumes. (Source: CLSA Asia-Pacific Markets)

Although FIIs pulled out US $ 9.77 billion of the Indian equity markets during FY 09, they have been quick to return in FY 10 and within just the first four months they have nearly made up for the exit, reinvesting US $ 8.50 billion or 87 % of the amount that they had pulled out in FY 09. (Source: CLSA Asia-Pacific Markets)

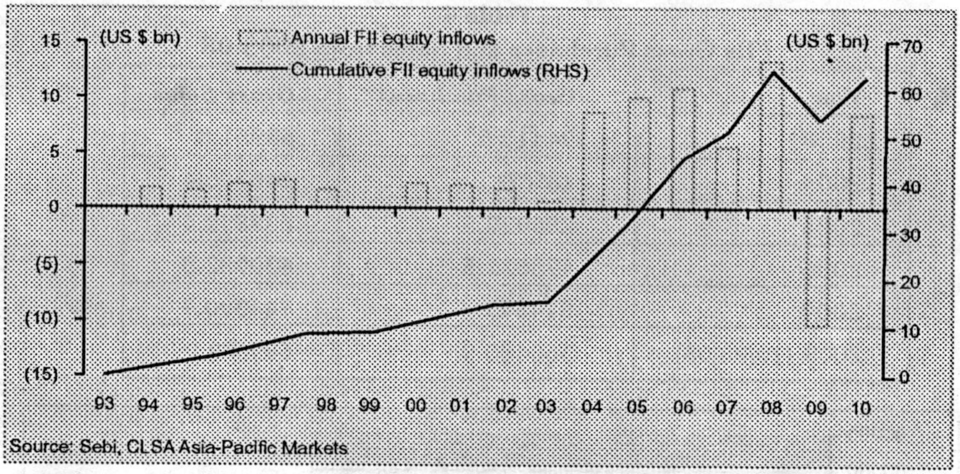

Fig. 5: FII Inflows

India is well placed to attract FII flows over the long term. With FIIs holding 16 per cent of equity of India's biggest 500 companies (Source: India Brand Equity Foundation) and as growth in the Indian economy accelerates, FII sentiment is expected to remain positive towards India.

The last three years in India have witnessed virtual bull-run in terms of rising inflow of investments from the FIIs. The number of registered FIIs have also shown an increasing trend (Table-5). In the Financial year 2005-2010, the number of registered FIIs increased from 686 to 1713. This huge increase in the number of FIIs shows their continuing interest in investing in Indian stock market.

Table 5

No. of Foreign Institutional Investors Registered

Year	*No. of FIIs*
1993	18
1994	158
1995	308
1996	367
1997	439
1998	496
1999	450
2000	506
2001	527

2002	490
2003	502
2004	540
2005	685
2006	882
2007	996
2008	1319
2009	1626
2010	1713

Source: SEBI Bulletin, February 2005, May 2006, October 2009, July 2010

FIIs are now looking at the economy as a whole, with the macroeconomic factors also playing their role in attracting foreign investors. Factors like a strong currency, key reforms in the banking, power and telecommunications sector, increased consumer spending and stable policies are expected to play a major role in attracting FIIs to India. The Securities Exchange Board of India (SEBI) along with the Institute of Chartered Accountants of India (ICAI) jointly monitor the markets and announces the regulatory measures thus making the Indian companies more transparent and more disciplined. The capital market reforms like improved market transparency, automation, dematerialization and regulations on reporting and disclosure standards were initiated because of the presence of the FIIs. But one aspect we should agree on is that the FII's increased role had changed the face of Indian stock market. It had brought both quantitative and qualitative change. It had also increased the market depth and breadth. With so much to benefit from, the FII investment in India is likely to increase in the future. But it essential to find the impact of FIIs in the stock market

Positive Feedback Traders:

FII flows can be considered both as the cause and the effect of capital market reforms.

The concern expressed about foreign investors is that they are positive feedback traders. A positive feedback trader is a trader who buys when the market increased and sells when the market fell. Investors can be positive feedback traders for rational reasons or because of behavioral biases. Investors who pursue portfolio insurance strategies as well as investors with extrapolative expectations are positive feedback traders. Investors with such strategies are often viewed to be destabilizing because their sales lead the market to fall further and their purchases increase prices further. In some models, positive feedback trading leads to bubbles where prices depart from fundamentals and to crashes when bubbles burst. Besides contributing to the volatility of stock returns, it is argued that such trading leads to destabilizing capital flows. This is because equity investors rush into countries whose stock markets are booming and flee from countries whose stock markets are falling. Foreign investors may act like positive feedback traders without destabilizing equity markets. One reason for this is that greater foreign ownership can lead to a lower risk premium for stocks in a country since the risks of these stocks can be better shared internationally. As a result, a period when foreign investors enter a market can also be a period when the market is doing well because of these investors. Equity markets also become more receptive to foreign investors as economies liberalize. Liberalization itself leads to stock market appreciation and in this scenario this appreciation is followed by inflows of foreign equity investments. Finally, in models that emphasize information asymmetries between domestic and foreign investors such as Brennan and Cao (1997), foreign investors learn more from stock returns than domestic investors do. This is because stock prices impound the information that domestic investors have and hence price increases reveal the domestic investors' favorable information to foreign investors. Since this information leads investors to have more favorable expectations for stock returns, it leads them to invest more without acting irrationally.

The period of mostly foreign net buying is one when stock prices are increasing and the periods of persistent net selling by foreign investors are periods of falling stock prices. There is evidence that foreign investors buy following a positive market return and sell following a negative market return. Finally, there are no significant differences between order imbalances for positive or negative lead market returns for either domestic investors or foreign investors. What is surprising, though, is that foreign investors sell more when the market is doing well than when it is doing poorly. Foreign investors have a significantly higher sell-order price-setting imbalance if the market was up the previous day than if it was down and they have a significantly higher sell-order imbalance if the market is up the same day than if it is down. Since domestic individual investors have large price setting net buy order imbalances when the market was up the previous day or is up the same day, foreign investors are selling the most when domestic demand is the highest. This cannot be viewed as destabilizing behavior.

LITERATURE REVIEW

The financial theory is that FII investments broadens the base of portfolio diversification and cause a long-term increase in the stock prices by reducing the equilibrium rate of return. It was however found that the FII behaviour played a significant role during East Asian Crisis. So, understanding the relationship between FII investment and Indian Stock Market is very important as it may have important policy implications. There have been some studies in the past that attempted to explain relationship between foreign investment flow and stock price, as follows:

Warther (1995) in his 'price pressure hypothesis' suggested that the increase in share prices associated with foreign investment flow is caused by temporary liquidity (i.e., excess demand) and predicts that this change in share price is subsequently reversed.

Merton (1997) shows that the expected return in the market with unrestricted investor base is higher than restricted investor base. Entry of foreign investors in the stock market broadens the investors' base, which increases diversification and risk sharing, lowering the risk premium for country specific volatility. Agarwal (1997), Chakrabarti (2001) and Trivedi and Nair (2003) found that the equity return has a significant and positive impact on the FII. But, given the huge volume of investments, foreign investors could play a role of market makers and book their profits, i.e., they can buy their financial assets when the price are declining, thereby jacking-up the assets price and sell when the assets price are increasing. Prasuna (1999) examined the determinants of FII investments in India using monthly data from January 1993 to March 1998. It was found that the relationship between lagged FII investment and percentage change in BSE sensex, and NSE Index is significant at 1% level. The FII relationship with exchange rate, interest rates, forward premia and foreign exchange reserves have been found to be insignificant. Kumar (2001) investigated the effects of FII inflows on the Indian Stock Market and concluded that FII investments did not respond to short-term changes or technical position of the market and they are more driven by Fundamentals. In order to study impact of Net FII Investment (NFI) on Sensex, a regression of NFI was estimated on lagged values of the first difference of NFI, first difference of sensex and one lagged value of the error correction term. The study concluded that Sensex causes Net FII Investment. Rai and Bhanumurty (2003) studied the determinants of foreign institutional investment in India during the period 1994-2002, by using monthly data and found that the equity returns is the main driving force for FII investment and is significant at all levels. Gordon and Gupta (2003) also examined causation running from FII inflows to return in BSE and conclude that FIIs act as market makers and book profits by investing when prices are low and selling when they are high. Report of the Expert Group on Encouraging FII Flows and Checking the Vulnerability of Capital Markets to Speculative Flows, GoI (November 2005) points out that one may foresee benefits of FII investment to the Indian economy in terms of reduced cost of equity capital, imparting stability to India's balance of payments, knowledge flows, strengthening corporate governance and improvement to market efficiency, while concerns have been expressed about herding and positive feedback trading, BoP Vulnerability, possibility of taking over companies and complexities of monetary management. In the considered view of the Expert Group, 'although there is scant evidence of FII flows destabilizing Indian capital market so far, just because it has not happened, does not mean that it cannot happen in future.' In the view of the Group, in order to build a consensus on the future of India's policies on the capital account, we need to initiate a program of research on "Capital flows and India's Financial Sector: Learning from Theory, International Experience, and Indian Evidence." It is in this context that this research, "FII Investment and Stock Market Performance — An Analysis using ARIMA Model" has been undertaken. The present chapter attempts to examine the relationship between FII investment and the Indian stock market performance. It aims to investigate whether average monthly BSE Sensex and NSE Index are dependent on the current and past FII net inflows. It also seeks to assess whether FII net inflows are dependent on the current and past market BSE Sensex and NSE Index.

LET TAKE THE CASE OF BSE SENSEX, NSE TO EXAMINE THEIR DEPENDENCY ON THE CURRENT FII INFLOWS:

For the purposes of this chapter, monthly net FII investment and monthly average BSE Sensex and NSE Index have been used. The multiple regression analysis has been used in the study. The following four regression models have been estimated.

Model-1

$$FIIt = \alpha + \beta_1 BSEt + \beta_2 BSEt{-}1 + \beta_3 BSEt{-}2 + \gamma_1 FIIt{-}1 + \gamma_2 FII(t-2) + et$$

Model-2

$$FIIt = \alpha + \beta_1 NSEt + \beta_2 NSEt{-}1 + \beta_3 NSEt{-}2 + \gamma_1 FIIt{-}1 + \gamma_2 FII(t-2) + et$$

Model-3

$$BSEt = \alpha + \beta_1 FIIt + \beta_2 FIIt{-}1 + \beta_3 FIIt{-}2 + \gamma_1 BSEt{-}1 + \nu 2\, BSE(t-2) + et$$

Model-4

$$NSEt = \alpha + \beta_1 FIIt + \beta_2 FIIt{-}1 + \beta_3 FIIt{-}2 + \gamma_1 NSEt{-}1 + \nu 2\, NSE(t-2) + et$$

Where FII_t = Net FII investment in month t

BSE_t = BSE Sensex for the month t

NSE_t = NSE index for month t

t refers to current month, t-1 refers to one month lag, t-2 means two months lag.

e_t refers to random stochastic error term

a, b_1 and g_1 refers to the constant and regression coefficients respectively.

Durbin-Watson Statistics:

The Durbin-Watson Statistics is used to test for a correlation (non-randomness) of the residuals. The null hypothesis that there is no correlation between the successive residuals is evaluated by:

$$d = \frac{\sum_{i-2}^{n} (e_i - e_{i-1})^2}{\sum_{i-1}^{n} e_i^2}$$

Thereby e_i is the residual corresponding to the observation *i* and e_{i-1} is the residual of the preceding observation. The *d* value is compared to the lower and upper critical values d_L and d_U proposed by Durbin and Watson. If the calculated *d* is smaller than the tabulated lower critical value d_L, the null hypothesis is rejected meaning that the residuals are correlated. If the calculated *d* is bigger than the tabulated upper critical value d_U, the correlation of the residuals is negligible and if the calculated *d* is between both tabulated critical values, the test is inconclusive.

Before any regression analysis can be applied to time series data, it is essential to find that these data are random or the error terms are free from auto correlation. The most popular test to ascertain the presence or absence of auto correlated error terms is the Durbin Watson d-statistics. For the formal test of significance, if there is no serial correlation, the DW statistics will be around 2. The DW statistics will fall below 2 if there is positive serial correlation. If there is negative correlation the statistics will lie somewhat in between 2 and 4. The study uses the d-statistics.

What is ARIMA Model?

The Acronym ARIMA stands for "Autoregressive – Integrated Moving Average" models are, in theory, the most general class of models for forecasting a time series is as fine-tuned versions of random-walk and random-trend models: the fine-tuning consists of adding *lags of the differenced series* and/or *lags of the forecast errors* to the prediction equation, as needed to remove any last traces of autocorrelation from the forecast errors. A non-seasonal ARIMA model is classified as an "ARIMA (p, d, q)" model, where:

- p is the number of autoregressive terms,
- d is the number of non-seasonal differences, and
- q is the number of lagged forecast errors in the prediction equation.

ARIMA (0, 1, 0) = random walk: which we first used in regression analysis, was the addition of lags of the stationarized series. For example, suppose we initially fit the random-walk-with-growth model to the time series Y. The prediction equation for this model can be written as:

$$\hat{Y}(t) - Y(t-1) = \mu$$

Where the constant term (here denoted by "μ") is the average difference in Y, This can be considered as a degenerate regression model in which DIFF(Y) is the dependent variable and there are no independent variables other than the constant term. Since it includes (only) a non-seasonal difference and a constant term, it is classified as an "ARIMA (0,1,0) model with constant."

ARIMA (1,1,0) = differenced first-order autoregressive model: If the errors of the random walk model are autocorrelated, perhaps the problem can be fixed by adding one lag of the dependent variable to the prediction equation—i.e., by regressing DIFF (Y) on itself lagged by one period. This would yield the following prediction equation:

$$\hat{Y}(t) - Y(t-1) = \mu + \phi(Y(t-1) - Y(t-2))$$

which can be rearranged to

$$\hat{Y}(t) = \mu + Y(t-1) + \phi(Y(t-1) - Y(t-2))$$

This is a first-order autoregressive, or "AR (1)", model with one order of non-seasonal differencing and a constant term—i.e., an "ARIMA (1,1,0) model with constant." Here, the constant term is denoted by "μ" and the autoregressive coefficient is denoted by "Ø", in keeping with the terminology for ARIMA models popularized by Box and Jenkins.

ARIMA (0, 1, 1) without constant = simple exponential smoothing: Another strategy for correcting auto correlated errors in a random walk model is suggested by the simple exponential smoothing model.

In non-stationary time series, the random walk model does not perform as well as a moving average of past values. The simple exponential smoothing model uses an *exponentially weighted moving average* of past values to achieve this effect. The prediction equation for the simple exponential smoothing model can be written in a number of mathematically equivalent ways, one of which is:

$$\hat{Y}(t) = Y(t-1) - \theta e(t-1)$$

Where $e(t-1)$ denotes the error at period $t-1$. This is also resembles the prediction equation for the ARIMA (1, 1, 0) model, except that instead of a multiple of the lagged difference it includes *a multiple of the lagged forecast error.* The coefficient of the lagged forecast error is denoted by "θ". "Theta" in this equation corresponds to the quantity "1-minus-alpha" in the exponential smoothing formulas.

When a lagged forecast error is included in the prediction equation it is referred to as a "moving average" (MA) term. The simple exponential smoothing model is therefore a first-order moving average ("MA (1)") model with one order of non seasonal differencing and no constant term —i.e., an "ARIMA (0, 1, 1) model without constant." We can actually fit a simple exponential smoothing by specifying it as an ARIMA (0, 1, 1) model without constant, and the estimated MA (1) coefficient corresponds to "1-minus-alpha" in the SES formula.

ARIMA (0, 1, 1) with constant = simple exponential smoothing with growth: The ARIMA (0, 1, 1) model *with* constant has the prediction equation:

$$\hat{Y}(t) = \mu + Y(t-1) - \theta e(t-1)$$

The one-period-ahead forecasts from this model are qualitatively similar to those of the SES model, except that the trajectory of the long-term forecasts is typically a sloping line (whose slope is equal to μ) rather than a horizontal line.

ARIMA (0, 2, 1) or (0, 2, 2) without constant = linear exponential smoothing: Linear exponential smoothing models are ARIMA models which use two non seasonal differences in conjunction with MA terms. The second difference of a series Y is not simply the difference between Y and itself lagged by two periods, but rather it is the *first difference of the first difference*—i.e., the change-in-the-change of Y at period t. Thus, the second difference of Y at period t is equal to (Y(t)-Y(t-1)) - (Y(t-1)-Y(t-2)) = Y(t) - 2Y(t-1) + Y(t-2). A second difference of a discrete function is analogous to a second derivative of a continuous function: it measures the "acceleration" or "curvature" in the function at a given point in time.

The ARIMA (0, 2, 2) model without constant predicts that the second difference of the series equals a linear function of the last two forecast errors:

$$\hat{Y}(t) - 2Y(t-1) + Y(t-2) = -\theta_1 e(t-1) - \theta_2 e(t-2)$$

Which can be rearranged as

$$\hat{Y}(t) = 2Y(t-1) - Y(t-2) - \theta_1 e(t-1) - \theta_2 e(t-2)$$

where theta-1 and theta-2 are the MA(1) and MA(2) coefficients. This is essentially the same as Brown's linear exponential smoothing model, with the MA(1) coefficient corresponding to the quantity 2*(1-alpha) in the LES model. To see this connection, recall that forecasting equation for the LES model is:

$$\hat{Y}(t) = 2Y(t-1) - Y(t-2) - 2(1-\alpha)e(t-1) + (1-\alpha)^2 e(t-2)$$

Upon comparing terms, we see that the MA (1) coefficient corresponds to the quantity 2*(1-alpha) and the MA (2) coefficient corresponds to the quantity -(1-alpha)^2 (i.e., "minus (1-

alpha) squared"). If alpha is larger than 0.7, the corresponding MA(2) term would be less than 0.09, which might not be significantly different from zero, in which case an ARIMA (0,2,1) model probably would be identified.

A "mixed" model—ARIMA (1, 1, 1): The features of autoregressive and moving average models can be "mixed" in the same model. For example, an ARIMA (1, 1,1) model with constant would have the prediction equation:

$$\hat{Y}(t) = \mu + Y(t-1) + \phi(Y(t-1) - Y(t-2)) - \theta e(t-1)$$

Normally, though, we will try to stick to "unmixed" models with either only-AR or only-MA terms, because including both kinds of terms in the same model sometimes leads to over fitting of the data and non-uniqueness of the coefficients.

ARIMA is a class of linear models capable of representing stationary as well as non-stationary time series. It does not involve independent variables in its constructions. Rather it makes use of the information in the series itself to generate forecasts. It relies heavily on auto correlation patterns of the data.

The autocorrelation of a series Y at lag K is estimated by

$$rk = \sum_{t=k+1}^{T} \frac{(y_t - \bar{y})(y_{t-k} - \bar{y})}{\sum_{t-1}^{T} (Y_t - \bar{y})^2}$$

Where $\bar{y}$ is the sample mean of y. This is the correlation coefficient for values of the series k periods apart. If r_1 is non-zero, it means that the series is first order serially correlated if r_k dies off more or less geometrically with increasing lag k, it is a sign that the series obeys a low order.

If the pattern of autocorrelation is one that can be captured by an autoregression of order less than k, then the partial autocorrelation at lag k will be close to zero. The partial autocorrelation at lag k recursively by

$$\Phi k = \frac{T_k^T 1 - \sum_{J=1}^{k-1} \Phi k-1, J_{k-j}^T}{1 - \sum_{J=1}^{k-1} \Phi k-1, J T j}$$

For k = 1 for k > 1

Where r_k is the estimated autocorrelation at lag k and

$$\Phi kj = \Phi k-1, J - \Phi k, \Phi k-1, k-j$$

In order to determine whether a series follow a purely autoregressive process or purely a moving average process, the Box-Jenkins methodology comes into picture.

ARIMA (Autoregressive Integrated Moving Average) models are generalizations of the simple AR model that use three tools for modeling the serial correlation in the disturbance.

The first tool is the auto regressive or AR term. An autoregressive model of order P, AR (P) has the form

$$U_t = P_1 U_{t-1} + P_2 U_{t-2} + \text{---------} + P_p U_{t-p} + \varepsilon_t$$

Where U_t is the time series and e_t is an uncorrelated random error term with zero mean and constant variance. Here, the value of U at time t depends on its value in the previous time period and a random error term.

The second tool is the integration order term. Each integration order corresponds to differencing the series being forecasted.

The third tool is the MA or moving average term. A moving average forecasting model uses lagged values of the forecast error to improve the current forecast. An MA (q) has the form:

$$U_t = a + \Phi_1 \varepsilon_{t-1} + \Phi_2 \varepsilon_{t-2} + \text{---------} + \Phi_q$$

Where a is constant

The autoregressive and moving average specifications can be combined to form an ARMA (p, q) specification.

$$U_t = a + P_1 U_{t-1} + P_2 U_{t-2} + \text{---------} +$$
$$P_p U_{t-p} + \varepsilon_t + \Phi_1 \varepsilon_{6-1} + \Phi_2 \varepsilon_{t-2} + \text{---------} \Phi_q \varepsilon_{t-q}$$

Where

U_t = dependent variable

U_{t-1}, U_{t-2} ——————— U_{t-p} = lagged variables upto P which is the number of auto regressive terms.

P_1, P_2, P_p = regression coefficients, φ_1, φ_2 is the weights.

ε_t is the residual or error term up to q which is the number of past error terms included in the model. 'a' represents a constant term. *ARMA* model use combinations of past values and past errors and offer a potential for fitting models that could not be adequately fitted by using an AR or MA model separately when the time series have to be differenced to make it stationary, the model is called *ARIMA* instead of *ARMA*. Q statistics is often issued, as a test of whether the series is white noise. There remains the practical problem of choosing the order of lag to use for the test. If too small a lag is chosen, the test may not detect serial correlation at high order lags. However, if too large a lag is chosen, the test may have low power since the significant correlation at one lag may be diluted by insignificant correlations at other lags.

The Q statistics at lag k is a test statistics for the null that there is no auto correlation up to order as is computed as:

$$QLB = T(T+2)\sum_{j-1}^{k}\frac{rj^2}{T-j}$$

Where rj is the jth auto correlation and T is the number of observations.

Selection Criteria for Best ARIMA Model: Although a lot of selection criteria may be used for choosing alternative ARIMA models but we have used the AIC (Akaike Information Criterion)/ Bayesian Information Criterion (BIC). The models with the lowest AIC/BIC is chosen for the analysis. BIC has been widely used for model identification in time series and linear regression. It can, however, be applied quite widely to any set of maximum likelihood-based models.

WHAT IS AIC AND BIC?

Akaike's information criterion, developed by Hirotsugu Akaike under the name of "an information criterion" (AIC) in 1971 and proposed in Akaike (1974), is a measure of the goodness of fit of an estimated statistical model. It is grounded in the concept of entropy, in effect offering a relative measure of the information lost when a given model is used to describe reality and can be said to describe the tradeoff between bias and variance in model construction, or loosely speaking that of accuracy and complexity of the model. The AIC is a test between models — a tool for model selection. Given a data set, several competing models may be ranked according to their AIC, with the one having the lowest AIC being the best. From the AIC value, one may infer that, e.g., the top three models are in a tie and the rest are far worse, but it would be arbitrary to assign a value above which a given model is 'rejected'.

In the general case, the AIC is:

$$AIC = 2\kappa - 2In(L)$$

Where k is the number of parameters in the statistical model and L is the maximized value of the likelihood function for the estimated model.

Over the remainder of this entry, it will be assumed that the model errors are normally independently distributed. Let n be the number of observations and RSS be:

$$RSS = \sum_{i=1}^{n}\hat{\varepsilon}_i^2$$

The residual sum of squares further assume that the variance of the model errors is unknown but equal for them all. Maximizing the likelihood with respect to this variance, the AIC becomes

$$AIC = 2k + n[In(2\pi RSS/n)+1]$$

This can be simplified by factoring out the term $n * \ln(2\pi)$. This is a constant term added to the AIC value of all the competing models. Therefore it can't affect the order in which we rank them and we can safely remove this term. When we also factor out the constant n, AIC simplifies to:

$$AIC = 2k + n[\text{In}(RSS)]$$

Bayesian information criterion (BIC) or **Schwarz Criterion** (also **SBC, SBIC**) is a criterion for *model selection* among a class of parametric models with different numbers of parameters. When estimating model parameters using *maximum likelihood estimation*, it is possible to increase the *likelihood* by adding parameters, which may result in *overfitting*. The BIC resolves this problem by introducing a penalty term for the number of parameters in the model.

The BIC was developed by Gideon E. Schwarz, who gave a Bayesian argument for adopting it. It is very closely related to the Akaike information criterion (AIC). In BIC, the penalty for additional parameters is stronger than that of the AIC.

The BIC is an asymptotic result derived under the assumptions that the data distribution is in the exponential family. Let:

- x = the observed data;
- n = the number of data points in x, the number of observations, or equivalently, the sample size;
- k = the number of free parameters to be estimated. If the estimated model is a linear regression, k is the number of repressors', including the intercept;
- $p(x|k)$ = the probability of the observed data given the number of parameters; or, the likelihood of the parameters given the dataset;
- L = the maximized value of the likelihood function for the estimated model.

The formula for the BIC is:

$$-2.\text{In}\, p(\chi|k) \approx BIC = -2.\text{In}\, L + k\ \text{In}(n)$$

Under the assumption that the model errors or disturbances are independent and identically distributed according to a normal distribution and that the boundary condition that the derivative of the log likelihood in respect to the true variance is zero, this becomes (up to an additive constant, which depends only on n and not on the model).

$$BIC = n \cdot \text{In}(\hat{\sigma}_e^2) + k \cdot \text{In}(n)$$

Where $\hat{\sigma}_e^2$ is the error variance

The error variance in this case is defined as

$$\hat{\sigma}_e^2 = \frac{1}{n}\sum_{i=1}^{n}(\chi_i - \overline{\chi})^2$$

Given any two estimated models, the model with the lower value of BIC is the one to be preferred. The BIC is an increasing function of σ_e^2 and an increasing function of k. So, unexplained variation of the dependent variable and the number of explanatory variables increase the value of

BIC. Hence, lower BIC implies either fewer explanatory variables, better fit, or both. It is important to keep in mind that the BIC can be used to compare estimated models only when the numerical values of the dependent variable are identical for all estimates being compared.

ANALYSIS

The regression Model-1 attempts to find whether currents months' Net FII investment is dependent on current and past BSE Sensex. The regression results are presented in the Table 3.

Table 3
Regression Analysis of Net FII Investment on Current and Past BSE Sensex and Past Net FII Investments

Predictor Variable	*Unstandardized B*	*Unstandardized S.E.B*	*Standardized b*	*t*	*Multiple R*	*R^2*	*$AdjR_2$*	*DW*	*F*
BSE_t	-.318	3.636	-.147	.664	.412	.170	-.014	1.970	.922
BSE_{t-1}	4.366	5.204	2.100	-.087					
BSE_{t-2}	-3.857	3.942	-1.995	.839					
BSE_{t-3}	.260	2.525	.144	-.979					
FII_{t-1}	.070	.283	.071	.103					
FII_{t-2}	-.115	.221	-.117	.249					
Constant	1656.873	2493.504		-.521					

The Table 3 shows that the one-month lag value, two-month lag and three-month lag values of BSE Sensex, and one-month, two-month lag value of net FII do not significantly affects the current month's investment pattern of FIIs.

The regression model-2 examines whether net FII investment is dependent on current and past NSE Index. The results are shown in Table 4.

Table 4
Regression Analysis of Net FII Investment on Current and Past NSE Index and Past Net FII Investments

Predictor Variable	*Unstandardized B*	*Unstandardized S.E.B*	*Standardized b*	*t*	*Multiple R*	*R^2*	*$AdjR_2$*	*DW*	*F*
NSE_t	1.917	10.100	.260	.190	.429	.184	.002	1.941	1.013
NSE_{t-1}	11.777	15.284	1.649	.771					
NSE_{t-2}	-14.715	13.919	-2.158	-1.057					
NSE_{t-3}	2.346	8.060	.366	.291					
FII_{t-1}	.099	.269	.100	.368					
FII_{t-2}	-.091	.228	-.093	-.399					
Constant	1746.299	2539.340		.688					

It is apparent from the Table 4 that the two-month lag and three-month lag NSE index and one month, two-month lag value of net FII do not significantly affects the current month's investment pattern of FIIs. The 't' value of these variables is not significant.

The regression model-3 examines whether current month's BSE sensex is caused by present and past FII investments. It is clear from the Table 5 that past FII investment have quite impact on current BSE sensex. It is also found from the analysis that one-month lag and two-month lag values of BSE sensex significantly affect current BSE sensex at 1% and 5% level of significance.

Table 5

Regression Analysis of Net FII Investment on Current BSE Sensex and Past BSE Sensex, Current and Past Net FII Investments

Predictor Variable	*Unstandardized B*	*Unstandardized S.E.B*	*Standardized b*	*t*	*Multiple R*	*R^2*	*$AdjR_2$*	*DW*	*F*
FII_t	.001	.010	.003	.138	.995	.989	.987	1.875	405.726
FII_{t-1}	-.054	.010	-.118	-5.502*					
FII_{t-2}	.016	.012	.035	1.377					
FII_{t-3}	-.026	.010	-.059	-2.721*					
BSE_{t-1}	1.288	.145	1.340	8.870*					
BSE_{t-2}	-.299	.137	-.334	-2.183*					
Constant	172.005			1.292					

* Significant 1% level

The regression model-4 examined whether NSE Index is dependent on past and present FII investment.

Table 6

Regression Analysis of Net FII Investment on Current NSE Sensex and Past NSE Index, Current and Past Net FII Investments

Predictor Variable	*Unstandardized B*	*Unstandardized S.E.B*	*Standardized b*	*t*	*Multiple R*	*R^2*	*$AdjR_2$*	*DW*	*F*
FII_t	.001	.004	.011	.406	0.989	0.979	0.974	1.840	298.054
FII_{t-1}	-.019	.003	-.140	-5.560*					
FII_{t-2}	.005	.004	.036	1.181					
FII_{t-3}	-.009	.003	-.069	-2.736*					
NSE_{t-1}	1.310	.161	1.351	8.144*					
NSE_{t-2}	-.319	.156	-.345	-2.049**					
Constant	60.536	46.414		1.304					

* Significant at 1% level

** Significant at 5% level

It is found from the Table 6 that past FII investment has significant impact over NSE index. But one-month and two-month lag NSE value significantly affect current NSE index at 1% and 5% level of significance. Now it is essential to find out that whether these results are in conformity to the ARIMA findings. It is evident from all the tables that the Durbin-Watson 'd' statistics for all the models are around 2. Hence, it can be conclude that the error terms in each of the models are not serially correlated.

The autocorrelation and partial correlation functions (ACF and PACFs) of the series of BSE sensex, NSE index and FII investment are presented in the Table 7 through Table 12.

Table 7
Autocorrelation: BSE Sensex

Lag	*AutoCorrelation*	*Standard Error*	*Box-Ljung*	*Prob.*
1	0.865	.158	29.987	0.000
2	0.719	.156	51.278	0.000
3	0.603	.153	66.734	0.000
4	0.496	.151	77.505	0.000
5	0.403	.149	84.822	0.000
6	0.332	.147	89.968	0.000
7	0.269	.144	93.460	0.000
8	0.205	.142	95.559	0.000
9	0.164	.139	96.940	0.000
10	0.134	.137	97.902	0.000
11	0.114	.134	98.627	0.000
12	0.101	.132	99.217	0.000
13	0.077	.129	99.573	0.000
14	0. 031	.126	99.635	0.000
15	-0.024	0.123	99.671	0.000
16	-0.075	0.121	100.058	0.000

Table 8
Partial Autocorrelation: BSE Sensex

Lag	*Partial Autocorrelation*	*Standard Error*
1	0.865	0.164
2	- 0.117	0.164
3	0.042	0.164
4	- 0.052	0.164
5	- 0.007	0.164
6	0.024	0.164

7	- 0.025	0.164
8	- 0.043	0.164
9	0.044	0.164
10	0.003	0.164
11	0.022	0.164
12	0.007	0.164
13	- 0.055	0.164
14	- 0.092	0.164
15	- 0.068	0.164
16	- 0.042	0.164

Table 9
Autocorrelation: NSE Index

Lag	*Autocorrelation*	*Standard Error*	*Box-Ljung*	*Prob.*
1	0.860	0.158	29.679	0.000
2	0.722	0.156	51.142	0.000
3	0.601	0.153	66.491	0.000
4	0.484	0.151	76.740	0.000
5	0.385	0.149	83.409	0.000
6	0.311	0.147	87.915	0.000
7	0.251	0.144	90.948	0.000
8	0.191	0.142	92.771	0.000
9	0.157	0.139	94.042	0.000
10	0.139	0.137	95.071	0.000
11	0.122	0.134	95.898	0.000
12	0.111	0.132	96.607	0.000
13	0.098	0.129	97.188	0.000
14	0.049	0.126	97.336	0.000
15	- 0.013	0.123	97.348	0.000
16	- 0.68	0.121	97.669	0.000

Table 10
Partial Correlation: NSE Index

Lag	*Partial Autocorrelation*	*Standard Error*
1	0.860	0.164
2	- 0.073	0.164

3	- 0.008	0.164
4	- 0.064	0.164
5	- 0.007	0.164
6	0.029	0.164
7	- 0.002	0.164
8	- 0.043	0.164
9	0.052	0.164
10	0.030	0.164
11	- 0.002	0.164
12	0.008	0.164
13	- 0.016	0.164
14	- 0.143	0.164
15	- 0.075	0.164
16	- 0.033	0.164

Table 11
Autocorrelation: FII Investment

Lag	*Autocorrelation*	*Standard Error*	*Box-Ljung*	*Prob.*
1	0.115	0.158	0.534	0.465
2	- 0.232	0.156	2.749	0.253
3	0.033	0.153	2.795	0.424
4	- 0.058	0.151	2.944	0.567
5	- 0.144	0.149	3.882	0.566
6	- 0.121	0.147	4.564	0.601
7	- 0.124	0.144	5.298	0.624
8	- 0.062	0.142	5.489	0.704
9	0.015	0.139	5.501	0.789
10	- 0.093	0.137	5.963	0.818
11	- 0.002	0.134	5.963	0.876
12	0.157	0.132	7.389	0.831
13	0.017	0.129	7.406	0.880
14	0.109	0.126	8.148	0.881
15	0.129	0.123	9.239	0.865
16	0.129	0.121	10.378	0.846

Table 12

Partial Autocorrelation

Lag	*Partial Autocorrelation*	*Standard Error*
1	0.115	0.164
2	- 0.248	0.164
3	0.102	0.164
4	- 0.149	0.164
5	- 0.086	0.164
6	- 0.155	0.164
7	- 0.153	0.164
8	- 0.106	0.164
9	- 0.065	0.164
10	- 0.197	0.164
11	- 0.057	0.164
12	- 0.002	0.164
13	- 0.099	0.164
14	0.104	0.164
15	0.007	0.164
16	0.192	0.164

Table 7 and Table 9 indicate that there is very high autocorrelation between current and past BSE Sensex as well as NSE market index. These findings are also in conformity with the regression results of significant (at 1% level) impact of past BSE Sensex and NSE Index on present BSE Sensex and NSE Index respectively.

Table 7 and Table 9 shows that BSE sensex and NSE index series is non-stationary and differencing and log transformation is needed to make the series stationary. The Table 11 and Table 12 reveal that the FII series is stationary and requires no differencing. The Table 11 and Table 12 showed the presence of mixed ARMA process.

Similarly, the Table 13 and Table 15 after log transformation indicated mixed ARMA process. The reliability of the ACFs and PACFs can also be checked through the findings of various ARIMA model.

Table 13

Autocorrelation: BSE Sensex Transformations: Log Transformation and Differencing (1)

Lag	*Autocorrelation*	*Standard Error*	*Box-Ljung*	*Prob.*
1	0.335	0.160	4.381	0.036
2	0.220	0.158	6.323	0.042
3	0.181	0.155	7.688	0.053

4	- 0.090	0.153	8.035	0.090
5	- 0.289	0.151	11.712	0.039
6	- 0.091	0.148	12.091	0.060
7	- 0.252	0.146	15.084	0.035
8	- 0.133	0.143	15.944	0.043
9	- 0.102	0.140	16.476	0.058
10	- 0.058	0.138	16.651	0.082
11	- 0.033	0.135	16.711	0.117
12	0.155	0.132	18.075	0.113
13	- 0.029	0.130	18.124	0.153
14	- 0.002	0.127	18.124	0.201
15	- 0.011	0.124	18.133	0.256
16	- 0.112	0.121	18.990	0.269

Table 14

Partial Autocorrelation: BSE Sensex Transformations: Log Transformation and Differencing (1)

Lag	*Partial Autocorrelation*	*Standard Error*
1	0.335	0.167
2	0.121	0.167
3	0.087	0.167
4	- 0.221	0.167
5	- 0.292	0.167
6	0.113	0.167
7	- 0.137	0.167
8	0.065	0.167
9	- 0.128	0.167
10	- 0.020	0.167
11	- 0.004	0.167
12	0.137	0.167
13	- 0.141	0.167
14	- 0.107	0.167
15	- 0.051	0.167
16	- 0.083	0.167

Table 15
Autocorrelation: NSE Index Log Transformation and Difference (1)

Lag	*Autocorrelation*	*Standard Error*	*Box-Ljung*	*Prob.*
1	0.300	0.160	3.509	0.061
2	0.229	0.158	5.612	0.060
3	0.139	0.155	6.416	0.093
4	- 0.054	0.153	6.540	0.162
5	- 0.351	0.151	11.982	0.035
6	- 0.112	0.148	12.552	0.051
7	- 0.317	0.146	17.301	0.016
8	- 0.102	0.143	17.811	0.023
9	- 0.118	0.140	18.516	0.030
10	0.052	0.138	18.656	0.045
11	0.029	0.135	18.703	0.067
12	0.105	0.132	19.333	0.081
13	0.011	0.130	19.340	0.113
14	0.054	0.127	19.519	0.146
15	- 0.104	0.124	20.226	0.163
16	- 0.074	0.121	20.597	0.195

Table 16
Partial Autocorrelation: NSE Index Log Transformation and Differencing (1)

Lag	*Partial Autocorrelation*	*Standard Error*
1	0.300	0.1679
2	0.152	0.167
3	0.040	0.167
4	- 0.150	0.167
5	- 0.384	0.167
6	0.101	0.167
7	- 0.195	0.167
8	0.148	0.167
9	- 0.121	0.167
10	0.059	0.167
11	0.000	0.167
12	- 0.085	0.167

13	0.009	0.167
14	- 0.112	0.167
15	- 0.041	0.167
16	- 0.088	0.167

After differencing once, the ACF and PACF for BSE Sensex and NSE index show that the series have become stationary which is depicted in the Table 13 and Table 14 and these for NSE index series are shown in Tables 15 and 16.

Table 17

Summary of *ARIMA* (p, d, q) Models For BSE Sensex Regressed on FII

ARIMA (p, d, q)	*Standard Error*	*AIC*	*ARIMA (p, d, q)*	*SE*	*AIC*
1, 0, 0	0.060	-94.422	1,1,7	0.043	-111.679
1, 0, 1	0.052	-104.204	1,1,9	0.043	-108.846
1, 0, 2	0.052	-103.351	2, 1, 2	0.020	-172.568
1, 0, 3	0.048	-104.108	2,0,0	0.048	-109.384
1, 0, 4	0.044	-110.282	2, 0,2	0.048	-107.941
1, 0, 5	0.044	-108.824	2, 0,4	0.044	-108.945
1, 0, 7	0.047	-104.666	2, 0,5	0.046	-106.00
1, 0,9	0.046	- 102.794	2, 1,0	0.0145	-116.793
1, 1,0	0.044	-118.460	2,1,2	0.046	-112.518
1, 1, 1	0.045	-116.736	2,1,4	0.042	-113.963
1, 1, 2	0.045	-115.276	2,1,5	0.041	-115.233
1,1,5	0.039	-117.828			

The Table 17 shows the summary results of ARIMA model. The AIC in Table 17 indicates that BSE sensex follows the ARIMA (1, 0, 0) when regressed on Net FII investment since the AIC value of –94.422 are closest to zero. The Table 18 reveals that NSE index follow the ARIMA (1, 0, 0) when regressed on FII investments, since the AIC value of –94.439 is closest to zero. But ARIMA output shows a warning that the order of the process may not be correctly estimated. This indicates that current BSE sensex depends on the just preceding months' BSE Sensex as well as on FII investment as was found using multiple regression analysis.

Table 18

Summary of *ARIMA* (p, d, q) ModelsFor NSE Index Regressed on FII

ARIMA(p, d, q)	*Standard Error*	*AIC*	*ARIMA (p, d, q)*,	*SE*	*AIC*
1, 0, 0	0.061	-94.439	1, 1, 9	0.043	-107.722
1, 0, 1	0.054	-101.228	2,0,0	0.043	-107.722
1, 0, 2	0.053	-101.714	2, 0, 2	0.046	-105.603
1, 0, 4	0.045	-108.117	2, 0, 4	0.044	-108.448

1, 0, 5	0.045	-107.i63	2, 0, 5	0.047	-104.429
1, 0, 7	0.045	-104.771	2, 0, 7	0.046	-102.662
1,0,9	0.049	-94.740	2,0,9	0.045	-98.954
1,1,0	0.046	-115.39	2, 0, 0	0.043	-107.722
1, 1, 1	0.046	-113.901	2, 0.2	0.046	-105.603
1, 1, 2	0.047	-112.682	2, 1, 0	0.046	-114.192
1, 1, 3	0.046	-111.854	2, 1, 2	0.043	-114.659
1, 1, 4	0.039	-118.249	2, 1, 5	0.039	-116.514
1, 1, 6	0.041	-113.605	2, 1, 7	0.042	-110.879

Table 19

Summary of *ARIMA* (p, d, q) ModelsFor Net FII Investment Regression BSE Sensex

ARIMA (p, d, q)	*Standard Error*	*AIC*	*ARIMA (p, d, q)*	*SE*	*AIC*
1, 0, 0	0.603	59.914	1, 1, 3	0.672	68.862
1, 0, 1	0.611	61.748	1, 1, 4	0.635	68.052
1, 0, 2	0.612	63.193	2, 0, 0	0.609	61.567
1, 0, 4	0.573	63.205	2, 0, 1	0.620	63.711
1, 0, 5	0.568	64.571	2, 0, 3	0.566	64.390
1, 0, 6	0.604	67.790	2, 0, 5	0.593	67.373
1,0,9	0.603	72.464	2, 1, 0	0.644	64.740
1, 1, 0	0.649	64.707	2, 1, 3	0.631	68.760
1, 1, 2	0.662	66.901	2, 1, 5	0.677	73.537

Table 20

Summary of *ARIMA* (p, d, q) Models for Net FII Investment Regressed on NSE Index

ARIMA (p, d, q)	*Standard Error*	*AIC*	*ARIMA (p, d, q)*	*SE*	*AIC*
1, 0, 0	0.599	59.419	2, 0, 1	0.616	63.242
1, 0, 1	0.606	61.285	2, 0, 4	0.577	64.617
1, 0, 3	0.599	63.574	1, 1, 0	0.644	64.307
1, 0, 4	0.569	62.677	1, 1, 2	0.641	65.740
1, 0, 5	0.583	64.759	1, 1, 5	0.618	69.798
1, 0, 7	0.598	68.587	2, 1, 0	0.633	63.709
1,0,8	0.592	71.648	2, 1, 1	0.649	65.832
2, 0, 0	0.604	61.109	2, 1, 3	0.667	69.513

The Table 19 reveals that the ARIMA (1,0, 0) on the AIC value is 59.914 which is minimum and Table 20 depicts ARIMA (1, 0, 0) in the AIC value's 59.419 is minimum. This result is also confirmed by regression results. Table 20 indicate that FII also follows autoregressive process of order 1 and moving average process of order 0 and 1 respectively when regressed on BSE and NSE index as given by the minimization of AIC values. It is to be noted here that ARIMA (1, 0, 0) for FII (when regressed on BSE and NSE is having lowest AIC value) but the ARIMA output shows a warning that the order of the process may not be correctly estimated. The immediate next minimum AIC is for ARIMA (2, 0, 0). These results also reinforce the findings of regression models 1 and 2.

CONCLUDING OBSERVATION

The present chapter examined the impact of Net FII investment on the Indian stock market represented by BSE Sensex and NSE index. This chapter case shows that past FII investment makes significant impact on current BSE Sensex and NSE Index; but there is no significant impact of current FII investment on current BSE Sensex and NSE Index. An important implication of these findings is that the FII investments in India deserve a well-calibrated policy response while the daily movement of stock market in India should be better explained by other factors than FIIs. Our study reinforces the need for expediting research program, "Capital flows and India's Financial Sector: Learning from theory, international experience, and Indian evidence" recommended by the GoI's Expert Group on FII (2005).

REVIEW QUESTIONS

1. What is the motivation behind to study FII investment?
2. How do you select the model criteria?
3. Elucidate the implication of BSE and NSE in relation to FII investment?
4. What is ARIMA Model? Why it is used in stock market?
5. Write short notes on:
   (a) Price pressure hypothesis
   (b) Performance of BSE
6. Quiz
   (a) ____ is the oldest stock exchange in Asia and has the greatest number of listed companies in the ____.
   (b) India, the second fastest growing economy after ____, has recently seen positive foreign institutional investor (FII) inflows driven by the sound fundamentals and growth opportunities.
   (c) The number of registered FIIs in the year 2009 is ____.
   (d) ____ is a trader who buys when the market increased and sells when the market fell.
   (e) The Acronym ARIMA stands for ____.
   (f) Which hypothesis suggests that the increase in share prices associated with foreign investment flow is caused by temporary liquidity and predicts that this change in share price is subsequently reversed?

10

Dividend Policies and Practices in Indian Stock Market

Variations in stock prices are largely explained by changes in the cash flow of companies. Dividend constitutes the cash flows that accrue to stockholders. Dividend policy determines the decision of earning between payment to stockholders and reinvestment in the firm. But dividend decisions during a period are taken on the basis of both current and past earnings. Therefore, this chapter justify that the Lintner's model of dividend behavior seems suitable enough to Indian data and also to analyse the current dividend that depends on current as well as past earnings.

INTRODUCTION

Economic reforms have brought in tremendous growth in the Indian stock market. India has today become an important market in the emerging markets of the world, next only to Malaysia, Mexico, Taiwan, Brazil, Korea and Thailand in terms of market capitalization and turnover. A number of measures are being taken not only to cope with the rapid quantitative strides in the growth of the market but also to ensure a qualitative change in the market by rendering it fair, transparent and efficient. In the regulated environment, price controls the amount of money being raised by the corporate sector, which lagged far behind the amount of money coming into the market leading to a scarcity in the equity stock. So, the corporate sector started raising money through the convertible debenture by giving a coupon rate, which is lower than the market rates, which ultimately get converted into equity shares at low price. This is due to change in price rather than their levels. But the price of a share at any point of time consists of a permanent component and a transitory component. The permanent component is the true value related to company specific factors such as its earnings, dividends, asset structure, management efficiency, competitive position etc. and other government factors such as government policies towards the industry. So, the permanent component can be approximated by the trend. However, market share index, which is expected to be the reflection of shareholders' mood, does not have any significant relationship with individual share price because of the volatility of the transitory component of share price. So, due to this national investors generally made portfolio investments by minimizing the risk and maximizing profit. Further, unfavorable behaviour of share price may induce the management of a company to increase dividend rate with a view to stimulating the price of its share on the stock market.

DIVIDEND POLICY

Corporate saving is one of the most significant sources of funds for financing corporate growth. While allocating the corporate profit, firms may decide either to retain it to meet their growth needs or treat it as payout to the shareholders as dividend. A dividend is a cash payment from a company's earnings; it is announced by a company's board of directors and distributed among stockholders. In other words, dividends are an investor's share of a company's profits, given to him or her as a part-owner of the company. Apart from option strategies, dividends are the only way for investors to profit from ownership of stock without eliminating their stake in the company. There is another motivation for a company to pay dividends: a steadily increasing dividend payout is viewed as a strong indication of a company's continuing success. The great thing about dividends is that they can't be faked. They are paid or not paid, increased or not increased. The company's board of directors decides what percentage of earnings will be paid out to shareholders, and then puts the remaining profits back into the company. Although dividends are usually dispersed quarterly, it is important to remember that the company is not obligated to pay a dividend every single quarter. In fact, the company can stop paying a dividend at any time, but this is rare, especially for a firm with a long history of dividend payments. A dividend decision is widely regarded as one of the most important financial decisions and the basic components of corporate financial management policy. The dividend decision, which is determined by a firm's dividend policy, affects the level of equity retained in a firm (Lease, John, Kalay, Loewenstein and Sarig 1999:1). If dividends that are paid out are not replaced in value terms by new equity, then this decision also influences the financial structure of the firm. In fact, dividend policy decision is a complex decision having numerous implications for the firm. It is closely related to the investment and financing decision of the company. Dividend decisions involve the periodic determination of proportion of a firm's total distributable earnings that is payable to its ordinary shareholders. The larger the dividend paid, the fewer funds are retained for reinvestment and the more the company will have to rely on other sources of long-term funds to finance projects. But dividends constitute the cash flow that accrues to stockholders. Hence, both growth and dividends are desirable. The relationship between dividends and value of the firm should therefore be the criterion for taking a dividend policy decision. In developed countries, the decision between paying dividend and retaining earnings has been taken seriously by both investors and management, and has been the subject of considerable research by economists in the last four decades. [Lintner, 1956; Brittain, 1964; Modigliani and Miller, 1961; Pettit, 1972; Black and Scholes 1973, Michael, Thaler and Womack, 1995; Dhillon and Johnson, 1994; Amibud and Murgia, 1997; Charitou and Vafeas, 1998]

The examination of dividend policy has always been one of the main topics in corporate finance research. During the last fifty years, corporate finance researchers have embarked on a considerable theoretical and empirical investigation concerning the dividend policy of firms. There are a variety of reasons why dividend policy is so interesting. The company's dividend decision has a direct impact on its financial mix. Additionally, the volume of the distributed dividend may affect the market value of the firm. There are three basic views regarding the dividend payment's effect on stock price. The first view implies that an increase in dividend payout has a positive impact on the value of the firm; the second suggests that there exists a negative effect on the value of the company and the third that dividend policy has no influence on the total price of the firm.

Corporate dividend policy has captured the interest of economists of this century and over the last five decades has been the subject of intensive theoretical modeling and empirical examination. A number of conflicting theoretical models (all lacking strong empirical support) define current attempts to explain corporate dividend behavior. Over the last century, three schools of thought have emerged. One section sees dividends as attractive and as a positive influence on stock price. A second community believes that stock prices are negatively correlated with dividend payout levels. The third group of theories maintains that firm dividend policy is irrelevant in stock price valuation. The purpose of this chapter is to examine the academic efforts to model dividend policy and to test the empirical validity and significance of the paradigms they fashion.

The Dividend Payout Ratio:

The dividend policy of firms can be analyzed in many different ways. One way to explore dividends is by considering the amount of money that firms pay to their shareholders. From another point of view, dividends can be seen from a shareholders' side, which emphasizes on the realized dividend yield, i.e., the dividend per share over the stock price. Another, widely used, element that helps to investigate the dividend policy of firms is the firms' dividend payout ratios. The payout ratio is the portion of earnings that firms distribute to their shareholders, thus it is a variable which captures the policy of firms by comparing their earnings with their total distributed dividends. Many researchers use this ratio as dependent variable in their econometric models and try to explain the dividend policy of firms by finding corporate variables which significantly affect the level of the distributed dividend.

Short-run Dividend Policies:

Dividend policy needs also to be analyzed in the short-run period. Short-run dividend policy refers to year-to-year corporate dividend strategies. Firms could set their payout policy according to their earnings; the second firms could consider their dividend in accordance with their share and, finally, the third is about firms that determine their policy after considering the dividend policy of other firms. Firms either distribute constant per share dividend, or constant per share dividend which increases over time at a constant rate. The first one is about the reasons according to which the firms choose to determine their dividend policy according to their shares. There are a lot of reasons for a choice like this; one can claim that these firms try to meet the preferences of their investors either for future capital gains or current income; another reason could be that firms use a specific dividend policy in order to reveal information about the quality of the investments that they undertake, or to give away an indication about their future results.

The second issue concerns regarding firms that had their short-run dividend payout policy as a constant per share dividend which increases over time at a constant rate. There is a variety of factors which can be used by firms to decide the level of distributed dividend growth; these factors can be either macroeconomic like expected inflation and economic growth, or microeconomic like the expected growth of the firm. Some firm's growth rate per share dividend is appointed by the expected growth of the firm; inflation could affect its per share dividend growth. The main reason why dividend affects share price of this affection is the difference between dividend and capital gain risk. There are also other reasons which can help to explain this distinct impact of dividends on share price, like asymmetric information, incomplete markets, transaction costs etc.

Models of Information Asymmetries: Signaling Models

The market imperfection of asymmetric information is the basis for three distinct efforts to explain corporate dividend policy. The mitigation of the information asymmetries between managers and owners via unexpected changes in dividend policy is the cornerstone of dividend signaling models. Agency cost theory uses dividend policy to better align the interests of shareholders and corporate managers. The free cash flow hypothesis is an *ad hoc* combination of the signaling and agency costs paradigms; the payment of dividends can decrease the level of funds available for perquisite consumption by corporate managers. The proponents of signaling theories believe that a corporate dividend policy used as a means of putting the message of quality across has a lower cost than other alternatives. The use of dividends as signals implies that alternative methods of signaling are not perfect substitutes.

Behavioral Models

Investor behavior is substantially influenced by societal norms and attitudes (Shiller,1984). Unfortunately, this motivation has been ignored by financial theorists for the most part because of the difficulty of introducing investor behavior into traditional financial pricing models (Arbel, Carvell and Postnieks, 1988). According to Shiller (1989), including these influences in modeling efforts can enrich the development of a theory to explain the endurance of corporate dividend policy. Ordinary investors are faced not with risk, but with uncertainty—a lack of concise judgment and sense of objective evidence (Knight, 1964). Social pressures can lead to errors in judgment and trading activities by shareholders that cannot be logically explained. These errors in judgment are only mistakes, not lapses of rational investment activity. Mass investor psychology profoundly influences aggregate market activity (Shiller, 1984). Dividend policy is inconsistent with wealth maximization of the shareholder and is better explained by the addition of a socio-economic behavior paradigm into economic models. Dividend payouts can be viewed as the socio-economic repercussion of corporate evolution—the information asymmetries between managers and shareholders cause dividends to be paid to increase the attractiveness of equity issues (Frankfurter and Lane, 1992). The systematic relation between industry type and dividend policy reported by Michel (1979) implies that managers are influenced by the actions of executives from competitive firms when determining dividend payout levels.

Managers, realizing that shareholders desire dividends, pay or increase dividends to mollify investors (Frankfurter and Lane, 1992). Dividend payments to shareholders should help increase the corporation's stability by serving as a ritualistic reminder of the managerial and owner relationship (Ho and Robinson, 1992). As Frankfurter and Lane (1992) contend, dividends are partially a tradition and partially a method to allay investor anxiety.

Theoretical Behavioral Models:

Feldstein and Green (1983) model the corporate dividend decision as the last step in a process that evaluates inputs from five sources. First, dividend policy is a consequence of investor consumption needs. The tax liabilities from dividend payment are less than the transaction costs of selling shares to provide income if earnings are retained. Second, the market value of retained earnings is less than the market value of dividends. Third, dividend payment is consistent with steady state growth and an optimal debt/equity ratio. Fourth, dividend payments are a by-product of the separation of corporation owners and managers; dividend payments help to diminish the agency costs arising from separation of corporate owners and managers and are used for signaling activities. Finally, although asymmetric information and agency costs are present in the model, the paradigm is not dependent on these market imperfections. The involvement of shareholders with diverse tax liabilities and diversification goals in an equilibrium with uncertainty results in dividend payments.

Shefrin and Statman (1984) explain dividend preference by using the theory of self-control (Thaler and Shefrin, 1981) and the descriptive theory of choice under uncertainty (Kahneman and Tversky, 1982). Information models are used to justify the presence of corporate dividends while the tax liability of dividends is used as a counter-argument. This model is also consistent with dividend clienteles. Dividends and capital gains are not always perfect substitutes because of a lack of self-control to delay gratification (Thaler and Shefrin, 1981). In financial theory, dividends and capital gains have the same value.

Dividend Discount Model

When investors buy stock in publicly traded companies, they generally expect to get two types of cash flows — dividends during the holding period and an expected price at the end of the holding period. Since this expected price is itself determined by future dividends, the value of a stock is the present value of dividends through infinity. This is given by the following formula:

$$\text{Value per share of stock} = \sum_{t=1}^{t=x} \frac{E(DPS_t)}{(1+K_e)^t}$$

Where: E(DPS) = expected dividends per share in period t

K_e = cost of equity

The features of dividend discount model are:

- It is too conservative.
- Expected dividends are estimated by assuming the growth rates in earnings and payout ratio which is itself a big assumption.
- Rate of return is estimated by riskiness, market beta, factor beta.

Valuations in Dividend Discount Model

Gordon growth model

The use of the Gordon growth model is limited to stable firms which have stable growth rates. The only considerations which have to be kept in mind are that growth rate of dividend cannot exceed that of economy and other measures of the company can also grow. The value of the firm is given by the following formula:

$$\text{Value of Stock} = \frac{\text{Expected Dividends next period}}{(\text{Cost of equity} - \text{Expected growth rate in perpetuity})}$$

Two stage growth model

This model considers that the growth of a firm takes place in two stages. First phase is where growth rate not stable and second phase is that of steady growth rate. Therefore, the final value of the firm is sum of two values one of first phase of variable growth and second stage of stable growth.

$$P_o = \sum_{t-1}^{i-n} \frac{E(DPS_t)}{(1 + \text{Cost of Equity})^t} + \frac{P_n}{(1 + \text{Cost of Equity})^n} \quad P_n = \frac{E(DPS_{a-1})}{(\text{Cost of Equity} - g)}$$

H model

This model was presented by Fuller and Hsia. It is suitable for firms that have high initial growth rate. This model assumes that growth rate declines linearly over time in initial stage. And other assumptions are that dividend payout and cost of equity are taken constant over time this exposes the result to risk, the payout ratio constant in both the phases. This model is inappropriate for firms which have low or no dividend at present.

$$P_o = \frac{DPS_o * (1 + g_o)}{(r - g_o)} + \frac{DPS_o * H * (g_o - g_o)}{(r - g_o)}$$

Where:

g_n = final stable growth

g_a = initial high growth

r = rate of return

Disdvantages of DDM

- When companies hold back cash, then cash flows to equity exceed dividends.
- Undervalue firms with large and increasing cash balances.
- Few firms pay huge dividends by funding through debt or equity thus giving a more optimistic picture.

Advantages of DDM

- Simplicity
- Dividends are the only cash flow for shareholders
- Fewer assumptions about:
  - * Capital expenditure
  - * Depreciation
  - * Working capital
- Dividends remain stable for most of the firm
- Valuations is less volatile

Usefulness of DDM

- Yield a conservative estimate
- Realistic estimate for firms that pay equity in dividends
- Where cash flow estimation is difficult
  - * Estimating capex and WC requirements for financial services which is difficult.
  - * Retained earnings and book value have real consequences for financial services.

Lintner's Model

The earliest major attempt to explain dividend behavior of companies has been credited to John Lintner (1956) who conducted his study on American Companies in the middle of 1950s. Since then there has been an ongoing debate on dividend policy in the developed markets resulting in mixed, controversial and inclusive results. John Lintner (1956) conducted a series of interviews with corporate managers about dividend policies of their companies. The total number of companies that he used was 600 from which he finally has chosen only 28, to survey and interview. In his study, Lintner made a number of important observations concerning the dividend policies of these companies. One of the most important conclusions is that companies have a long-run target dividend payout ratio. That meant that companies aim to distribute, in the long run, a constant portion of their earnings each year. Another interesting remark of Lintner's study concerns the managers that proved to be more interested on changes on dividend than on absolute levels. Additionally, managers avoid changing their dividend policy if they are not certain that they will be able to keep the new policy constant for a reasonable period. That is to say that manager avoids changing the companies' dividend policy very often since it is likely to give a negative signal to investors as uncertainty increases. In 1956, John Lintner stated that most of the firms think primarily in terms of the portion of earnings that should be paid out as dividends rather than in terms of the proportion of earnings that should be ploughed back into the firm. Secondly, firms try to reach the target payout ratio gradually over a period of time because stockholders prefer a steady progression in dividends.

John Lintner states that dividend policy has two parameters:

- The target payout ratio
- he rapidity (speed) by which current dividends adjust to the target.

Lintner developed this theory based on two important things that he observed about dividend policy:

- Companies tend to set long-term target dividend payout ratios in line with the amount of positive net present value (NPV) projects they have available.
- Increases in earnings are not always sustainable. As a result, managers are reluctant to change the dividend policy until they see a sustainable growth in earnings level.

Based on these observations, Lintner stated the following model of dividend behaviour:

Model 1:

$$D_t = crEPS_t + (1\text{-}c)\, D_{t\text{-}1}$$

Where D_t = dividend per share for year t

c = adjustment rate

r = target payout ratio

EPS_t = earnings per share for year t

$D_{t\text{-}1}$ = dividend per share for year t-1

In his empirical analysis, Lintner developed a partial adjustment model that captures the above findings. According to Lintner, each firm i has a target dividend payout ratio (ri). Using this payout ratio, Lintner, computed the target dividend at time t (Dit*) as a proportion of the real earnings of the firm i at time t (Eit), i.e. Dit*= ri Eit. In real world the dividend, which the firm finally pays, at time t, (Dit) differs from the target one (Dit*). Thus, it is more reasonable to model the change between the actual dividend at time t and time t-1, instead of the actual dividend at time t only. Taking the change in actual dividends into account, it is realistic and consistent with the long-run target payout ratio, to assume that the actual change in dividend at time t, (Dit - Di,t-1), equals to a constant portion (αi) plus the speed with which the dividend, at time t-1, has adjusted to the target dividend at time t, (Dit* - Di,t-1). Since the target dividend at time t is a proportion of the real earnings at time t, the final model is as follows:

$$D_{it} - D_{it\text{-}1} = a_i + C_i\, r_i\, E_{it} - C_i D_{i\,t\text{-}1}$$

Where Dit = the actual dividend payment during period t, Eit = the earnings of the firm during period t, ci = the adjustment factor (which indicates the speed with which the dividend, at time t-1, has adjusted to the optimal target dividend at time t), and ri = the target payout ratio. This theoretical model can be estimated using the following econometric model:

$$\Delta D_{it} = a_{i\,i}\beta E_{it} + \beta_2 D_{it\text{-}1} + \bullet_{it}$$

Where ΔDit = the change in dividend from time t-1 to time t, for the firm i, β1 represents the product ci times ri of the theoretical model, β2 = the variable ci of the theoretical model with negative sign (that is, β2 = - ci), and εit = the error of the model 5. Lintner's estimation of the above model appeared fairly good, explaining 85% of the dividend changes in his sample of companies. Fama and Babiak (1968) undertook a more comprehensive study of Lintner model's performance. Their starting point was the work of Lintner (1956). Their sample consists of 392 industrial firms over the period 1946 through 1964. Fama and Babiak tested the Lintner's model with their data and methodology and found that it performed well but it can be improved by introducing, as an additional explanatory variable, the earnings from the previous year without the constant term. Keeping in view the present chapter has undertaken to study the behaviour of stock prices in BSE Sensex for different dividend policies of 27 firms listed on the Bombay Stock Exchange during the period 2004-2008. Thirdly to examine the relationship between stock prices and dividends, to determine the relevance of the Lintner's model in predicting stock prices and judge the stability of dividend policy in general.

LITERATURE REVIEW

When a company earns profits from operations, management can do one of two things with the profits. It can choose to retain them — essentially reinvesting them into the company with the hope of creating more profits and thus further stock appreciation. The other alternative is to distribute a portion of the profits to shareholders in the form of dividends. The payment of dividends has received much attention from researchers internationally. The crux of debate on the dividend policy is the division of retained earnings, i.e., profit after tax (PAT) between dividend and earnings as internal resources. According to a widely discussed theory, the value of a firm is not subject to the dividend policy followed but depends on the earnings power of the firm. Hence instead of deciding on how to split the earnings between dividends and retained earnings, the firm should endeavor towards having an optimal investment policy resulting in optimal return (Modgliani and Miller, 1961). Miller and Modigliani (1961) argued that dividends are irrelevant and cannot be used to determine the value of a firm's shares (and therefore change shareholder value). On the other hand, Gordon (1963) and Lintner (1962) were the first supporters of the relevance of dividends in creating shareholder wealth. They suggested that there is a direct relationship between a firm's dividend policy and its market value. Investors' world normally prefer low dividends as the dividends are subject to higher tax rate than that in the case of capital gains resulting out of earnings capitalization (Farrar and Selwyn, 1967). But the investors in lower or no-tax bracket would prefer higher dividend rates since they consider the dividends as a source of regular income. A rational investor would normally discount the future of distant dividends at a higher rate than near dividends as a matter of averting risk. Hence, a company paying a higher dividend will always command a higher price for its share than a company having same earning power but paying lesser dividend (Gordon, 1962). The growing firm where, internal rate of return is more than the cost of raising finance from outside would normally opt for paying minimum possible rate of dividend and ploughing back more profits for further investment opportunities. A growing firm can maximize its shareholders' wealth by retaining all the profits. It is reverse in the case of a declining firm (Walter, 1963). Lintner in his empirical study on USA companies found out that the firms establish their dividends in accordance with the level of current earnings as well as dividend of the previous year. More preference is given to the proportion of earnings to be paid as dividend (dividend payout ratio or DPR) than the dividend per share (DPS). Firms normally prefer changing their DPS slowly and gradually with the changes in earnings per share (EPS) (Lintner, 1956). After Lintner (1956) proposed the so-called two-variable dividend model, Fama and Babiak (1968) tested this model on the dividend data of 392 major North American industrial firms for the years 1946-1964. Lintner's dividend model succeeded fairly well in explaining the dividend changes of individual firms. Various researchers have studied the important area of dividend policy in an international context. Despite extensive research being undertaken on the issue, the effect of dividends on share prices remains one of the unsolved issues of finance (Correia, Flynn, Uliana and Wormald 1993). Noe and Rebello (1996) studied the impact of asymmetric information and managerial opportunism on firms' financing and payout policies. They found that the signaling mechanisms that shareholders prefer most are the restriction of dividends, followed by equity financing and, finally, the under pricing of securities. When managers determine policies on their own, a reversal of this hierarchy may prevail. Pettit (1977) studied the clientele effect of dividends. Retired investors and pension funds, for example, tend to prefer cash income, and may therefore want the firm to pay out a high percentage of its earnings. On the other hand, shareholders in their peak earning years prefer the reinvestment of cash and low dividend payments. Ang (1998) presented an interesting interpretation of Lintner's dividend model by introducing the concept of equilibrium dividends that is not only time dependent, but also utilizes a firm's specific parameters to greater effect. This time-dependent equilibrium dividend should be distinguished from the more familiar notion of desired dividend, and is useful for both pedagogical and theoretical reasons. This distinction indicates the usefulness of Lintner's dividend model. Sealy and Knight (1987) appeared to have found a negative preference for dividends, which is understandable in view of the differential tax treatment of income and capital gains that prevailed in South Africa at that juncture. Botha, Bosch and Van Zyl (1987) found that dividend policy has no effect on changes in shareholders' wealth. Firer (1988) found that investors do not believe that growth companies are entitled to withhold dividends from their shareholders. Investors also appear to support the 'bird in the hand' approach to dividend payment. Uliana (1988) found that owner-controlled companies pay out significantly lower percentages of earnings (average 25%) than either conglomerate-controlled companies (42%) or foreign-controlled companies (49%). Until March 1990, dividends were taxed in the hands of all but the lowest income earners in the economy (Ross, Westerfield, Jordan and Firer, 2001). The national budget of that year witnessed the elimination of tax on dividends. Then, in March 1993, the Secondary Tax on Companies (STC) was introduced, in terms of which a certain percentage of dividends, currently 12,5%, is payable as tax if a dividend is declared. The intention of STC was to increase profit retention in companies, thereby moderating dividend behaviour. Van Rensburg, Slaney and Hardy (1997) concluded that researchers that study the impact of dividends on share prices should guard against misrepresenting the economic timing of shareholder return. Bhana (1997) found that a significant increase in a company's share price follows an announcement of a share dividend and concluded that investors interpret share dividends to be an important signaling device. Bhana (1998) found that the announcement of special dividends conveys value-increasing information to the market and that the gains from this positive information accrue to shareholders. More recently, Auret and De Villiers (2000) determined that earnings per share (EPS) have greater explanatory power than dividends per share (DPS) in the interpretation of share prices. Wolmarans (2001) found that portfolio strategies that are based on earnings yield significantly outperform those that are based on dividend yield.

TAKE CASE OF TWENTY-SEVEN COMPANIES LISTED IN BSE SENSEX

The chapter using the dividend discount model, a sample of 27 firms across sectors. Firm's valuation using Dividend discount Model.

ANALYSIS

An analysis has been made on the 27 BSE companies. The dividend payout for 27 firms for the last 5 years is shown in the Fig. 1.

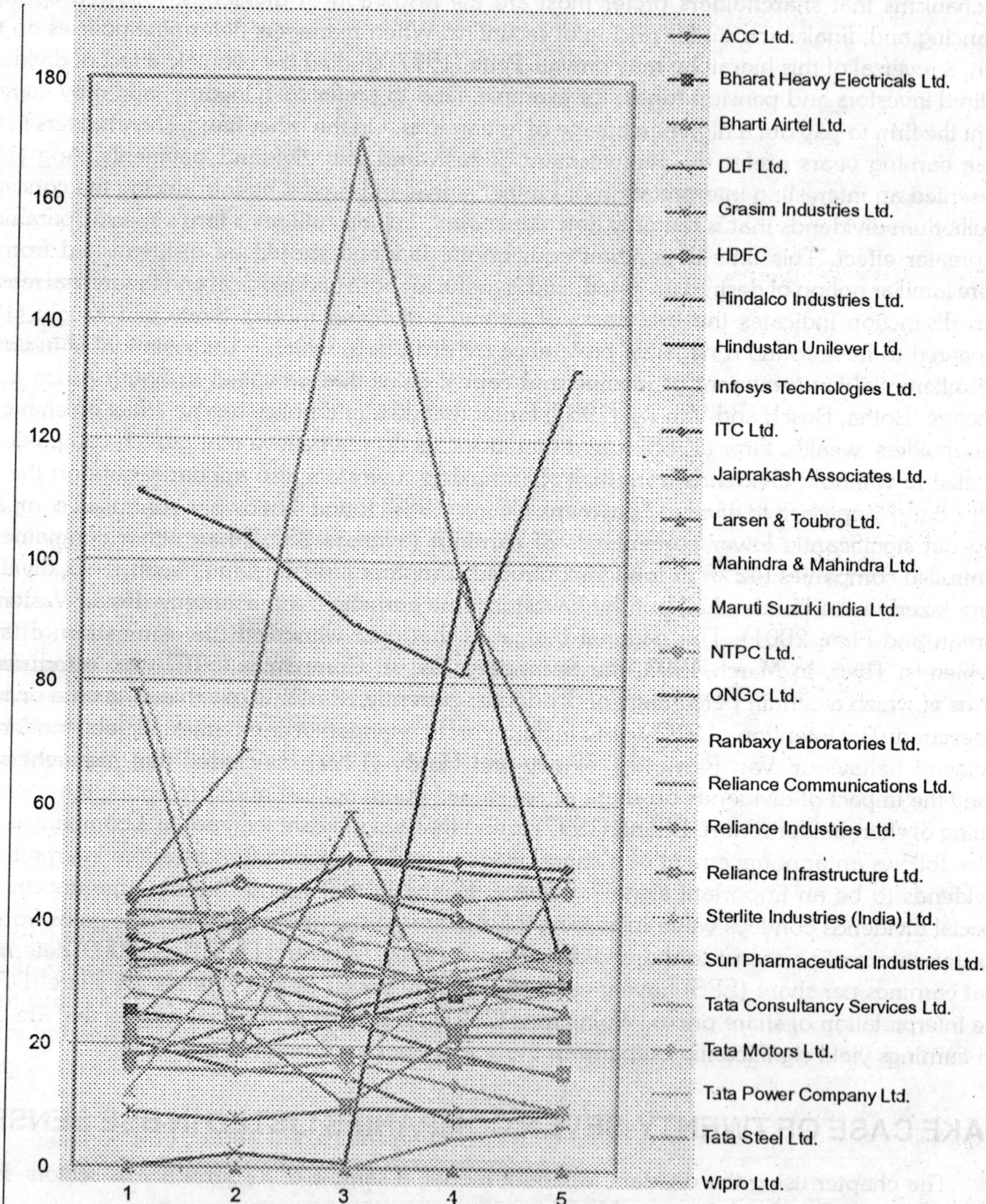

Fig. 1

A first look at the graph shows in Fig. 1 that the most of the firms maintain a fixed dividend payout ratio. Firms like Infosys Ltd., Ranbaxy, HLL and Wipro Ltd. show a considerable variation in dividend payout.

Based on Lintner's theorem, the dividend payout ratio of the current year is compared with the operating ratio in the current year and dividend payout of the last year.

Table 1

Regression Test Results for Lintner's Dividend Stability Test

Year	*2005*	*2006*	*2007*	*2008*
R Square	0.527599	0.580853	0.466759	0.512369
Dividend payout of last year	0.614864	1.187327	0.484797	0.723115
Operating margin of current year	0.016553	-0.12167	0.286691	-0.18014

As indicated Lintner's model test is significant for the firms in SENSEX and confirms the presence of a target dividend payout policy of firms. The Table 1 shows that the dividend payout of the company is fairly explained by dividend payout of the last year and operating margin of current year. Further, the Table 1 shows a strong positive correlation of dividend payout in the current year with the dividend payout in the last year. In the year 2006 and 2008, a negative values of operating margins in the current year shows that those companies paid a higher dividend despite of reduction in their operating margins. The R-square value of around 50% suggests that this model explained 50% variation in the dividend payout of a firm. This suggests that some variations which may be the consequence of biases introduced by unobserved effects on the dividend behavior. To summarize, the estimation of the Lintner model tested on BSE-Sensex listed firms accepts Lintner's hypothesis since dividend decisions are based on long-term target payout. There is a clear indication that firms in the BSE place a higher importance on last year's dividends payout to signal their future profitability or to minimize agency costs. Lintner's model states that the companies try to maintain a target dividend payout ratio. In this present analysis it is seen that the dividend payout in the last year is the major determinant of the dividend to be paid in the current year. To maintain the dividend payout, the companies paid dividend which is inversely proportional to the operating margin of the company.

The same result is also verified from the coefficient of variation of dividend payout of those 27 companies. The coefficient of variation represents the ratio of the standard deviation to the mean, and it is a useful statistic for comparing the degree of variation from one data series to another, even if the means are drastically different from each other. The coefficient of variation of the dividend payout ratio is shown in Table 2.

Table 2

Values of Coefficient of Variation for Dividend Payout for the Period 2004-2008 in Sensex

Name	*Coefficient of Variation*
ACC Ltd.	0.146000487
Bharat Heavy Electricals Ltd.	0.117648623

Bharti Airtel Ltd.	-
DLF Ltd.	1.593658565
Grasim Industries Ltd.	0.164682678
HDFC	0.117157889
Hindalco Industries Ltd.	0.376303002
Hindustan Unilever Ltd.	0.189670486
Infosys Technologies Ltd.	0.5718588
ITC Ltd.	0.157882597
Jaiprakash Associates Ltd.	0.278731364
Larsen & Toubro Limited	0.199345541
Mahindra & Mahindra Ltd.	0.064094724
Maruti Suzuki India Ltd.	0.094874317
NTPC Ltd.	0.238755131
ONGC Ltd.	0.049344738
Ranbaxy Laboratories Ltd.	0.566054484
Reliance Communications Ltd.	1.402111838
Reliance Industries Ltd.	0.204550482
Reliance Infrastructure Ltd.	0.105331035
Sterlite Industries (India) Ltd.	0.429545611
Sun Pharmaceutical Industries Ltd.	0.069242164
Tata Consultancy Services Ltd.	0.093860697
Tata Motors Ltd.	0.094900884
Tata Power Company Ltd.	0.012792978
Tata Steel Ltd.	0.100876458
Wipro Ltd.	0.51520116

Bharati Airtel didn't pay any dividend in those 5 years. A relatively high value in the coefficient of variation of DLF is explained by the fact that it didn't pay dividend in the year 2004 and hence the subsequent dividend lead to the jump in the standard deviation and hence the coefficient of variation. Similarly, Reliance Communications Ltd. which was founded in the year 2004 didn't pay any dividend in years 2004-2006. A list of dividend yield of all the 30 companies in the Sensex is given follows:

Table 3
Dividend Yield Value for the Firms in Sensex

Name	*Dividend yield*
Hindustan Unilever Ltd.	4.55
ACC Ltd.	3.96

ONGC Ltd.	3.92
Tata Motors Ltd.	3.67
Mahindra & Mahindra Ltd.	2.61
Tata Power Company Ltd.	2.26
Tata Steel Ltd.	2.22
State Bank of India	2.1
NTPC Ltd.	2.09
Infosys Technologies Ltd.	1.94
ITC Ltd.	1.91
Bharat Heavy Electricals Ltd.	1.81
ICICI Bank Ltd.	1.7
Ranbaxy Laboratories Ltd.	1.68
Tata Consultancy Services Ltd.	1.65
Grasim Industries Ltd.	1.57
Wipro Ltd.	1.44
HDFC	1.37
Sun Pharmaceutical Industries Ltd.	1.35
Hindalco Industries Ltd.	1.27
Sterlite Industries (India) Ltd.	1.08
HDFC Bank Ltd.	0.88
Maruti Suzuki India Ltd.	0.79
Reliance Infrastructure Ltd.	0.75
Larsen & Toubro Limited	0.64
Reliance Industries Ltd.	0.64
Jaiprakash Associates Ltd.	0.53
DLF Ltd.	0.51
Reliance Communications Ltd.	0.1
Bharti Airtel Ltd.	0.0

The regression analysis for the Lintner's model shows that dividend payout of last year and operating margin of current year explains 46% to 58% variation in the values of the dividend payout in the current year. It says that there are some other factors also which contribute in determination of dividend payout in the current year. Some other factors like debt to equity ratio of the firm, owner's fund in the company and the liquidity ratio (current ratio) also contributes in determination of this dividend payout. It is observed from the analysis that dividend and debt are direct substitutes. So, it is expected that degree of leverage will be negatively associated with dividend distribution in the BSE. It is also found that dividend policy relies upon a firm's earnings power so more profitable firms should pay more dividends in the BSE. Dividends do not reduce managerial discretion in a system where ownership is concentrated, such as in India. Hence, ownership concentration will have no impact on dividend payments in the BSE. It is also observed that dividend payment depends on the current liquidity position of the firm. Lintner's model states that the dividend payout is dependent on the last year's dividend made by the firm.

A theoretical relationship which can be established for the dividend payout with respect to those determinants can be represented as:

Table 4
Determinants of Dividend Payout for a Firm

Characteristics	*Variables*	*Predicted Relationship*
Profitability	Operating Margin	Positive relationship
Leverage ratio	Debt to Equity Ratio	Negative relationship
Ownership	Owner's Fund as % of total fund*	No impact
Liquidity Ratio	Current Ratio	Positive relationship
Maintenance of dividend	Last year's dividend	Positive relationship

Again this chapter tries to predict the relationship between dividend payout in the current year with 5 variables to find out how sensex behaves with respect to dividend payout. Again a regression analysis is done taking dividend payout of current year as dependent variable and operating margin, debt-equity ratio, owner's fund, current ratio and last year's dividend payout as independent variables.

Table 5
Regression Test Results for Determinants of Dividend Payout in Sensex for the Period 2004-2008

Year	*2005*	*2006*	*2007*	*2008*
R-Square	0.559187	0.584952	0.879061	0.653023
Operating Margin	-0.09925	-0.1914	-0.2214	-0.13297
Debt/Equity	3.226781	1.751368	11.81624	22.07673
Owners' Fund	-0.06949	0.174847	0.362683	0.909661
Current ratio	-1.14726	-0.01031	-3.57097	-2.86878
Dividend Payout last yr	0.644814	1.14525	0.537128	0.747162

The results are shown in Table 5 that there is some improvement in predication of dividend payout in the current year using those 3 extra independent variables. The improvement is significant in the year 2008 but in rest of the years it doesn't show any major improvements. Further, it shows a negative relationship with operating margin, positive relationship with debt to equity ratio, positive relation with owner's fund, negative relationship with current ratio and a positive relationship with the last year's dividend payout. This result contradicts the theoretical findings that dividend payout for a given year should be positively co-rrelated with the operating margin, negatively co-rrelated to debt-equity ratio and positively correlated to current ratio. This finding also suggests that since there is no major improvements in prediction of dividend payout in the current year compared to our prior results. The major reason behind this is the maintaining of a target dividend payout ratio of the managers of those firms. As already explained by Lintner's theory those companies try to maintain a target dividend payout. So, other factors like operating margin, owner's fund and debt-equity ratio doesn't matter much for those companies. The target dividend payout principal of those firms can be further explained by the graph of the dividend payout of those firms in the last 5 years. The regression result is further shows that last year's dividend payout plays a significant role in determining dividend payout for the current year. However, dividend policy in our sample is positively affected by owner's fund, which means that Indian firms pay more attention to please the owner's of the firm. This finding shows that the coefficient on ownership concentration is significant which supports the hypothesis that dividend payment is also used as a device to reduce agency costs in the BSE. Finally, the results indicate that stock market liquidity is negatively correlated with dividend payment, which is in accordance with Gonzalez's (2003) theoretical model. In fact, the introduction of an electronic quotation system in the BSE improved liquidity and thus facilitated capital gains that replaced somewhat dividend payments.

Again the study is made to identify the relationship between the marginal tax rate faced by the company and the dividend payout ratio of the company. In India, dividend income is free of tax to shareholders. Therefore, higher the marginal tax rate faced by the company, higher should be the dividend payout ratio. The companies in Sensex (30 companies) are analyzed to identify the relationship between the effective tax rate of the company and the dividend payout ratio.

Method Followed for Marginal Tax Rate and Dividend Payout Model

The effective tax is computed rate faced by using the operating margin, net profit margin and interest coverage ratio of the companies.

Net Profit Margin = Net Profit / Revenue

Operating Margin = Earnings before Interest and Tax / Revenue

Interest Coverage = Earnings before Interest and Tax / Interest

Operating Margin / Net Proft Margin (ON) = Earnings before Interest and Tax/Net Profit –[1]

[1] / Interest coverage ratio = Interest / Net Profit – [2]

[1] – [2] = (Earnings before interest and tax – Interest)/Net Profit –[3]

= (Net Profit + tax) / Net profit

1/[3] = Net Profit / (Net Profit + Tax) –[4]

1 – [4] = 1 – Net Profit/(Net Profit + Tax)

= Tax/(Net Profit + Tax)

= Effective Tax Rate

Table 6
The Sensex 30 Companies and their Dividend Payout Ratios in the Past 5 Years

Name	*2004*	*2005*	*2006*	*2007*	*2008*
ACC Ltd.	36.2	30.49	26	30.92	37.65
Bharat Heavy Electricals Ltd.	30.54	28.67	24.09	23.33	25.2
Bharti Airtel Ltd.	0	0	0	0	0
DLF Ltd.	30.99	98.3	0.77	2.34	0
Grasim Industries Ltd.	15.45	18.71	24.21	18.92	18.57
HDFC	34.1	41.46	45.26	46.58	44.09
Hindalco Industries Ltd.	9.27	7.88	14.93	15.94	20.51
Hindustan Unilever Ltd.	131.8	81.45	89.49	104.07	111.37
Infosys Technologies Ltd.	49.77	19.85	58.32	18.48	78.24
ITC Ltd.	49.45	50.53	50.76	40.29	35.08
Jaiprakash Associates Ltd.	21.99	21.91	10.34	23.22	17.57
Larsen & Toubro Limited	26.29	30.04	34.05	41.32	42.15
Mahindra & Mahindra Ltd.	29.1	30.39	32.45	33.54	33.79
Maruti Suzuki India Ltd.	9.78	9.72	9.69	7.73	9.02
NTPC Ltd.	45.53	44.11	45.23	38.69	23.3
ONGC Ltd.	47.94	48.85	50.7	49.91	44.55
Ranbaxy Laboratories Ltd.	60.06	94.95	170.28	68.3	44.8
Reliance Communications Limited	7	4.96	0	0	0
Reliance Industries Ltd.	9.8	13.75	17.52	15.73	15.98
Reliance Infrastructure Ltd.	15.93	17.68	18.37	19.01	21.25
Sterlite Industries (India) Ltd.	34.84	32.49	15.59	35.38	12.32
Sun Pharmaceutical Industries Ltd.	25.11	23.57	25.29	26	28.44
Tata Consultancy Services Limited	35.55	34.46	27.72	34.21	32.54
Tata Motors Ltd.	32.51	35.34	37.13	41.68	39.27
Tata Power Company Ltd.	30.84	31.6	31.41	30.81	30.73
Tata Steel Ltd.	29.39	26.15	23.39	23.64	23.83
Wipro Ltd.	33.47	35.2	40.23	26.83	83.23

The pattern of dividend payout of the past years is shown in the below Fig. 2.

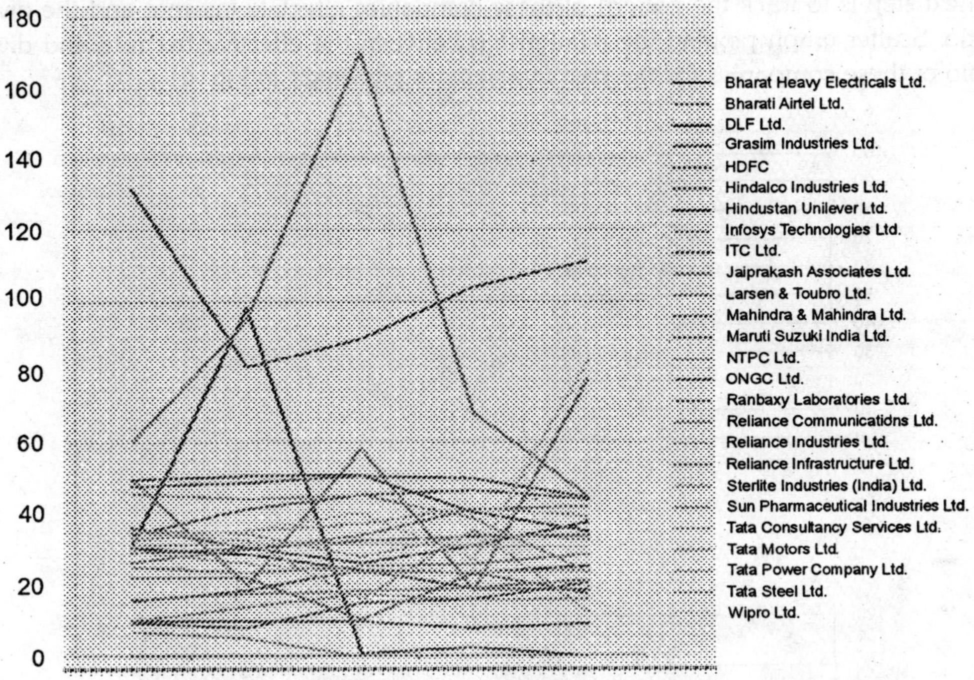

Fig. 2

It can be noted from above that some companies maintain more or less a constant dividend payout. We eliminate those companies and come out with companies which have a varying dividend payout ratio.

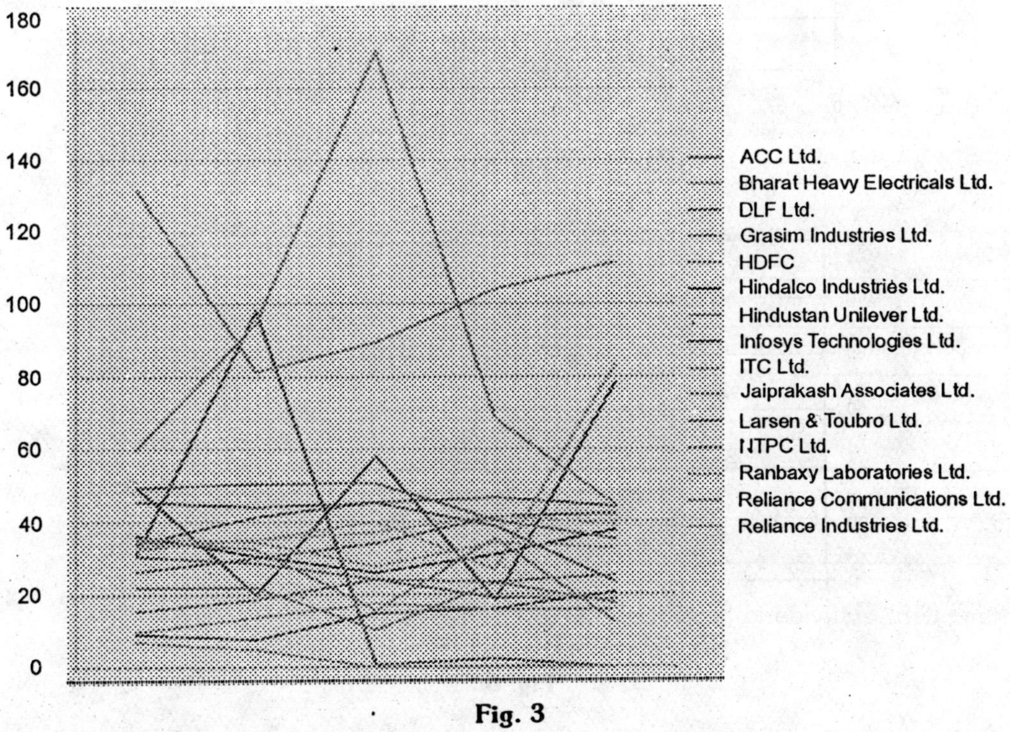

Fig. 3

The next step is to track the pattern of these companies effective tax rate and the dividend payout ratio. Scatter graph plotting the relationship between the effective tax rate and dividend payout ratio of these companies for the past five years is presented in Fig. 4.

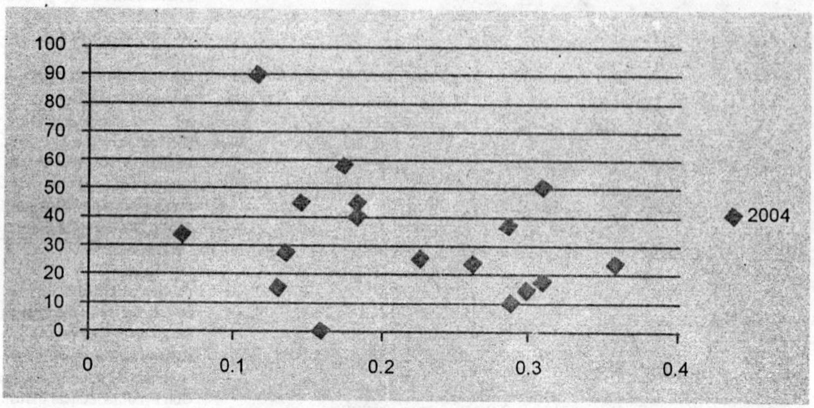

Fig. 4

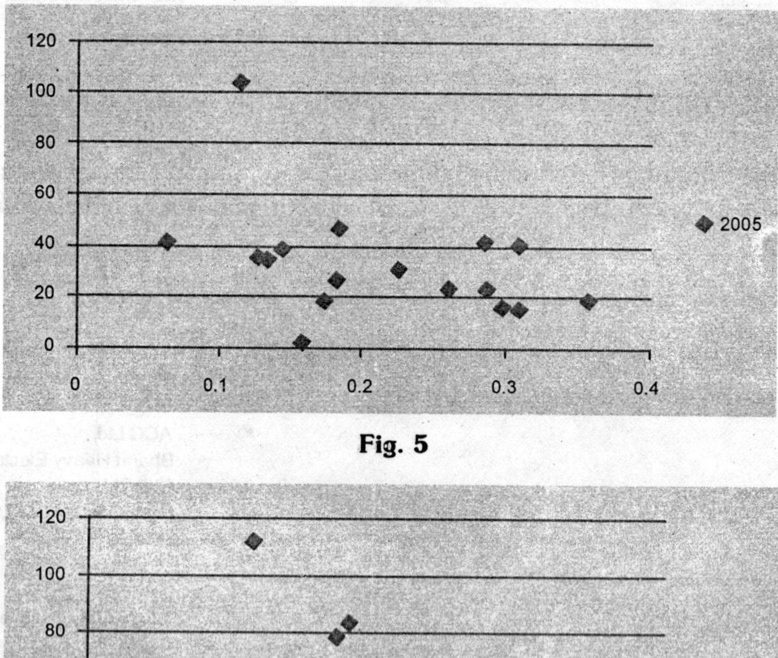

Fig. 5

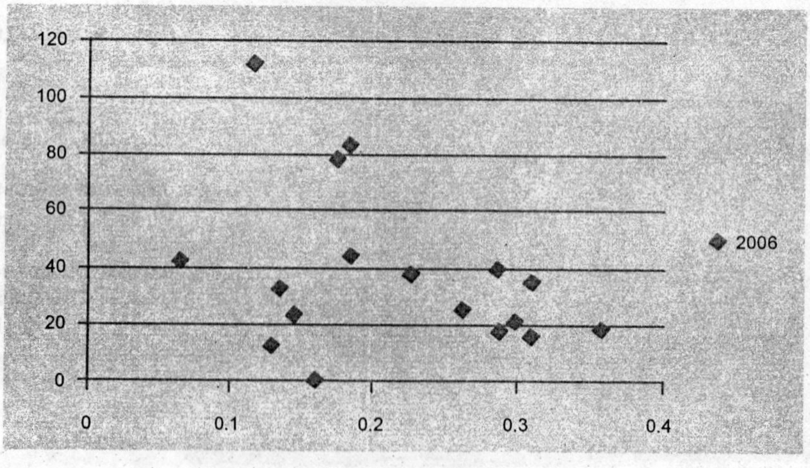

Fig. 6

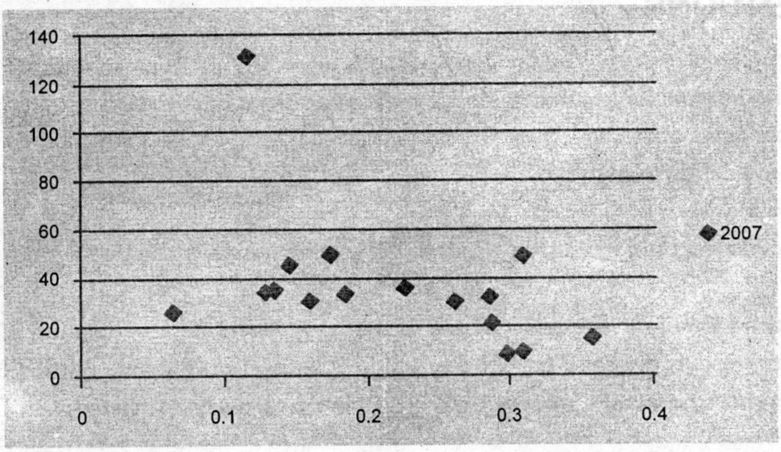

Fig. 7

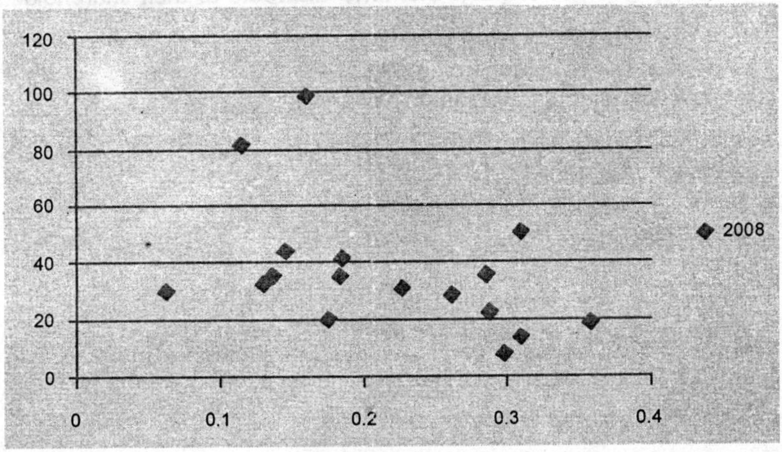

Fig. 8

All graphs show a clear downward sloping patter indicates that the companies which face a high marginal tax rate have less dividend payout ratio. So, it is inferred from the analysis that companies which already give out huge amounts of money as tax, are less willing to pay out high amount of dividends.

CONCLUDING OBSERVATION

Many researchers with different streams have worked on dividends and proposed several theories to explain dividend behavior. While many earlier studies pointed to the tax preference theory, many recent studies have emphasized rather signaling and agency cost hypotheses. However, the dividend set remains puzzling. Many questions are either still unanswered or answered in conflicting ways. The stock market's main game is making judgments about the earning potential of companies, which are subjective. It has been observed that the share price depends on the dividend policy of the firm. Hence, it requires time and efforts to research the stocks and ther monitor the performance.

REVIEW QUESTIONS

1. What is dividend policy? Why dividend policy is important for corporate firms?
2. Explain the relevance of Lintner's Model in dividend decision?
3. Write short notes on:
   (a) The dividend payout ratio
   (b) Signaling Models
   (c) Dividend discount model
4. Quiz
   (a) Dividend decision is closely related to the ______ and ______ decision of the company.
   (b) An increase in dividend payout has a ______ impact on the value of the firm.
   (c) A second community believes that ______ are negatively correlated with Dividend payout levels.
   (d) ______ hypothesis is an ad hoc combination of the signaling and agency costs paradigms.
   (e) ______ is the portion of earnings that firms distribute to their shareholders.

11

Indian Stock Market Reaction to Announcement of Bonus Issues

The chapter examines the stock market reaction to the information contain of bonus issues with a view to determine whether Indian market is semi-strong efficient or not. This chapter found support to the hypothesis that Indian stock market is semi-strong efficient.

INTRODUCTION

Firms announcing bonus experiences rise in their stock prices on an average supporting semi-strong form Efficient Market Hypothesis (EMH). EMH is highly debated issue among researchers and finance professionals. It is not only having implications for the investors but also for the financial managers. It is assumed that the semi-strong form efficiency leads the security prices to react immediately to any new information. Bonus issue announcements, should not lead to arbitrage opportunity as reserve, from which the bonus issue is announced, is believed to be reflected in price. The bonus announcement doesn't impact company's economic prospects. The interpretation of daily stock price reaction to announcement of bonus issue has documented significant market price reaction. So, it is a subject of interest for empirical discussion within the financial literature today.

WHAT ARE BONUS SHARES?

The term *bonus* means an extra dividend paid to shareholders in a company out of surplus profit. The directors decided to distribute a part of profit among the shareholders in the form of bonus either in cash or in the form of shares. Cash bonus is paid by the company when it has large accumulated profits as well as cash to pay dividend. Many a time, a company is not in a position to pay bonus in cash in spite of sufficient profits because of its adverse effects on the day to day cash position of the company. In such a position, the company pays a bonus to its shareholders in the form of shares known as a bonus share. Bonus shares are additional shares given without any cost to existing shareholders. So, a 5 for 1 bonus would mean you get five additional shares on free of cost for holding one share in the company. The issue of bonus shares increases the total number of shares of existing shareholders but it does not increase the value of the company. Although the total number of issued shares increases, the ratio of number of shares held by each shareholder remains constant. Bonus shares do not directly affect a company's performance. But share capital gets increased according to the bonus issue ratio because of bonus issue. Secondly, liquidity in the stock increases. Thirdly, Effective Earnings per share, Book Value and other per share values stand reduced. Fourthly, market price gets adjusted on issue of bonus shares and accumulated profits get reduced. A bonus issue adds to the total number of shares in the market and equity shares get diluted. Since the profits remain the same but the number of shares has increased, the EPS will decline. Hypothetically, the stock price should also reduce proportionately to the number of new shares. But, in reality, it may not happen. That's because the stock is now become more liquid and there are so many more shares available to buy and sell. Further, a bonus issue is a signal that the company is in a position to service its larger equity and it is regarded as a sign of the good health of the company. Whenever a company announces a bonus issue, it also announces a Book closure Date/Record Date. The record date is the date on which the bonus takes effect, and shareholders on that date are entitled to the bonus. It is the date after which the company will not handle any transfer of shares requests until the benefits are transferred. A company generally announces such a date along with the announcement of the bonus issue/splits/dividend announcement. After the announcement of the bonus but before the record date, the shares are referred to as cum-bonus. After the record date, when the bonus has been given effect, the shares become ex-bonus. There is not much difference between *bonus issue and stock split*. When a bonus issue is made, the company's share capital is increased with a related decrease in its Reserves and Surplus. But when a share is split, say, from ₹ 10 denomination to Re. 1 denomination, there would neither be an increase in the share capital nor simultaneous decrease in the reserves of the company. Stock split may, therefore, become visible to be more deceptive than bonus issue. But it does make the shares more inexpensive in the market. In an efficient market as per the efficient market hypothesis (EMH), the effect of the price change due to bonus issue or splits or dividend as on the Book Closure date gets adjusted in the price of the stock in the market effective with the opening of the trade floor on the book closure date.

HOW DOES A STOCK'S PRICE CHANGE AFTER A BONUS ANNOUNCEMENT?

Let's take an example: The record date for Max Labs' 5 for 1 bonus was January 13, 2009. At the time, the stock price was around ₹ 2,110. Ex-bonus, the stock adjusted to ₹ 352. ₹ 352 is ₹ 2,110 divided by 6, which is entirely appropriate because there are now 6 stocks where there used to be 1. Usually, bonus shares are issued with the intent of rewarding the investor. Although it is having said that the ex-bonus (post bonus) price of the share is adjusted to bonus ratio. So if the price of a share before bonus is ₹ 100 and a bonus of 1:1 is issued, then ex-bonus share price would adjust to ₹ 50, which means that the total market value will remain the same. There is generally a case where the price of the share increases after bonus effect is incorporated. The main financial effect of bonus share is that it increases the number of shares outstanding and reduces the earnings per share (EPS).

LITERATURE REVIEW

Ball and Brown (1992) found earnings information of the companies effect the share prices. The better than the expected earnings is increased the share price and the worse decrease the share price. The interesting result was that about 85% of the informational content of the annual earnings announcements were reflected in the stock price prior to the release of the actual annual earnings figure indicating insider information and inefficiency. A Canadian study by Masse *et al.* (1997) investigated the impact of stock dividend announcements on the value of firms listed on the Toronto Stock Exchange, acknowledged significant and positive abnormal returns around the announcement date. As mentioned earlier, issue of bonus is merely an accounting entry of transfer from free reserves to share capital and does not have any real impact on company future earnings. However, it does have a signaling effect about company's ability in future to maintain same or better earnings per share on enhanced no. of outstanding share. Rankine and Stice (1997) confirms the positive signaling value of stock dividends by documentation that for the stock distribution of the same size, those accounted for as stock dividends and associated with a significant larger announcement negative return than those accounted for as stock splits. Frank and Jagannathan (1998) and Bali and Hite (1998) analyze stock returns on the ex-dividend day for US and Hong Kong firms, respectively. Both studies develop models of investor behavior which are based on microstructure arguments and report positive abnormal returns consistent with such arguments. A few studies have been carried out in recent years to test the semi-strong form of the efficiency in the Indian stock market. Ramachandran (1985) studied the impact of the announcements of the bonus issues on equity stock prices and found mixed evidences of the semi-strong form of the efficiency of the Indian stock market. Obaidullah (1992) observed positive stock market reaction to the equity bonus announcements. He found evidence to support the semi-strong form of the EMH. Srinivasan (2002), found the extremely large positive abnormal returns on ex-bonus and ex-right dates for the equity stocks. Rao (1994) estimated the cumulative abnormal returns of 6.31% around the three days of the announcement day. He reported that the Indian stock market responds in an expected direction to corporate announcements and it supported the semi-strong form of the EMH for the Indian stock market. Budhraja I., Parekh P. and Singh T. (2004) confirms that abnormal returns in stock prices around the bonus issue announcement date over three-day trading period starting one day before the announcement is significant at 95% confidence limit. Their study on BSE listed stocks also further say that much of the information in the bonus announcement gets impounded into stock by the time of the announcement of the bonus issue, refute the strong form of EMH and signal trading on insider information. Mishra (2005) discussed the market reaction around the bonus issue announcements and found that on an average, the stock starts showing positive abnormal returns eight to nine days before the announcement date. This study also supports the signaling hypothesis consistent with the findings in the United States, Sweden, Canada, and New Zealand.

The effect of the information of the bonus issue announcement is found mixed. Many researchers have conducted the empirical tests to challenge the Efficient Market Hypothesis.

TAKE CASE OF 30 PUBLICLY LISTED COMPANIES OF NSE TO FIND OUT THE ANNOUNCEMENT EFFECTS OF BONUS ISSUES ON STOCK PRICES

This chapter analyses stock bonus issue announcements made during the years 2004 and 2005. Following criteria have been considered to select the bonus issue announcement as an eligible one for the sample:

- The bonus issue announcement date is the date on which the stock exchange that is National Stock Exchange of India Ltd. is informed that the bonus issue is recommended by the Board of Directors.
- The bonus issue had to be an issue of new fully paid ordinary shares which costs nothing to shareholders and not issued with a rights issue or bonus option issue.
- The bonus must have not been issued in part or whole as a consideration in a merger or reconstruction or acquisition.
- There shouldn't be any cash dividend announcement along with the bonus issue announcements.

This chapter tests the following hypothesis:

* Here are no significant abnormal returns around bonus announcement date.
* Bonus issues do not increase liquidity of Indian stock markets.

In order to ascertain the influence of company/industry-specific information on the returns of individual portfolio, it needed a means of adjusting the changes in the stock market movements as a while without which, it was not possible to distinguish between price changes that were due to a security's co-movement with the overall market and changes caused by the arrival of new information about a company or industry. Fortunately, the market provides a convenient means of making this adjustment. The returns on security "i" in period "t", "R_{it}" can be seen as being equal to the expected return plan an unexpected element. Algebraically, this is summarized in the following relationship.

Return on security "i" in period "t" is given by:

$$R_{it} = I_n (P_{it} / P_{it-1})$$

The announcement effect on the stock price is measured by the standard market model event study methodology. The model describes the linear relationship between the return of the security to the return of the market portfolio. The impact on market price due to bonus announcement is estimated by the difference between the realized post-announcement period return and the return predicted by the market model.

The closing prices of the sampled stock were considered to arrive at daily returns for 20 days before and after the announcement of the bonus issue. Hence, the total event window considered for the bonus issue is 20 days before and after the announcements. If the announcement date is denoted to be **t=0**, 20 days before the announcement is **t-20** and 20 days after the announcement date is **t+20**.

Abnormal Returns:

The abnormal return has been calculated for each stock on a daily basis by subtracting expected return from the actual return. Abnormal return for each day is consolidated for all companies and average abnormal return is calculated. Market model Abnormal Return (AR) for the "i[th]" firm on day "t" given by

$$AR_{it} = R_{it} - (\alpha_1 - \beta_1 R_{mt})$$

Where α_1 and β_1 are the estimated coefficients

$$\alpha_1 = \bar{r}_i - \beta_i \bar{r}m$$

$$\beta_1 = cov(r_i, r_m / var(r_m))$$

The parameters α_1, and β_1 have been estimated from the following OLS regression of the event firm's returns on the index returns during the estimation period for firm i.

$$R_{it} = \alpha_i + \beta_i R_{mt} + e_{it}$$

Where

R_{it} is the rate return of the stock i on the day T .

R_{mt} is the rate of return of the market index (m) on the day T.

e_{it} is the error term of the stock is on the day T, having zero mean $\sigma^r e_i$ variance. Under the assumption of joint normality and independently and identically distributed returns, the error of the regression is well behaved, i.e.,

E (e_{it}) = 0 and VAR (e_{it}) = $\sigma^r e_i$

The cumulative effect of the event over a specified number of days is determined by calculating cumulative average abnormal returns or CAARs.

CAAR = ΣAAR_t

Where AAR_t = average abnormal return for each time period

$$AAR_t = \frac{1}{N}\sum_{i=1} AR_{it}$$

i = 1

Where N = Number of Securities studies, t is defined in trading days relative to the event day and ARR_t denotes the average of the abnormal return crossing events.

Again the traditional t-statistics for each daily reform AAR_t have been computed. "t" test is applied to test the hypothesis. The t-test tests weather the mean of a normally distributed population has a value, specified in a null hypothesis.

$$SAR_{it} = \frac{AR_{it}}{\sigma_{ei}} \sim t(k_{1-2})$$

Where SAR_{it} is the maximum likelihood estimate of the variance of AR_{it} and

$$\sigma_{ei} = \sqrt{\frac{\sum_{t=1}^{k}(AR_t)^2}{k}} \times \sqrt{1+\frac{1}{k}+\frac{(R_{mt}-R_m)^2}{\sum_{t=1}^{k}(R_{mt}-R_m)^2}}$$

Where R_{mt} and R_m are the return and mean return on the market during the k-day estimation period.

The Total Standardized Abnormal Return ($TSAR_t$)

$$TSAR_t = \sum_{i=1}^{N} SAR_{it}$$

The individual prediction errors are assumed to be cross sectionally independent and distributed normally, so standardized prediction error has a student t-distribution.

ANALYSIS

Table 1 presents the results of event study of 30 publicly listed companies' bonus issues announcement.

Table 1
Average Abnormal Returns and Cumulative Abnormal Returns around Announcement of Bonus Issues of Sample Company

Event Day	*ARR*	*CARR*	*t-Test*
-20	0.04523	0.04523	1.183**
-19	0.04255	0.08778	1.403
-18	0.03695	0.12473	1.860**
-17	0.03498	0.15971	1 .753**
-16	0.03003	0.18974	1.872**
-15	0.00828	0.19802	1.770**
-14	-0.00992	0.18810	1.464
-13	0.00469	0.19279	1.281
-12	0.00972	0.20251	1.159
-11	0.04832	0.25083	1.453
-10	-0.00121	0.24962	1.594
-9	0.00015	0.24977	1.645
-8	0.00351	0.25328	1.842**

-7	-0.01036	0.24292	1.835**
-6	-0.01330	0.22962	1.792**
-5	-0.27008	-0.04046	1.548
-4	-0.01810	-0.05856	1.518
-3	-0.01668	-0.07524	1.764**
-2	-0.38496	-0.46020	2.022*
-1	-0.41460	-0.87480	2.056*
0	35	-0.85645	-0.473
1	0.01859	-0.83786	-0.403
2	0.01759	-0.82027	-0.295
3	0.30575	-0.51452	-0.376
4	0.01789	-0.49663	-0.553
5	0.00225	-0.49438	-0.513
6	0.02591	-0.46847	-0.184
7	0.01969	-0.44878	-0.574
8	0.02250	-0.42628	-0.418
9	0.02482	-0.40146	-0.477
10	0.02259	-0.37887	-0.436
11	0.00498	-0.37389	-0.574
12	0.01770	-0.35619	-0.828
13	0.02530	-0.33089	-0.926
14	0.02371	-0.30718	-1.208
15	0.02148	-0.28570	-1.223
16	0.02437	-0.26133	-1.126
17	0.02402	-0.23731	-1.111
18	0.02687	-0.21044	-1.281
19	0.02640	-0.18404	-1.595
20	0.02356	-0.16048	-1.631

** Significant at 10% level

* Significant at 5% level

It is evident from the table that most of the values of CAAR are negative both before and after the day of announcement. However before the announcement, it shows somewhat positive return but it continues stayed negative till the announcement. All AARs after the announcement day are statistically insignificant at any conventional level by applying traditional t-statistics. On the announcement day onwards, AAR shows positive returns which implies that there was leakage of information, substantial before the event. It is also found from the analysis that pre-event announcement have positive CAAR and is significant on $t_{-20}t_{-18\,t-17\,t-16,\,t-15,\,t-8,t-7\,t-6\,t-3,t-1}$ etc. If the information related to the event leaks out prior to the announcement, the CAAR will gradually increase in the day prior to the announcement and then decrease on the day of the announcement, reflecting the response of those stocks for which information did not leak out. So, it appears to be no announcement affect associated with bonus announcement in India. However, it is evident from the analysis that there is no chance of gaining any abnormal return based on this event.

The results indicate that bonus issue announcements do not provide any significant opportunity to arbitrage in Indian market. It is assumed that there is clear indication of an insider trading in some of those stocks.

Table 2
Average Abnormal Returns and Cumulative Abnormal Returns around Announcement of Record Date Event of Sample Company

Event Day	*ARR*	*CARR*	*t-test*
-20	0.01318	0.01318	1.01
-19	0.014882	0.028061	0.974
-18	0.01937	0.047431	1.052
-17	0.013803	0.061234	1.138
-16	0.016042	0.077276	1.178
-15	0.022083	0.099359	1.244
-14	0.024466	0.123824	1.294
-13	0.023079	0.146903	1.392
-12	0.026142	0.173045	1.272
-11	0.026151	0.199195	1.188
-10	0.023561	0.222757	1.064
-9	0.021714	0.24447	1.095
-8	0.018413	0.262883	1.267
-7	0.021934	0.284818	1.274
-6	0.024528	0.309346	1.178
-5	0.019384	0.32873	1.113
-4	0.020631	0.34936	0.962
-3	0.021523	0.370883	0.891
-2	0.021202	0.392085	0.671
-1	0.022378	0.414463	0.663
0	0.02367	0.438133	0.71
1	0.025747	0.46388	1.248
2	0.023228	0.487108	1.079
3	0.025747	0.512855	1.055

4	0.028388	0.541243	1.183
5	0.03887	0.580113	1.29
6	0.040388	0.620501	1.179
7	0.03854	0.659041	1.16
8	0.039405	0.698446	1.052
9	0.04039	0.738836	1.139
10	0.037844	0.77668	1.083
11	0.0371	0.81378	1.133
12	0.037718	0.851498	1.022
13	0.039513	0.891012	1.084
14	0.044154	0.935166	1.023
15	0.04302	0.978186	0.997
16	0.040692	1.018878	1.033
17	0.036139	1.055017	1.014
18	0.036608	1.091625	1.042
19	0.036517	1.128142	1.059
20	0.036029	1.164171	0.937

This chapter has also been taken to review the status of the market efficiency in the case of record date for the bonus issue as an event. But as an event, record date is a day before which an investor can make fresh purchase of shares of a company announcing bonus issue and being shareholder has right to get bonus shares. It has been found in the literature that there may be signaling effect behind announcing bonus issue. Bonus issue may be considered to be an indication of healthy and sound financial position of the company as hypothesized in Signaling Effect Theory.

It is found from the analysis that all company has shown positive return. But the study does not find any underlying logic related to bonus issue. It can be assumed that there can be altogether a different set of information available after the record date. On the basis of this information there can be increased interest in the stocks of the respective companies.

Further analysis of liquidity is also as a factor affecting the efficiency of the market. Liquidity is the lagging indicator of the fact that information has come into the market. Low level of the liquidity enables the players having higher investment capacity to take advantage against of the participants having lower investment capacity. Thus, the lower liquidity of the market adds to the inefficiency of the market. The Table 3 reveals that almost all the companies have shown the decrease in the volume of trading. Out of total 30 companies, only 6 companies have shown increase in the volume of trading of their stocks. The liquidity has decreased by on an average by 76%. So, it is to believe that bonus issue announcement affects the liquidity to decrease. The underlying logic could be leakage of the information of the bonus issue announcement.

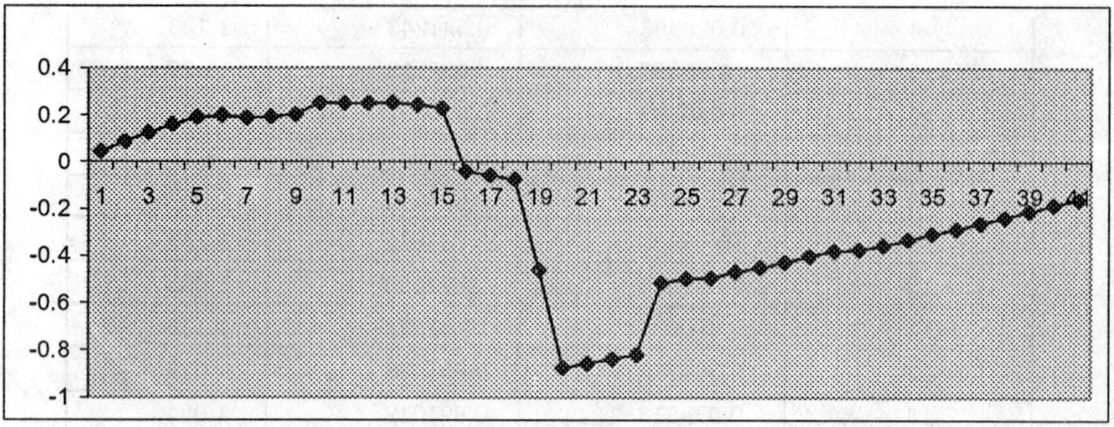

Fig. 1: CAAR for Bonus Announcement of Sample Company

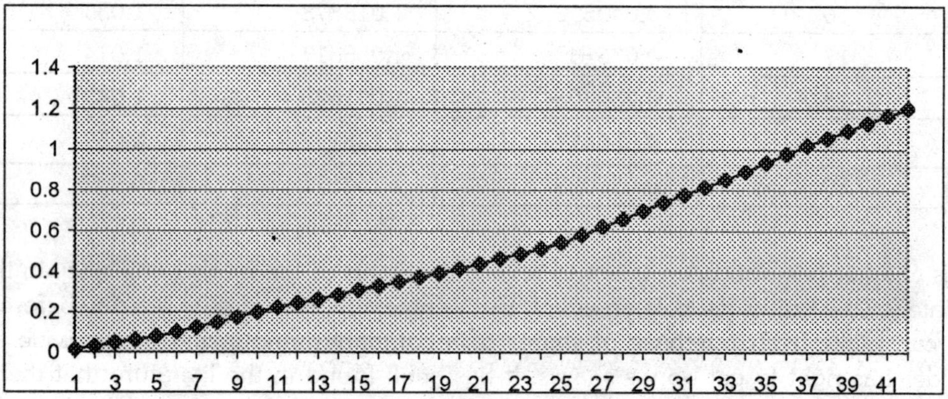

Fig 2: CAAR for Record Event of Sample Company

Table 3
Liquidity in the Stocks with Bonus Issue Announcement

Name of the Company	*Avg no. of shares before announcement*	*Avg no. of share after announcement*	*Change %*
Aarti Industries Ltd.	322429	137939	-133.75
Aftek Infosys Ltd.	408479	227414	-79.62
Asahi India Ltd.	77684	87827	11.55
Alembic Ltd.	17370	29151	40.41
Berger Paints Ltd.	21279	12880	-65.21
Cranes Software Int .Ltd.	7465	4860	-53.60
DCM Shriram Consolidated Ltd.	24118	17026	-41.65
Federal Bank Ltd.	220969	220591	-0.17
Goodlass Nerolac Paints	5513	5573	1.08

Gujarat Ambuja Cement	674275	364500	-84.99
Gujarat NRE Coke Ltd.	857374	333361	-157.19
Helios & Matheson	373610	84464	-342.33
Hevells India Ltd.	68113	56578	-20.39
Hindustan Sanitary & Ind.	28802	8511	-238.41
Hi-tech Gears Ltd.	15018	3975	-277.81
Infosys Technologies Ltd.	493505	397866	-24.04
Kotak Bank	165471	84223	-96.47
Liberty Shoes Ltd.	103216	42313	-143.93
Mahindra & Mahindra Ltd.	591417	515478	-14.73
Mahavir Spinning Mills	34851	25320	-37.64
Motherson Sumi Systems	256972	82902	-209.97
Mphasis BFL	77802	282469	72.46
Opto Circuits Ltd.	89367	75658	-15.34
Orchid Chemicals	463880	217060	-113.71
Sah Petroleum Ltd.	789916	203182	-288.77
Sesa Goa Ltd.	460155	269904	-70.49
Swaraj Engines Ltd.	4992	22221	77.53
Vishal Exports Overseas	2241338	3318848	32.47
Zodiac Clothing Ltd.	6272	4942	-26.91
Wipro	661236	561333	-17.80
Average Turnover Change	-	-	-76.80

Table 4
Announcement and Record Dates for the Companies Announcing Bonus Issue (Considering the Years 2004 and 2005)

Name of the Company	*Announcement Date*	*Record Date*
Aarti Industries	29/12/2004	10/2/2005
Aftek Infosys	29/11/2004	28/1/2005
Asahi India Glass Ltd.	24/05/2005	2/9/2005
Cranes Software International Ltd.	22/08/2005	11/11/2005
DCM Shriram Consolidated Ltd.	08/09/2005	5/10/2005
Gujarat Ambuja Cement Ltd	20/04/2005	25/06/2005
Gujarat NRE Coke Ltd.	09/11/2005	10/2/2005
Hewells India Ltd.	12/05/2005	6/8/2005
Helios and Matheson	25/07/2005	29/9/2005

Hindustan Sanitary and Industries Ltd.	29/10/2004	6/1/2005
Hi-Tech Gears Ltd.	24/01/2005	17/3/2005
Kotak Mahindra Bank Ltd.	07/06/2005	26/8/2005
Liberty Shoes Ltd.	18/07/2005	14/10/2005
Mahindra and Mahindra Ltd.	14/06/2005	2/9/2005
Mahavir Spinning Mills Ltd.	17/06/2005	16/9/2005
Motherson Sumi Systems Ltd.	07/01/2005	26/2/2005
Mphasis BFL Ltd.	12/04/2005	14/11/2005
Opto Circuits India ltd.	09/05/2005	17/8/2005
Orchid Chemicals and Pharmaceuticals Ltd.	18/07/2005	17/9/2005
Sah Petroleum Ltd.	22/08/2005	21/10/2005
Sesa Goa Ltd.	17/12/2004	17/02/2005
Swaraj Engines Ltd.	17/06/2005	16/08/2005
Vishal Export Overseas Ltd.	14/06/2005	26/08/2005
Wipro Technologies Ltd.	22/04/2005	23/8/2005
Zodiac Clothing Company	13/04/2004	25/10/2005
Infosys Technology	05/07/2005	02/07/2005
Alembic Ltd.	12/2/2004	27/03/2005
Berger Paints Ltd.	4/2/2004	25/3/2004
The Federal Bank	7/6/2004	30/11/2004
Goodlass Nerolac Paints Ltd.	30/4/2004	16/8/2004

CONCLUDING OBSERVATION

The present chapter analyzed the market reaction of stock prices around announcement of bonus issues of India by taking sample of thirty publicly listed companies. This chapter used the event study methodology to study the accuracy of stock price reaction to bonus issues announcement. It is found from the analysis that on an average many stocks showing positive abnormal return before the announcement date. It is assumed that this may be due to leakage of information. The study also reveals that CAAR is negative on the announcement date. Apart from this, the study also reviews the market efficiency with respect to record data but does not find any underlying logic related to bonus issues. This chapter also reveals that liquidity of the market around the bonus issue announcement has shown 76 per cent decrease in the volume on the basis of number of shares traded. This chapter found support to the hypothesis that Indian stock market is semi-strong efficient.

REVIEW QUESTIONS

1. What are Bonus shares? How does stock price change after bonus announcements?
2. How do you determine the efficiency of Stock market after bonus announcement?

3. What is abnormal return? How do you determine it?
4. What is event study methodology?
5. Quiz
   a. ______ means an extra dividend paid to shareholders in a company out of surplus profit.
   b. Bonus shares are ______ shares given without any cost to existing shareholders.
   c. ______ is the date on which the bonus takes effect, and shareholders on that date are entitled to the bonus.
   d. After the record date, when the bonus has been given effect, the shares become______.
   e. The abnormal return has been calculated for each stock on a daily basis by subtracting ______from the ______.

12

GDR Market in India

This chapter explains the relationship between GDR price and Domestic price to encourage Indian companies to integrate with global market. It also highlights the significance of the difference of variance in average GDR price and average domestic price to tap the international capital market with greater confidence and resource strength.

INTRODUCTION

The structure of global equity markets has changed considerably over the past few decades. The technological progress and the liberalization of capital flows have lowered the barriers that insulated national markets from each other. The segmentation of markets that results from these barriers is creating incentives for corporate managers to adopt financial policies such as international cross-listing, whereby a firm lists its shares for trading on at least two stock exchanges located in different countries. Since 1991, India has introduced major reforms to improve the efficiency of resources allocation and expand the productive capacity of the economy. An important element of the financial reform policy is the encouragement to the flow of foreign capital for the promotion of new units and financing the increasing capital requirements of the existing units. The inflow of foreign funds with entry of foreign institutional investors (FII) has changed the approach of performance of the Indian stock market. Moreover, it has forged an important linkage between the capital and the forex markets. During this phase, investment norms for non-resident Indians (NRIs), persons of Indian origin (PIOs) and overseas corporate bodies (OCBs) have been largely liberalized. An integration of world financial market has been the distinct feature of the recent global development. There is a remarkable change in the GDRs. Further, the Indian corporate have been allowed to tap the global market with global depository receipt (GDR), American depository receipt (ADR) and foreign currency convertible bond (FCCB) since 1993.

The capital market has become very active and Financial Institutions (FIs), Foreign Investment banks, Asset management companies have shown increasing interest in investing in India. What a view to achieve the goal, Euro-issue is taken as one of the viable alternatives. GDR is envisaged as an innovative and easily accessible route to reach the international capital market by Indian corporate sector. The response of foreign investment flows to reforms was a great encouraging. The total flows of foreign investment direct and portfolio is depicted in the Table-1. It clearly shows that the size of euro-issues has grown tremendously just after new economy policy measures announced.

Table 1

Foreign Investment Inflows

Year	*A. Direct investment*		*B. Portfolio investment*		*Total (A+B)*	
	Rupees crore	*US $ million*	*Rupees crore*	*US $ million*	*Rupees crore*	*US $ million*
1991-92	316	129	10	4	326	133
1992-93	965	315	748	244	1713	559
1993-94	1838	586	11188	3567	13026	4153
1994-95	4126	1314	12007	3824	16133	5138
1995-96	7172	2144	9192	2748	16364	4892
1996-97	10015	2821	11758	3312	21773	6133
1997-98	13220	3557	6794	1828	20014	5385
1998-99	10358	2462	-257	-61	10101	2401
1999-00	9338	2155	13112	3026	22450	5181
2000-01	18406	4029	12609	2760	31015	6789
2001-02	29235	6130	9639	2021	38874	8151
2002-03	24367	5035	4738	979	29105	6014
2003-04	19860	4322	52279	11377	72139	15699
2004-05	27188	6051	41854	9315	69042	15366
2005-06	39674	8961	55307	12492	94981	21453
2006-07	103367	22826	31713	7003	135080	29829
2007-08	140180	34835	109741	27271	249921	62106
2008-09	161536	35180	-63618	-13855	97918	21325
2009-10	176304	37182	153511	32375	329815	69557

Data for 2008-09 and 2009-10 are provisional.

Source: Handbook of Statistics on Indian Economy 2009-10

THE RATIONALE FOR CROSS-BORDER LISTINGS

It is generally believed that increased marketability of a firm's securities is the main benefit of pursuing cross-listing, while compliance with foreign reporting requirements is cited as a major cost. But however, it is always noticed that net benefits of cross-listing is positive, although not necessarily substantial.

- Cross-border listings have gained in importance over the past few decades as many companies have become more international in their orientation. As well, technological progress and the liberalization of capital flows have fostered considerable competition among global stock exchanges for equity listings and trades.
- The geography of cross-border listings has changed considerably since the mid-1980s, with US exchanges attracting an increasing share of cross-listed firms.
- Empirical studies suggest that the cost of equity capital generally declines following a foreign listing. This can be explained by a decline in transactions costs or by an improvement in the quality and quantity of firm-specific information available to investors.
- Informational asymmetries across countries prevent simultaneous price discovery on foreign exchanges.
- Improve the liquidity of its existing shares and support a liquid secondary market for new equity issues in foreign markets.
- Increase its share price by overcoming mispricing in a segmented and illiquid home capital market.
- Increase the firm's visibility and political acceptance to its customers, suppliers, creditors, and host governments.
- Establish a secondary market for shares used to acquire other firms in the host markets.
- Create a secondary market for shares that can be used to compensate local management and employees in foreign subsidiaries – in case company has foreign subsidiaries and wishes to use stock options and share purchase compensation plans for local management and employees, cross-listing should reduce transaction and foreign exchange costs for the local beneficiaries.

ADVANTAGES OF CROSS-LISTING AND ISSUING OF GDR/ADR

The advantages of cross-listing on foreign exchanges and issuing of GDR/ADR in foreign market are an accessible and attractive market for both international issuers and investors. It has many advantages to offer companies seeking to raise capital and to claim a greater share of the attention of international investors worldwide. The advantages of cross-border listings include an enlarged investor base, increased marketability of firm's securities, enhanced local market trading for shares, and the opportunity to raise new capital. These benefits include:

- Access to the world's largest pool of international investment capital.
- Strong international outlook.
- Experienced international investors, across a wide range of industry sectors.
- The world's most liquid and active secondary market in international equities.
- Worldwide visibility for international companies.
- Worldwide dissemination of corporate news via the Exchange's Regulatory News Service which is carried by major international news vendors around the world.

- A flexible and cost-effective means of raising capital.
- High and well-respected standards of regulation.
- Arrangement of products — equities, depository receipts and debt issues — to meet the varied capital raising requirements of different issuers.
- The ability to list securities in a range of currencies, including the yen and euro.
- It can help introduce a company to the international investment community, or serve to strengthen existing ties with global investors. It confirms to the world that the company is a truly global and well-managed business, and increases investor interest and confidence. As a result, a cross-listing or issuing of GDR/ADR has the potential to enhance both the day-by-day trading in an Indian company's shares, and its ongoing corporate funding opportunities.
- They are a very valuable source of capital, particularly as they tend to take a longer-term view on companies, thus providing greater stability — especially in volatile market conditions.

WHAT ARE DEPOSITORY RECEIPTS?

A depositary receipt (DR) is a type of negotiable (transferable) financial security that is traded on a local stock exchange. It represents a security, usually in the form of equity, which is issued by a foreign publicly-listed company. The DR, which is a physical certificate, allows investors to hold shares in equity of other countries. One of the most common types of DRs is the American depositary receipt (ADR), which has been offering to companies, investors and traders and provides global investment opportunities since the 1920s.

An American Depositary Share ("ADS") is a dollar denominated form of equity ownership in a non-US company. It represents the foreign shares of the company held on deposit by a custodian bank in the company's home country and carries the corporate and economic rights of the foreign shares, subject to the terms specified on the ADR certificate. ADRs provide US investors with a convenient way to invest in non-US securities without having to worry about the complex details of cross-border transactions. It offer the same economic benefits enjoyed by the domestic shareholders of the non-US company. ADRs are issued by depositary bank. A specific number or fraction of shares in the-non-US Company backs each ADR. ADRs can be listed on any of the US exchanges, such as the NYSE and the AMEX, and may be quoted for trading on the NASDAQ. They can also be privately placed and traded as Rule 144A securities.(Rule 144A was implemented in order to induce foreign companies to sell securities in the US capital markets. The objective of Rule 144A is to increase the liquidity and efficiency of the US equity and debt markets for securities issued in private placements. Thus, large institutional investors are able to trade restricted securities more freely with other institutional investors without registering the trade with the SEC. The rule was designed to develop a more liquid and efficient institutional resale market for unregistered securities.)

The concept of the ADR has been extended to other geographical markets, resulting in structures known as GDRs, International depositary receipts (IDRs), and European depositary receipts (EDRs), which are generally traded or listed in one or more international markets.

Companies, across the world are increasingly tapping international markets to enhance their global presence and raise capital at competitive rates abroad. Further, with increasing globalisation, and diversification of business across the globe, companies are seeking listings in international markets in order to enhance their profile. At the same time, investors around the world are looking across their national borders to take advantage of new opportunities for capital growth and to add an element of geographic diversification to their portfolios by investing in international securities. While the mechanics of cross-border investment flows are often complex, ADR, offers a convenient, easy to use avenue for adding global exposure to US portfolios. Like the capital markets themselves, the ADR has evolved in sophistication and in importance. Today the ADR is an instrument used widely by non-US companies to offer and trade their shares conveniently and efficiently in the US equity markets.

DRs have spread to other parts of the globe in the form of global depositary receipts (GDRs) (the other most common type of DR), European DRs and International DRs. ADRs are typically traded on a U.S. national stock exchange, such as the New York Stock Exchange (NYSE) or the American Stock Exchange, while GDRs are commonly listed on European stock exchanges such as the London Stock Exchange. Both ADRs and GDRs are usually denominated in U.S. dollars, but can also be denominated in euros.

How Does the DR Work?

The DR is created when a foreign company wishes to list its already publicly-traded shares or debt securities on a foreign stock exchange. Before it can be listed to a particular stock exchange, the company is required to meet certain requirements put forth by the exchange. Initial public offerings, however, can also issue a DR. DRs can be traded publicly or over-the-counter exchange.

Pricing and Cross-Trading

When any DR is traded, the broker tries to find the best price of the share as very often an investor compare the U.S. dollar price of the ADR with the U.S. dollar equivalent price of the local share on the domestic market. If the ADR of the Russian gas company is trading at US$12 per share and the share trading on the Russian market is trading at $11 per share, a broker feel comfortable to buy more local shares from Russia and issue ADRs on the US market. This action then causes the local Russian price and the price of the ADR to reach parity.

The continual buying and selling in both markets, however, usually keeps the prices of the ADR and the security on the home market in close range of one another. Because of this minimal price differential, most ADRs are traded by means of intra-market trading. A U.S. broker may also sell ADRs back into the local Russian market. This is known as cross-border trading. When this happens, an amount of ADRs is canceled by the depository and the local shares are released from the custodian bank and delivered back to the Russian broker who bought them. The Russian broker pays for them in roubles, which are converted into dollars by the U.S. broker.

THE BENEFITS OF DEPOSITORY RECEIPTS

The functions of DR are to increase global trade, which in turn can help increase not only volumes on local and foreign markets but also the exchange of information, technology, regulatory procedures as well as market transparency. Thus, instead of being faced with impediments to foreign investment, as is often the case in many emerging markets, the DR investor and company can both benefit from investment abroad. Let's take a closer a look at the benefits:

For the Company

A company is opting to issue a DR to obtain greater exposure and raise capital in the world market. DRs issuing boosted the company's prestige on its local market and added the benefit of increasing the share's liquidity in the market. Depositoary receipts encourage an international shareholder base, and provide expatriates living abroad with an easier opportunity to invest in their home countries. Moreover, in many countries, especially those with emerging markets, obstacles often prevent foreign investors from entering the local market. By issuing a DR, a company can still encourage investment from abroad without having to worry about barriers to entry that a foreign investor might face.

These benefits can be categorized as:

- A DR program can stimulate investor interest, enhance a company's visibility, broaden its shareholder base, and increase liquidity.
- The DR offers a new avenue for raising capital, often at highly competitive costs by enabling the company to participate in international equity markets.
- DRs is enhancing communications with global investors and shareholders.
- ADRs provide an easy way for US employees of non-US companies to invest in their companies' employee stock purchase plans.
- DR ratios ensured that an issuer's DRs trade in a comparable range with those of its peers in the international market.

For the Investor

Buying into a DR immediately turns an investors' portfolio into a global one. Investors gain the benefits of diversification, while trading in their own market under familiar settlement and clearance conditions. More importantly, DR investors will be able to reap the benefits of these usually higher-risk, higher-return equities, without having to endure the added risks of going directly into foreign markets, which may pose lack of transparency or instability resulting from changing regulatory procedures. It is important to remember that an investor will still bear some foreign-exchange risk, stemming from uncertainties in emerging economies and societies. On the other hand, the investor can also benefit from competitive rates the U.S. dollar and euro have to most foreign currencies.

The core benefits for investors are:-

- DRs make it easy to purchase and hold a non-US issuer's securities.
- DRs trade easily and conveniently in dollars and settle through US/ international clearing houses.
- Publicly traded DRs are registered with the international regulators.

GDRs allow issuers to raise capital in two or more markets simultaneously, thus broadening their shareholder base. They can be settled outside the US and can be traded in the Rule 144A private market. Under SEC Regulations, securities offered or sold to investors outside the US are not subject to SEC registration requirements.

Benefits of ADRs over GDRs

The choice of an ADR offering or a GDR offering is driven by a number of considerations of an Indian issuer. There are a number of strategic benefits in accessing the US capital markets and seeking a listing in the US some of which include: enhancing company's profile and visibility, particularly if there is existing business or business opportunity in that region; currency for acquisitions; opportunity for US employees to benefit from an employee stock option plan etc. In addition to the strategic benefits, it has also been observed that ADR programmes has more active trading in the aftermarket, while in case of GDRs, they trading is sporadic and in a number of cases, the DR is converted in the underlying equity shares.

ADRs Typically Trade at a Premium

It is observed that DRs enjoy a considerable premium over their underlying stock price. This is particularly noteworthy since over a period of time, the Indian market is opened up to foreign institutional investors and such premiums may have presented arbitrage opportunities. Several studies have also investigated the effect of ADR issue on underlying stock returns. The general trend appears to be that ADR issuance increases stock prices permanently - probably by reducing cost of capital and increasing liquidity.

There are a number of factors that could be considered as influencing ADR returns including return on the underlying stock, the US-India exchange rate, the movement of two important US indices — the S&P 500 and NASDAQ and variations in trading volumes as also the return expectations of investors between the American and Indian markets.

GLOBAL DEPOSITORY RECEIPTS

A GDR is a dollar denominated instrument traded on a stock exchange in Europe or the US or both. It represents a certain number of underlying equity share. Though the GDR is quoted and traded in dollar terms, the underlying equity shares are denominated in rupees. GDR are issued through the under writers, who arrange to sell the GDR to the investors. After the final issue, a depository is chosen and the company registers the equivalent equity shares of GDR issue in the name of this depository. Though the shares are registered in the name of this depository, the physical possession of the shares is with the local custodian, who acts as the trustee of the depository. The depository subsequently issues the GDR to the under-writer who distributes these negotiable instruments to the investors. The Reliance Industries Ltd, in May 1992, made the first GDR issue of $150 million. Till March 1997, as many as 63 GDR issues have been launched which could mobilize $5933.58 million with an additional amount of $1035.50 million through 10 Euro bond issues. Starting with the maiden issue of the Reliance Industries in May 1992, around 81-odd Indian companies have so far tapped the global market with a cumulative mobilization of Rs. 37,417.35 crore by the end of 2001-02 through 115 issues (Table 3). Indeed, India has the distinction of issuing the maximum number of DRs among the emerging economies. The genesis of Indian multinational corporations (MNCs) with not only international operations but also a global ownership is logical fallout of this process.Table-2 presents the Indian GDR issues.

Table 2
Foreign Investment Inflows

(US $ in million)

Item	*2009-10 (P)*												
	Apr.	***May***	***Jun.***	***Jul.***	***Aug.***	***Sep.***	***Oct.***	***Nov.***	***Dec.***	***Jan.***	***Feb.***	***Mar.***	***Apr.-Mar.***
1	***2***	***3***	***4***	***5***	***6***	***7***	***8***	***9***	***10***	***11***	***12***	***13***	***14***
A. Direct Investment (I+II+III)	2,339	2,095	2,471	3,476	3,174	1,512	2,332	1,700	1,542	2,042	1,717	1,209	37,763
I. Equity (a+b+c+d)	2,339	2,095	2,471	3,476	3,174	1,512	2,332	1,700	1,542	2,042	1,717	1,209	27,149
a. Government (SIA/FIPB)	931	101	85	248	643	111	302	179	51	588	93	139	3,471
b. RBI	1,150	1,916	2,337	1,757	2,477	1,355	1,726	1,367	1,233	1,292	1,364	1,016	18,990
c. Acquisition of shares *	258	78	49	1,471	54	46	304	154	258	162	260	54	3,148
d. Equity capital of unincorporated bodies #	..	..	..	..	..	..	..	..	..	..	..	..	1,540
II. Reinvested earnings +	..	..	..	..	..	..	..	..	..	..	..	..	8,669
III. Other capital ++	..	..	..	..	..	..	..	..	..	..	..	..	1,945
B. Portfolio Investment (a+b+c)	2,278	5,639	353	3,032	1,574	5,095	2,922	1,274	1,533	3,139	230	5,306	32,376
a. GDRs/ADRs # #	33	-	10	965	1,603	96	-	381	94	46	-	100	3,328
b. FIIs **	2,245	5,639	343	2,067	-29	4,999	2,922	893	1,439	3,093	230	5,206	29,048
c. Offshore funds and others	-	-	-	-	-	-	-	-	-	-	-	-	-
Total (A+B)	4,617	7,734	2,824	6,508	4,748	6,607	5,254	2,974	3,075	5,181	1,947	6,515	70,139

Source: RBI Bulletin, February 2011

The first Indian GDR issues made by Reliance Industries and Grasim Industries were at a premium. So it is evident that the Indian capital market has remarkably changed through the issue of GDRs and able to mobilize considerable foreign investment. But the year 1995 remained dull throughout with four issues where 3 being at discount, mobilizing only $ 304 million have given the impression of drying GDR market. However, it again picked up in 1996 through nine issues mobilizing $1890 million. In the financial year 2003-04 (April 03-July 03), actual outflows on account of overseas investments was US$ 224.58 million as compared to US$ 370.49 million in the corresponding period of last year.

Indian companies have started venturing into other countries for marketing, production, acquisition, and even research and development. Investments abroad by Indian companies in 2004-05 were US$ 2.5 billion. The table-4 depicts the ADRs issued by India.

Table 3
Euro-issues by Indian Companies

(Amount in ₹ crore)

Item	*Amount Raised*	*No. of Euro-issues*
1992-93	702.32	2
1993-94	7,897.82	27
1994-95	6,743.23	31
1995-96	1,296.69	5
1996-97	5,594.27	16
1997-98	4,009.46	7
1998-99	1,147.78	3
1999-00	3,487.21	6
2000-01	4197.07	13
2001-02	2341.50	5
Total	37,417.35	115

Source: Handbook of Statistics on Indian Economy, RBI, Various Issues.

Table 4
ADR Issue by Indian Companies

Company	*Issue Day*	*Stock Exchange*	*Lead Manager*	*Offer Price*	*Amount Mobilised ($ million)*	*ADR: Domestic Share*
Infosys	11 March 1999	Nasdaq	BT Alex Brown	55.7	70.4	2:1
Satyam Infoway	19 Oct 1999	Nasdaq	DSP Marill Lynch	n.a	150 .0	1:2
Rediff.com	13 June 2000	Nasdaq India	Goldman Sachs	12.0	55.2	2:1
ICICI	22 Sept 1999	NYSE	DSP Marill Lynch	9.8	275.0	1:5
ICICI Bank	28 March 2000	NYSE	DSP Marill Lynch	11.0	175.0	1:2
Silverline	20 June 2000	NYSE	Saloman Smith Barney	25.0	130.0	1:2
VSNL	15 August 2000	NYSE	Saloman Smith Barney	11.0	n.a.	1:2
Wipro	19 Oct 2000	NYSE	Morgan Stanley	41.4	135	1:1
Dr. Reddy's	11 April 2001	NYSE	Marill Lynch	10.1	Rs. 619.1	1:1

Satyam Computers	15 May 2001	NYSE	Marill Lynch	9.7	140.0	1:2
HDFC Bank	20 July 2001	NYSE	Marill Lynch	13.8	172.5	1:3
MTNL	28 Sept 2001	NYSE	Goldman Sachs	5.9	n.a	1:2

Source: Monthly Review of Indian Economy, Centre for Monitoring Indian Economy, Various Issues.

Initially, companies seeking to float DRs were required to obtain prior permission from the Department of Economic Affairs, Ministry of Finance, and the Government of India (GOI). Only those companies are eligible to issue who have a consistent track record of good performance for a minimum period of 3 years. The infrastructure companies were exempted from the latter requirement in June 1996. The restrictions on number of DR issues were also removed in June 1996. The Euro issue proceeds were subject to a number of end-use restrictions modified from time to time before their withdrawal in May 1998. However, such proceeds were not to be invested in stock market and real estate. In December 1999 Indian software companies, in March 2000 other knowledge-based companies, and in April 2001 all types of companies were permitted to undertake overseas business acquisition through ADR/GDR stock swap. In January 2000, companies were made free to access the GDR/ADR market through an automatic route operated by the RBI, without the prior approval of the GOI or the track record condition. The issuing company needs to furnish full particulars of the issue to the GOI and the RBI within 30 days of completion of such transactions. The main objective of this chapter is to find out the relationship between the movements of GDR price and corresponding domestic prices of the underlying shares. Secondly an attempt has been made to highlight the causes of the significant deviations of GDR price from the domestic prices.

Eligibility for issue of Global Depository Receipts (GDR):

The eligibility criteria for the company to issue their GDRs are:

(1) An issuing company desirous of raising funds by issuing Foreign Currency Convertible Bonds or ordinary shares for equity issues through Global Depository Receipts is required to obtain prior permission of the Department of Economic Affairs, Ministry of Finance, and Government of India.

(2) An issuing company seeking permission under sub-paragraph (1) shall have a consistent track record of good performance (financial or otherwise) for a minimum period of three years, on the basis of which an approval for finalizing the issue structure would be issued to the company by the Department of Economic Affairs, Ministry of Finance.

(3) On completion of finalization of issue structure in consultation with the Lead Manager to the issue, the issuing company shall obtain the final approval for proceeding ahead with the issue from the Department of Economic Affairs.

(4) The Foreign Currency Convertible Bonds shall be denominated in any freely convertible foreign currency and the ordinary shares of an issuing company shall be denominated in Indian rupees.

(5) When an issuing company issues ordinary shares or bonds under this Scheme, that company shall deliver the ordinary shares or bonds to a Domestic Custodian Bank who will, in terms of agreement, instruct the Overseas Depository Bank to issue Global

Depository Receipt or Certificate to non-resident investors against the shares or bonds held by the Domestic Custodian Bank.

(6) A Global Depository Receipt may be issued in the negotiable form and may be listed on any international stock exchanges for trading outside India.

(7) The provisions of any law relating to issue of capital by an Indian company shall apply in relation to the issue of Foreign Currency Convertible Bonds or the ordinary shares of an issuing company and the issuing company shall obtain the necessary permission or exemption from the appropriate authority under the relevant law relating to issue of capital.

Limits of foreign investment in the issuing company

The ordinary shares and foreign currency convertible bonds (means bonds issued in accordance with the scheme and subscribed by a non-resident in foreign currency and convertible into ordinary shares of the issuing company in any manner, either in whole, or in part, on the basis of any equity related warrants attached to debt instruments) issued against the Global Depository Receipts is to be treated as direct foreign investment in the issuing company. The aggregate of the foreign investment made either directly or indirectly shall not exceed 51% of the issued and subscribed capital of the issuing company.

Listing of the Global Depository Receipts

The Global Depository Receipts issued may be listed on any of the Overseas Stock Exchanges, or Over the Counter Exchanges or through Book Entry Transfer Systems prevalent abroad and such receipts may be purchased, possessed and freely transferred by person who is a non-resident within the meaning of Section 2(q) of the Foreign Exchange Regulation Act, 1973 (46 of 1973) subject to the provisions of the Act.

Transfer and redemption

The clauses pertaining to transfer and redemption are:

(1) A non-resident holder of Global Depository Receipts may transfer those receipts, or may ask the Overseas Depository Bank to redeem those receipts. In the case of redemption, Overseas Depository Bank shall request the Domestic Custodian Bank (means a banking company which acts as a custodian for the ordinary shares or foreign currency convertible bonds of an Indian company which are issued by it against global depository receipts or certificates) to get the corresponding underlying shares released in favour of the non-resident investor, for being sold directly on behalf of the non-resident, or being transferred in the books of account of the issuing company in the name of the non-resident.

(2) In case of redemption of the Global Depository Receipts into underlying shares, a request for the same will be transmitted by the Overseas Depository Bank (means a bank authorized by the issuing company to issue global depository receipts against issue of Foreign Currency Convertible Bonds or ordinary shares of the issuing company) to the Domestic Custodian Bank of India, with a copy of the same being sent to the issuing company for information and record.

(3) On redemption, the cost of acquisition of the shares underlying the Global Depository Receipts shall be reckoned as the cost on the date on which the Overseas Depository Bank advises the Domestic Custodian Bank for redemption. The price of the ordinary shares of the issuing company prevailing, i.e., the Bombay Stock Exchange or the National Stock Exchange on the date of the advice of redemption shall be taken as the cost of acquisition of the underlying ordinary shares.

(4) For the purposes of conversions of Foreign Currency Convertible Bonds, the cost of acquisition in the hands of the non-resident investors would be the conversion price determined on the basis of the price of the shares at the Bombay Stock Exchange, or the National Stock Exchange, on the date of conversion of Foreign Currency Convertible Bonds into shares.

Fungibility

Fungibility means division or conversion into smaller parts. Two-way fungibility means conversion into smaller parts and vice versa. The term is becoming very popular now-a-days because; Reserve Bank of India has announced guidelines to facilitate two-way fungibility of ADRs and GDRs. After a initial shyness there were umpteen number of transactions in the capital markets with respect to two-way fungibility.

The Reserve Bank of India issued the operative guidelines on February 13 permitting the re-issuance of the depository receipts. However, domestic and financial institutional investor had not taken any advantage till August 2002. The first ever two- way fungibility was concluded in the shares of Chennai based India Cements Ltd. Though it was a very small transaction, yet it paved the way for two-way fungiqility in Indian capital markets.

Two-way fungibility of depository receipts is crucial for providing a boost to FIIs and institutional trading through arbitrage in domestic and global capital markets. Two-way fungibility of depository receipts, allow investors to convert local shares into American and Global depository receipts.

Indian companies have started venturing into other countries for marketing, production, acquisition, and even research and development. Investments abroad by Indian companies in 2004-05 were US$ 2.5 billion.

TAKE CASE OF TWENTY EIGHT COMPANIES TO EXAMINE THE RELATIONSHIP BETWEEN MOVEMENT OF GDR PRICE AND DOMESTIC SHARE PRICE

The required data for analysis have been collected from the daily "Economic Times" The statistical tools like mean, standard deviation, co-efficient of variation, skew ness and kurtosis have been used to determine the price behavior of GDR and domestic price. Further correlation has been made to find the presence of higher explanatory power for domestic price and GDR price. Again to test the integration between average GDR price and domestic price, single factor regression has been used. Moreover `t' test and `F' test has been applied to examine the significance of the difference of variance in the average GDR price and average domestic price.

ANALYSIS

The mean and standard deviation for GDR and domestic price are presented in Table-5. It is found that the mean market price of GDRs is higher than the domestic price in case of 22 companies out of 28 sample companies. It shows that the market price performance of about 79% of the companies has been higher in GDR market than in the domestic market. Therefore at the overall level the average GDR price has been much higher than the domestic price. The GDR discount to domestic price on an average of the weekly prices of 6 months period (Jan-June 98) ranged between 0.02 percent and 0.24 percent, while the premium to domestic price ranged between 0.01 percent and 0.81 percent. The discount was the highest in respect of Himanchal Futur followed by GNFC at 0.18 percent, but the premium is highest in case of Crompton Greaves followed by Flex Industries at 0.62 percent.

Compared to the domestic price the variability has been at a higher level in the case of GDR price of 19 (67%) companies falling in the sample. This is evident from the figures of standard deviation and coefficient of variation set out in Table-5 on comparative basis for the GDR and domestic prices.

The normality of distribution is measured by co-efficient of skewness and kurtosis. If the distribution is normal, the co-efficient of skewness will be equal to '0' and that of kurtosis 3. But it is found from the Table-6 that there is lack of normality in GDR. Table-7 exhibit the correlation coefficients of GDR and Domestic price of share of sample companies. It is found from the analysis that the behaviour of correlation between GDR and domestic price is high and it is significant at 5% and 1% level. So the above analysis shows that the movement of the price of GDRs and domestic price of shares are in same direction. The results are tabulated in Table-8. The observed 'F' value is higher than the theoretical F at 1% and 5% level of significance. So the regression is significant and domestic price is a significant explanatory factor of the variation in the GDRs price. The adjusted R2 is very low in case of G.N.F.C.Com.Ltd. The beta coefficient in almost all the cases shows positive and fall in acceptable ranges. In most of the cases the 't' value of intercept and beta coefficient is statistically significant at 1%, 2% and 5% level. The table-9 presents the GDR issues made by different companies.

Table 5

Mean Standard Deviation and Coefficient Variation of Weekly GDR Prices and Domestic Prices

Sl. No.	*Name of the Company*	*Mean Price (₹)*			*Standard Deviation*		*Coefficient Variation*	
		GDR	*Domestic*	*Prem/Dis*	*GDR*	*Domestic*	*GDR*	*Domestic*
1	Arvind Mills	69.72	65.91	0.06	11.73	12.56	137.63	157.67
2	Ashok Leyland	40.91	42.33	-0.03	9.38	8.29	88.02	68.78
3	B.S.E.S Ltd.	220.34	182.8	0.21	34.02	23.49	1157.14	551.58
4	Bajaj Auto	711.32	578.19	0.23	84.1	42.91	7073.27	1841.02
5	Bombay Dying	102.05	92.53	0.10	13.21	13.98	174.41	195.44
6	C.E.S.C	38.04	34.86	0.09	10.14	6.92	102.88	47.92
7	Century Text	576.2	562.06	0.03	595.28	591.41	354362.24	349765.75
8	Core Health	21.08	15.08	0.40	6.14	4.71	37.68	22.14
9	Crompton	71.1	39.21	0.81	14.35	10.24	205.8	104.94

10	D.C.W	15.89	15.75	0.01	0.63	2.19	0.4	4.81
11	Dr. Reddy's	513.53	392.06	0.31	71.47	58.67	5107.52	3442.57
12	E.I.D. Parry	79.88	89.76	-0.11	2.23	10.21	4.97	104.33
13	E.I. Hotels	436.5	352.83	0.24	102.75	47.16	10556.89	2224.45
14	Finolex Cable	152.16	155.48	-0.02	41.88	38.54	1754.15	1485.3
15	Flex Industries	29.95	18.5	0.62	0.83	2.49	0.7	6.21
16	G.A. Cement	275.88	271.95	0.01	30.74	28.04	944.96	786.29
17	G.E. Shipping	48.01	40.59	0.18	5.72	4.39	32.72	19.24
18	G.N.F.C	19.71	24.17	-0.18	1.36	3.84	1.84	14.76
19	Garden Silk	13.98	15	-0.07	0.39	1.6	0.15	2.56
20	Grasim (New)	337.94	312.7	0.08	57.46	25.35	3301.82	642.47
21	Grasim (Old)	337.94	312.17	0.08	57.46	25.35	3301.82	642.47
22	Himachal Futur	17.34	22.89	-0.24	0.87	11.61	0.75	134.86
23	Hind Develop	11.98	10.85	0.10	0.33	2.47	0.11	6.08
24	Hindalco (New)	716.44	678.5	0.06	89.41	56.8	7993.95	3226.06
25	Hindalco (Old)	716.44	678.5	0.06	89.41	56.8	7993.95	3226.06
26	ICICI	114.83	90.41	0.27	15.99	13.01	255.58	169.35
27	I.P.C.L	67.12	66.75	0.01	10.02	9.2	100.45	84.62
28	I.T.C	877.73	689.03	0.27	123.82	83.7	15331.5	7005.03

Table 6

Co-efficient of Skewness and Kurtosis for GDR and Domestic Price

Sl. No.	*Name of the Company*	*GDR Price*		*Domestic Price*	
		Coefficient of Skewness	*Coefficient of Kurtosis*	*Coefficient of Skewness*	*Coefficient of Kurtosis*
1	Arvind Mills	0.128	0.368	0.204	-0.048
2	Ashok Leyland	0.589	-1.254	0.483	-1.209
3	B.S.E.S Ltd.	-1.055	1.171	-0.112	-0.838
4	Bajaj Auto	-0.798	-0.028	-0.733	-0.682
5	Bombay Dying	-0.469	0.366	0.302	0.005
6	C.E.S.C	0.594	-0.845	0.447	-1.090
7	Century Text	0.351	-2.005	0.375	-1.949
8	Core Health	5.032	5.523	0.844	0.007
9	Crompton	-1.280	2.158	0.439	-1.427
10	D.C.W	-1.041	4.847	0.570	0.971
11	Dr. Reddy's	0.039	-1.949	0.328	-1.661
12	E.I.D. Parry	1.278	0.692	0.659	-0.450

13	E.I. Hotels	0.243	2.672	-0.816	0.333
14	Finolex Cable	0.225	-1.921	0.299	-1.689
15	Flex Industries	1.279	0.698	0.382	0.254
16	G.A. Cement	-0.801	-0.723	-0.399	-0.906
17	G.E. Shipping	-0.162	1.826	-0.983	1.029
18	G.N.F.C	-1.796	4.482	0.936	0.138
19	Garden Silk	1.279	0.691	0.232	-0.696
20	Grasim (New)	0.363	-1.140	-0.099	-1.250
21	Grasim (Old)	0.363	-1.140	0.099	-1.250
22	Himachal Futur	-2.512	11.080	1.235	0.280
23	Hind Develop	1.286	0.709	0.628	-0.766
24	Hindalco (New)	-0.033	-0.684	0.887	0.387
25	Hindalco (Old)	-0.33	-0.684	0.887	0.387
26	ICICI	-0.35	-0.291	0.318	-0.814
27	I.P.C.L	0.098	-1.238	0.016	-0.972
28	I.T.C	-0.093	-1.077	0.106	-1.544

Table 8
Single Factor Regression for GDR and Domestic Price

Sl.No.	*Name of the Company*	*R Square*	*Adjusted R Square*	*Intercept*	*Beta Coeff*	*'F' value*	*'T'*
1	Arvind Mills	0.93	0.93	-6.33	1.03	358.74*	18.94*
2	Ashok Leyland	0.95	0.94	7.04	0.86	475.53*	21.80*
3	B.S.E.S Ltd.	0.66	0.65	58.65	0.56	47.84*	6.91*
4	Bajaj Auto	0.60	0.58	269.33	0.39	—	—
5	Bombay Dying	0.67	0.65	3.98	0.86	49.13*	7.01*
6	C.E.S.C	0.70	0.69	13.08	0.57	56.96*	7.54*
7	Century Text	0.97	0.97	-4.54	0.98	115.47*	33.99*
8	Core Health	0.01	-0.03	13.66	0.06	0.18	0.43
9	Crompton	0.14	0.10	20.03	0.26	3.99**	1.99**
10	D.C.W	0.09	0.05	32.95	-1.08	2.58**	-1.60
11	Dr. Reddy's	0.72	0.71	32.49	0.70	64.03*	8.002*
12	E.I.D. Parry	0.05	0.01	2.16	1.09	1.45	1.20
13	E.I. Hotels	0.47	0.45	214.51	0.31	21.84*	4.67*
14	Finolex Cable	0.90	0.90	22.11	0.87	234.83*	15.32*
15	Flex Industries	0.05	0.01	38.88	-0.68	1.315	-1.147
16	G.A. Cement	0.74	0.73	55.16	0.78	69.04*	8.309*
17	G.E. Shipping	0.24	0.21	22.43	0.37	7.71*	2.77*

Table 7

Correlation of GDR and Domestic Price of Sample Company

	1	2	3	4	5	6	7	8	9	10	11	12	13	14	15	16	17	18	19	20	21	22	23	24	25	26	27	28
1.	1.00																											
2.	0.36	1.08																										
3.	0.49*	-0.15	1.00																									
4.	0.70*	0.36	0.83*	1.00																								
5.	0.92**	0.40*	0.50**	0.65**	1.00																							
6.	0.13	0.88**	-0.12	0.22	0.18	1.00																						
7.	0.20	-0.66**	0.32	-0.02	-0.22	-0.78**	1.00																					
8.	-0.27	-0.03	-0.39	-0.26	-0.28	0.12	-0.23	1.00																				
9.	0.65**	0.43*	0.71**	0.66**	0.70**	0.34	0.07	-0.33	1.00																			
10.	-0.59**	0.20	-0.62**	-0.50**	-0.55**	0.34	-0.56**	0.36	-0.50**	1.00																		
11.	-0.08	0.77**	-0.40*	0.01	-0.09	0.83**	-0.88**	0.32	-0.03	0.55**	1.00																	
12.	-0.48*	0.18	-0.30**	-0.48**	-0.53**	0.28	-0.58**	0.46*	-0.76*	0.78*	0.60*	1.00																
13.	0.63*	0.36	0.61**	0.66**	0.66**	0.13	0.15	-0.29	0.68*	-0.56*	-0.11	-0.58*	1.00															
14.	0.26	0.91**	0.08	0.43*	0.29	0.87*	-0.78*	0.01	0.46*	0.23	0.79*	0.14	0.30	1.00														
15.	-0.48*	0.18	-0.30*	-0.48*	-0.53*	0.29	-0.58*	0.46*	-0.76*	0.79**	0.60**	1.00**	-0.58*	0.14	1.00													
16.	0.43*	0.63**	0.33	0.70*	0.36	0.55**	-0.45*	0.05	0.28	-0.05	0.53**	0.30	0.41*	0.61**	0.10	1.00												
17.	0.52*	0.52*	0.55*	0.71*	0.56*	0.52*	-0.24*	0.12	0.67*	-0.11	0.30	-0.25	0.39*	0.62*	-0.25	0.63**	1.00											
18.	-0.56*	0.26	-0.369	-0.37*	-0.43*	0.52*	-0.57*	0.23	-0.19	0.80**	0.52*	0.52*	-0.45*	0.35	0.52*	-0.04	0.13	1.00										
19.	-0.48*	0.18	-0.30*	-0.45*	-0.53*	0.28	-0.57*	0.43*	-0.76*	0.79	0.60*	1.00*	-0.58*	0.14	0.99*	0.10	-0.25	0.52*	1.00									
20.	0.37*	0.65*	0.22	0.52*	0.73*	0.41*	-0.05*	-0.21	-0.55*	-0.45*	0.20	-0.26*	0.64*	0.45*	-0.26*	0.50*	0.32	-0.45*	0.26*	1.00								
21.	0.37*	0.65*	0.22	0.52*	0.73*	0.41*	-0.05*	-0.21	-0.55*	-0.45*	0.20	-0.26*	0.64*	0.45*	-0.26*	0.50*	0.32	-0.45*	0.26*	1.00**	1.00							
22.	-0.20	0.24	-0.09*	-0.45*	-0.25*	0.29	-0.49*	0.29	-0.40*	0.46*	0.47*	0.62*	-0.41*	0.22	0.62*	0.03	-0.24	0.29	0.62*	-0.09	-0.09	1.00						
23.	-0.49*	0.18	-0.80*	-0.48*	-0.53*	0.28	-0.58*	0.46*	-0.76*	0.78*	0.60*	1.00	0.58*	0.14	1.00*	0.30	-0.25	0.52*	0.99*	-0.27*	-0.27	0.62*	1.00					
24.	0.61*	0.35	0.73**	0.79*	0.53*	0.35	-0.02	-0.24	0.74*	-0.49*	0.002	-0.53*	0.56*	0.35	-0.53*	0.60*	0.67*	-0.28*	-0.53*	0.52*	0.25*	-0.44*	-0.53*	1.00				
25.	0.61*	0.35	0.73**	0.79*	0.53*	0.35	-0.02	-0.24	0.74*	-0.49*	0.002	-0.53*	0.56*	0.35	-0.53*	0.60*	0.67*	-0.28*	-0.53*	0.52*	0.25*	-0.44*	-0.53*	1.00				
26.	0.34	0.65*	0.56*	0.68*	0.41*	0.65*	-0.39*	-0.06*	0.70*	-0.10*	0.44*	-0.28	0.43*	0.74*	-0.28	0.69*	0.83*	0.15	-0.28	0.39*	0.39*	-0.28*	-0.28*	0.72*	1.00			
27.	0.64*	0.73*	0.45*	0.76*	0.60*	0.65*	-0.47*	-0.15*	0.69*	-0.19*	0.45*	-0.24*	0.57*	0.79*	-0.24	0.72**	0.71*	-0.06	-0.24	0.64*	0.64*	-0.006	-0.24	0.72*	0.72*	1.00		
28.	0.17	0.18	0.83*	0.74*	0.17	0.17	-0.11	-0.22	0.57*	-0.26	-0.03	-0.49*	0.44*	0.35	-0.49*	0.47*	0.59*	-0.06	-0.49*	0.05	-0.56	-0.48*	0.69*	0.73**	0.53	1.00		

*Significance of 5% level

**Significance of 1% level

18	G.N.F.C	0.02	-0.01	15.22	0.45	0.63	0.796
19	Garden Silk	0.04	0.0001	26.48	-0.82	1.00	-1.002
20	Grasim (New)	0.78	0.77	180.32	0.39	86.25*	9.28*
21	Grasim (Old)	0.78	0.77	180.32	0.39	86.25*	2.507***
22	Himachal Futur	0.207	0.17	-82.97	6.10	6.28***	1.890**
23	Hind Develop	0.13	0.09	-21.10	2.63	3.57**	4.652*
24	Hindalco (New)	0.47	0.45	365.10	0.43	21.63*	4.652*
25	Hindalco (Old)	0.47	0.45	365.10	0.43	21.63*	4.652*
26	ICICI	0.79	0.78	7.17	0.72	91.79*	15.274*
27	I.P.C.L	0.90	0.90	8.08	0.87	233.30*	4.269*
28	I.T.C	0.43	0.40	299.22	0.44	18.227*	

* Significant at 1% level

** Significant at 10% level

*** Significant at 2% level

Table 9

GDR Companies # euro convertible bond ** adjusted for bonus	***Industry Segregation***	***Date of GDR issue***	***Size of GDR issue US $***	***Shares per GDR Mil!***	***GDR Issue Price **(US$)***
Arvind Mills	Textiles	03-Feb-94	125.00	1.0	9.78
Ashok Leyland	Autos	20-Mar-95	137.77	3.0	12.79
Bajaj Auto	Autos	27-Oct-94	110.00	1.0	16.89
Ballarpur Ind.#	Paper	27-May-94	35.00	1.0	8.77
Bombay Dye	Textiles	16-Nov-93	50.00	1.0	9.20
BSES Ltd	Power	04-Mar-96	125.00	3.0	14.40
Century Textiles	Diversified	21-Sep-94	100.00	2.0	254.00
CESC	Power	14-Apr-94	125.00	1.0	10.67
Core Parent	Pharma	21-Jun-94	70.00	1.0	12.60
Crompton Greaves	Electrical	02-Jul-96	50.00	1.0	7.56
DCW	Diversified	19-May-94	25.00	5.0	13.55
Dr. Reddy's	Pharma	18-Jul-94	48.00	1.0	11.16m
E. I. Hotels	Hotels	07-Oct-94	40.00	1.0	9.30
EID Parry	Fertiliser	07-Jul-94	40.00	1.0	8.39
Finolex Cab	Cables	19-Jul-94	55.00	1.0	16.60
Flex Industries	Packaging	30-Nov-95	30.00	2.0	8.05
G.E. Shipping	Shipping	17-Feb-94	100.00	5.0	15.94
G.N.F.C	Fertiliser	06-Oct-94	61.11	5.0	12.75

GAIL	Oil & Refineries	04-Nov-99	22.50	6.0	9.67
Garden Silk	Textiles	04-Mar-94	45.00	5.0	26.28
Grasim (1st)	Diversified	25-Nov-92	90.00	1.0	12.98
Grasim (2nd)	Diversified	09-Jun-94	100.00	1.0	20.50
Guj Ambuja #	Cement	26-Nov-93	80.00	1.0	5.95
Himachal Futuri	Telecomm.	02-Aug-95	50.00	4.0	9,30
Hindalco (1st)	Aluminium	22-Jul-93	72.00	1.0	10.73
Hindalco (2nd)	Aluminium	08-Jul-94	100.00	1.0	16.00
Hindustan Dev.	Diversified	21-Sep-94	76.00	1.0	2.05
India Cements	Cement	11-Oct-94	90.00	1.0	4.23
Indian Alum.	Aluminium	22-Feb-94	60.00	1.0	6.77
Indian Hotels	Hotels	28-Apr-95	86.25	1.0	16.60
Indian Rayon	Diversified	25-Jan-94	125.00	1.0	15.01
Indo Gulf	Fertiliser	18-Jan-94	100.00	1.0	4.51
Indo Rama	Textiles	21-Mar-96	50.00	10.0	11.37
ICICI	Finance	02-Aug-96	230.00	5.0	11.50
ICICI (ADR)	Finance	22-Sep-99	315	5.0	9.80
Infosys	IT	11-Mar-99	70.38	0.5	34
IPCL	Petrochemicals	08-Dec-94	85.00	3.0	13.87
ITC	Cigarettes	13-Oct-93	68.85	1.0	7.65
J.K. Corp	Diversified	17-Oct-94	55.00	1.0	8.00
Jain Irrig	Plastics	25-Feb-94	30.00	1.0	11.13
JCT Ltd.	Textiles	29-Jul-94	45.00	10.0	16.96
Kesoram Ind	Diversified	31-Jul-96V	30.00	1.0	1.60
L&T (1st)	Diversified	18-Nov-94	150.00	2.0	16.70
L&T (2nd)	Diversified	01-Mr-96	135.00	2.0	15.35
Mah & Mah	Autos	30-Nov-93	74.75	1.0	4.46
MTNL	Telecom	04-Dec-97	418.53	2.0	11.958
NEPC Micon	Diversified	07-Nov-94	47.70	1.0	3.18
Nippon Denro#	Steel	03-Mar-94	125.00	10.0	21.36
Oriental Hotels	Hotels	14-Dec-94	30.00	1.5	12.75
Ranbaxy Labs	Pharma	29-Jun-94	100.00	1.0	19.38
Raymond Woolen	Textile	09-Nov-94	60.00	2.0	10.61
Reliance	Diversified	27-May-92	150.00	2.0	16.35
Reliance (2nd)	Diversified	15-Feb-94	300.00	2.0	23.50
Reliance Petroleum	Diversified	18-Oct-99	100	15.0	23.0
S.A.I.L	Steel	07-Mar-96	125.00	15.0	12.97

Satyam Infoway	IT	19-Oct-99	75.00	1.0	18.0
S.I.E.L.	Diversified	14-Oct-94	40.00	3.0	14.64
Sanghi Poly	Textiles	28-Jul-94	50.00	5.0	9.56
SIV Ind.	Textiles	01-Aug-94	45.00	1.0	6.37
SPIC	Fertiliser	28-Sep-93	65.00	5.0	11.15
SBI	Banking	03-Oct-96	369.95	2.0	14.15
Sterlite India#	Diversified	22-Dec-93	100.00	1.0	17.86
Tata Electric	Power	22-Feb-94	65.00	100.0	710.00
Telco (1st)	Autos	15-Jul-94	115.00	1.0	8.25
Telco (2nd)	Autos	06-Aug-96	200.00	1.0	14.25
Tube Invest	Cycles & Acc.	20-May-94	45.60	1.0	6.58
United Phos.	Pesticides	25-Feb-94	55.00	1.0	20.50
Usha Beltron	Cables	06-Oct-94	35.00	1.0	10.70
Videocon Int.	Electronics	26-Mar-97	90.00	1.0	8.10
VSNL	Telecomm.	24-Mar-97	527.00	0.5	13.93
Wockhardt	Pharma	25-Feb-94	75.00	1.0	14.35

CONCLUDING OBSERVATION

This chapter presents some stylized facts of GDR and Domestic price of shares of sample companies. The evidence is that there is high correlation between GDR and Domestic price. There has been a tendency to move in the same direction, which turned out as significant. So volatility in the BSE Sensex leads to decline in GDR market and price rigging before GDR issues is causing volatility of the scripts in the domestic market. Further the variability at the overall level in GDR market has been significantly higher than in the domestic market. Therefore, the crash in GDR market affects the liquidity in the domestic capital market. So there should be price stability in both pre and pro GDR issues, in both domestic and international market to proliferation of international funds through Euro-issues.

REVIEW QUESTIONS

1. What is the Rationale for Cross-Border Listings?
2. What is GDR?
3. How do you evaluate the movement of GDR price and Domestic prices?
4. Quiz:
   a. —- is a dollar denominated instrument traded on a stock exchange in Europe or the US or both.
   b. The first Indian GDR issues made by —and —were at a premium.
   c. ——— Made the first GDR issue of $150 million in –year.
   d. In 2000-2001 how many Euro Issue made by Indian Companies?
   e. Which companies are eligible to issue GDRs?

13

Emerging Market and Developed Market — A Study

The International capital market facilitated cross-country financial flows, which contribute to a more efficient allocation of resources. Keeping in view, the present chapter analyses the relationship between emerging markets and developed markets movement in the global context.

INTRODUCTION

The past twenty-five years have witnessed a process of accelerating change in the world's financial markets. Driven by an interacting process of liberalization and innovation, regulations have been removed; new products have emerged in the market. And developing countries have found new ways to mobilize domestic and international savings. The dynamics of globalization is now a major force in shaping development of nations. Capital formation plays an important role in the process of development. To overcome the vicious circle of low capital formation and low growth, developing countries seek to look for help from external sources. Foreign capital fills the resource gap of developing countries. In recent years, there is a trend towards internationalization of financial markets. Financial integration leads to rapid flows of funds from 'less returns markets' to 'high returns markets' and in this process it brings about equality in returns.

Financial integration depends upon the flow of funds from one market to another and one country to another. Financial integration is subject of perpetual interest to policy makers, investors and academics. The latter interest group has provided strong evidence on interaction among international financial markets. Investors are return-oriented and therefore highly interested in studies that examine co-movements of financial markets. Due to tendency of financial integration, investors are incapable to earn extra returns in long term. However, cross-border diversification presents remarkable opportunity to maximize profits as well as minimize risks. Policy makers' interest is partly based on prudence caused by possible spillover effects in case of integrated financial markets. It has been observed in some research that developed equity markets are more integrated than emerging ones. While strong arguments can be made in case of progressive integration of developed European financial markets, where periods of similar trend co-movements of equity market indices are interchanged with periods of short-run country specific volatility (Fratzscher, 2001.), integration between emerging markets as well as between emerging and developed markets are not accompanied with credible empirical evidence.

The increased flow of funds in the international financial market is due to techno-financial innovation. In April 1992, Government permitted Indian companies to raise equity capital by issuing their programmes in the international financial markets. The emerging markets are an increasing part of today's investment opportunities. Emerging stock markets play an increasingly important role in developing countries. The developing economies have now become market-oriented in approach. So, integration of emerging markets with developed markets is of global interest.

HOW EMERGING MARKET IS DIFFERENT FROM DEVELOPED MARKET?

An emerging, or developing, market economy (EME) is defined as an economy with low-to-middle per capita income. Such countries constitute approximately 80% of the global population, representing about 20% of the world's economies. Countries whose economies fall into this category are usually considered emerging because of their developments and reforms. Emerging markets are countries that are restructuring their economies along market-oriented lines and offer a wealth of opportunities in trade, technology transfers, and foreign direct investment. According to the World Bank, the five biggest emerging markets are China, India, Indonesia, Brazil and Russia. Other countries that are also considered as emerging markets include Mexico, Argentina, South Africa, Poland, Turkey, and South Korea. These countries made a critical transition from a developing country to an emerging market (by Chuan Li,). Emerging market indicators are usually the opposite indicators for the developed markets which creates both opportunities and threats. High growth rates and a bourgeoning middle class lead to new markets for goods and services. Whereas developed markets are homogeneous as a group. The developing counties desperately needed capital. In the past, developing countries normally borrowed either from commercial banks or from foreign governments and multilateral lenders like the IMF and the Word Bank to finance their development. But however many developing countries failed to fuel the development process and demonstrates their inability to well manage and efficiently operate the borrowed funds to support economic growth. This often resulted in heavy debt overload and led to a severe economic imbalance. In light of the unsatisfactory results of government borrowing, developing countries began to rely on equity investment as a means of financing economic growth. They seek to attract equity investment from private investors who will become their partners in development. To attract equity financing, a developing country has to establish the preconditions of a market economy and create a business climate that meets the expectations of foreign investors. This change in financing sources thus became another factor leading to the rise of emerging markets. The rise of emerging markets is changing the traditional view of development, as investing in the emerging markets is no longer associated with the traditional notion of providing development assistance to poorer nations. Further, emerging markets are rationalizing their trade relations and capital investment with industrialized countries. Trade and capital flows are directed more toward new market opportunities, and less by political consideration. As a result, the increasing two-way trade and capital flows between emerging markets and industrialized countries reflect the transition from dependency to global interdependency. The accelerated information exchange, especially with the aid of the Internet, is integrating emerging markets into the global market at a faster pace.

PORTFOLIO INVESTMENT AND RISKS

Emerging markets offer an opportunity to investors who are looking to add some risk to their portfolios. The possibility for some economies to fall back into a not-completely-resolved civil war or a revolution sparking a change in government could result in a return to nationalization, expropriation, and the collapse of the capital market. Delicate exchange rate fluctuations could transform into an all-out devaluation resulting merely from investors speculating in the possibility of political disorder or losing faith in the banking system. Because the risk of an EME investment is higher than one of a developed market, panic, speculation and knee-jerk reactions are also more common. During 1997 Asian crisis, international portfolio flows into these countries actually began to reverse themselves, which clearly indicates that how EMEs can be high-risk investment opportunities. However, the bigger the risk, the bigger the reward, so emerging market investments have become a standard practice among investors aiming to diversify while adding risk.

IMPORTANCE OF EMERGING MARKET

The emerging market economies, which were seen as a seemingly endless source of instability, fragility and chronic shortages of capital for so long, are now an important part of global resilience. Today, the emerging world has become an important source for the global supply of goods and services, and of savings. Through a combination of better policies, better economic performance, the emerging world appears considerably less likely to be an independent source of volatility for the global financial system during the years. Financial innovations like emergence of new financial markets, institutions and new financial instruments have led to the financial integration according to literature. The national financial systems of various countries get increasingly integrated across the borders and have influence on each other national financial markets. The national financial markets of major industrial countries are fast integrating globally and there is considerable weakening of the distinction between emerging and developed markets. Hence, the present chapter finds out the important features that distinguishes between the emerging markets and developed markets. This chapter also evaluates the performance and integration of emerging market and developed market in the framework of risk and return characteristics.

LITERATRE REVIEW

Financial integration of equity markets means that assets of equal risk offer investors with the same expected return. Financial integration in the short-run is identified with consistency among the markets considered. On the contrary, segmentation is a result of lack of integration. There is a wide literature that tries to assess the degree of equity market integration. Studies based on price equalization for financial market assets have used uncovered interest parity (Fratzschner, 2001) or capital asset pricing model (Bekaert and Harvey 1995, Dumas and Solnik 1995, Ferson and Harvey 1991, Hardouvelis *et al.*, 1999.). Robert Korajczyk (1995) investigated financial integration between equity markets using multifactor equilibrium Arbitrage Pricing Theory to define risk and to measure deviations from the 'law of one price'. According to results of the study, the measure of market segmentation tends to be much larger for emerging markets than for developed markets which is consistent with large barriers to capital flows into or out of the emerging markets. However the measure shows tendency to decrease over time, which is in line with growing levels of integration. International linkages between equity markets can be as well tested with a theoretical VAR models (King and Wadhwani 1990, Koch and Koch 1993, Eum and Shim 1993). Co-integration analysis is used to notice degree of integration by measuring the stability of long-run relationships across financial markets (Dickinson 2000, Richards 1996). Gilmore, Lucey and Mcmanus (2005) and Voronkova (2004) examined bilateral and multilateral co-integration properties of the German stock market on the one hand and Polish, Czech and Hungarian stock market on the other hand. Both studies suggest that the process of integration of the Central and Eastern European countries into the EU is leading to a closer integration of their equity markets with those of major EU countries but also in case of Voronkova (2004) with USA equity markets. Many studies put in line the degree of real integration and financial integration (Fama and French 1989, Ferson and Harvey 1991, Jagannathan and Wang 1996) emphasizing that extent of national financial integration depends on the extent of real and financial convergence with other economies as well as on country's performance. Furthermore, financial integration tends to be highest during periods when observed countries or the dominant country are in recession (Erb *et al.*, 1994, Ragunathan *et al.* 1999.). Some studies conducted in developed and emerging markets provide strong evidence that removal of legal and non-legal barriers to capital flows induces financial integration (Bekaert and Harvey, 1995.).

LET TAKE THE CASE OF SIXTEEN EMERGING MARKETS AND TWENTY DEVELOPED MARKETS FOR EVALUATING THE PERFORMANCE AND INTEGRATION OF MARKET

To test this, present chapter used statistical tools like mean, S.D., coefficient of variation, Skewness and Kurtosis used to determine the behaviour of emerging and developed market. Further, correlation has been determined to find the presence of higher explanatory power for emerging and developed market.

A brief description has been provided of all the methods used.

Regression Equation

A regression equation indicates the nature of the relationship between two (or more) variables algebraically. In particular, it points out the extent to which you can predict some variables by knowing others, or the extent to which some are associated with others.

A linear regression equation is usually written

$$Y = a + bX + e$$

Where

Y is the dependent variable

a is the intercept

b is the slope or regression coefficient

X is the independent variable (or covariate)

e is the error term

The equation will specify the average magnitude of the expected change in Y given a change in X.

Residual

Residual (or error) represents unexplained (or residual) variation after fitting a regression model. It is the difference between the observed value of the variable and the value suggested by the regression model.

Multiple Regression Correlation Coefficients

The multiple regression correlation coefficients, R^2, are a measure of the proportion of variability explained by, or due to the regression (linear relationship) in a sample of paired data. It is a number between zero and one and a value close to zero suggests a poor model.

A very high value of R^2 can arise even though the relationship between the two variables is non-linear. The fit of a model should never simply be judged from the R^2 value.

Correlation Coefficient

A correlation coefficient is a number between -1 and 1, which measures the degree to which two variables are linearly related. If there is perfect linear relationship with positive slope between the two variables, we have a correlation coefficient of 1; if there is positive correlation, whenever one variable has a high/low value, so does the other. If there is a perfect linear relationship with negative slope between the two variables, we have a correlation coefficient of -1; if there is negative correlation, whenever one variable has a high/low value; the other has a low (high) value. A correlation coefficient of "0" means that there is no linear relationship between the variables.

The required data for sixteen emerging markets and twenty developed markets have been collected from the emerging market database of the International Finance Corporation and Morgan Stanley Capital International perspectives. MSCI excludes investment companies and foreign domiciled companies, to avoid double counting. All returns are computed on month-end values, assuming dividend reinvestment, and are denominated in US dollars.

The returns are calculated in two ways:

The continuously compounded return is measured as $\log(P_t/P_{t-1})$ where P_t stands for the closing price of the stock on day t. This is referred to as the 'Price Series'.

The simple return in the log scale are constructed as $\dfrac{\log(P_t)-\log(P_{t-1})}{\log(P_{t-1})}$

Where P_t stands for the closing price of the stock on day t. This is referred to as the 'Return Series'.

Harry M. Markowitz got the Nobel Prize for his contribution to the Theory of Portfolio Choice. In his acclaimed portfolio theory, Markowitz tried to show how the concept of portfolio selection can be distinguished from security selections and also devised methods to arrive at all efficient portfolios that save the time involved in trial and error methods. It was on the basis of his work, William Sharpe and Lintner later developed the popular Capital Asset Pricing Model. So, Markowitz called it as the foundations of portfolio theory. Markowitz's framework led to the concept of efficient portfolios. An efficient portfolio is expected to yield the highest return for a given level of risk or lowest risk for a given level of return. Markowitz attempted to lessen the risk of an investment portfolio by mathematical methods, while maintaining the possibility of reward. This model mathematically described ways to distribute risk in an 'optimal' portfolio by diversifying investment among a number of different products, such as stocks and bonds and future contracts. This model is able to quantify risk for the first time. In the model, it was called 'beta'. The size of beta was supposed to convey an accurate assessment of risk. The quantification of risk and the need for optimization of return with lowest risk are the contributions of Markowitz. This led to what is called the modern portfolio theory, which emphasizes the tradeoff between risk and return.

The single factor Capital Asset Pricing Model (CAPM) as proposed by Sharpe (1964), Lintner (1965) and Mossin (1965) applied in the international context. Capital market theory basically begins where the Markotwitz efficient frontier ends. Equilibrium is assumed between risk and expected return for each security due to the behaviour of risk-averse investors. There are many models to explain the relationship between expected risk and return for any asset when markets are in equilibrium. The relationship between expected return and unique risk instead of total risk and the valuation of securities that follows is the essence of the capital asset pricing model (CAPM). Sharpe defines the market portfolio as a portfolio consisting of all securities where the proportion invested in each security corresponds to its relative market value. The relative market value of a security is simply equal to the aggregate market value of the security divided by the sum of the aggregate market value of all securities. Sharpe (1964), John Lintner (1965) and Mossin (1966) starting with the normative models of Markowitz and Tobin have developed similar theories of capital market equilibrium under conditions of risk.

The following assumption underlined these models are

- Every investor is one-period expected utilities maximize and exhibits diminishing marginal utility of terminal wealth.
- All investors have the same one-period time horizon.
- Every investor feels that he can evaluate a portfolio solely in terms of the mean and dispersion or variance of one-period returns.
- It is assumed that there are no transaction or information costs that the borrowing and lending rates are equal and the same for all individuals and those investors will only select portfolios with optimal combinations of risk and return.
- All investors hold identical or homogeneous expectations about the distributions of future returns.
- The capital market is in equilibrium.

Under these assumption, Sharpe and Lintner has shown that the expected return for asset on portfolio is related to the expected return on the market portfolio by the following equation:

$$R_p - R_f = \beta(R_m - R_f)$$

Where

R_p =expected return for asset on portfolio

R_f =risk-free rate

R_m =expected return on the market portfolio

β is defined as the cov (R_p,R_m) divided by Var (R_m). The variable β is a measure of systematic risk. Emerging and developed market return is explained in terms of a benchmark portfolio. Emerging and developed market equity is priced relative to the world index. The international CAPM assumes that assets in different markets are identically priced. ICAPM tests the joint test of the integration of world markets. It links the expected return on a risky asset to its risk in an efficient portfolio.

The estimable forms of ICAPM is

$$R_P = a + b_P R_m + e_P$$

a = constant return

β_P = beta

e_P = error term

R_P = return of the fund

R_m = return of the market

Again to test the integration between emerging and developed market, single factor regression has been used. Moreover, 't' test and 'F' test have been applied to examine the significance of the difference of variance in the emerging and developed markets.

t-Test

A ***t*-test** is any statistical hypothesis test for two groups in which the test statistic has a Student's *t*-distribution if the null hypothesis is true. A test of the null hypothesis is that the means of two normally distributed populations are equal. Given two data sets, each characterized by its mean, standard deviation and number of data points; we can use some kind of *t*-test to determine whether the means are distinct, provided that the underlying distributions can be assumed to be normal. All such tests are usually called Student's *t*-tests. There are different versions of the *t*-test depending on whether the two samples are independent of each other (e.g., individuals randomly assigned into two groups), or paired, so that each member of one sample has a unique relationship with a particular member of the other sample. If the *t*-value that is calculated is above the threshold chosen for statistical significance (usually the 0.05 level), then the null hypothesis is that the two groups do not differ is rejected in favor of an alternative hypothesis. Once a *t*-value is determined, a *P*-value can be found using a table of values from Student's t-distribution.

F-Test

An F-test is any statistical test in which the test statistic has an F-distribution if the null hypothesis is true. A great variety of hypotheses in applied statistics are tested by F-tests. The hypothesis is that the means of multiple normally distributed populations, all having the same standard deviation, are equal. This is perhaps the most well-known of hypotheses tested by means of an F-test, and the simplest problem in the analysis of variance (ANOVA). The hypothesis that the standard deviations of two normally distributed populations are equal, and thus they are of comparable origin.

Apart of it, if it is equality of variances or standard deviations that is being tested, the F-test is extremely non-robust to non-normality. In many cases, the F-test statistic can be calculated through a straightforward process. Two regression models are required, one of which constrains one or more of the regression coefficients according to the null hypothesis. The test statistic is then based on a modified ratio of the sum of squares of residuals of the two models as follows:

Given *n* observations, where model U has *k* unrestricted coefficients, and model R restricts *m* of the coefficients (typically to zero), the F-test statistic can be calculated as

$$F = \frac{\left(\frac{RSS_R - RSS_U}{m}\right)}{\left(\frac{RSS_U}{n-k}\right)}$$

Where RSS_i is the residual sum of squares of model *i*.

ANALYSIS:

Volatility relates to the variability in the price of a security. In the context of international financial market, volatility of the market refers to the volatility of the indices of the securities within the international financial market. The most common measure of stock market volatility is the standard deviation. Standard deviation measures the deviation of the return of equity from its mean returns. International portfolio investment can increase volatility of emerging and developed markets, if foreign investors make investment decisions based on short-term gain.

The Table 1 presents return and risk of the emerging and developed markets. From, the table it is evident that the returns of all emerging markets are much higher than developing markets. The mean of Malaysia is highest. Jordan and Pakistan is having negative return, i.e.,-.38% and -.40%. The average return of emerging market is 3.5% against 1.44% for developed market. Out of sixteen emerging markets, nine emerging markets (56%) witnessed a sharp drop in mean return than average mean return. So, it suggests that emerging market returns is time varying. In case of developed markets, the highest returns have been observed in Austria and New Zealand at 3.32% and 2.8% respectively. Out of twenty developed markets, eleven developed markets (45%) shows higher return than the average return. So, it is observed from the analysis that the emerging market return and developed market return are identical during this period.

The Table 1 also depicts that higher level of volatility as compared to accompany return in emerging markets developed markets. Average volatility for emerging markets is 14.23% as against 7.46% for developed market. Malaysia is having highest volatility among the emerging markets with standard deviation being 32.39%. The volatility for Venezuela, Turkey, Taiwan, Chile and Argentina are higher than average. These countries also show higher mean return. So, it is apparent that higher return is noticed in these countries due to high volatility. Spain has the highest volatility among the developed markets with standard deviation being 18.22%. The volatility of Sweden, Norway, Italy, Hong Kong, Germany, Finland and Austria is higher than average. But it is observed that the volatility is more in Spain but shows negative return. So, it is inferred from the analysis that sometimes volatility does not lead to get high return.

The variance of Spain is much higher, i.e., 331.98%. Similarly, the variance of Malaysia is highest, i.e., 1049.54%. The mean return of all emerging market except Jordan and Pakistan is higher than the benchmark level. Similarly, the mean return of all developed countries except UK, USA, Spain, and Netherlands is higher than the benchmark level. The volatility of 75% developed countries is higher than the benchmark level. Similarly, the volatility of all emerging countries is higher than the benchmark level.

The time varying shifts of mean and volatility in both global and local is tested through the normality of the return distribution. Skewness and Kurtosis is the simplest form of measurement to the normality of a distribution. If the distribution is normal, the coefficient of Skewness will be equal to 0 and that of Kurtosis 3. Some measures of normality deploy a combination of Skew ness and Kurtosis also. In a symmetrical distribution, the Skewness will be identical where the mean=median=mode. The Table 2 presents the coefficient of Skewness and Kurtosis of emerging and developed markets. Most emerging and developed markets exhibit Skewness and Kurtosis values higher than the benchmark level. It is observed from the table that the coefficient of Skewness of nine emerging markets out of sixteen shows negative values and Kurtosis exhibit higher value in ten out of sixteen markets. When the mean>median, distribution is positively skewed and *vice versa*.

Both the emerging and developed market is negatively skewed because their median value is greater than mean values. So, it may be necessary to run a more rigorous test of normality. Similarly, in case of developed market, thirteen developed markets out of twenty exhibit negative skewness and kurtosis has increased in four out of twenty markets. So, it is evident that the emerging and developed market returns are not normally distributed. Standard errors of Skewness and Kurtosis shows the degree to which the sample is reliable. It represents that lesser the standard error; the more is the reliability of the sample. The standard error of skewness of emerging market and developed market is .472 and standard error of Kurtosis of both the market is .918. The correlation coefficient measures the degree of relationship among the various countries. It also identifies how change in one variable affects the change in other variable.

The Table 3 exhibit the correlation coefficients of emerging market. It is found from the table that Argentina exhibits a significant correlation of .71 with Thailand and .44 with India. Brazil's correlation with Mexico is .63. India is having a significant correlation, i.e., .55 with Thailand. Korea exhibits a significant correlation of .69 and .43 with Mexico and Colombia. Mexico's correlation with Indonesia, Thailand and Jordan is .62, .44 and .47 respectively. Thailand is significantly correlated with Turkey. Colombia exhibits significant correlation of .41, .45 and .58 with *Jordan*,

Pakistan and Indonesia. Jordan is highly correlated with Malaysia, Pakistan, Indonesia and Taiwan. Malaysia is having negative significance correlation with Pakistan and Indonesia but positively correlated with Taiwan. Pakistan is positively correlated with Indonesia but negatively correlated with Taiwan and Turkey. Indonesia is positively correlated with Venezuela but negatively correlated with Taiwan. Taiwan exhibits significant correlation with Turkey. All these countries are having significant correlation at 5% and 1% level. Brazil, Korea, Mexico, Thailand, Taiwan is highly correlated with MSCI India. As some of the emerging market is highly correlated with each other, the benefits from international diversification may not arise. There may not be ample scope for global investment. It is also inferred from the table that some of the emerging countries show no correlation at all. The Table 4 shows the correlation between developed markets over a two-year period. Australia is highly correlated with USA. It exhibits a correlation of .66 with Belgium, .74 with Canada, .60 with Denmark, .54 with Finland, .71 with France .66 with Germany, .71 with Netherlands, .53 with New Zealand, .54 with Singapore, .70 with Sweden, .61 with Switzerland, .78 with USA and .76 with UK. Belgium is also significantly correlated with Canada, Denmark, Finland, France, Germany, Netherlands, New Zealand, Norway, Singapore, Sweden, Switzerland, USA and UK. Canada's correlation with Denmark, Finland, France, Germany, Japan, Netherlands, New Zealand, Singapore, Spain, Sweden, Switzerland, USA and UK is .54, .45, .45, .67, .55, .43, .68, .62, .51, .41, .67, .52, .74 and .64 respectively. Denmark exhibits highest correlation of .74 with Norway. Similarly, Finland is highly correlated with UK. But the developing country Hong Kong, Italy and Japan shows no correlation at all with other countries. It is observed from the analysis that some of the European markets have higher correlation with one another. Hence, from the results, it can be generalized that developed markets are strongly integrated and there is less arbitrage opportunities among them. Most of these countries are significantly correlated at 5% and 1% level.

The Table 5 depicts the correlation of emerging markets with developed markets. It is inferred from the table that Korea and Mexico is highly correlated with all developed markets except Austria, Canada, Denmark, and Germany and New Zealand. Brazil is highly correlated with Australia, Belgium, Denmark, France, Germany, Netherlands, UK, USA, Switzerland, Sweden and Singapore. Brazil is negatively correlated with Hong Kong. India is correlated with Hong Kong and New Zealand. Thailand is correlated with Australia, Austria, Belgium, Canada, Finland, France, Japan, Netherlands, Norway, Sweden, Switzerland, USA and UK. Indonesia is also significantly correlated with some of the developed countries. So, it is observed from the analysis that international diversification of portfolio investment would be less effective in these countries. Malaysia and Pakistan exhibited very low and negative correlation with developed countries. So, it is well documented that benefits from international diversification arises out of the low correlation that markets exhibit with one another.

From the above analysis, it is evident that emerging markets and developed markets are not integrated with each other and also they are not moving in same direction. The emerging market Korea and Mexico is correlated with developed countries; the diversification benefit is expected to have decreased considerably. So, these countries may remain closed for foreign investment. As most of the emerging and developed markets are not interrelated, it clearly brings out the scope for risk reduction in a portfolio of developed market by including emerging market. From the correlation analysis, it is apparent that the behaviour of correlation between is mixed both in case of developed and emerging market. Most of the emerging market and developed market are not correlated with each other.

The test of integration and asset pricing of emerging and developed market is determined by using ICAPM framework. The Table 6 presents the single-factor regression of emerging market. The observed 'F' value is higher than the theoretical 'F' at 5% level of significance only in Korea and Mexico. So, MSCI is not a significantly explanatory factor of the variation in emerging market return except in Korea and Mexico. The adjusted $R^{2\ \text{value}}$ is very low and negative in case of India, Colombia, Jordan, Malaysia, Pakistan, Philippines, and Venezuela. Both intercept and beta coefficient is presented with 't' value. The 't' value is significant statistically at 5% level only in Korea and Mexico. So, it is apparent from the analysis that if the risk and return attributes are time varying, it is difficult to test asset pricing. Table 7 depict the summary results of single factor regression of developed markets. The observed 'F' value is higher than the theoretical 'F' at 5% level of significance in case of Australia, Belgium, Canada, France, Germany, Netherlands, Sweden, Switzerland, USA and UK. The regression is significant for these countries. So for the ten countries, MSCI world is an explanatory variance of developed market returns. The adjusted R^2 is indicative weakness of the attempted regression in only 10 countries. For this market, MSCL does not explain returns. In case of only ten countries, the beta coefficient is statistically significant. The 't' value for these countries is significant at 5% level of significance. It is inferred from the analysis that MSCI world is poor explanatory variable for emerging and developed market returns. So, it concludes that several emerging markets have faced destabilizing effects in terms of having investment from the developed countries in these markets. Further, multi-factor model may better explain asset pricing in both the markets.

CONCLUDING OBSERVATION

This chapter have examined the distinguished characteristics of emerging market and developed markets in terms of risk, return, volatility, and normality of distribution, correlation. This chapter concludes that the return and volatility of emerging markets are higher than developed markets. There is a lack of normality of distribution both in emerging and developed market. The emerging markets and developed markets are not correlated with each other. They are not moving in the same direction.

The findings of this chapter have important implications for both investors and policy makers. For investors, the high degree of integration means it has become a more attractive place for investment. However, higher integration also implies that there are fewer opportunities to diversify portfolios within the area, thus providing incentives to focus more on diversifying across sectors or across regions. For policy makers, the process of global financial integration poses some challenges. Financial integration has increased competition and market efficiency and, at the same time, continuing financial integration has made individual markets increasingly interdependent and subjected to spillovers resulting from endogenous and exogenous shocks. However in this study, MSCI world is extremely poor explanatory variable of emerging market return than developed market returns. So, it concludes that international capital market is not completely integrated. So, there is an arbitrage opportunities among them and international diversification would be more efficient in these markets.

Table 1

Risk and Return of Emerging and Developed Market

Emerging	*Market Mean(%)*	*Std. Dev.*	*Variance*	*Developed*	*Market Mean(%)*	*Std. Deviation*	*Variance*
Argentina	8.24	22.67	514.07	Australia	1.63	3.75	14.09
Brazil	6.95	11.12	123.70	Austria	3.31	7.58	57.46
Chile	6.88	24.53	601.63	Belgium	1.46	6.91	47.74
India	2.62	7.53	56.64	Canada	1.85	4.02	16.17
Korea	0.64	8.31	69.17	Denmark	1.99	7.33	53.71
Mexico	1.68	5.41	29.24	Finland	1.06	11.62	135.15
Thailand	3.04	8.39	70.55	France	1.20	6.88	40.74
Colombia	2.93	7.46	55.62	Germany	1.37	9.27	86.01
Jordan	-0.38	12.46	147.57	Hong Kong	1.24	10.23	104.77
Malaysia	9.67	32.39	1049.54	Italy	1.83	10.75	115.62
Pakistan	-0.40	8.83	77.92	Japan	1.04	5.51	30.44
Philippines	-1.04	8.38	70.32	Netherland	0.55	6.67	44.45
Indonesia	0.83	13.32	177.44	Newsland	2.80	3.59	12.92
Taiwan	3.97	18.46	341.09	Norway	2.33	10.92	119.23
Turkey	3.52	22.21	493.53	Singapore	1.04	4.83	23.30
Venezuela	4.75	16.21	262.79	Spain	-1.23	18.22	331.98
Average	3.50	14.23		Sweden	2.45	8.22	67.71
				Switzerland	1.17	4.11	16.96
				USA	0.87	4.65	21.64
				UK	0.91	4.73	22.33
				MSCI World	1.01	5.02	25.25
				Average	1.44	7.46	

Table 2

Coefficient of Skewness and Kurtosis for Emerging and Developed Markets

Emerging Market	*Coefficient of Skewness*	*Coefficient of Kurtosis*	*Developed Market*	*Coefficient of Skewness*	*Coefficient of Kurtosis*
Argentina	4.15	19.15	Australia	0-.08	0.33
Brazil	-1.26	5.32	Austria	0.81	5.40
Chile	4.34	20.27	Belgium	0-.45	1.99
India	0-.36	0.33	Canada	-1.14	1.92
Korea	-.08	-1.09	Denmark	0-.38	1.29
Mexico	-.22	1.25	Finland	0-.19	0-.07

Thailand	1.49	4.25	France	0.02	0.45
Colombia	0.22	0.55	Germany	0-.16	2.39
Jordan	-3.78	16.45	Hong Kong	-.68	4.79
Malaysia	4.51	21.29	Italy	1.11	4.93
Pakistan	-1.11	2.91	Japan	0.40	0-.73
Philippines	0-.11	0-.45	Netherland	0-.52	1.39
Indonesia	-1.81	6.02	Newsland	0-.66	-.143
Taiwan	1.98	5.95	Norway	0.57	1.47
Turkey	-1.49	5.21	Singapore	0-.45	0.74
Venezuela	1.21	7.73	Spain	-3.91	7.42
Average	0.48	7.23	Sweden	0.06	0.64
			Switzerland	0.26	0.11
			USA	0-.38	1.04
			UK	0-.17	0.61
			MSCI World	0-1.2	2.12
			Average	0-.29	1.85

Table 3

Correlation of Emerging Market Return

	MSCI	Arg.	Brazil	Chile	India	Korea	Mexico	Thailand	Colombia	Jordan	Malaysia	Pakistan	Philippines	Indonesia	Taiwan	Turkey	Venezuela
MSCI	1.00																
Arg.	.235	1.00															
Brazil	.490*	.245	1.00														
Chile	.343	.045	.206	1.00													
India	.166	.446*	.144	.247	1.00												
Korea	.758**	.089	.288	.393	.402	1.00											
Mexico	.721**	.322	.631**	.290	.205	.691**	1.00										
Thailand	.542**	.717**	.357	.208	.559**	.280	.445*	1.00									
Colombia	.184	.217	.078	.133	.312	.436*	.325	.093	1.00								
Jordan	-.023	.082	.224	.051	.214	.219	.470*	.031	.418*	1.00							
Malaysia	.158	.009	.024	-.011	-.113	-.088	-.264	.115	-.347	-.895**	1.00						
Philippines	-.049	.278	.027	.225	.390	.155	.275	.226	.345	.324	-.304	.254	1.00				
Indonesia	.253	.193	.389	.168	.307	.343	.624**	.229	.584**	.809**	-.743**	.437*	.375	1.00			
Taiwan	.583**	-.010	-.015	.051	.055	.390	.082	.294	-.159	.664**	.705**	.434*	-.191	-.436*	1.00		
Turkey	.377	.344	-.120	.198	.129	.222	.120	.432*	.068	.317	.332	-.305	-.009	-.014	.432*	1.00	
Venezuela	.169	-.087	-.036	.147	.225	.237	.024	.164	.341	.152	.142	.025	.100	.419*	.014	.107	1.00

* Significant at the 0.05 level (2-tailed)

** Significant at the 0.01 level (2-tailed)

Table 4
Correlation of Developed Market Return

	MSCI	Australia	Austria	Belgium	Canada	Denmark	Finland	France	Germany	Hong Kong	Italy	Japan	Netherland	News Land	Norway	Singapore	Spain	Sweden	Swizer Land	USA	UK
MSCI	1.00																				
Australia	.474**	1.00																			
Austria	171	.150	1.00																		
Belgium	.631**	.667**	.353	1.00																	
Canada	.734**	.746**	.304	.556**	1.00																
Denmark	.501*	.605**	.277	.705**	.543**	1.00															
Finland	.462*	.542**	.375	.419*	.451*	.355	1.00														
France	.793**	.712**	276	.899**	.673**	.601**	.496*	1.00													
Germany	.796**	.663**	.204	.840**	.551**	.502*	.454*	-.935**	1.00												
Hong Kong	.003	-.034	-.138	-.155	-.016	-.043	.157	-.091	-.192	1.00											
Italy	.331	.396	153	.278	.232*	.163	.124	.304	.460	-.114	1.00										
Japan	.262	.318	.334	.093	.430*	.043	-.100	.116	.054	.132	.200	1.00									
Netherlands	.815**	.718**	.279	.880**	.681**	.637**	.478*	.967**	.921**	-140	.368	.185	1.00								
Newsland	.400	.535**	.344	.486*	.629**	.322	.352	.412	.354	-.171	.147	.151	.431*	1.00							
Norway	.422*	.370	.152	.619**	.228	.749**	.205	.570**	.542**	.040	.196	-.054	.568*	.075	1.00						
Singapore	.547**	.542**	.145	.563**	.513*	.404	.331	.616**	.642**	.014	.259	.344	.660**	.397	.354	1.00					
Spain	.365	.205	.127	.634	.413*	.062	.191	.476*	.427*	.011	.336	.237	.438*	.277	.222	.292	1.00				
Sweden	.576**	.704**	.235	.766**	.672**	.468*	.505*	.896**	.859**	-.020	.415*	.240	.905**	.381	.404	.540**	.447*	1.00			
Switzerland	.693**	.614**	.320	.899**	.524*	.548**	.370	.869**	.823**	-.065	.191	.315	.848**	.412	.515*	.518*	.367	.812**	1.00		
USA	.891**	.786**	.238	.733**	.741**	.604**	.484*	.917**	.871**	-094	.355	249	.957**	.409	.498*	.615**	.343	.930**	.777**	1.00	
UK	.705	.760**	.233	.893**	.648**	.681**	.515	.926**	.866**	-.055	.352	.143	.912**	.414*	.609**	.628**	.383	.824**	.853**	.880*	1.00

* Significant at the 5%level (2-tailed)

** Significant at the 1% level (2-tailed)

Table 5
Correlation between Developed and Emerging Market

	Australia	Austria	Belgium	Canada	Denmark	Finland	France	Germany	Hong Kong	Italy	Japan	Nether-land	News-land	Norw-ay	Singap-ore	Spain	Sweden	Swifzer land	USA	UK
Argentina	.475*	.204	.298	.294	.165	.028	.307	.212	-.036	.189	.229	.299	.388	.085	.184	.234	.394	.378*	.339	.348
Brazil	.518*	.151	.657**	.328	.487*	.264	.665*	.725**	-.587**	.268	-.099	.683**	.293	.357	.532**	.152	.586*	.477*	.639**	.602**
Chile	.549**	.111	.306	.397	.317	.268	.377	.403	.189	.328	.172	.350	.036	.348	.333	.150	.328	.219	.382	.450*
India	.331	.010	.178	.373	.116	.078	.193	.173	.028	.312	.601**	.271	.370	.204	.441*	.363	.255	.200	.270	.228
Korea	.599**	.145	.581**	.625**	.400	.530	.687**	.699**	.106	.447*	.502*	.732**	.259	.460*	.560*	.482*	.754**	.655**	.736**	.610**
Mexico	.686**	.096	.861**	.552**	.728**	.620**	.853**	.852**	-.103	.451*	.054	.876**	.332	.618**	.572**	.321	.839**	.865**	.827**	.875**
Thailand	.642**	.142	.450*	.538**	.406*	.056	.524**	.450*	.104	.213	.324	.560**	.440*	.301	.481*	.217	.536**	.501*	.611**	.532**
Colombia	.149	.226	.391	.094	.231	.152	.263	.292	.119	-.057	.333	.261	.177	.441*	.381	.108	.245	.518*	.230	.355
Jordan	.126	.162	.432*	.097	.297	.274	.329	.284	-.050	.116	.209	.386	.111	.194	.458*	-.011	.247	.443*	.283	.501*
Malaysia	.072	-.005	-.158	.092	-.133	-.157	-.110	-.062	-.074	-.046	-.190	-.168	.163	-.118	-.161	.068	-.099	-.246	.130	-.325
Pakistan	-.064	-.087	.074	-.091	.135	.091	.033	.030	.113	-.080	.302	.115	-.205	133	217	-.301	018	.248	.091	.120
Philippines	.142	.283	.328	.626	.229	-.258	.070	.109	-.018	.458*	.329	.132	.011	.256	.038	.001	.148	.264	.097	.236
Indonesia	.336	.107	.589**	.260	.446*	.379	.495	.472	.038	.163	.224	.514*	.256	.384	.536**	.150	.476*	.584**	.481*	.693**
Taiwan	.273	-.094	.046	.332	.053	.164	.173	.186	.214	.110	.073	.197	.166	.101	.036	.166	.349	.076	.290	-.015
Turkey	.353	.118	.185	.391	.675	.132	.307	.190	.578**	.111	.215	.165	.200	.119	.125	.328	.341	.214	.240	.241
Venezuela	.174	.101	.131	.285	.120	.050	.109	.073	.273	-.162	.328	.143	.198	.067	.445*	.118	.119	.123	.216	.209

* Significant at the 5%level (2-tailed)

** Significant at the 1% level (2-tailed)

Table 6
Single-factor Regression Statistics for Emerging Market with MSCI World Index

Emerging Market	R^2	*Ad* R^2	*Observed F*	*Intercept*	*Beta Coefficient*	*t value*
Argentina	.055	.012	1.287	.583	.235	1.134
Brazil	.240	.204	6.646	-.539	.490	2.578
Chile	.117	.077	2.928	.529	.343	1.711
India	.028	-.017	.625	.721	.166	.791
Korea	.574	.555	29.672*	.715	.758	5.447*
Mexico	.519	.496	22.673*	-.672	.721	4.762*
Thailand	.293	.261	9.134	-.248	.542	3.022
Colombia	.034	-.010	.773	.647	.184	.879
Jordan	.001	-.045	.012	1.009	-.023	-.108
Malaysia	.025	-.019	.566	.775	.158	.753
Pakistan	.008	-.037	.176	.992	-.084	-.420
Philippines	.002	-.043	.053	1.043	-.049	-.229
Indonesia	.064	.022	1.507	.932	.253	1.227
Taiwan	.340	.310	11.349	.382	.583	3.369
Turkey	.142	.103	3.637	.712	.377	1.907
Venezuela	.029	-.016	.649	.763	.169	.805

* Significant at 1% level.

Table 7
Single-factor Regression Statistics for Developed Market With MSCI World Index

Emerging Market	R^2	*Ad* R^2	*Observed F*	*Intercept*	*Beta Coefficient*	*t value*
Australia	.559	.539	27.938*	-.623	.748	5.286*
Austria	.030	-.014	.684	.631	.174	.527
Belgium	.398	.371	14.539*	.343	.631	3.813*
Canada	.539	.518	25.716	-.684	.734	5.071*
Denmark	.251	.216	7.355	.326	.501	2.712
Finland	.214	.178	5.985	.800	.462	2.446
France	.628	.611	37.153	.262	.793	6.095*
Germany	.634	.618	38.157*	.422	.796	6.177*
Hong Kong	.003	-.045	.001	1.014	-.003	-.013
Italy	.109	.069	2.702	.729	.331	1.644
Japan	.069	.026	1.621	.765	.262	1.273
Netherlands	.665	.649	43.577*	.672	.815	6.601*

Newsland	.160	.120	4.001	-747	.400	2.000
Norway	.178	.141	4.764	.559	.422	2.183
Singapore	.299	.268	9.403	.420	.547	3.066
Spain	.133	.094	3.375	1.137	.365	1.837
Sweden	.767	.756	72.24*	-.297	.876	8.499*
Switzerland	.481	.456	19.436*	-8.098	.693	4.409*
USA	.793	.784	84.497*	.172	.891	9.192*
UK	.497	.474	21.738*	.329	.705	4.662*

* Significant at 1% level.

REVIEW QUESTIONS

1. What is emerging and developed market? How they are different? What is the importance of emerging market?
2. What is portfolio risk and investment?
3. Why " t" and "F" test is used? What are its significance?
4. Quiz
   (a) _____ called as the foundations of portfolio theory.
   (b) William Sharpe and Lintner later developed the popular _____ Model.
   (c) A correlation coefficient is a number between _____ which measures the degree to which two variables are linearly related.
   (d) The single factor Capital Asset Pricing Model (CAPM) as proposed by _____,_____ and _____ applied in the international context.

14

Performance Evaluation of Mutual Funds in India

The Indian financial system in general and the Mutual Fund (MF) industry in particular continue to take turnaround from early 1990s. Growth and development of various mutual fund products in Indian capital market have proved to be one of the most catalytic instruments in generating momentous investment growth in the capital market. In this context, close monitoring and evaluation of mutual funds has become essential. Therefore, the present Chapter evaluates the performance of 31 tax planning schemes in India.

INTRODUCTION

With the growth of the economy and the capital market in India, the size of investors has also increased rapidly. New innovative instruments and institutions have emerged which have been playing the role of financial intermediaries. With the emphasis on increase in domestic savings and improvement in deployment of investment through markets, the need and scope for mutual fund operation has increased tremendously. In this context, close monitoring and evaluation of mutual funds has become essential for fund managers to make this instrument as the strongest and most preferred instrument in Indian capital market in the coming years.

Mutual funds have a fund manager who invests the money on behalf of the investors by buying / selling stocks, bonds etc. The United States leads with the number of mutual fund schemes. There are more than 8000 mutual fund schemes in the USA. Comparatively, India has around 1000 mutual fund schemes, but this number has grown exponentially in the last few years. The Total Assets under Management in India of all Mutual funds put together touched a peak of ₹ 6,27,999 Crore. during April to September 2009-10.

WHAT IS MUTUAL FUND?

A mutual fund is a professionally managed type of collective investment scheme that pools money from many investors and invests it in stocks, bonds, short-term money market instruments and other securities. It is trust that pools the savings of a number of investors who share a common financial goal. Money collected is invested in capital market instruments. Income earned and capital appreciations are shared by its unit holders. MF gives an opportunity to invest in: Diversified, Professionally managed, Basket of Securities and At Low Cost.

HISTORY OF MUTUAL FUND

The modern mutual fund was first introduced in Belgium in 1822. This form of investment soon spread to Great Britain and France. Mutual funds became popular in the United States in the 1920s and continue to be popular since the1930s, especially open-ended mutual funds. Mutual funds experienced a period of tremendous growth after World War II, especially in the 1980s and 1990s. As of October 2007, there are 8,015 mutual funds that belong to the Investment Company Institute (ICI), a national trade association of investment companies in the United States, with combined assets of $ 12.356 trillion. In early 2008, the worldwide value of all mutual funds totaled more than $ 26 trillion.

MUTUAL FUNDS STRUCTURE IN INDIA

Mutual Funds in India follow a 3-tier structure. There is a Sponsor (the First tier), who thinks of starting a mutual fund. The Sponsor approaches the Securities and Exchange Board of India (SEBI), which are the market regulator and also the regulator for mutual funds. Not everyone can start a mutual fund. SEBI checks whether the person is of integrity, whether he has enough experience in the financial sector, his net worth etc. Once SEBI is convinced, the sponsor creates a Public Trust (the Second tier) as per the Indian Trusts Act, 1882. Trusts have no legal identity in India and cannot enter into contracts, hence the Trustees are the people authorized to act on behalf of the Trust. Contracts are entered into in the name of the Trustees. Once the Trust is created, it is registered with SEBI after which this trust is known as the mutual fund. It is important to understand the difference between the Sponsor and the Trust. They are two separate entities. Sponsor is not the Trust, i.e., Sponsor is not the Mutual Fund. It is the Trust which is the Mutual Fund. The Trustee's role is not to manage the money. Their job is only to see, whether the money is being managed as per stated objectives. Trustees may be seen as the internal regulators of a mutual fund.

TYPES OF MUTUAL FUND

The existing types of schemes in the Industry are:

By Structure:

A mutual fund scheme is classified into open-ended scheme or close-ended scheme depending on its maturity period.

Open-ended Fund

An open-ended Mutual fund is one that is available for subscription and repurchase on a continuous basis. These Funds do not have a fixed maturity period. Investors can conveniently buy and sell units at Net Asset Value (NAV) related prices which are declared on a daily basis. The key feature of open-ended schemes is liquidity.

Close-ended Fund

A close-ended Mutual fund has a stipulated maturity period, e.g., 5-7 years. The fund is open for subscription only during a specified period at the time of launch of the scheme. Investors can invest in the scheme at the time of the initial public issue and thereafter they can buy or sell the units of the scheme on the stock exchanges where the units are listed. In order to provide exit route to the investors, some close-ended funds give an option of selling back the units to the mutual fund through periodic repurchase at NAV related prices. SEBI Regulations stipulate that at least one of the two exit routes is provided to the investor, i.e., either repurchase facility or through listing on stock exchanges. These mutual funds schemes disclose NAV generally on weekly basis.

Interval Schemes:

Interval Schemes are that scheme, which combines the features of open-ended and close-ended schemes. The units may be traded on the stock exchange or may be open for sale or redemption during predetermined intervals at NAV related prices.

Risk Return Matrix

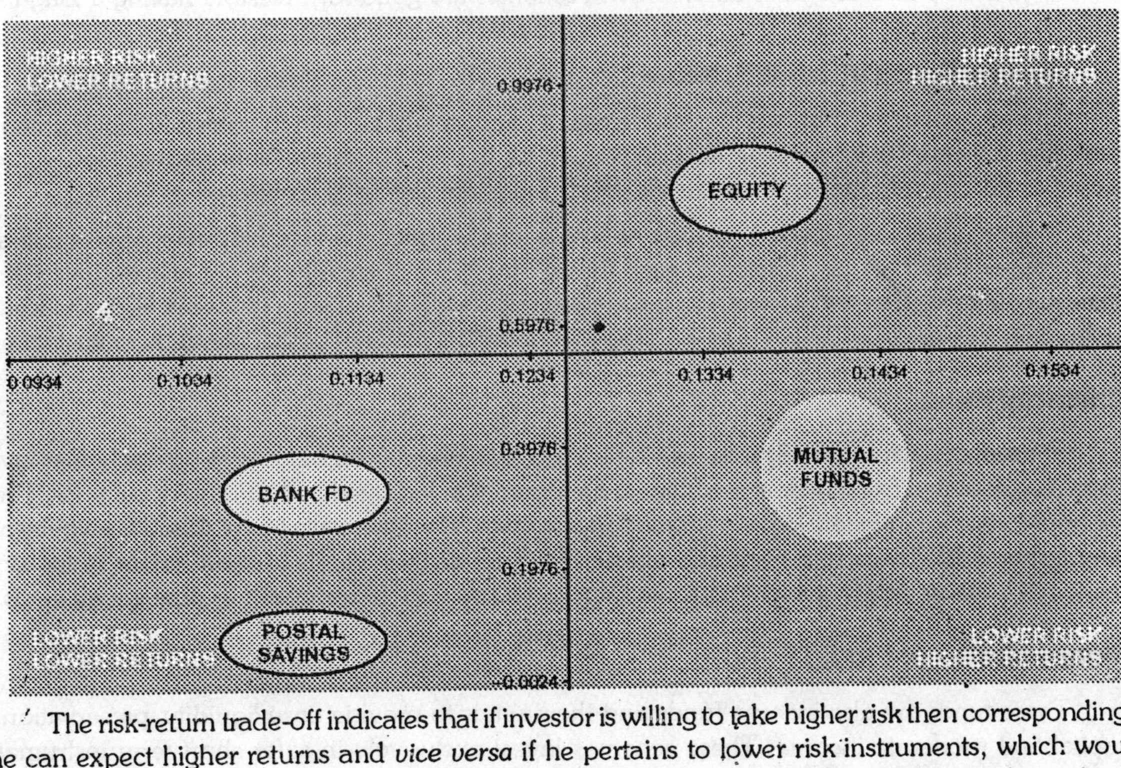

The risk-return trade-off indicates that if investor is willing to take higher risk then correspondingly he can expect higher returns and *vice versa* if he pertains to lower risk instruments, which would be satisfied by lower returns. For example, if an investor opt for bank FD, which provide moderate return with minimal risk. But as he moves ahead to invest in capital protected funds and the profit-bonds that give out more return which is slightly higher as compared to the bank deposits but the risk involved also increases in the same proportion.

Thus investors choose mutual funds as the primary means of investing, as Mutual funds provide professional management, diversification, convenience and liquidity. That doesn't mean mutual fund investments risk free. This is because the money that is pooled in are not invested only in debts funds which are less riskier but are also invested in the stock markets which involves a higher risk but can expect higher returns. Hedge fund involves a very high risk since it is mostly traded in the derivatives market which is considered very volatile.

By Investment Objective:

A scheme can also be classified as growth fund, income fund, or balanced fund considering its investment objective. Such schemes may be open-ended or close-ended schemes as described earlier. Such schemes may be classified mainly as follows:

Growth/Equity Oriented Scheme

The aim of growth funds is to provide capital appreciation over the medium to long-term. Such schemes normally invest a major part of their corpus in equities. Such funds have comparatively high risks. These schemes provide different options to the investors like dividend option, capital appreciation, etc. and the investors may choose an option depending on their preferences. The investors must indicate the option in the application form. The mutual funds also allow the investors to change the options at a later date. Growth schemes are good for investors having a long-term outlook seeking appreciation over a period of time.

Income/Debt Oriented Scheme

The aim of income funds is to provide regular and steady income to investors. Such schemes generally invest in fixed income securities such as bonds, corporate debentures, Government securities and money market instruments. Such funds are less risky compared to equity.

These funds are not affected because of fluctuations in equity markets. However, opportunities of capital appreciation are also limited in such funds. The NAVs of such funds are affected because of change in interest rates in the country. If the interest rates fall, NAVs of such funds are likely to increase in the short run and *vice versa*. However, long-term investors may not bother about these fluctuations.

Balanced Fund

The aim of balanced funds is to provide both growth and regular income as such schemes invest both in equities and fixed income securities in the proportion indicated in their offer documents. These are appropriate for investors looking for moderate growth. They generally invest 40-60% inequity and debt instruments. These funds are also affected because of fluctuations in share prices in the stock markets. However, NAVs of such funds are likely to be less volatile compared to pure equity funds.

Money Market or Liquid Fund

These funds are also income funds and their aim is to provide easy liquidity, preservation of capital and moderate income. These schemes invest exclusively in safer short-term instruments such as treasury bills, certificates of deposit, commercial paper and inter-bank call money, government securities, etc. Returns on these schemes fluctuate much less compared to other funds. These funds are appropriate for corporate and individual investors as a means to park their surplus funds for short periods.

Other Schemes:

Tax-Savings Schemes

It aims to minimize tax bills, such as keeping turnover levels low or shying away from companies that provide dividends, which are regular payouts in cash or stock that, are taxable in the year that they are received. These funds still shoot for solid returns; they just want less of them showing up on the tax returns.

Index Funds

Index Funds replicate the portfolio of a particular index such as the BSE Sensitive index, S&P NSE 50 index (Nifty), etc. These schemes invest in the securities in the same weight age comprising of an index. NAVs of such schemes would rise or fall in accordance with the rise or fall in the index, though not exactly by the same percentage due to some factors known as "tracking error" in technical terms. Necessary disclosures in this regard are made in the offer document of the mutual fund scheme. There are also exchange traded index funds launched by the mutual funds which are traded on the stock exchanges.

The types of Mutual Fund are also presented in the Fig. 1

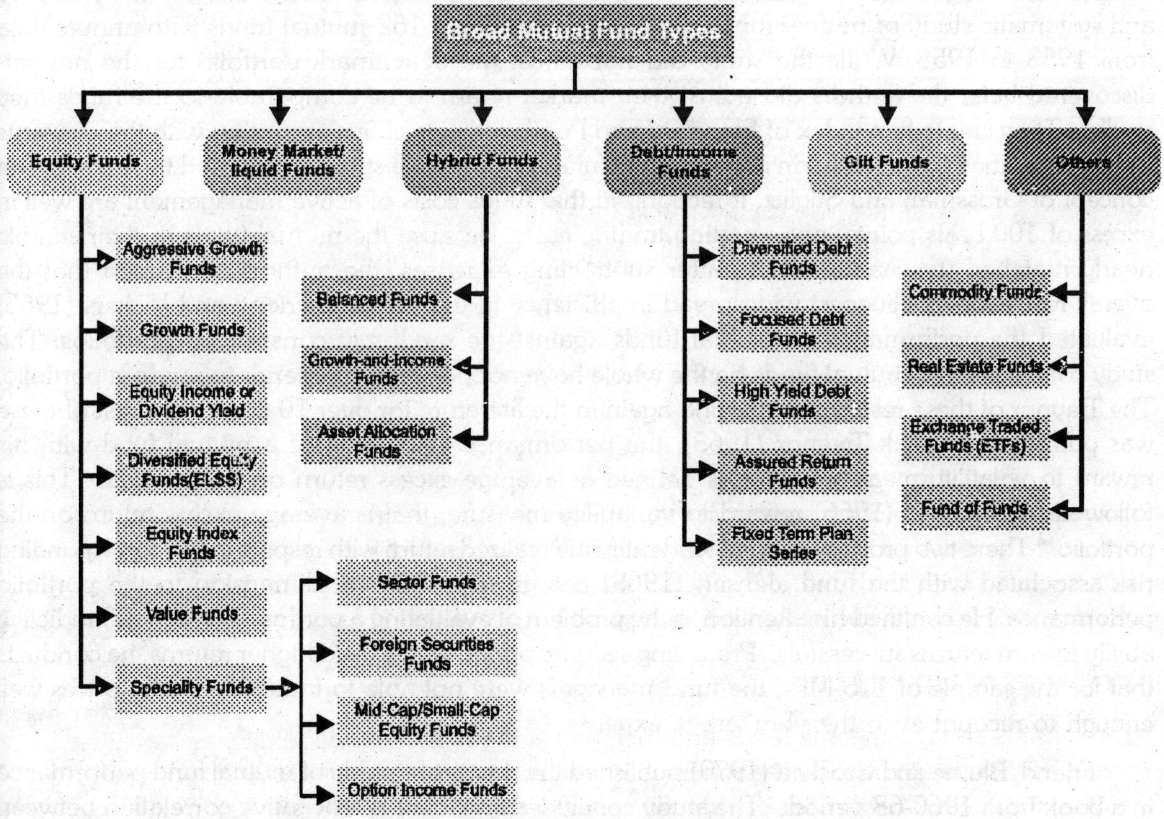

Fig. 1: Types of Mutual Fund

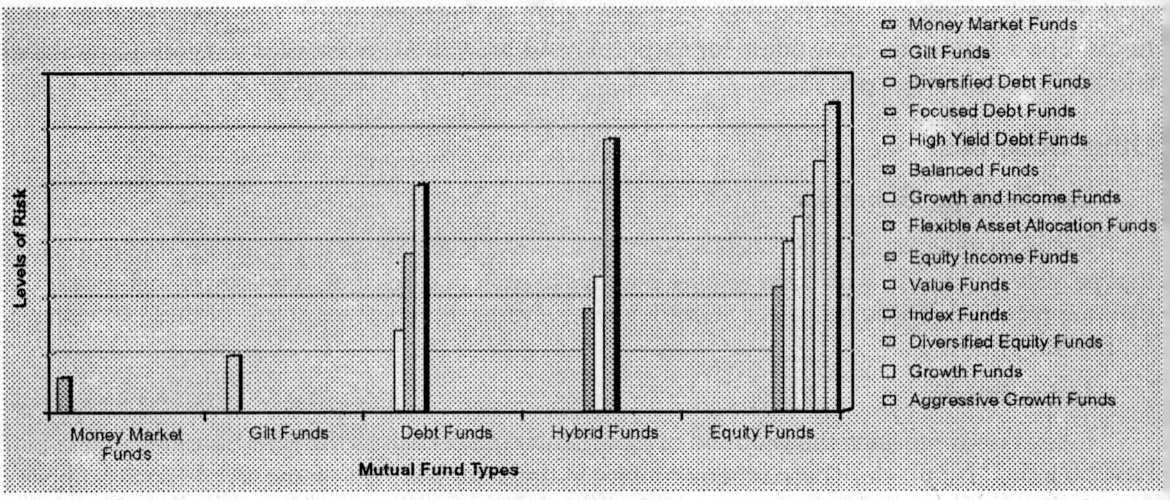

Fig. 2: Risk Hierarchy of Different Mutual Funds

LITERATURE REVIEW

In keeping with the economic frames, several scholars have investigated whether or not mutual funds outperform the market. Friend, Brown, Herman and Vickers did the first extensive and systematic study of mutual funds. The study considered 152 mutual funds with annual data from 1953 to 1958. While the study did not adjust the benchmark portfolio for the not-yet-discovered beta, the authors did adjust their market return to be comparable to the funds they studies. They created an index of Standard and Poor's indexes of five securities, with the elements weighted by their representation in the mutual funds sample. The study anticipated the equilibrium concept of Grossman and Stiglitz. It recognized that funds costs of active management are well in excess of 100 basis points, not counting trading costs. Because the mutual funds in their sample nearly matched the market index, after subtracting expenses, the authors concluded that the overall results do not suggest widespread in efficiency in the industry. Friend and Vickers (1965) evaluated the performance of mutual funds against the randomly constructed portfolios. The study concludes that mutual funds on the whole have not performed superior to random portfolio. The Treynor of these results is not found again in the literature for over 10 years. The first of these was published by Jack Treynor (1965), the performance evaluation of a mutual fund with his reward to volatility measure which is defined as average excess return on the portfolio. This is followed by Sharpe's (1966) reward to variability measure, that is average excess return on the portfolio. [4] There two procedures tried to identify the realized return with respect to the corresponding risk associated with the fund. Jensen (1968) has given a different dimension to the portfolio performance. He confined his attention to the problem of evaluating a portfolio manager's predictive ability to earn returns successfully. Predicting security prices, which yield higher returns, he conducts that for the sample of 115 MFs, the fund managers were not able to forecast security prices well enough to recount even their brokerage expense.

Friend, Blume and Crockett (1970) published the results of a study of mutual fund performance in a book from 1960-68 periods. The study concludes that there is a negative correlation between fund performance and management expense measures. Also it found that results for the period 1960-68 as a whole provide some evidence of a slight positive relation between performance and turnover. Risk-adjusted performance evaluation is made by Carlsen (1970) emphasized that the conclusions drawn from calculations of return depend on the time period, type of fund and the choice of benchmark. Carlsen essentially recalculated the Jensen and Sharpe results using annual data for 82 common stock funds over the 1948-67 periods. His results contradicted both Sharpe and Jensen. Risk-adjusted performance evaluation is also made by SEC study (1971) and concluded that some of the funds had outperformed the benchmarks but there was no consistency in performance. John McDonald (1974) examined the relationship between the stated fund objectives and their risk and return attributes. The study concludes that, on an average, the fund managers appeared to keep their portfolios within the stated risk. Some funds in the lower risk group possessed higher risk than funds in the most risky group. James RF Guy (1978) evaluated the risk-adjusted performance of UK investment trusts through the application of Sharpe and Jensen measures. The study concludes that no trust had exhibited superior performance compared to the London Stock Exchange Index. Kon and Jen (1979) explored the possibility of market-related risk over a period of time for mutual funds. The authors separated the data sample based on the risk regimes and applied OLS (Ordinary Least Square) method on each sample. The findings showed different betas for 37 out of 49 funds which indicates active manager's timing activities for maximizing the fund's yield. Peasnell, Skerratt and Taylor (1979) had remarked the Jensen investigation into mutual fund performance using the insights of Arbitrage theory and this exercise appeared to provide independent confirmation of Jensen's findings that professionally managed funds are systematically unable to outperform the market.

Henriksson and Merton (1981) reported that mutual fund managers were not able to follow an investment strategy that successfully times the return on the market portfolio. Again Henriksson (1984) conclude there is strong evidence that the funds market risk exposures change in response to the market indicated. But the fund managers were not successful in timing the market.

Berkowitz, Finney and Logue (1988) studied mutual fund performance using quarterly data over the 1976-83 periods. They measured a higher alpha for growth funds; they assumed the findings are evidence of the small firm effect. Grinblatt and Titman (1989) conclude that some mutual funds consistently realize abnormal returns by systematically picking stocks that realize positive excess returns. So, one must consider the caveat that the measures used require that returns be drawn from a stationary distribution. Richard A. Ippolito (1989) concludes that mutual funds on an aggregate offer superior returns. But expenses and load charges offset them. This characterizes the efficient market hypothesis. Peter Oertmann and Heinz Zimmermann (1966) conclude that the relation between average fund returns and the traditional measures of risk, such as volatility and beta, is positive and thereby predict, the relationship postulated by the CAPM to be surprisingly strong. Ariff and Johnson (1990) made an important study in Singapore and found that the performance of Singapore unit trusts spread around the market performance with approximately half of the funds performing below the market and another half performing above the market on a risk-adjusted basis. Cole and IP (1993) investigated the performance of Australian equity trusts. They found evidence that portfolio managers were unable to earn overall positive excess risk-adjusted returns. Allen and Tan (1998) studied for UK and found that both raw returns and risk-adjusted returns exhibited strong evidence of persistence in the long run but this evidence appears to reverse in the short run. A number of academics, professionals have written articles explaining the concept, function and importance of mutual funds in the development of the capital market in India. Barua and Varma (1991) evaluated the performance of master share (1987-1991) using CAPM approach. The study had used ET Index as a proxy for market behavior. The risk-adjusted performance is measured by using Sharpe, Jensen and Treynor measures. The study concluded that the fund performed better than the market, but the fund did not do well when compared to Capital Market Line (CML). Ajay Shah and Susan Thomas (1994) studied the performance evaluation of 11 mutual fund schemes and concluded that except one scheme other schemes earned inferior returns than the market in general. Bhosale and Adhikary (1994) evaluated the performance of growth schemes using Sharpe, Treynor, Jensen and Fama's measures. The study has used Fama's measures for identifying returns due to diversification and systematic risk. Jaideep and Sudip Majumdar (1994) evaluated the performance of five growth oriented schemes for the period February 1991 to August 1993. They have used CAPM and Jensen measures to evaluate the performance. They conclude that the selected mutual fund schemes have not offered superior returns during the study period than the market in general. Kaura and Jaydev (1995) evaluated the performance of growth oriented schemes by using Jensen, Treynor and Sharpe measures and found that the schemes have not performed well. Tripathy., Nalini. P (1996) has evaluated the performance of growth oriented schemes by using CAPM model and Jensen, Treynor, Sharpe measures and concluded that performance appraisal is not a difficult task rather return of the scheme will depend upon the performance of mutual funds. So, the fund may produce returns either above or below average, but it may be superior over the long run. Again in her further study (1998), concluded that the involvement of mutual funds in the transformation of Indian economy has made it urgent to view their services not only as financial intermediary but also as a pace setter as they are playing a significant role in spreading equity culture. R. A. Yadav and Biswadeep Mishra (1996) have evaluated performance of 14 mutual fund schemes using monthly data. It uses three risk-adjusted performance measures namely Sharpe Index, Treynor Index and Jensen measure. The study concluded that the funds as a whole performed well in terms of non-risk-adjusted measure of average returns and the fund managers of growth schemes adopted a conservative investment policy and maintained a low profile beta. M. Thiripalraju and Prabhakare R. Patil (1997) made a study from 1994 to 1999 and concluded that none of the schemes rewarded the investors and the portfolio managers cannot book the profits when the market is in boom phase due to lack of depth in the market. K. V. Rao and K. Venkateswarlu (1997) concluded that the performance of the UTI is mixed, indicating outperformance in only some of the schemes. G. Ramachnadran (1997) suggests that external influences together with imperfections of Indian stock markets are turning portfolio performance measures less reliable. So, he rejects CAPM under predictive and non-predictive forms. So, he concludes that median of returns and mean absolute deviation of returns might be considered as an alternative to mean and standard deviation of returns, while evaluating mutual fund schemes risk-adjusted performance meaningfully wherever normality is violated with high peakedness and long tails. When both methods are individually applied, performance rankings of mutual fund schemes found to differ significantly. Amitabh Gupta (2000) has examined the investment performance of Indian mutual funds in terms of six performance measures, using weekly NAV data for 73 mutual fund schemes from 1994 to 1999. He found that the schemes have shown a mixed performance during the period. Worldwide fund managers are under scrutiny of sponsors, investors, regulators and researchers. Again in Gupta (2002) examined the growth, regulatory framework and performance evaluation of Indian mutual funds and reported poor performance. The present chapter has been undertaken with the object of examining the market timing abilities of Indian fund managers to reward higher return to the investors. This chapter has been test the following hypothesis in respect of performance evaluation of the Indian mutual funds. In India, very little work has been done to investigate fund managers forecasting abilities. Active fund managers are expected to reward higher return. If the fund manager identifies undervalued stocks, he will buy them and earn expected return. If the fund manager feels that market on the whole overvalued, then he would get out of the market. Hence, the present study has the objective of finding out the necessary facts, which can benefit the investors and fund managers. This paper evaluates the performance of mutual fund schemes in the framework of risk and return.

This chapter tests the following hypothesis in respect of performance evaluation of the Indian mutual funds:

- The sample mutual funds are earning higher returns than the market portfolio returns (benchmark returns) in terms of risk.
- The sample mutual funds are offering the advantages of diversification and superior returns due to selectivity to their investors.
- The investment objectives of the mutual fund schemes are related to their systematic risk and total variability.
- Mutual fund managers display distinct market-timing abilities.
- Managers of tax saving schemes are more likely to exhibit market-timing abilities.
- Fund Managers of closed-ended schemes are likely to be more successful in timing the market.

Risk can be hard to quantify and assessing attitudes to risk even more so. Nevertheless, finance theory tells us that risk and risk aversion are critical factors in the determination of most investors' portfolios.

It is difficult to provide a single best summary measure of the risk attached to a particular investment such as a mutual fund because the best measure of risk depends on whether the mutual fund is held in isolation or is part of a larger portfolio of assets. In the latter case, risk can actually be lower than the sum of the risks attached to the investments held separately. This is because a portfolio generally contains investments with offsetting risks: when one investment is doing well, another might be doing badly and *vice versa*, and so the overall risk from combining the two investments can be reduced. The process of combining investments in a way that reduces overall risk is called diversification.

Standard deviation is one commonly used measure of risk. It is useful both when considering an asset held in isolation and when considering a portfolio as a whole. In the case of a single asset, standard deviation measures the dispersion of an asset's returns around its mean or average value. It is equal to the square root of the variance of the asset's returns. The variance of the returns on a portfolio comprising two assets is equal to the weighted sum of the variances of the two assets' returns plus twice the covariance between these returns. Again, the standard deviation is the square root of the variance.

Hence, while standard deviation may be an appropriate measure of risk for a single asset, the presence of covariance terms means that when two or more assets are held in combination, the individual assets' standard deviations are no longer sufficient measures of the risk of the combined asset holdings.

Generally, investors invest in mutual fund by considering capital appreciation, better liquidity, less risk and tax liability.

TAKE THE CASE OF THIRTY-ONE EQUITY-LINKED SCHEMES FOR EVALUATING PERFORMANCE:

So, this chapter takes 31 schemes, i.e., The UTI, LIC, CanBank, IND Bank, PNB Bank, SBI, and BOI Bank for comprehensive evaluation of schemes. The risk is calculated on the basis of month-end Net Asset Values. Further, BSE national index is assessed as market index or benchmark. The returns are computed on the basis of the Net Asset Values (NAVs) of the different schemes and returns in the market index are computed on the basis of the BSE National Index on the respective date. The NAVs are adjusted assuming dividends are reinvested at the ex-dividend NAV. In this study, the weekly yields on 91-day Treasury bills have been used as a surrogate for risk-free rate of return.

Return: The returns are computed as follows:

$$R_{pt} = \ln\left[\frac{NAV_{t+1} - NAV_t}{NAV_t}\right]$$

Where R_{pt} is return on the fund during the period 't', where 't' stands for time and NAV stands for Net Asset Value of the fund. 'In' is the natural logarithm to the base 'e'.

The average return on the market portfolio is determined as follows:

$$R_p = \sum_{t=1}^{n} R_{pt} / n$$

Where R_p is the average return on the mutual fund schemes.

BSE national index is taken as benchmark. Similarly, return on index is computed by the following formula.

$$R_{mt} = \ln\left[\frac{Index_{t+1} - Index_t}{Index_t}\right]$$

Where 'R_m' is the returns on the basis of the BSE National Index. 'In' is the natural logarithm to the base 'e'.

The average return on market index is as follows:

$$R_m = \sum_{t=1}^{n} R_{mt} / n$$

Where R_m is the average return on the market.

Risk standard deviation of monthly returns is to be taken as risk. Sharpe pointed out, "It is generally highly correlated with familiar measures and thus provides an adequate surrogate."

$$\sigma_p = \left\{ \frac{1}{n} \sum_{t=1}^{n} (R_{pt} - R_p)^2 \right\}^{1/2}$$

Where σ_p is total risk of the scheme portfolio. The logarithmic standard deviation is to be expressed in percentage after multiplying it by 100. The total risk on the market line portfolio is

$$\sigma_m = \left\{ \frac{1}{n} \sum_{t=1}^{n} (R_{mt})^2 \right\}^{1/2}$$

Where σ_m is total risk of the market portfolio

In order to obtain systematic risk (Beta) of the portfolio, CAPM version of market model is applied. The estimable form of CAPM is:

$$R_p = a + \beta_p R_m + ep$$

Where, R_p is the return on the mutual fund scheme

R_m is the return on the market index

a is the constant term

β_p is the systematic risk (Beta)

ep is the error term

Higher β indicates a high sensitivity of fund returns against marker returns, the lower value indicates a low sensitivity.

Performance Evaluation Measures

The performance of sample mutual fund schemes has been evaluated by using the following six performance measures. A brief description of these measures is as follows:

Treynor Measrue

This model measures the relationship between fund's additional return over risk-free return and market risk measured by beta. This is called as reward to volatility measure ($RVOL_p$).

$$RVOL_p = (R_p - R_f)/\beta_p$$

If the $RVOL_p$ is greater than the benchmark comparison ($R_m - R_f$), the portfolio has outperformed the market.

Sharpe Measure

This measure indicates the relationship between the portfolio's additional return over risk-free return and total risk of the portfolio measured in terms of standard deviation. This is called as reward to variability measure ($RVAR_p$).

$$RVAR_p = (R_p - R_t)/\sigma_p$$

Where R_p = Average return on the portfolio

R_f = Risk-free rate

σ_p = Total risk of the scheme portfolio

The benchmark comparison is $RVAR_M = (R_M - R_f)/$

If $RVAR_p$ is greater than the benchmark comparison, the fund's performance is superior over the market. If the $RVAR_p$ is less than $RVAR_M$, the fund's performance is not good as the market. A fund, which may have outperformed according to Treynor measure, may indicate inferior performance according to Sharpe measure. Because it is based on systematic risk and Sharpe measure is based on total risk. Such risk is not a factor in determining a value of the Treynor measure, as market risk is only the denominator of Treynor measure. But, in case of Sharpe measure, total risk is the denominator. So, a fund with a low amount of market risk could have a high amount of total risk resulting a high Treynor measure and low Sharpe measure.

Differential Return Measure

The differential return measures of Jensen and Sharpe are obsolete measures of performance and reflect whether or not fund managers are able to generate returns in excess of equilibrium returns.

Jensen Differential Measure

Jensen attempts to construct a measure of absolute performance on a risk-adjusted basis that a definite standard against which performance of various funds can be measured. This standard is based on CAPM measures the portfolio manager's predictive ability to achieve higher return than expected for the given riskiness. The basic model is:

$$R_p - R_f = \alpha + \beta(R_m - R_f) + ep$$

Where, R_p = Average return on the portfolio

R_f = Risk-free rate

R_m = Average return on the market

α = Intercept measuring the forecasting ability of the manager

= Systematic risk measure

ep = Error term

A positive value of Alpha for a portfolio would indicate that the portfolio has an average return greater than the benchmark return indicating the superior performance. Alternatively, a negative value of alpha would indicate that the fund has a return less than the benchmark.

Sharpe Differential Return Measure

Sharpe has applied this measure to know the incremental returns earned by the mutual fund manager for the given level of risk. The Sharpe Differential Return measure may be computed by using following formula:

$$R_p - [R_f + (R_m - R_f)\sigma_p / \sigma_m]$$

The Sharpe measure is based on the Capital Market Line (CML). One of the major characteristics of CML is that only efficient portfolio can be plotted here. So it is assumed that, a managed portfolio (mutual fund scheme) is an efficient portfolio. If a portfolio is well diversified, the two measures (Jensen and Sharpe) should indicate same level of differential return. If the portfolio is imperfectly diversified, the Sharpe differential return will be smaller.

The differential return will be difference between the actual average return of the mutual fund scheme ad its expected return for the given level of risk. Sharpe measure therefore takes into consideration not only the manager's stock selection ability but also his ability to provide diversification. A comparison of Sharpe's differential returns and Jensen's alpha reveals the impact of selectivity and diversification on the fund returns.

Fama's Decomposition Measure

Eugene Fama provides a framework that allows for a more detailed breakdown of the performance of a fund. The total return is decomposed into: (i) risk-free rate, (ii) compensation for systematic risk, (iii) compensation for inadequate diversification, and (iv) Net superior return. Net selectivity is defined as the excess return adjusted for all risk. This is same as the difference between selectivity and the compensation for inadequate diversification. The fund manager or the mutual funds asset management company can select undervalued securities to earn higher return and can be determined with the help of the following formula:

(a) Risk-free Return : R_f

(b) Compensation for Systematic Risk : $\beta(R_m - R_f)$

(c) Compensation for Inadequate Diversification : $(R_m - R_f)(\sigma_p / \sigma_m - \beta$

(d) Net Selectivity : $(R_p - R_f) - (\sigma_p - \sigma_m)(R_m - R_f)$

If it shows positive feature, then the investors are benefited out of the selectivity exercised by the fund manager and assume that it has achieved superior returns.

Methods of Market Timing:

The market timing of sample mutual fund schemes has been evaluated by using the two measures. A brief description of these measures are as follows:

Treynor and Mazuy Model:

These are several procedures that have been proposed to correct the effect of timing ability on the estimate of beta. The first is a quadratic regression proposed by Treynor and Mazuy. This regression is:

$$R_p - R_f = \alpha + \beta(R_m - R_f) + \gamma(R_m - R_f)^2 + \varepsilon$$

Where, R_{f} = Risk—free Return

E_{p} = Random error term

α, β and γ are parameters of the model.

The parameters in the above model can be estimated by using standard regression methodology. Treynor and Mazuy have argued that estimated value of parameter γ in the above formula act as a measure of market-timing skill of the fund manager. If fund managers could able to select the time correctly, the estimated value of γ would be significantly positive. On the contrary if the estimated value of γ should not be significantly different from zero, the fund managers are not be able to select the market timing correctly. The average beta of the portfolio would be constant when the fund manager is not engaged in market timing and only concentrates in stock selection. In this case, the fund return and market return would be a linear relationship. Even if the fund manager changed the beta and would not be successful in assessing the market timing, still it shows the linear relationship. Treynor and Mazuy argued that in case the fund manage was able to successfully assess the market direction and changes the portfolio beta, it would find a higher than normal beta. In that situation, it implies that the fund is doing better. When the market declines, the fund has a lower than normal beta. In such situations the plots of the fund returns against the market returns would lie above the linear relationship and would give a curvature to the scatter of points.

Henriksson and Merton Model:

Another return-based approach for estimating timing performance is the option approach developed by Merton and Hendrickson. The regression used is similar to the Treyner-Mazuy regression. In contrast to the linear beta, adjustment of the Treynor and Mazuy framework, the portfolio beta in the Henrikson and Merton study is assumed to switch between two betas. A large value if the market is expected to do well, i.e., when $R_m > R_f$ (up market) and a small value otherwise, i.e., when $R_m < R_f$ (down market). Therefore, it is argued that a successful market timer would select a high up-market beta and a low down-market beta. Thus, such a relationship can be estimated by equation using a dummy variable.

$$R_p - R_f = \alpha_+ \beta (R_m - R_f) + \gamma [D (R_m - R_f)] + E_p$$

Where D is a dummy variable that equals o for $R_m > R_f$ and –1 otherwise.

So that beta of the portfolio is b in a up market and (b-g) in a down market. Parameter g indicates the difference between the two betas and significant value of g would indicate market timing ability of the fund managers.

ANALYSIS

Risk and Return Analysis:

The Table 1 presents return and risk of the thirty-one tax planning schemes together with market return and risk. From the table, it is evident that out of the thirty-one schemes only nine schemes, i.e., Magnum Gift, Plan-A, Magnum Gift Plan-B, Canpep-92, Canpep-93, MEP-93, Indtaxshild Plan-A, Magnum Tax Profit-94, Canpep-94, MELS-95, MELS-96, MEP-95, MEP-96, have earned higher return than the market return and rest of the 22 schemes have earned lower return than the market return. It is also seen from the Table 1 that 12 schemes have earned positive returns while the remaining schemes exhibited negative returns. The average return earned by the sample schemes is 2.87% whereas average risk-free return for the same scheme is 3.11%. The average return for the market is 2.39%. This implies that the sample scheme on an average performed poorer than the risk-free asset. The average risk of the sample scheme is 38.92% whereas the market risk is 68.31%. It is evident from the Table 2 that the total risk of ten schemes, i.e., Canpep-93, MEP-91, Indshelter Plan-A, Indshelter Plan-B, PNBELSS-92, LIC Dhan 80cc B(2) Plan-B, Canster 80L-90, MEP-93, Indtaxshield Plan-A, MEP-96 is higher than the market risk and remaining 21 schemes are lower than the market risk on the whole, 13 schemes have an above average beta which indicates that mutual fund returns are highly volatile.

Table 1

Risk and Return of Mutual Fund Schemes vs. Benchmark Comparison

Sl. No.		*Fund Return*	*Risk-free Return*	*Fund Risk*	*Market Return*	*Market Risk*
1	MELS-91	-0.054361	-0.031111	0.102452	0.023839	0.683189
2	Magnum Gift Plan - A	0.071483	-0.031111	0.130533	0.023839	0.683189
3	Magnum Gift Plan - B	0.045151	-0.031111	0.103530	0.023839	0.683189
4	Boinanza 80 cc (B) Plan-B	-0.050996	-0.031111	0.155541	0.023839	0.683189
5	Canpep-91	-0.081650	-0.031111	0.103149	0.023839	0.683189
6	Canpep-92	0.024801	-0.031111	0.102814	0.023839	0.683189
7	Canpep-93	0.021149	-0.031111	0.855117	0.023839	0.683189
8	MEP-91	-0.032112	-0.031111	0.813722	0.023839	0.683189
9	MEP-92	-0.022055	-0.031111	0.114662	0.023839	0.683189
10	Indshelter Plan-A	-0.189047	-0.031111	0.973572	0.023839	0.683189
11	Indshelter Plan-B	-0.091636	-0.031111	0.757626	0.023839	0.683189
12	PNBELSS-92	-0.155634	-0.031111	0.686240	0.023839	0.683189
13	PNBELSS-91.80 cc B	-0.125718	-0.031111	0.645905	0.023839	0.683189
14	LIC Dhan 80 cc B (1) Plan-A	-0.102592	-0.031111	0.636388	0.023839	0.683189
15	LIC Dhan 80 cc B (1) Plan-B	-0.102593	-0.031111	0.627806	0.023839	0.683189
16	LIC Dhan 80 cc B (1) Plan-C	-0.013662	-0.031111	0.105988	0.023839	0.683189

17	LIC Dhan 80 cc B (2) Plan-A	-0.081844	-0.031111	0.144359	0.023839	0.683189
18	LIC Dhan 80 cc B (2) Plan-B	-0.081844	-0.031111	0.857196	0.023839	0.683189
19	LIC Dhan 80 cc B (2) Plan-C	-0.064391	-0.031111	0.125927	0.023839	.683189
20	Boinanza 80 cc (B) Plan-A	-0.068854	-0.031111	0.101407	0.023839	0.683189
21	Canster 80L-90	-0.053053	-0.031111	0.725951	0.023839	0.683189
22	MEP-93	-0.009382	-0.031111	0.928416	0.023839	0.683189
23	Indtax Plan-A	0.008787	-0.031111	0.694095	0.023839	0.683189
24	Indtax Plan-B	-0.003381	-0.031111	0.118480	0.023839	0.683189
25	Magnum Tax Profit-94	0.103063	-0.031111	0.103578	0.023839	0.683189
26	Canpep-94	0.026824	-0.031111	0.112271	0.023839	0.683189
27	MELS-95	0.065246	-0.031111	0.150691	0.023839	0.683189
28	MELS-96	0.116866	-0.031111	0.110306	0.023839	0.683189
29	MEP-94	-0.116330	-0.031111	0.130270	0.023839	0.683189
30	MEP-95	0.059985	-0.031111	0.114369	0.023839	0.683189
31	MEP-96	0.045626	-0.031111	0.732672	0.023839	0.683189
	Average	-0.028710	-0.031111	0.389195	0.023839	0.683189

Risk-Return Grid of Sample Schemes

The sample schemes have been classified into four categories on the basis of their return and risk characteristics. The Figure 1 presents four-quadrant picture on returns and risk.

- Quadrant I present schemes, which have earned higher returns than the market. (High return/Low risk). In this category out of 31 schemes, eight schemes are falling under this. They are magnum Gift Plan A, Magnum Gift Plan B, Canpep-92, Magnum taxprofit-94, Canpep-94, MELS-95, MELS-96, MEP-95. These schemes have earned higher returns by taking lower risk in the market.
- Quadrant II consists of those schemes whose returns are higher than the market also fund risk are higher than that of the market (High return/high risk). Surprisingly, only one fund, i.e., MEP-96 is falling under this category earning higher return by taking higher risk.

	I	II
High	$R_p > R_m$ $\sigma_p < \sigma_m$ Magnum Gift Plan – A Magnum Gift Plan – B Canpep – 92 Magnum Tax Profit – 94 Canpep – 94 MELs – 95 MELs – 96	$R_p > R_m$ $\sigma_p < \sigma_m$ MEP-96
Return	MEP - 95	

	IV	III
Low	$R_p > R_m$ $\sigma_p < \sigma_m$ MELs – 91 Boinananza 80 cc (B) Plan-B Canpep – 91 MEP – 92 PNBELSS-91-80 cc B LIC Dhan 80 cc B (1) Plan – A LIC Dhan 80 cc B (1) Plan - B LIC Dhan 80 cc B (1) Plan - C LIC Dhan 80 cc B (2) Plan - A LIC Dhan 80 cc B (2) Plan - C LIC Dhan 80 cc (B) Plan - A Indtaxshield Plan – B MEP – 94	$R_p > R_m$ $\sigma_p < \sigma_m$ Canpep – 93 MEP – 91 Ind Shelter Plan – A Ind Shelter Plan – B PNBELSS – 92 LIC Dhan 80 cc B (2) Plan – B Canster 80 L – 90 MEP – 93 Indtaxshield Plan - A
Low	Risk	High

Figure I: Risk-Return Grid of Mutual Fund Scheme

- Quadrant III contains all those schemes whose returns have been found to be lower than the market returned but funds risks are higher than the market risk (Low return/high risk). So, nine schemes are falling in this category. They are Canpep-93, MEP-91, Ind shelter Plan-A, Ind shelter Plan-B, PNB ELSS-92, LIC Dhan 80 cc B(2) Plan-B, Canster 80L-90, MEP-93, Indtaxshield Plan-A. These schemes have earned lower returns than the market returns by taking higher risk in the market.
- Quadrant IV presents those schemes whose returns is less than the market return and funds risks are also lower than the market risk (Low return/Low risk). 13 schemes out of 31 schemes are falling under this category. These schemes have earned lower return than the market by taking low risk.

According to the modern portfolio policy, the risk and return are to be in the linear form. So, the risk and return are expected to be in tandem with the investment policy. As the tax planning schemes are expected to invest 80% of their corpus in equity shares, these schemes are expected to earn higher returns with higher risk. So, it is highly essential to examine if the risk characteristics of these schemes are consistent with their stated objectives. The relationship has been examined in terms of standard deviation and systematic risk, which is called beta.

Investment Objective and Risk

The risk- return analysis indicates that some of the schemes are not in conformity with their stated objectives. Table 2 presents the stated objectives of the funds with their average betas and average total risk. But there is considerable overlap between the schemes. Some of the schemes in the lowest risk possessed considerably higher betas than the funds. It is seen from the Table 2 that beta for the tax planning schemes varies from a minimum of 0.30 for Indtaxshield Plan-B to 0.87 for MELS-95. The average beta is 0.51, which indicates one per cent change in the market portfolio, results in a change of 0.51 per cent in the portfolio. Though the average is 0.51, only 3 schemes, i.e., Boinanza 80 cc (B), Magnum tax profit-94. Ind tax shield Plan-A, have an aggressive beta value more than 0.7 and 11 schemes have beta of 0.5 to 0.7. These schemes are magnum Gift Plan-A, Canpep-93, MEP-91, LIC Dhan 80 cc B(2) Plan-A, LIC Dhan 80 cc B(2) Plan-C, MEP-93, Magnum tax profit 99, Canpep-94, MELS-96, MEP-95, MEP-96. So, on the whole, mutual funds are holding less risky portfolios than the market in general. It can be concluded that the returns and risk are not always in conformity with the stated objectives and investment objectives are only indicative. So, it is felt that selection of the scheme purely on the basis of investment objective may mislead the investor.

Risk and Diversification

Table 3 presents the unique risk and diversification of the sample scheme. It is evident that the degree of diversification is linked with unsystematic risks. Funds, which have high R2 value, have low unsystematic risk and *vice versa*. Diversification is linked with superior returns also. The average unique risk of the sample scheme is 54.53% and diversification is 13.56%. There are 13 schemes, i.e., Canpep-93, MEP-91, PNBELSS-92, LIC Dhan 80 cc B(1) Plan-A, LIC Dhan 80 cc B(1) Plan-B, LIC Dhan 80 cc B(2) Plan-B, MEP-93, Ind Tax Shield Plan-A, Magnum tax profit-94, Canpep-94, MELS-96, MEP-95, MEP-96 which have low unique risk than the average and high value of diversification, which is more than the average. 12 Schemes, i.e., MELS-91, Magnum Giftplan-A, Magnum Giftplan-B, Boinanza 80 cc (B) Plan-B, Canpep-91, Canpep-92, MEP-92, LIC Dhan 80 cc B(1) Plan-C, LIC Dhan 80 cc B (2) Plan-A, LIC Dhan 80 cc B(2) Plan-C, Boinnanza 80 cc (B) Plan-A, Indtax shield Plan-B have more unique risk which is greater than the average and low diversification. However, six schemes have demonstrated a relationship of high risk, high diversification or low risk, low diversification.

Sharpe Measure

Table 4 indicates the Sharpe measure of mutual funds. Out of 31 schemes, nine schemes, i.e., Magnum Giftplan-A, Magnum Giftplan-B, Canpep-92, Magnum tax profit-94, Canpep-94, MELS-95, MELS-96, MEP-94, MEP-96, have higher return than the benchmark portfolio. 13 schemes which found place in the fourth quadrant (low risk/low return) have lower value than the benchmark. As the risk taken is less than the benchmark portfolio, with respect to the given level of risk, the funds have underperformed the benchmark. The scheme falling in the 1st quadrant (high return/low risk), eight schemes, i.e., Magnum Giftplan A, Magnum Giftplan B, Canpep-92, Magnum taxprofit-94, Canpep-94, MELS-95, MELS-96, MEP-95 outperformed their concerned benchmark. Here, the fund managers have taken relatively lower risk but have been able to generate higher returns, thereby showing superior performance. In the schemes which fall in the 2nd quadrant (high return/high risk) only one scheme earned returns that are commensurate with the risk. The scheme MEP-96 has earned higher return than the market portfolio by taking additional risk. However, the performance of the scheme lying in the 3rd quadrant (low return/high risk) is not satisfactory. Despite taking higher risk in the market, none of the schemes outperformed the benchmark.

Table 2
Risk and Return of Sample Scheme

Sl. No.	Scheme Name	Fund Return	Std. Fund	Fund Beta (β)	Beta (t)
1	MELS-91	-0.054361	0.102452	0.459207	2.671965
2	Magnum Gift Plan - A	0.071483	0.130533	0.596827	2.731404
3	Magnum Gift Plan - B	0.045151	0.103530	0.4131782	2.354027
4	Boinanza 80 cc (B) Plan-B	-0.050996	0.155541	0.777056	3.016237
5	Canpep-91	-0.081650	0.103149	0.446474	2.571385
6	Canpep-92	0.024801	0.102814	0.395415	2.26202
7	Canpep-93	0.021149	0.855117	0.530702	3.8888
8	MEP-91	-0.032112	0.813722	0.587428	4.709407
9.	MEP-92	-0.022055	0.114662	0.431803	2.1157
10	Indshelter Plan-A	-0.189047	0.973572	0.438765	2.68817
11	Indshelter Plan-B	-0.091636	0.757626	0.398783	3.20123
12	PNBELSS-92	-0.155634	0.686240	0.400007	3.606152
13	PNBELSS-91.80 cc B	-0.125718	0.645905	0.346016	3.26679
14	LIC Dhan 80 cc B (2) Plan-A	-0.102592	0.636388	0.404878	4.009018
15	LIC Dhan 80 cc B (2) Plan-B	-0.102593	0.627806	0.404459	4.071671
16	LIC Dhan 80 cc B (2) Plan-C	-0.013662	0.105988	0.487788	2.751326
17	LIC Dhan 80 cc B (2) Plan-A	-0.081844	0.144359	0.501343	2.028792
18	LIC Dhan 80 cc B (2) Plan-B	-0.081844	0.857196	0.497042	3.583825
19	LIC Dhan 80 cc B (2) Plan-C	-0.064391	0.125927	0.549871	2.596250
20	Boinanza 80 cc (B) Plan-A	-0.068854	0.101407	0.389078	2.174341
21	Canster 80L-90	-0.053053	0.725951	0.300603	2.268329
22	MEP-93	-0.009382	0.928416	0.674194	4.086924
23	Indtaxshield Plan-A	0.008787	0.694095	0.417795	3.44605
24	Indtaxshield Plan-B	-0.003381	0.118480	0.300077	1.334266
25	Magnum Tax Profit-94	0.103063	0.103578	0.573197	2.810967
26	Canpep-94	0.026824	0.112271	0.643613	2.896328
27	MELS-95	0.065246	0.150691	0.872626	2.908098
28	MELS-96	0.116866	0.110306	0.595645	2.674227
29	MEP-94	-0.116330	0.130270	0.733132	2.809362
30	MEP-95	0.059985	0.114369	0.582873	2.499002
31	MEP-96	0.045626	0.732672	0.542615	4.005451
	Average	-0.028710	0.389195	0.506210	

Table 3
Unique Risk and Diversification of Mutual Fund Schemes

Sl.No.	Name of the Schemes	Unique Risk	Diversification
1	MELS-91	0.665864	0.093767
2	Magnum Gift Plan - A	1.076354	0.097574
3	Magnum Gift Plan – B	0.694515	0.074340
4	Boinanza 80 cc (B) Plan-B	1.496247	0.116491
5	Canpep-91	0.679654	0.087447
6	Canpep-92	0.688878	0.069037
7	Canpep-93	0.419838	0.179776
8	MEP-91	0.350758	0.243243
9	MEP-92	0.859408	0.066193
10	Indshelter Plan-A	0.094801	0.094801
11	Indshelter Plan-B	0.349840	0.129314
12	PNBELSS-92	0.158581	0.158581
13	PNBELSS-91.80 cc B	0.133948	0.133949
14	LIC Dhan 80 cc B (2) Plan-A	0.188925	0.188924
15	LIC Dhan 80 cc B (2) Plan-B	0.193723	0.193723
16	LIC Dhan 80 cc B (2) Plan-C	0.708612	0.056294
17	LIC Dhan 80 cc B (2) Plan-A	1.376657	0.056931
18	LIC Dhan 80 cc B (2) Plan-B	0.433632	0.156931
19	LIC Dhan 80 cc B (2) Plan-C	1.011252	0.088995
20	Boinanza 80 cc (B) Plan-A	0.560998	0.075369
21	Canster 80L-90	0.264637	0.086994
22	MEP-93	0.402129	0.236241
23	Indtaxshield Plan-A	0.217206	0.180269
24	Indtaxshield Plan-B	0.747429	0.031916
25	Magnum Tax Profit-94	0.377791	0.161580
26	Canpep-94	0.427204	0.173361
27	MELS-95	0.746452	0.178204
28	MELS-96	0.411284	0.154957
29	MEP-94	0.564564	0.168311
30	MEP-95	0.451001	0.138027
31	MEP-96	0.152141	0.291471
	Average	0.545301	0.135643

Treynor Measure

This measure evaluates the performance with respect to systematic risk. Table 5 presents treynor measure of mutual fund schemes and benchmark portfolio. It is seen from the table that out of 31 schemes, 13 schemes outperformed their respective benchmark. These schemes are Magnum Giftplan-A, Magnum Giftplan-B, Canpep-92, Canpep-93, MEP-93, Ind taxshield Plan-A, Ind taxshield Plan-B, Magnum tax profit-94, Canpep-94, MELS-95, MELS-96, MEP-95, and MEP-96. Interestingly, most of the schemes outperformed in respect of Sharpe measure too. Thus, 9 schemes, i.e., Magnum Giftplan-A, Magnum Giftplan-B, Canpep-92, Magnum tax profit-94, Canpep-94, MELS-95, MELS-96, MEP-95, MEP-96 have outperformed both in terms of total risk and systematic risk. Only four schemes exhibited superior performance in terms of systematic risk but did not do so in respect of total risk. So, it is possible that a portfolio might have outperformed the market in terms of treynor measure whereas in terms of sharpe measure, it did not. The reason for this deviation is that the portfolio under consideration may have a relatively larger amount of unique risk. The presence of unique risk in the portfolio does not affect the treynor measure, but it would affect the sharpe measure as it is based on total risk.

Table 4
Sharpe Measure of Mutual Fund Scheme

Sl.No.	*Name of the Schemes*	*Sharpe Measure*	*Benchmark*
1	MELS-91	0.226936	0.536349
2	Magnum Gift Plan - A	0.78592	0.420966
3	Magnum Gift Plan – B	0.736617	0.530764
4	Boinanza 80 cc (B) Plan-B	-0.127844	0.353283
5	Canpep-91	-0.489961	0.532725
6	Canpep-92	0.543812	0.534456
7	Canpep-93	0.061114	0.064260
8	MEP-91	-0.001230	0.067529
9	MEP-92	C.078979	0.479235
10	Indshelter Plan-A	-0.162223	0.056442
11	Indshelter Plan-B	-0.079888	0.072529
12	PNBELSS-92	-0.181457	0.080074
13	PNBELSS-91.80 cc B	-0.146472	0.085079
14	LIC Dhan 80 cc B (1) Plan-A	-0.112323	0.086347
15	LIC Dhan 80 cc B (1) Plan-B	-0.113858	0.087519
16	LIC Dhan 80 cc B (1S) Plan-C	0.164632	0.581455
17	LIC Dhan 80 cc B (2) Plan-A	-0.351436	0.380648
18	LIC Dhan 80 cc B (2) Plan-B	-0.351436	0.064104
19	LIC Dhan 80 cc B (2) Plan-C	-0.264288	0.436364
20	Boinanza 80 cc (B) Plan-A	-0.372193	0.541876

21	Canster 80L-90	-0.030225	0.075694
22	MEP-93	0.041386	0.056162
23	Indtaxshield Plan-A	0.057482	0.079168
24	Indtaxshield Plan-B	0.234048	0.463791
25	Magnum Tax Profit-94	1.295391	0.530518
26	Canpep-94	0.516028	0.489441
27	MELS-95	0.639434	0.364653
28	MELS-96	1.341514	0.498159
29	MEP-94	-0.772569	0.421815
30	MEP-95	0.699284	0.480462
31	MEP-96	0.104734	0.074999

Jensen Measure

Table 6 presents the Jensen Measure of mutual fund schemes. Out of the 31 schemes, only 13 schemes, i.e., Magnum Giftplan-A, Magnum Giftplan-B, Canpep-92, Canpep-93, MEP-93, Indtaxshield Plan-A, Indtaxshield Plan-B, Magnum tax profit-94, Canpep-94, MELS-95, MELS-96, MEP-95, MEP-96 have positive alpha values indicating superior performance of the schemes. The value of an alpha is an absolute, which indicates different return of the fund, between equilibrium return and actual return. Equilibrium return is the return the benchmark portfolio is expected to earn with the given level of systematic risk. The additional return over equilibrium return earned by the fund manager can be attributed to his ability to select securities. The average alpha value in the sample scheme is –0.025. It is evident from Table 7 that out of 31 schemes alpha value of schemes are less than '0' (a<o) and thirteen schemes are having alpha greater than O (a>o). So this indicates that one-third of the fund managers are able to earn superior returns. In the sample, MELS-96 has the highest return of 11.52% out of ability to identify the securities.

Table 5
Treynor Measure of Mutual Fund Scheme

Sl.No.	*Name of the Schemes*	*Treynor Measure*	*Benchmark*
1	MELS-91	-0.050631	0.05495
2	Magnum Gift Plan - A	0.171899	0.05495
3	Magnum Gift Plan – B	0.184574	0.05495
4	Boinanza 80 cc (B) Plan-B	-0.025590	0.05495
5	Canpep-91	-0.113196	0.05495
6	Canpep-92	0.141401	0.05495
7	Canpep-93	0.098473	0.05495
8	MEP-91	-0.0017040	0.05495
9	MEP-92	0.020973	0.05495
10	indshelter Plan-A	-0.359956	0.05495

11	Indshelter Plan-B	-0.151774	0.05495
12	PNBELSS-92	-0.311307	0.05495
13	PNBELSS-91.80 cc B	-0.273418	0.05495
14	LIC Dhan 80 cc B (1) Plan-A	-0.176549	0.05495
15	LIC Dhan 80 cc B (1) Plan-B	-0.175732	0.05495
16	LIC Dhan 80 cc B (2) Plan-C	0.035772	0.05495
17	LIC Dhan 80 cc B (2) Plan-A	-0.101194	0.05495
18	LIC Dhan 80 cc B (2) Plan-B	-0.102069	0.05495
19	LIC Dhan 80 cc B (2) Plan-C	-0.060525	0.05495
20	Boinanza 80 cc (B) Plan-A	-0.097006	0.05495
21	Canster 80L-90	-0.072993	0.05495
22	MEP-93	0.060061	0.05495
23	Indtaxshield Plan-A	0.095496	0.05495
24	Indtaxshield Plan-B	0.092409	0.05495
25	Magnum Tax Profit-94	0.23408	0.05495
26	Canpep-94	0.090015	0.05495
27	MELS-95	0.110422	0.05495
28	MELS-96	0.248431	0.05495
29	MEP-94	-0.116239	0.05495
30	MEP-95	0.156288	0.05495
31	MEP-96	0.1416120	0.05495

Sharpe Differential Return Measure

Table 7 presents the differential returns of mutual fund schemes of the 31 schemes. 11 schemes reflect positive differential returns indicating superior performance. These schemes are Magnum Giftplan-A, Magnum Giftplan-B, Canpep-92, LIC Dhan 80 cc (B)(1) Plan-C, Indtaxshield Plan-B, Magnum tax profit-94, Canpep-94, MELS-95, MELS-96, MEP-95 and MEP-96. These are the returns earned by selection of undervalued securities and diversifying the portfolio. Out of the 13 schemes which have higher returns according to Jensen measure, 10 schemes also have higher returns according to Sharpe differential measure which indicates that these portfolios are diversified and the rest of the schemes Canpep-93, MEP-93, Indtaxshield Plan-A and LIC Dhan 80 cc B(1) Plan-C have not well diversified their portfolios hence returns are low.

Table 6

Jensen Measures of Mutual Fund Schemes

Sl.No.	*Name of the Schemes*	*Actual Fund Return*	*Equilibrium Returns*	*Alpha Value*
1	MELS-91	-0.054361	0.005878	-0.060239
2	Magnum Gift Plan - A	0.071483	0.001685	0.069798

3	Magnum Gift Plan – B	0.045151	-0.008407	0.053558
4	Boinanza 80 cc (B) Plan-B	-0.050996	0.011588	-0.062584
5	Canpep-91	-0.081650	-0.006577	-0.075073
6	Canpep-92	0.024801	-0.009383	0.034184
7	Canpep-93	0.021149	-0.001949	0.023098
8	MEP-91	-0.032112	0.001168	-0.03328
9	MEP-92	-0.022055	-0.007383	-0.014672
10	Indshelter Plan-A	-0.189047	-0.007001	-0.182046
11	Indshelter Plan-B	-0.091636	-0.009197	-0.082439
12	PNBELSS-92	-0.155634	-0.009131	-0.146503
13	PNBELSS-91.80 cc B	-0.125718	-0.012097	-0.113621
14	LIC Dhan 80 cc B (1) Plan-A	-0.102592	-0.008863	-0.093729
15	LIC Dhan 80 cc B (1) Plan-B	-0.102592	-0.008886	-0.093707
16	LIC Dhan 80 cc B (2) Plan-C	-0.013662	-0.004307	-0.009355
17	LIC Dhan 80 cc B (2) Plan-A	-0.081844	-0.003562	-0.078282
18	LIC Dhan 80 cc B (2) Plan-B	-0.081844	-0.003798	-0.078046
19	LIC Dhan 80 cc B (2) Plan-C	-0.064391	-0.000896	-0.063495
20	Boinanza 80 cc (B) Plan-A	-0.068854	-0.009731	-0.059123
21	Canster 80L-90	-0.053053	-0.014592	-0.038461
22	MEP-93	-0.009382	0.005936	0.003446
23	Indtaxshield Plan-A	0.008789	-0.008153	0.01694
24	Indtaxshield Plan-B	-0.003381	-0.014622	0.011241
25	Magnum Tax Profit-94	0.103063	0.000386	0.102677
26	Canpep-94	0.026824	0.004255	0.022569
27	MELS-95	0.065246	0.016839	0.048407
28	MELS-96	0.116866	0.001619	0.115247
29	MEP-94	-0.116330	0.009175	-0.125505
30	MEP-95	0.059985	0.000918	0.059067
31	MEP-96	0.045626	-0.001294	0.04692

Fama's Break-up of the Funds

Table 8 presents Fama's components of investment performance of sample schemes, the nine schemes, i.e., Magnum Giftplan-A, Magnum Giftplan-B, Canpep-92, Magnum tax profit-94, Canpep-94, MELS-95, MELS-96, MEP-95, MEP-96, have outperformed according to Sharpe measure, have higher returns due to selectivity only. In case of Canpep-93, MEP-93, Indtaxshield Plan-A, Indtaxshield Plan B which outperformed according to Treynor measure and Jensen measure but not Sharpe, have higher returns due to impact of Beta. Thus, they have outperformed in terms of systematic risk. However, other nine schemes have higher returns due to selectivity only. Thus the fund managers are efficient in identifying the undervalued securities. A positive net selectivity will indicate superior performance. If it is negative selectivity, then it is to be assumed that fund managers have taken diversifiable risk that has not been compensated by extra returns. Out of 31 schemes, 15 schemes show negative selectivity due to impact of imperfect diversification of the fund. The fund managers are not able to recognizing turning points in the market and failed to adopt market-timing strategy.

Table 7
Sharpe Differential Returns of Mutual Fund Schemes

Sl.No.	*Name of the Schemes*	*Actual Fund Return*	*Equilibrium Returns*	*Alpha Value*
1	MELS-91	-0.054361	-0.022776	-0.031585
2	Magnum Gift Plan - A	0.071483	0.018939	0.052544
3	Magnum Gift Plan – B	0.045151	-0.022689	0.06784
4	Boinanza 80 cc (B) Plan-B	-0.050996	-0.018515	-0.032481
5	Canpep-91	-0.081650	-0.022720	-0.05893
6	Canpep-92	0.024801	-0.022747	0.047548
7	Canpep-93	0.021149	0.037528	-0.016379
8	MEP-91	-0.032112	0.034206	-0.066318
9	MEP-92	-0.022055	0.060928	-0.082983
10	Indshelter Plan-A	-0.189047	0.047038	-0.236085
11	Indshelter Plan-B	-0.091636	0.029704	-0.12134
12	PNBELSS-92	-0.155634	0.023923	-0.179557
13	PNBELSS-91.80 cc B	-0.125718	0.020735	-0.146453
14	LIC Dhan 80 cc B (1) Plan-A	-0.102592	0.019971	-0.122563
15	LIC Dhan 80 cc B (1) Plan-B	-0.102592	0.019928	-0.12252
16	LIC Dhan 80 cc B (2) Plan-C	-0.013662	-0.022603	+0.008941
17	LIC Dhan 80 cc B (2) Plan-A	-0.031844	-0.019523	-0.062321
18	LIC Dhan 80 cc B (2) Plan-B	-0.081844	-0.037695	-0.044149
19	LIC Dhan 80 cc B (2) Plan-C	-0.064391	-0.021003	-0.047851
20	Boinanza 80 cc (B) Plan-A	-0.068854	-0.022971	-0.045883
21	Canster 80L-90	-0.053053	-0.027678	-0.025375
22	MEP-93	-0.009382	0.047425	-0.038043
23	Indtaxshield Plan-A	0.008789	0.024603	-0.015816
24	Indtaxshield Plan-B	-0.003381	-0.021601	0.01822
25	Magnum Tax Profit-94	0.103063	-0.022797	0.12586
26	Canpep-94	0.026824	-0.022098	0.004892
27	MELS-95	0.065246	-0.019015	0.08426

28	MELS-96	0.116866	022257	0.139123
29	MEP-94	-0.116330	-0.020654	-0.095676
30	MEP-95	0.059985	-0.021929	0.081914
31	MEP-96	0.045626	-0.027447	0.073073
	Average			-0.013387

Table 8

Fama's Components of Investment Performance

Sl.No.		*Fund Return*	*Risk-free Return*	*Impact of Beta*	*Imperfect Diversifi -cation*	*Net Selectivity*
1	MELS-91					
2	Magnum Gift Plan - A	-0.054361	-0.031111	0.025233	-0.016993	-0.031490
3	Magnum Gift Plan – B	0.071483	-0.031111	0.032796	-0.022296	0.092095
4	Boinanza 80 cc (B) Plan-B	0.045151	-0.031111	0.022704	-0.014377	0.067935
5	Canpep-91	-0.050996	-0.031111	0.042699	-0.030189	-0.032395
6	Canpep-92	-0.081650	-0.031111	0.024534	-0.016254	-0.058835
7	Canpep-93	0.024801	-0.031111	0.021728	-0.013458	0.047642
8	MEP-91	0.021149	-0.031111	0.029162	0.039616	-0.016518
9	MEP-92	-0.032112	-0.031111	0.032279	0.033169	-0.066450
10	Indshelter Plan-A	-0.022055	-0.031111	0.023727	-0.014505	-0.000166
11	Indshelter Plan-B	-0.189047	-0.031111	0.024110	0.054196	-0.236242
12	PNBELSS-92	-0.091636	-0.031111	0.021913	0.039024	-0.121462
13	PNBELSS-91.80ccB	-0.155634	-0.031111	0.02198	0.033215	-0.179718
14	LIC Dhan 80 cc B (1) Plan-A	-0.125718	-0.031111	0.019013	0.032937	-0.146558
15	LIC Dhan 80 cc B (1) Plan-B	-0.102592	-0.031111	0.022248	0.028937	-0.122667
16	LIC Dhan 80 cc B (2) Plan-	-0.102593	-0.031111	0.022225	0.028270	-0.121976
17	C	-0.013662	-0.031111	0.026804	-0.018279	0.008924
18	LIC Dhan 80 cc B (2) Plan-A	-0.081844	-0.031111	0.027549	-0.015938	-0.062344
19	LIC Dhan 80 cc B (2) Plan-B	-0.081844	-0.031111	0.027312	0.041633	-0.119678
20	LIC Dhan 80 cc B (2) Plan-	-0.064391	-0.031111	0.030215	-0.020086	-0.043403
21	C	-0.068854	-0.031111	0.021379	-0.013196	-0.045899
22	Boinanza 80 cc (B) Plan-A	-0.053053	-0.031111	0.016518	0.041871	-0.080331
23	Canster 80L-90	-0.009382	-0.031111	0.037047	0.041648	-0.037765
24	MEP-93	0.008787	-0.031111	0.022958	0.032869	-0.015929
25	Indtax Plan-A	-0.003381	-0.031111	0.016489	0.006959	0.018200

26	Magnum Tax Profit-94	0.103063	-0.031111	0.031497	0.031784	0.125843
27	Indtax Plan-B	0.026824	-0.031111	0.035366	--0.026336	0.048905
28	Canpep-94	0.065246	-0.031111	0.047951	-0.035830	0.084236
29	MELS-95	0.116866	-0.031111	0.032731	-0.023858	0.139105
30	MELS-96	-0.116330	-0.031111	0.040285	-0.029808	-0.095697
31	MEP-94	0.059985	-0.031111	0.030288	-0.022829	0.081897
	MEP-95	0.045626	-0.031111	0.029817	-0.026147	0.073066
	MEP-96					

The Table 9 presents the empirical results for the Treynor and Mazuy model. The Table 3 depicts that out of thirty-one mutual fund schemes investment managers of only two schemes, viz., Dhan 80 cc B (2) P-C, Boinanza 80 cc(B) Plan-A appear to be successful market timers. The observed t-value for their gamma coefficients is found to be significant and positive at five per cent level. There are other six schemes for which the t-values are significant but are negative. These schemes are MELS- 95, MELS-96, MEP-95, MEP-96, Canpep-94, Magnum tax profit-94. So, in terms of Treynor and Mazuy formulation, majority of the Indian fund managers does not seem to be engaged in market timing activities, Also the fund managers market the time in the wrong direction.

Table 9
Results of Treynor & Mazuy Model

S. No.	*Scheme Name*	*Beta*	*S.E Beta*	*t-beta*	*Gamma*	*S.E.*	t-Gamma	R^2
1	LIC Dhan 80CCB(2)P–A	.695	.162	4.305	.225	1.383	.162	.215
2	LIC Dhan 80CCB(2)P–B	.642	.108	5.919	–4.266	.929	–.005	.341
3	LIC Dhan 80CCB(2)P–C	.935	.189	4.938	3.353	1.622	2.068	.304
4	LIC Dhan P–C	.671	.140	4.805	–. 607	1.195	–. 508	.254
5	LIC Dhan P–A	.652	.085	7.717	–3.630	.724	–. 050	.467
6	LIC Dhan P–B	.637	.085	7.467	9.479	.731	.130	.452
7	PNB ELSS–91	.664	.093	7.113	.187	.799	.234	.428
8	PNB ELSS–92	.691	.093	7.402	.416	.800	.520	.450
9	Indshelter–B	.669	.103	6.521	1.050	.879	1.195	.397
10	Indshelter–A	.664	.129	5.138	1.263	1.106	1.142	.294
11	MEP–92	.742	.153	4.840	–6.214	1.312	–. 047	.257
12	MEP–91	.830	.099	8.348	.363	.851	.430	.509
13	Canpep–93	.723	.109	6.605	–. 106	.937	–. 011	.391
14	Canpep–92	.837	.138	4.634	.329	1.178	.280	.242
15	Canpep–91	.700	.137	5.097	.159	1.176	.135	.278
16	Boinanza 80cc P–B	.493	.189	2.607	–. 611	1.622	–. 377	.091

17	MagGift P–B	.760	.139	5.480	–. 538	1.188	–. 453	.307
18	MagGift P–A	.979	.165	5.916	–1.248	1.417	–. 881	.342
19	MELS–91	.824	.136	6.041	.140	1.168	.120	.350
20	Boinanza 80 cc (B) P–A	.663	.125	5.303	2.209	1.071	+2.063*	.316
21	Canster 80L–90	.553	.097	5.720	1.089	.827	1.316	.342
22	Indsheild P–B	.535	.147	3.627	.122	1.263	.096	.163
23	Indsheild P–A	.594	.087	6.854	.590	.742	.795	.415
24	MEP–93	.814	.109	7.487	.119	.931	.128	.453
25	Magnum tax profit–94	.476	.103	4.639	–2.092	.878	–2.383*	.278
26	Canpep–94	.440	.108	4.067	–2.095	.925	–2.264*	.234
27	MEP–96	.436	.070	6.255	–2.124	.596	–3.561*	.422
28	MEP–95	.425	.101	4.210	–3.697	.864	–4.281*	.335
29	MEP–94	.467	.124	3.764	–1.478	1.062	–1.392	.187
30	MELS–96	.485	.109	4.451	–1.870	.933	–2.004*	.253
31	MELS–95	.651	.140	4.635	–3.319	1.202	–2.763*	.291

* Significant at 5% level.

Table 10
Results of Heriksson & Merton Model

S. No.	Scheme Name	Beta	S.E	t-beta	Gamma	S.E. Gamma	t-Gamma	R^2
1	LIC Dhan 80 cc B(2) P-A	1.004	.263	3.809	6.923	.047	1.460	.239
2	LIC Dhan 80 cc B(2) P-B	.836	.177	4.716	4.370	.032	1.370	.358
3	LIC Dhan 80 cc B(2) P-C	1.212	.321	3.774	5.792	.058	1.002	.272
4	LIC Dhan P-C	.598	.231	2.587	-1.548	.042	-.372	.253
5	LIC Dhan P-A	.859	.136	6.295	4.663	.025	1.900	.494
6	LIC Dhan P-B	.832	.138	6.019	4.382	.025	1.761	.475
7	PNB ELSS-91	.745	.154	4.834	1.809	.028	.652	.431
8	PNB ELSS-92	.807	.154	5.237	2.546	.028	.919	.454
9	Indshelter-B	.691	.172	4.020	3.382	.031	.109	.385
10	Indshelter-A	.585	.216	2.713	-1.948	.039	-.502	.283
11	MEP-92	.616	.253	2.433	-2.830	.046	-.621	.261
12	MEP-91	.928	.164	5.647	2.150	.030	.727	.511
13	Canpep-93	.843	.180	4.672	2.716	.032	.837	.397
14	Canpep-92	.749	.227	3.295	2.476	.041	.605	.245
15	Canpep-91	.745	.227	3.276	9.904	.041	.242	.278

16	Boinanza 80 cc B P-B	2.423	.306	.079	-.105	.055	-1.907	.136
17	MagGift P-B	.898	.229	3.919	3.178	.041	.771	.311
18	MagGift P-A	1.122	.275	4.086	3.401	.049	.688	.339
19	Mels-91	.995	.224	4.436	3.853	.040	.954	.359
20	Boinanza 80 cc (B) P-A	.997	.207	4.816	7.817	.037	2.099*	.317
21	Canster 80L-90	.802	.158	5.084	5.485	.028	1.931	.360
22	Indsheild P-B	.605	244	2.479	1.566	.044	.357	.164
23	Indsheild P-A	.753	.142	5.288	3.495	.026	1.365	.425
24	MEP-93	1.046	.177	5.921	5.214	.032	1.640	.474
25	Magnum tax profit-94	.671	.174	3.855	4.675	.031	1.494	.242
26	Canpep-94	.527	.185	2.847	2.246	.033	.675	182
27	MEP-96	.457	.126	3.637	7.571	.023	.335	.316
28	MEP-95	.262	.187	1.402	-3.171	.034	-.942	.167
29	MEP-94	.686	.205	3.341	5.146	.037	1.392	.187
30	MELS-96	.623	.184	3.381	3.368	.633	1.015	.220
31	MELS-95	.833	.243	3.426	4.561	.044	1.042	.224

* Significant at 5% level

The Table 10 shows the results of Henriksion and Merton model. It is found that only one scheme, viz., Boinanza 80 cc (B) p-A showed market timing skills. The t-value for gamma was found to be statistically significant and positive at 5 per cent level. Other schemes exhibited wrong market timing abilities of fund managers. Thus in terms of both the model the results indicated that only one scheme Boinanza 80 cc (B) plan-A was found to be reflect market-timing abilities. So, the empirical results do not lend support to the hypothesis that Indian fund managers are able to time the market. These results are similar to those repeated by other researchers utilising data from Indian mutual funds. In a nutshell, it is to be said that none of the schemes rewarded the investors and the main constraint on the portfolio managers is that they cannot book the profits when the market is boom phase due to lack of depth in the market. At the same time, there are no hedging instruments available for them to hedge the market uncertainties.

CONCLUDING OBSERVATION

This chapter has examined the investment performance of Indian mutual funds in terms of six performance measures. The empirical results reported here do not lend support to the hypothesis taken in the study. There is only one scheme in conformity with the linear relationship of return and risk. All other schemes do not demonstrate this relationship. On the whole, 13 schemes have an alone average beta, which indicates that mutual fund returns are highly volatile. About 10 schemes have outperformed both in terms of Treynor measure and Sharpe measure. However, four schemes exhibited superior performance in terms of systematic risk but did not do so in respect of total risk. According to Jensen measure, 13 schemes have positive alpha values indicating superior performance of the schemes. Stock selection is one of the most important characteristics of a fund manager. Selectivity techniques bring out stock selection abilities and the reward thereof. The analysis made by the application of Fama's measure indicates that the returns out of diversification are very less. Nine schemes out of 31 schemes have higher returns due to selectivity only. All other schemes show lack of net selectivity and diversification. So, it was found that proper balance between selectivity and diversification is not maintained. This is due to fund manager's acumen of selectivity and poor investment planning of the fund. This chapter has also empirical analysed the market-timing abilities of Indian fund manager in the form of two models, i.e., one by Treynor and Mazuy and the other by Henriksson and Merton. The results indicated here do not lend support to the hypothesis that Indian fund managers are able to time the market correctly. There is only one scheme where market-timing ability of the fund managers was exhibited. These results are also similar with earlier research, which was conducted by the developed capital market.

REVIEW QUESTIONS

1. What are mutual funds? How many types of mutual funds are available?
2. How do you evaluate the performance of mutual funds?
3. Write short notes on:
   (a) Treynor model
   (b) Sharpe model
   (c) Jensen model
4. Quiz:
   (a) The modern mutual fund was first introduced in _____ 1822.
   (b) Mutual Funds in India follow a _____ structure.
   (c) Who is the market regulator of mutual funds?
   (d) Which fund is one that is available for subscription and repurchase on a continuous basis?
   (e) Which schemes invest exclusively in treasury bills and certificates of deposit?
   (f) Which provide regular and steady income to investors?

15

Mutual Fund Investor's Behavior Model in Indian Stock Market

This chapter determines the investor's behavior model, systematic inadequacies in stock market. This chapter suggests an integrated marketing approach to be developed to protect and enhance investor's confidence in the mutual funds in the coming years.

INTRODUCTION

There are various investment avenues available to an investor such as real estate, bank deposits, post office deposits, shares, debentures, bonds etc. A Mutual fund is one more type of Investment Avenue available to investors. There are many reasons why investors prefer mutual funds. Buying shares directly from the market is one way of investing. But this requires spending time to find out the performance of the company whose share is being purchased, understanding the future business prospects of the company, finding out the track record of the promoters and the dividend, bonus issue history of the company etc. An informed investor needs to do research before investing. However, many investors find it cumbersome and time-consuming to pore over so much of information, get access to so much of details before investing in the shares. Investors therefore prefer the mutual fund route. They invest in a mutual fund scheme which in turn takes the responsibility of investing in stocks and shares after due analysis and research. The investor need not bother with researching hundreds of stocks. He leaves it to the mutual fund and its professional fund management team.

Another reason why investors prefer mutual funds is because mutual funds offer diversification. An investor's money is invested by the mutual fund in a variety of shares, bonds and other securities thus diversifying the investor's portfolio across different companies and sectors. This diversification helps in reducing the overall risk of the portfolio. It is also less expensive to invest in a mutual fund since the minimum investment amount in mutual fund units is fairly low (₹ 500 or so). With ₹ 500, an investor may be able to buy only a few stocks and not get the desired diversefiction. These are some of the reasons why mutual funds have gained in popularity over the years.

Indians have been traditionally savers and invested money in traditional savings instruments such as bank deposits. Against this background, if we look at approximately ₹ 5 lakh crore which Indian Mutual Funds are managing, then it is no meant an achievement. A country traditionally putting money in safe, risk-free investments like Bank FDs, Post Office and Life Insurance, has started to invest in stocks, bonds and shares – thanks to the mutual fund industry.

However, there is still a lot to be done. The ₹ 5 lakh crore stated above includes investments by the corporate sector as well.

Going by various reports, not more than 5% of household savings are channelized into the markets, either directly or through the mutual fund route. Not all parts of the country are contributing equally into the mutual fund corpus. 8 cities account for over 60% of the total assets under management in mutual funds. The total number of certified Mutual Funds Advisors is around 50,000 – whereas there are over 20 lakh life insurance advisors. These are issues which need to be addressed jointly by all concerned with the mutual fund industry. Market dynamics are making industry players to look at smaller cities to increase penetration. Competition is ensuring that costs incurred in managing the funds are kept low and fund houses are trying to give more value for money by increasing operational efficiencies and cutting expenses. As of today, there are 41 Mutual Funds in the country. Together they offer over 1000 schemes to the investor. Many more mutual funds are expected to enter India in the next few years. In a rapidly changing stock market, it is essential to respond positively and quickly to events, which tend to move share prices. The search for maximum returns has to be balanced against the need to control risk.

A mutual fund is able to reduce such risk associated with investment by investing in a large number of companies across different industries. The guiding factor behind investment decision of a mutual fund is the fundamental strength of a share determined by the overall economic situation. The sizeable presence of mutual funds is an essential feature of any major stock exchange the world over. During the last few years, the MF industry grew by leaps and bounds. The growing small investors' population and the spreading equity cult call for unrestricted growth of mutual funds in the country. Mutual funds are ideally suitable to a developing economy like India. This is because the mutual funds, on the one hand, help investors by taking right investment decisions for their money and providing them better returns, and on the other hand, the economy on which huge funds are made available. Thus, in view of the increasing importance of mutual funds in the Indian context, it becomes very necessary to examine as to how the investors perceive the investments in MFs.

This chapter has been undertaken with the objective of analyzing the perceptions of the investors towards mutual fund through marketing variables and also to evaluate the investor's expectation of returns, grievances from the difficulty faced during the application and period of investment.

RECENT TRENDS IN MUTUAL FUND

The mutual fund industry in India is a little over three decades old evolutions but the real impetus has come after the change in the mutual fund regulation way back in 1993. At the end of 1993, the mutual fund industry had assets under management of 470.04 billion. With the entry of private sector funds in 1993, a new era started in the Indian Mutual Fund Industry, giving the Indian investors a wider choice of fund families. The number of mutual fund houses went on increasing, with a many foreign mutual funds setting up funds in India and also the industry has witnessed several mergers and acquisitions. As at the end of January 2003, there were 33 mutual funds with total assets of 1218.05 billion. In February 2003, following the repeal of the Unit Trust of India Act 1963, UTI was bifurcated into two separate entities. Today, the Industry consists of the Unit Trust of India, mutual funds sponsored by public sector banks and Insurance Corporation and that set up by private and foreign funds. It still continues to be the largest player in the domestic mutual fund industry. The entry of private sector mutual funds has imparted competitive efficiency in the industry, helped investors to choose from funds with different maturity periods, and offered different risk-return trade-offs. The Table 1shows the amount mobilized by the different mutual funds for the period 1987-88 to 1999-2005.

Table 1
Gross Mobilisation by Mutual Funds

(₹ in crore)

Year	*UTI*	*Public Sector Mutual Funds*	*Private Sector Mutual Funds*	*Total*
1987-88	1763.00	258.00	N/A	2021.00
1988-89	3483.00	301.00	N/A	3784.00
1989-90	5504.00	1204.00	N/A	6708.00
1990-91	3182.00	2967.00	N/A	6149.00
1991-92	8686.00	2580.00	N/A	11266.00
1992-93	11051.00	1978.00	N/A	13029.00
1993-94	51000.00	9527.00	1549.00	62076.00
1994-95	9500.00	2143.00	2084.0	13727.00
1995-96	5900.00	296.00	312.00	6508.00
1996-97	4280.00	151.00	346.00	4777.00
1997-98	9100.00	332.00	1974.00	11406.00
1998-99	13193.00	1671.00	7847.00	22711.00
1999-2000	13698.00	3817.00	43726.00	61241.00
2000-2001	12413.00	5535.00	75009.00	92957.00
2001-2002	4643.00	12082.00	147798.00	164523.00
2002-2003	7096.00	23515.00	284095.00	314706.00
2003-2004	23992.00	31543.00	534649.00	590190.00

2004-2005	46,656	56,589	7,36,463	839708
2005-06	73127	110319	914703	1098149
2006-07	142280	196340	1599873	1938493
2007-08	337498	346126	3780753	4464377
2008-09	423131	710472	4292751	5426354
2009-10	423774	660988	3655375	4740137

Source: SEBI Bulletin, February 2005, October 2010

Table 2
Investment by Mutual Fund

(₹ in crore)

Year	*Equity*	*Debt*	*Total*	*Asset under Management*
2004-05	448	16981	17429	149600
2005-06	14308	36486	50794	231862
2006-07	9062	52543	61605	326292.13
2007-08	16306	73790	90096	505152.44
2008-09	6984.60	81803.3	88786.90	417299.68
2009-10(Apr-Sept)	3230.40	94002.70	97233.10	627998.80

Source: SEBI Bulletin October 2009, October 2010

The Table 1 shows the growth trend of mutual funds during these years. Total investments by mutual funds has been ₹ 92233.10 crore of which ₹ 3230.40 crore was invested in equity and ₹ 94000.70 crore was invested in debt exhibited in Table 2. The growth in size, as reflected in the assets under management, speaks for its growing prominence. The industry has moved on from traditional product offerings like equity, debt and balanced funds to liquid, money market funds, sector specific, index and gilt funds. This apart, the industry, which in 1993 had less than 10 schemes, today has 460 schemes offered by mutual funds catering to varied needs of investors. A booming economy and favourable regulatory environment have added to the growth of mutual fund industry in India.

TAKE A SAMPLE OF 300 RESPONDENTS FROM DIFFERENT GROUP OF DEMOGRAPHIC PROFILE OF INDIA TO TEST THE INVESTORS PERCEPTION OF MUTUAL FUNDS INVESTMENTS

This case is based on the combination of three sampling methods – Convenience, Judgment and Heuristic. Majority of the respondents were from the "Service Class" which include bank employees, academicians, corporate executives, students and businessmen.

In order to determine the investors' perceptions towards mutual fund, the analyses were made by using Likert's Scale, Spearman's Rank Correlation and the covariability. Also Chi-square test is used to test the association between two or more variables. If the observed value for a given degree of freedom is less than table value at a certain level of significance, the null hypothesis is true otherwise false at 5% level of significance. The Pearson's Coefficient of Contingency is also determined to have a clear view on various aspects of study. Further, the agreement measures the strength of association between the attributes as a rule of thumb C<0.5, 0.25<C<0.5 and C<0.25 indicate strong, moderate and weak.

ANALYSIS

Here in the analysis, the respondents are classified into five classes on the basis of their total holding of mutual funds, which is presented in the following table along with the investment range.

Table 3
Investment Size of Mutual Fund in the Sample

Class	*Investment Range (in Rupees)*	*No. of Respondent*	*Percentage*
A	Upto 10,000	96	33.33
B	10,001 to 20,000	66	22.92
C	20,001 to 30,000	48	16.67
D	30,001 to 40,000	42	14.58
E	Above 40,000	36	12.50

Table 4
Investment in Different Mutual Funds

Types of Mutual Funds	*No. of Respondents*	*Percentage*
Public Sector Funds	108	37.5
Private Sector Funds	36	12.5
Foreign Tie-up Funds	24	8.34
All types of Funds	120	41.67

It is clear from the above. Table 4 that majority of the respondents invested in all types of funds followed by public sector, private sector and tie-up funds. This is analyzed by using Likert's Scale taking total holding of investors with these funds. So, it is viewed that all types of funds are so successful to win the investors' confidence.

Table 5
Investments in Different Types of Scheme

Types of Scheme	*Ranking (Responses)*					*Total Points*	*Rank*
	1	2	3	4	5		
Growth Scheme	126	96	06	06	0	1044	2
Tax Scheme	162	78	36	0	0	1230	1
Income Scheme	30	36	66	12	6	522	3
Balanced Scheme	6	6	30	66	12	288	4
Other Schemes	0	12	0	18	60	144	5

It shows that maximum weightage is given to tax plan scheme because majority of respondents are from service class who are interested in the investments, which provide some deduction from income tax. The growth scheme is also popular among investors in comparison to other schemes due to capital appreciations, bonus and dividends etc.

Table 6

Preference for Different Types of Schemes of MFS in India

Types of Scheme	*Ranking (Responses)*					*Total Points*	*Rank*
	1	**2**	**3**	**4**	**5**		
Growth Scheme	186	90	12	0	0	1326	1
Tax Scheme	78	114	48	42	06	1080	2
Income Scheme	30	54	138	66	0	912	3
Balanced Scheme	0	24	102	156	06	720	4
Other Schemes	0	0	0	36	222	294	5

It is evident from the above table by using Likert's scaling that the growth scheme ranks first indicates that it is most preferred by investors due to capital gain but income schemes have perceived secondly only from maximum tax savings benefit angle. However, different users according to their requirements perceive the mutual fund schemes differently.

Table 7

Testing of Spearman's Rank Correlation between Investment and Preference

Types of Scheme	*Ranks*		*d*	*d²*
	Preference	*Investment*		
Growth Scheme	1	2	-1	1
Tax Plan Scheme	2	1	1	1
Income Scheme	3	3	0	0
Balanced Scheme	4	4	0	0
Other Schemes	5	5	0	0
				Sd2 = 2

$R = 1 - 6\ Sd^2/n\ n\ (n^2-1) = 0.9$

The table value of Spearman's rank correlation coefficient at 5% level of significance is 0.9 and the calculated value of rank correlation coefficient is 0.9. So, the null hypothesis is rejected and there is co-relation between the preference and investment in different types of schemes.

Table 8

Investor's Perception towards Mutual Funds

Perception	*Class Response*					*Total Response*	*Percentage*
	A	*B*	*C*	*D*	*E*		
Equity share	18	6	12	6	2	54	18.75
Fixed deposit schemes	18	0	12	6	12	48	16.67

Investment Institution	50	50	16	18	10	144	50.00
Lack of awareness/ can't express	0	0	12	12	18	42	14.58

It is observed that 50 per cent investors perceive that mutual fund organization is an investment institution which pools the money from the public to channelize funds to the corporate sectors, 18.75 per cent investors opined that it is an equity share and 16.67 per cent investor gave their opinion that it is nothing but a fixed deposit scheme. But interestingly 14.58 per cent investors cannot perceive the mutual funds in a proper perspective due to lack of understanding among the investors about the correct nature of MF investments. So, it is apparent that the mutual fund is getting better investor awareness from the institutional investors only.

Table 9

Investor's Attitude towards New Mutual Funds

Opinion	*Class (Response)*					*Total Response*	*Percentage*
	A	*B*	*C*	*D*	*E*		
Yes	60	30	30	30	24	174	60.42
No	48	36	18	6	6	114	39.58

The above table depicted that 60.42 per cent investors like to invest in newly floated mutual funds. The main reason is that investors population have substantially raised along with investments. Further, SEBI has undertaken a number of supervisory measures for mutual funds, which has created a confidence among investors to get the benefit of profitability, safety and liquidity. But 39.58 per cent investors do not like to invest in newly floated mutual funds due to lack of investor education to differentiate between MF products and initial primary issue of a company. So, AMFI is required to create a fund for investor education programme to bring more confidence in MFs in near future.

Interpretation and Analysis of Degree of Association between Demographic Variables and Investment Class:

Here, the analysis was made of degree of association between age, income, occupation, qualification of the investors to which they belong with the help of chi-square test. The relevant tables are presented below:

Chi-square Test: Age and Investment of Investors

Table 10

Observed Frequency

Age Group	*Response of Investment*					*Total*
	A	*B*	*C*	*D*	*E*	
Below 30	24	6	0	0	0	30
31-35	24	18	6	6	6	60
36-40	36	30	12	12	6	96

41-45	12	12	18	12	12	66
Above 46	0	0	12	12	12	36
Total	*96*	*66*	*48*	*42*	*36*	*288*

Table 11

Expected Frequency

Investment Class	*Response of Investment Class*					*Total*
	A	*B*	*C*	*D*	*E*	
Below 30	10	6.875	5	4.375	3.75	30
31-35	20	13.75	10	8.75	7.5	60
36-40	32	22	16	14	12	96
41-45	22	15.125	11	9.625	8.25	66
Above 46	12	8.25	6	5.25	4.5	36
Total	*96*	*66*	*48*	*42*	*36*	*288*

C^2_{16} = 104.769

Degree of freedom = 16 *i(coefficient of contingency) = 0.5164*

Table 12

Occupation and Investment Pattern Observed Frequency

Occupation	*Response of Investment*					*Total*
	A	*B*	*C*	*D*	*E*	
Banker	30	30	6	12	6	84
Academician	18	12	12	6	6	54
Corporate executive	18	12	12	6	12	60
Self-employed	12	6	18	18	12	66
Student	18	6	0	0	0	24
Total	*96*	*66*	*48*	*42*	*36*	*288*

Table 13

Expected Frequency

Occupation	*Response of Investment*					*Total*
	A	*B*	*C*	*D*	*E*	
Banker	28	19.25	14	12.25	10.5	84
Academician	18	12.38	9	7.87	6.25	54
Corporate executive	20	13.75	10	8.75	7.5	60
Self-employed	22	15.13	11	9.62	8.25	66
Student	8	5.5	4	3.5	3	24
Total	*96*	*66*	*48*	*42*	*36*	*288*

Degree of freedom = 16

c^2_{16} = 69.0768 and i = 0.4398

Table 14
Qualification and Investment Pattern Observed Frequency

Qualification	*Response of Investment Class*					*Total*
	A	**B**	**C**	**D**	**E**	
Undergraduate	0	6	6	18	6	36
Graduate	30	30	6	6	12	84
Postgraduate	42	18	18	12	18	108
Doctorate/Post doctorate	24	12	18	6	0	60
Total	*96*	*66*	*48*	*42*	*36*	*288*

Table 15
Expected Frequency

Qualification	*Response of Investment Class*					*Total*
	A	**B**	**C**	**D**	**E**	
Undergraduate	12	8.25	6	5.25	4.5	36
Graduate	28	19.25	14	12.25	10.5	84
Postgraduate	36	24.75	18	15.75	13.5	108
Doctorate/Post doctorate	20	13.75	10	8.75	7.5	60
Total	*96*	*66*	*48*	*42*	*36*	*288*

Degree of freedom = 12

c^2_{12} = *80.2136 and i = 0.4667*

Table 16
Income and Investment Pattern Observed Frequency

Income Class	*Response of Investment*					*Total*
	A	**B**	**C**	**D**	**E**	
Below 5000	36	12	6	6	0	60
5001 to 10,000	36	30	12	6	6	90
10,001 to 15,000	24	18	18	6	6	72
15,001 to 20,000	0	6	6	12	12	36
Above 20,000	0	0	6	12	12	30
Total	*96*	*66*	*48*	*42*	*36*	*288*

Table 17
Expected Frequency

Investment Class	*Response of Investment Class*					*Total*
	A	**B**	**C**	**D**	**E**	
Below 5000	20	13.75	10	8.75	7.50	60
5001 to 10,000	30	20.63	15	13.12	11.25	90

10,001 to 15,000	24	16.50	12	10.50	9.0	72
15,001 to 20,000	12	8.25	6	5.25	4.5	36
Above 20,000	10	6.87	5	4.38	3.75	30
Total	*96*	*66*	*48*	*42*	*36*	*288*

Degree of freedom = 16

$C^2_{12} = 112.933$ *and* $i = 0.5307$

Testing of Hypothesis

Table 11 reveals that the calculated value of C^2_{16} is 104.769 and tabular value is 26.3 at 5 per cent level. Hence, null hypothesis is rejected. Further, the coefficient of contingency is 0.5164. It is concluded that there is strong association between the age and investment pattern of mutual fund investments.

From Table 13, it is found that the calculated value of C^2_{16} is 69.0768 and tabular value is 26.3 at 5 per cent level. So the null hypothesis is rejected. Again the coefficient of contingency is less than 0.5, which indicates there is moderate association between occupation and investment pattern. Similarly, it is evident from Table 15 that the calculated value of C^2_{16} is 80.2136 and the tabular value is 21.026. Hence, null hypothesis is rejected. Further coefficient of contingency is 0.4667. So, it is concluded that there is a moderate association between the qualification and investment pattern of mutual fund investors. It is found from Table 17 that the calculated value of C^2_{16} is 112.933, which is higher than the tabular value at 5 per cent level of significance indicating rejection of null hypothesis. Again the coefficient of contingency is 0.5307 and indicates a strong association between the post-tax monthly income of the family and the investment pattern of mutual fund investors.

Observation

It is observed that the perception of investors is very encouraging from the institutional investors only. The retail investors are not able to perceive the product in a proper perspective. Further, investors invested in the mutual funds without understanding their mechanics, which misguided endeavors to distorted investors' perception. Also a few funds, which have not performed well unfortunately, demoralized the investing public. Thus, there is needed to take some strategy to bring more confidence among investors for which mutual funds would be able to project the image successfully.

INTEGRATED MARKETING STRATEGY

The mutual funds operate in an imperfect market where many mutual funds operate, each competing with everyone else almost with similar product lines. So, the mutual fund industry would require framing a marketing mix so that a fine-fusion is made possible between the interests of the mutual funds and their customers. The elements of marketing mix are put into model form in Figure 1. Secondly, the savings environment is becoming more dynamic due to change in saving habit. So in such a situation the role of mutual funds is to peruse a market development strategy by monitoring and reaching prospective investors, seeking innovation in ways to convince to stay on with mutual funds. Thirdly, the mutual funds always endeavor to innovating new schemes suitable to the savings needs of different cross-sections of the public and their financial needs. Therefore, it is essential to have a deep study of the changing psychology of prospective investors, increasing their level of earnings. Fourthly, another area which need great attention is that it is essential to create a work culture in the workforce, and behavioral management of the employees should be improved to keep overall public image of the institution. Fifthly, owing to lack of low awareness and usage of recent developments the potential investors are deprived to move to other financial institution. So, the mutual funds have to revamp their promotional strategies through personal promotion as well as through impersonal promotion. In addition to this, due to operations of many mutual funds, there will be need for appropriate guidelines for self-regulations in respect of publicity/advertisement and inter-scheme transactions within each mutual fund. Further infrastructure bottlenecks have to be removed and banking and postal systems have to be developed for growth of mutual funds. So, mutual funds need to take advantage of modern technology like computer and telecommunications to render service to the investors. Lastly, investors, and investors' interest ought to be paramount which can be increased by setting make mutual funds standard of behaviours and professionalism.

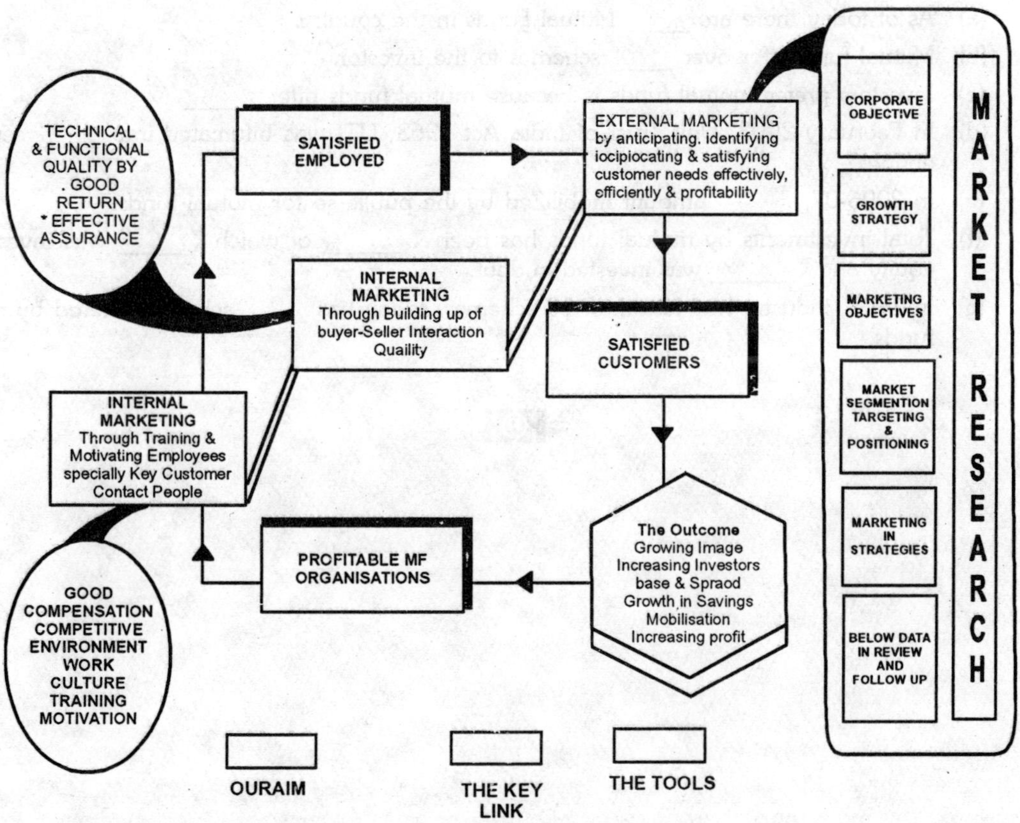

Fig. 1

CONCLUDING OBSERVATION

The keyword in success of mutual fund business is the perceived confidence of the investors in the organization in totality taking into account both the historical quality of the product in terms of return as well as the way the account is perceived to be managed in terms of concern and customer servicing. So if the past is any indicator of the future, the mutual fund industry will no doubt, have an explosive growth, if it is able to match the investor's expectations. Therefore, mutual funds will have to equip themselves materially and personally to come up to the expectations of the investors. Thus, all the above aspects need close review to transform this potential into reality to become a sophisticated market in terms of technology regulations and investors' protection in future.

REVIEW QUESTIONS

1. How do you evaluate the perception of investors towards mutual fund investment?
2. Explain the integrated approach for optimal functioning of mutual funds.
3. Quiz
   (a) As of today there are _____ Mutual Funds in the country.
   (b) Mutual fund offer over _____ schemes to the investor.
   (c) Investors prefer mutual funds is because mutual funds offer ______.
   (d) In February 2003, Unit Trust of India Act 1963, UTI was bifurcated into _____ separate entities.
   (e) In 2006-07, ______ amount mobiliZed by the public sector mutual funds.
   (f) Total investments by mutual funds has been ₹ ______ of which ₹ _____ was invested in equity and ₹ ______ was invested in debt.
   (g) In 1993, industry had less than 10 schemes, today has _____ schemes offered by mutual funds.

16

A Service Quality Model for Customers in Public Sector Banks

There is proliferation of banking companies and their products. The recent trends show that most banks are shifting from a "Product-centric model to a customer centric model" as customer satisfaction is becoming one of the major targets in the hands of the banks. This chapter analyze the factors that are essential in influencing the investment decision of the customers in the public sector banks also suggests some measures to formulate marketing strategies to lure customers towards them.

INTRODUCTION

Banking and financial services form the core of the economic system of a country. The banking sector in India has made remarkable progress since the economic reforms in 1991. New private sector banks brought the necessary competition into the industry and spearheaded the changes towards higher utilization of technology, improved customers service and innovative products. The banking area has been almost flooded with new entrants including private banks, foreign banks, non-banking finance companies, the merchant bankers, chit funds etc. The three major sub groups, the public sector, the private sector and foreign banks have posted impressive increases in various broad parameters. The total income of the nationalized banks increased by 7.7% compared to 2002-2003. Private sector banks have recorded a growth of 9.81% in their total income while foreign banks increase it by 9.41% over the last financial year, public sector banks have registered a marginal downfall of 1.05% in their interest income in the case of public sector banks, has registered an increase of 14.05%. The share of public sector banks in the deposits pie declined from 78 to 76% even as that of the private sector banks increased from 16 to 18%. So the competition is tough. Better service quality, innovative products, better bargains are all greeting the Indian customers. In order to provide service in the present-day world of competition, the banks will have to formulate marketing strategies in a way to encourage the customers towards them. Keeping in view the above, the present chapter has made an attempt to study the preferences and priorities towards types of service provided by the public sector banks. Secondly to identify key features and service attributes that is essential for customer satisfaction. Thirdly to suggest some measures to increase the level of customer satisfaction to enhance their market share.

TAKE SAMPLE OF FOUR PUBLIC SECTOR BANKS FOR EVALUATING THEIR SERVICES PROVIDED TO CUSTOMERS

Four public sector banks are taken. The banks which selected is one have maximum number of branches in each city. After studying the banking facilities provided by these banks, of which the customer is the main focus, a questionnaire is designed. A sample of 200 customers is taken for the study. Most of the questions are designed having a 7-point scale. The data which is collected have been clarified, tabulated and processed for factor analysis, which is the most appropriate multi-variety technique to identify the groups of determinants.

Factor analysis identifies common dimensions of factors from the observed variables that link together the seemingly unrelated variables and provides insight into the underlying structure of the data. In this study, Principal Component analysis has been used since the objective is to summarize most of the original information in a minimum number of factors for prediction purposes. A Principal Component Analysis is a factor model in which the factors are based upon the total variance. Another concept in factor analysis is the rotation of factors. Various rotations are one of the most popular methods used in the study to simplify the factor structure by maximizing the variance of a column of the pattern matrix. Another technique called latent root criteria is used, under this, only the factors having latent roots (Eigen value) greater than one are considered. An Eigen value is the column sum of squares for a factor. It represents the amount of variance in data. After determination of the common factors, factor scores were estimated for each factor. The common factors themselves on are expressed as linear combinations of the observed variables.

Factor Model: $F_i = W_{i1}X_1 + W_{i2} + \text{------------} W_{ik}X_k$

Where

F_i = estimate of the ith factor

W_i = weight or factor score coefficient

K = no. of variables

The next step is the naming of factors.

Analysis

A customer takes into account various factors while deciding about investing in a bank. These ranges of factors begin with customer's perception, the promised return and to the attractiveness of the offer. So from informal discussions with customers, all the relevant variables are included in the study. Twenty statements are generated for measuring respondent's opinion on a 7-point scale for preferring bank investment. Factor matrix and their corresponding factor loading after the varimax rotation are presented in the table.

Table 1

Eigen Values and Percentage of Variance of Trace of PSB Customers

Attribute	Eigen Value	Percent of Variation	Cumulative Per Cent
1. Waiting time	3.367	16.834	16.834
2. Speed of depositing money	2.638	13.191	30.026
3. Speed of withdrawals	2.470	12.350	42.376
4. Service charge	2.290	9.760	53.824
5. Atmosphere in the Bank	1.952	11.760	63.584
6. Interest on loans	1.485	7.425	71.009
7. Interest on savings	1.210	6.051	77.060
8. Technology innovation in the Bank	.0903	4.517	81.577
9. Behavior of staff towards customer	.640	3.200	84.777
10. Site of the bank	.633	3.167	87.944
11. Knowledge of staff regarding bank services	.511	2.555	90.499
12. Sound of operational efficiency	.404	2.020	92.519
13. Availability of staff for enquiry and assistance	.511	1.894	94.413
14. Layout of the Bank	.404	1.477	95.890
15. Sitting and lighting arrangement in the bank	.379	1.213	97.103
16. Banks innovation towards introducing new service	.221	1.103	98.206
17. Parking facility	.141	.703	98.909
18. Banks publication regarding performance	.115	.577	99.485
19. Relationship with customer	.067	.336	99.822
20. Banks advertising regarding services	.036	.178	100.00

Table 2

Loading of Selected Variables on Key Factors (Loading criteria>0.5)

Attribute	F1	F2	F3	F4	F5	F6	F7
1. Waiting time	.907						
2. Speed of depositing money	.588						
3. Speed of withdrawal	.702						
4. Service charge							
5. Atmosphere in the Bank					.702		
6. Int. on loan		.796					
7. Int. on savings		.680					

8.	Technology innovation in the Bank							.774
9.	Behaviour of the staff toward customer			.855				
10.	Site of the Bank				.782			
11.	Knowledge of staff regarding bank services				.793			
12.	Sound of operational efficiency			.741				
13.	Availability of staff for enquiry and assistance			.858				
14.	Layout of the Bank	.810						
15.	Sitting and lighting arrangement in the Bank					.581		
16.	Banks innovation towards introducing new services							.691
17.	Parking facility						.832	
18.	Banks publication regarding performance							
19.	Relationship with customer			.644				
20.	Banks advertising regarding services	.914						
	Eigen values	8.806	2.695	1.487	1.144	2.336	1.124	

The grouping of variables with a factor coefficient >.5 are shown in the Table 3. Factor 1 has an Eigen value of 8.806 and explains 44.03% of total variance. The Eigen value of the second factor, third factor, fourth, fifth and sixth factor are 2.695, 1.487, 1.144, 2.336 and 1.124 respectively. The total variable accounted for by all the six factors is 75.74%, which is quite high, and it establishes the validity of the study. Naming the factors has been done on the basis of the size of factor loading of the variables.

Table 3

Grouping of Factor Loading for Identifying Key Features

No.	*Attributes*	*F1*	*F2*	*F3*	*F4*	*F5*	*F6*	
1.	Waiting time	.907						
2.	Speed of depositing money	.588						
3.	Speed of withdrawals	.702						
14.	Layout of the Bank	.810						
20.	Bank's advertising regarding services	.914						
6.	Interest on loans		.796					
7.	Interest on savings		.680					
13.	Availability of staff for enquiry			.858				
9.	Behaviour of staff towards customer			.855				
12.	Sound of operational efficiency			.741				

19. Relationship with customer			.644				
10. Site of the bank				.782			
11. Knowledge of staff regarding bank services				.793			
5. Atmosphere in the bank					.702		
15. Sitting and lighting arrangement in the bank					.581		
17. Parking facility					.832		
8. Technology innovation in the bank						.774	
16. Banks innovation towards introducing new services						.691	

The factors are named after grouping the key variables and looking at the communality of the variables in explaining at typical attribute of a Bank.

Table 4

Factors of Customer Preference for Banks

Core Factor	***Price Factor***	**Services Behaviour**	**Situational Factor**	***Environmental Factor***	**Technology Factor**
Waiting time ♦ Speed of depositing money ♦ Speed of withdrawal ♦ Layout of the bank ♦ Banks advertising regarding services	Int. on loans ♦ Int. on ♦Savings	Behaviour of staff towards customer ♦ Ssound of operational efficiency ♦ Availability of staff for enquiry and assistance ♦ Relationship with customer	Site of the bank ♦ Knowledge of staff regarding bank services	Atmosphere in the bank ♦ Sittings lighting of arrangement in the a bank ♦ Parking facility	Technology innovation in the bank ♦ Banks innovation towards introducing new services

The Table 5 depicts the variables under each of the six derived factors. The first factor identified with waiting time; speed of deposit and withdrawal, layout of the bank and advertising services of the bank have been grouped under factor Fl and termed as core factor. These are the core factor of the bank, which are the common expectations of any customer while making investment in bank. The second factor is the price factor. It generates insignificant satisfaction because the public sector bank customers feel that they are not getting enough for the price they are paying to avail bank service. The third factor service behavior shows significance for behavior of staff towards customer, sound of operational efficiency, availability of staff for enquiry and assistance, relationship with customer. This factor suggest that the service and delivery should be prompt and on time. It is very important part of the bank to provide services in a continuous basis so that the customer stays loyal and happy. The customers are willing to pay more if the quality of service is appreciable. Communication gap is one of the root causes of all banking ills in the public sector banks. Regular and frequent meetings between the bankers and customers would help the banks in receiving proper feedback as to what the customers want on one hand and on the other hand it would help the customers to be loyal and co-operative with the bank.

The fourth factor is situation factor includes attributes such as site of the bank and knowledge of staff about bank services. If it lack of knowledge about rendering bank services even though it is situated in prime location, it cannot motivate the customers. So, site along with knowledge about bank services are equaled important for customers' preferences about the bank.

The fifth factor is environmental factor includes atmosphere in the bank, sittings and lighting arrangement, parking place within the bank premises. This is very important because the customer should feel comfortable, peace with themselves both physically and mentally in the premises.

The sixth factor clearly indicates the combination of two attributes such as technology innovation in the bank, bank's innovation towards introducing new services. This factor is termed as technology factor. Innovation and mechanism is the need of the hour for public sector banks to achieve the confidence of the customers.

The ranks of the factor are given in the Table 5.

Table 5

Ranking of Factors Representing Satisfaction Level of the Public Sector Bank Customer

Factor	*Average Score*	*Rank*
Core factor	3.08	5
Price factor	3.15	2
Service behavior	3.14	3
Situation factor	3.71	1
Environment factor	3.15	2
Technology factor	3.13	4

The satisfaction level of customer regarding situation factor ranks the highest on the list, which signifies the location of the bank and knowledge of the employees, are quite good. Also the customer appreciates environmental factor and price factor. So, it is noticed that public sector banks are taking keen interest with regard to environmental factor within the bank premises. Service behaviors of the bank are moderately satisfied by the customer. So, customer expectation statement should be vision for the organization to aspire for. Technology factor of the bank is also not satisfied by the customer. The technology factor pertains to the computerization and banks innovativeness in introducing newer and better services. But many of the public sector banks are lagging behind in this aspect, which increase the deskwork of the employees and thereby reducing the efficiency of the staff. The routine operation factors of the PSBs are very low which signified that customers are dissatisfied with their operational work of the PSBs. The customers are waiting for a long time to get their work done. Communication gap is the root cause of all banking ills in the PSBs. So, PSBs should gear up to promote their activities by proper trainings, educating employees in order to tune and in information technology attract their customers by providing quick services.

CONCLUDING OBSERVATION

The banking industries in today's scenario has transformed into a buyers' market, where the customer has the choice to select the bank. So, the present chapter highlights the necessary facts of customer's preferences, where the market is turning competitive due to large number of players with varied investment facilities. Now, it is the need of the hour of the PUBs to inculcate marketing orientation in their work culture. The bankers should more educate about the recent trends to meet the customer expectation and needs to go a long way in building the reputation and image of the public sector banks.

REVIEW QUESTIONS

1. Write short notes on:
   (a) Factors analysis
   (b) Principal component analysis
2. How do you evaluate the perception of customers towards services provided by public sector banks?
3. Briefly explain the services model of public sectors banks.

17

Holistic Approach for Plastic Card Consumers in India

Today, the plastic card segment is highly competitive one with almost all the banks offering debit cards in association with international or master card. Every bank is trying to gain a market share with aggressive promotional activities and additional value-added services. Keeping in view, the present chapter investigates the factors that are essential in influencing the decision-making styles of consumers in India.

INTRODUCTION

The economic development and technological advances lead to the impressive growth of service industry. It has changed the method of work, quality of products and services. It has brought about enormous saving in terms of time and money for the business. The plastic cards began to be widely used only after 1970, when specific standards for magnetic strip were set. In the late 1990s, plastic cards became very common and by 2001, plastic money has become an essential form of 'ready money'. There has been a growth on electronic payment due to growing access of internet among the customers and convenient modes of delivery and payment. In the present-day world, no one wants to carry cash and Indians are no exceptions. The benefits of plastic money have offered unmatched ways to create equilibrium and offer an amicable solution when it comes to purchases and the inability to carry cash. The unprecedented growth in the number of plastic card users' has stimulated the Indian economy by a significant extent. The advent of malls, multiplexes, online shopping stores and shopping complexes have contributed to the growth of the use of plastic cards. It is not wrong to say that Indian market is not driven by style statement and is driven more by needs. The modern day Indian customers find it easier to make physical payment rather than carrying too much cash. The introduction of credit card facilities to pay for mobile, electricity, movie tickets and other related transactions have also contributed to the growth of plastic money in the country. The changes in consumer behavior and tastes led to the tremendous growth of plastic cards. The plastic cards made of plastic are widely used by the consumers all around the globe. Nowadays, plastic cards have turned into the most common way to make payments, since they are secure, convenient, and accepted anywhere in the world. Plastic money also known as Plastic cards act as a vital tool for everyday transaction of people today.

WHAT IS PLASIC CARD?

Plastic money made out of plastic, is a new and easier way of paying for goods and services. 'Plastic cards are the physical carriers of electronic cash.' This card can be used by customers to pay for their shopping, transportation, parking, dining etc. Goods and services can be purchased over the Internet by using electronic cash card. Plastic money was introduced in the 1950s and is now an essential form of ready money which reduces the risk of handling a huge amount of cash. The various Plastic cards include ATM cards, Debit Card, TM-cum-Debit Card, Credit Cards, Smart Card, Charge Cards, and Co-branded cards, Add-on cards and so on.

ATM Cards

Automated Teller Machine (ATM) cards are capable of doing variety of functions. It can perform both cash and non-cash transactions in secured environment. ATM Cash Transactions includes deposits and withdrawals. Non-cash transactions include: Providing Mini Statement, Balance enquiry, Transfer of funds between accounts, Requisition of Cheque books, drafts etc. and Bill payments.

Debit Card

If the person has an account in the bank, the bank provides debit card facility. This card is useful to make payment from Member Establishments (ME) who has arrangements with the card issuing bank or agency. They check the balance and deduct the amount from the bank balance online. When a debit card is issued to make the payment, the total amount charged is instantly reduced from the bank balance of the account holder. All credit and debit cards are affiliated to two major issuers — VISA and Master Card. Master Card and VISA are global non-profit organizations who promote the growth of the card business throughout the world. They have built vast network of Member Establishments so that customers can use the cards worldwide for their debit and credit purchases.

Debit-cum-ATM Card

This is most common nowadays. The same debit card can be used to draw cash from the ATM and also make payment to the shops for purchases. This is two in one card.

Credit Cards

This card enables the client to obtain goods or services from the various shops having arrangement with the issuing agency even if there is no balance in his/her savings or current account. The bank assumes that the loan will be repaid by the customers at later date. The credit cardholder has to make payment for the dues before the due date. Otherwise interest is levied in the next billing statement. Normally, limit of the credit will be fixed by the bank for the amount of purchases to be made by the customer based on the net worth of the customer.

Master Card and Visa

Master Card and Visa are global non-profit organizations dedicated to promote the growth of the card business across the world. They have built a vast network of merchant establishments so that customer's world wide may use their respective credit cards to make various purchases.

Charge Cards

A Charge card has all features of credit card. In charge card, the entire payments of the bills has to be made in the due date. If the client failed to do so, then he is considered as a defaulter and he has to pay a sharp late payment charges. But in case of Credit cards, the client is not declared as a defaulter if he misses to pay by due date. In such case, a late fee is levied in the next billing statements of the credit card holder.

Co-branded Card

Co-branded cards are credit cards issued by card companies that have tied up with a popular brand for the purpose of offering certain exclusive benefits to the consumer.

AMEX (American Express) and Diners' Club Card

This is well-known branded charge cards. They have their own merchant establishments and tie-ups and does not depend on the network of Master Card or VISA. These cards are typically meant for the high-income group categories and companies. These cards are not acceptable at many outlets. But wide variety of special privileges is enjoyed by the AMEX cardholders and Diners Club Cardholders.

Smart Cards

A Smart Card is most useful to pay for small purchases. No identification, signature or payment authorization is required for using this card. The exact amount of purchase is deducted from smart card during payment. Currently, this product is available in very developed countries like US.

Affinity Card

The card issuer has a tie-up with popular organizations and institutions which are often non-profit organizations. When a card is used, a certain percentage is contributed to the organization or institution by the card issuer.

Photo Card

When a photo is imprinted on the card, it helps to identify the user of the credit card and is considered to be safer. In many cases, photo card can also be used as identity card.

Global Card

Global cards can be used as credit cards instead of cash and traveler cheques while traveling abroad to foreign countries for business or personal reasons.

Add-on Cards

Normally, an issuing bank offered two add-on cards per credit card to the spouse, parents, children or other family members of the original cardholder. All expenses incurred on add-on card are billed to the primary cardholder.

Petro Card

Some Petroleum companies offer a scheme of gifting the points to the customers to pay for the fuel through electronic medium. It is convenient, secured and speedy mode of transaction.

Prepaid Card

Prepaid card also called reloadable debit cards is a card paid for at Point of Sale and permits the holder to buy goods or services up to the prepaid value. Not all such cards show the identity of the bearer (e.g., phone cards). Prepaid debit cards use either the offline debit system or the online debit system to access these funds. Particularly for companies with a large number of payment recipients abroad, prepaid debit cards allow the delivery of international payments without the delays and fees associated with international checks and bank transfers.

Promotional Card

Promotional card is typically a card offering special benefits to users, e.g., discounts or rewards.

Protected Memory Card

Protected memory card is a smart card that requires a secret code or PIN number to be entered before the data can be sent/received from the chip.

Barcode Card

Barcode card is a card with printed codes made from vertical lines of different thickness used for fast error-free data entry printed somewhere on the face or reverse. There is an array of machine-readable rectangular bars and spaces arranged in a specific way defined in international standards to represent letters, numbers, and other human-readable symbols. Cards are either the usually 30 micron credit card type cards or alternatively can be 'pop out' cards.

Cheque Guarantee Card

Cheque guarantee card is a card issued by a bank or building society for the purpose of guaranteeing settlement of cheques to third parties or supporting the encashment of cheques at financial institutions up to a specified value. Most debit and some credit cards may also functions cheque guarantee cards (multifunction cards).

Unsecured Credit Cards

Unsecured credit cards are issuing to a person on good credit history. A credit company checks the credit records, number of working bank accounts, history of paid and missed bills, etc. of the person while issuing it and would be given a credit card with a credit limit. With this credit card in hand, one can make monthly expenses like paying various pills, shopping, etc., and later would receive a bill on the total expenses which he made in that month. The bill has to be paid monthly, but the customer has the privilege to pay money either partly or fully each month. To acquire an unsecured credit card, one does not have to deposit any money, but may have to pay a membership fee. Unsecured credit cards are good for people who have control over their finances and enough resources to pay back, what they have taken from the company.

Secured Credit Cards

Secured credit cards were introduced much later than unsecured credit cards and are given to individuals with no credit history. To acquire a secured credit card, one has to set a credit limit for oneself and deposit it in an account to get a credit card. While using the secured credit card, one can only spend money within that credit limit and sometimes 100% of the money present in the account. Secured credit cards are good for people who do not have a firm control on their expenses. Besides, people who receive a secured credit card do not have to worry about creating debts for themselves.

HISTORY OF PLASTIC CARD

As far back as the late 1800s, consumers and merchants exchanged goods through the concept of credit, using credit coins and charge plates as currency. It wasn't until about half a century ago that plastic payments as we know them today became a way of life. The period following the Second World War saw the USA become the world's first and the largest "service economy". To boost sales and increase the customer base, a reliable payment system was needed which led to the innovation of Credit Cards. The use of credit cards originated in the USA in the 1920s.The individual firms, such as Oil companies and hotel chains, began to issue credit cards to their customers for purchase made at their outlets. After World War II, the use of credit cards raised rapidly. Credit cards were not always been made of plastic. There have been credit tokens made from metal coins, metal plates, and celluloid, metal, fiber, paper, and now mostly plastic cards. The origin of the bank credit card concept can be traced to the launching of a credit plan called "charge-it" by John C. Biggins of the Flatbush National Bank of Brooklyn in New York. In 1946, Biggins invented the "Charge-it" program between bank customers and local merchants. Merchants could deposit sales slips into the bank and the bank billed the customer who used the card.

In 1949, Frank X McNamara, head of the Hamilton Credit Corporation had a business dinner at New York's Major's Cabin Grill with Alfred Bloomingdale, McNamara's long-time friend and grandson of the founder of the Bloomingdale's Store, and Ralph Sneider, McNamara's attorney. At the end of the dinner, when the bill arrived, Frank realized he had forgotten his wallet so immediately that he called his wife and asked her to bring some money for hotel payment. McNamara promised never to let this happen again. Merging the two concepts from that dinner, the lending of credit cards and not having cash on hand to pay for the meal, McNamara came up with a new idea — a credit card that could be used at multiple locations. What was particularly novel about this concept was that there would be a middleman between companies and their customers.

McNamara discussed the idea with Bloomingdale and Sneider and three pooled some money and started a new company in 1950 which called Diners' Club. The Diners' Club was going to be a middleman. Instead of individual companies offering credit to their own customers, the Diners' Club was going to offer credit to individuals for many companies. Previously, stores would make money with their credit cards by keeping customers loyal to their particular store, thus maintaining a high level of sales. However, the Diners' Club needed a different way to make money since they weren't actually selling anything. To make a profit without charging interest, the companies who accepted the Diners' Club credit card were charged 7 per cent for each transaction while the subscribers to the credit card were charged a $ 3 annual fee (begun in 1951). McNamara's new credit company focused on salesmen. Since salesmen often need to dine at multiple restaurants to entertain their clients, the Diners' Club needed both to convince a large number of restaurants to accept the new card and to get salesmen to subscribe. The first Diners' Club credit cards were given out in 1950 to 200 people (most were friends and acquaintances of McNamara) and accepted by 14 restaurants in New York. However, the concept of the card grew and by the end of 1950, 20,000 people were using the Diners' Club credit card. A customer could eat without cash at any restaurant that would accept Diners' Club credit cards. Diners' Club would pay the restaurant and the credit cardholder would repay Diners' Club. The Diners' Club card was at first technically a charge card rather than a credit card since the customer had to repay the entire amount when billed by Diners' Club. Though the Diners' Club continued to grow and by the second year was making a profit ($ 60,000), McNamara thought the concept was just a fad. In 1952, he sold his shares in the company for more than $ 200,000 to his two partners. The Diners' Club credit card continued to grow more popular and didn't receive competition until 1958. In that year, both American Express and the Bank America (later called VISA) arrived. American Express issued their first credit card in 1958. The credit card industry got a further boost with the arrival of American Express began selling their card as a prestige to hotels, restaurants, shops or airlines in America and slowly expanded the network across the world. In 1960, the Credit Card operating system was developed and an international bank card system known as "VISA" International was established. Another International Bank Card system called "Master Card" was also established. In the year 1965, the Barclays Bank, UK, launched Barclay Card with a Visa tie-up. The Access Card was launched in the year 1962 in the UK by a consortium of British and Scottish banks with a Master Card tie-up. With the amazing success of credit card system in UK, the Euro card was introduced in most of the West European countries with a tie-up with Access. In the year 1988, the first woman card was launched "My Card" by International Bank of Asia in Hong Kong. There was tremendous demand for that card. The card was introduced as "Ladys Card" in Malaysia. In 1990, Green Card was launched in UK and Europe.

The advancement of Information Technology has paved the way for a radical change in the nature and mode of banking operations. In order to meet the ever-increasing customer demand, Indian banks are concentrating on multi-channel delivery. Customers today have a wide range of products to choose from. The first credit card to enter India was the Diners' Club Card in the year 1964.

The first Indian banks to launch credit cards were "Andhra Bank and Central Bank". The first credit card introduced by Andhra Bank was VISA Classic in the year 1981, followed by Central Bank of India's credit card in collaboration with Master Card Corporation in the year 1981. Country first gold card was also issued from the same time. The other nationalized banks, Canara Bank, Bank of India, and Bank of Baroda gradually introduced their credit cards in India only later. Apart from these Indian Banks, many foreign banks such as Citibank, Standard Chartered Bank, ANZ Grindlays Bank, Bank of America and American Express Bank have also introduced their proprietary and other franchised cards through their Indian branches. Citibank issues Diners' Club Card. Andhra Bank now offers four types of credit cards for different categories of people, including the VISA ICC card for international usage. Similarly, Canara Bank has a range of cards from their proprietary Can Card to franchised cards such as Can Card Visa, Can Card Master, and VISA International Gold Cards etc. Bank of Baroda has started its BOBCARD Master, and today this bank issues four types of credit cards. SBI has made rapid strides in the credit card business as to come out with several Premium Cards. The bank issues regular card, international card, ATM card and the ATM-cum-Debit card. The other banks such as Indian Overseas Bank, Dena Bank, Corporation Bank and Vysya Bank have affiliated with the principal issuers like Canara Bank, Citibank, Bank of India etc. for issuing credit cards. In India, oil companies issue "petro cards" for easier payment at the company's petrol stations. Similarly the "Mahanagar Telephone Nigam Limited" (MTNL) has already introduced its "Virtual Calling Card" and has recently launched a co-branded telecom credit card to facilitate payment of telephone bills. India has 5.3 million credit cards and 6.5 lakh debit cards. The average spends on a credit card, at ₹ 22,000 a year.

The best credit cards in India are usually meant for specific user group such as women, students and small business owners. Statistics have clearly revealed that the numbers of credit cardholders in India are close to 22 million as of January, 2007. It has been also revealed that the increasing consumerism in the country has led to a twofold increase in the number of credit card transactions from FY 2003-04 to 2005-06. The trends were as favorable as ever in the financial years, FY 2006-07 and 2007-08 and the same.

RBI Guidelines on Credit Card Operations

The Reserve Bank of India has placed draft guidelines on credit card operations from the members of the public. The guidelines, when finally issued would be applicable to all commercial banks/non-commercial finance companies (NBFCs). It may be recalled that the Reserve bank had constituted a Working Group to evolve a regulatory mechanism for cards to ensure orderly growth of this segment of consumer credit and protect the interest of banks/NBFC and their customers. The report of the group was placed in public domain on April 23, 2005. The draft guidelines issued now have been framed taking into account the feedback received from media, member of the public and other on the report of the Working Group. The draft guidelines are as each Bank/NBFC has a well documented policy and a fair practices code for credit card and should widely disseminate contents towards plastic money.

Debit Cards *vs.* Credit Cards: Similarities and Differences

Credit Card is a card which enables the consumers to purchase products or services without paying immediately. This credit concept is based on the principle of "Buy now pays later. Pay now, or pay later with interest." That's the difference between a debit card and a credit card. Debit Cards or Credit Cards are electronic plastic cards that are used as a substitute for cash. The same banks offer both debit cards and credit cards. Both cards offer special rewards, such as points and cash back on purchases made through the card. Debit cards and credit cards are used to make online payments with the help of the Pin number assigned to customers. They are used to withdraw money from ATMs, depending on the cash limit available on these cards. Debit cards and credit cards differ in some significant ways. In the case of a credit card, the issuer offers credit and overdraft facilities. This facility is not available with a debit card, which will only debit payments from existing and available funds within the cardholders' account. A credit cardholder therefore has a monthly bill to pay in every month that the card is used. If they don't pay that bill, high interest charges are applied. A debit cardholder is free from the hassle of paying those bills and from the risk of building up large debts to credit card companies. Bank Debit Cards help reduce the need for carrying cash and cheques. Debit cards are directly linked to a cardholder's bank account. Whenever a cardholder withdraws money from an ATM or uses the debit card for making payments, his/her account balance is automatically reduced.

Every time customer uses a credit card actually is borrowing money from a bank that is made available to him. The institution pays the debt to the vendor and, in turn, customer pays the money back to the institution. Debit cards take funds directly from the money that customer have in his bank account — acting much like a cheque, just faster. With a debit card, it is very convenient to shop at a variety of places including gas stations, grocery stores, restaurants and retail stores. It provides instant access to money and is accepted worldwide.

ADVANTAGES AND DISADVANTAGES OF DEBIT AND CREDIT CARD

Debit cards and credit cards each have advantages and disadvantages. The biggest advantage of debit cards over credit cards is that customers need not to be worried about interest rates, monthly bills and finance charges. Debit card uses only the money customer actually have. Credit cards, after all, accrue interest on unpaid balances. Credit card limits are often quite high, sometimes significantly higher than the average monthly balance of a customer's account. Another advantage of the debit card is how easy it is to acquire one. Customer can get a debit card with pretty much any checking account, whereas customer can obtain a credit card only by applying for one. A debit card does not require an investigation of credit history; most credit cards do require a credit check of customers. Like credit cards, debit cards are accepted by merchants with less identification and scrutiny than personal checks, thereby making transactions quicker and less intrusive. Unlike personal checks, merchants generally do not believe that a payment via a debit card may be later dishonored. Unlike a credit card, which charges higher fees and interest rates when a cash advance is obtained, a debit card is used to obtain cash from an ATM or a PIN-based transaction at no extra charge, other than a foreign ATM fee. A person with poor credit can obtain a debit card without too much trouble. Debit cards can be used to make online purchases and payments. They provide freedom from carrying cash and cheques while traveling, thereby offering more safety. Debit cards come with lesser fraud protection facilities than credit cards. A customer can only use as many funds as available. Therefore, in case of an emergencies where credit is urgently needed beyond account balance, a debit card will not be enough to meet needs. A disadvantage of debit cards is the amount of buying protection provided to customer by law. Debit card transactions very much resemble cash transactions. The money changes hands quickly, and it's difficult to get it back. If customer want to return an unsatisfactory item which is purchased with a debit card, many businesses will only give an exchange or store credit. Many banks are now charging over-limit fees or non-sufficient funds fees based upon pre-authorizations, and even attempted but refused transactions by the merchant. In some countries, debit cards offer lower levels of security protection than credit cards. Theft of the users' PIN using skimming devices can be accomplished much easier with a PIN input than with a signature-based credit transaction. However, theft of users' PIN codes using skimming devices can be equally easily accomplished with a debit transaction PIN input, as with a credit transaction PIN input, and theft using a signature-based credit transaction is equally easy as theft using a signature-based debit transaction. One advantage of credit cards over debit cards is that credit card helps to make very large purchases that would be otherwise impossible. It is easy with credit cards to feel like can buy whatever customer want, whenever want. Live and spend within any means. However, debit cards are becoming more popular because they use the funds from the cardholder's savings or checking account, offering convenience and safety. Debit Card has been used as an alternative mode of payment these days.

THE DANGERS OF PLASTIC CARDS

Skimmers

A growing threat activity today is "skimming" to both credit card and debit card users. Skimming occurs when thieves set up a scanning device that captures the magnetic strip and keypad information from ATM machines, gas pumps, and retail and restaurant checkout devices. This allows for the duplication of the card enabling it to be used as either a debit or credit card. Example: After the waiter/shopkeeper takes debit card for payment, he skims (scans) the card before returning it to the table. With this number in hand, there exists the possibility of duplicating that number onto a fraudulent debit card. At this time, the new card may be swiped as a credit purchase without the need for a PIN number.

Key Logging

Key logging comes in two forms: the first form is a physical device which can be attached to a computer, most commonly via the keyboard input port. These devices tend to collect a finite number of key strokes. The device can then be removed and used by the thief to see every key stroke made on that computer. The second form of key logging is software-based. In other words, this is a program which may be added to the computer by logging into a website, receipt of a bogus email. This type of key logging will transmit customers' exact key strokes to a remote location where the thief can have access to it. This occurs whenever customers' computer is logged on to the internet. Example: Mr. Mohan is a travelling salesman staying at a well-known hotel equipped with a business centre. He uses the business centre computer to access various accounts. Once he leaves the computer, the thief comes by and removes the physical key logger device.

HOW CREDIT/DEBIT CARD WORKS?

A credit card is a type of borrowing. Firms lending money to customers must be licensed by the Office of Fair Trading (OFT) under The Consumer Credit Act, 1974. The Act requires certain credit and hires agreements to be set out in a particular way and to contain relevant information for the person borrowing.

Credit cards allow to 'buying on credit'. They aren't linked to your bank account. The bank offers a credit card. The credit card provider will normally run checks to see if the customer has problems repaying debts before offering.

The Risks of Using a Credit Card

A customer is to be careful before using a credit card. If he doesn't repay bill in full by the scheduled date shown, then interest will be charged on the whole amount of the bill for that month. The rates of interest — indicated by the APR (annual percentage rate) — are normally very high. If a customer takes cash out with a credit card, then he is going to charged daily interest from the moment take out the cash until the credit card bill is paid in full. This is an expensive way of borrowing money. Some credit cards also charge an annual fee simply for having the card. It is important to know that credit cards are owned by banks and are given to customers as per their financial position. The banks normally consider salary or total monthly income before issuing a credit card to customer. The banks will decide the maximum limit on credit card based on customers' past credit history and repayment capacity. Thus, a credit card is actually a small loan taken from a bank to fulfill the immediate necessities with a promise that customer will repay later. This is opposite to the principle of the debit card which customer use instead of cash.

Though credit cards can help to give immediate happiness by providing freedom to make quick purchases, simultaneously it will end up detrimental credit score in case of defaults in payments. In case if credit score is not good enough, a customer may face difficulties in securing loans from banks and other financial lenders as it would be difficult to prove creditworthiness in such situations. It is quite known that the rate of interest charged on credit cards is much higher as compared to other kinds of loans. So, many financial experts suggest people to go in for a personal loan instead of a credit card. Till date, many people have found it difficult to oppose the excitement of buying excessively with the use of a credit card which causes the credit card debt to increase.

Debit cards are linked directly to bank account. A customer can use them to buy goods or withdraw cash and the amount is taken from account instantly. Most bank accounts offer debit cards. Most debit cards double up as 'cheque guarantee cards', guaranteeing that customers' cheque will be honored by bank up to a stated amount.

RECENT TRENDS

An affluent economy, disposable incomes going up, rise in consumer expenditure, growing wealth levels, consumer sophistication and organised retail gaining prominence have all led to a robust growth in credit cards. According to a Nilson Report in April, 2009, 78 per cent of American households — about 91.1 million - had one or more credit cards at the end of 2008. "In less than 15 years, debit card transactions in the United States grew from 1 percent of non-cash transactions to more than 50 per cent." (Source: Tower Group, August 2009). Today, Visa reports there are 309 million Visa credit cards and 352 million Visa debit cards in circulation in the United States. Master Card states that as of Sept. 30, 2009, there were 211 million Master Card credit cards and

130 million debit cards). According to data from the US Census Bureau, there were 159 million credit cardholders in the United States in 2000, 173 million in 2006, and that number is grown almost to 181 million Americans by 2010.

The credit card market in India, which started out in 1981, is on the verge of an unprecedented boom. Between 1987 and 2000, the market has virtually grown to over 3.8 million cards with almost 25-30% growth in new cardholders. However, the credit card industry in India grown exponentially in its 15 years of business in the country it had issued 2.69 crore card till December 2003. However in just one year 2004, the figure has spurted to 4.33 crore. Banks and credit card issuers in India, such as Citibank, American Express and Standard Chartered, have registered a sharp 50% jump in card usage in FY 08. Even as consumers in India spend an average of ₹ 4,000 a month per card. The use of plastic money in India is gaining prominence and has started accelerating after holding on to steady growth for years. According to Credit Card Management Consultancy (CCMC), there are about 25 million credit cardholders in the country and the number was grown significantly in 2008-09. However, 40% of the cards are still inactive as a large number of consumers have multiple cards, while they use only one or two actively.

Though the financial year 2008-09 had been exceptionally challenging for the global economy, Indian payment card market seems to be not-so-affected by it. The number of credit and debit cards was estimated at 1,621 lakh as on March, 2009, posting an increase of over 321 lakh cards and registering a growth of 25% in the fiscal. The card acceptance infrastructure has been growing at a positive pace, registering a merchant terminal base of about 4.27 lakh. The debit card base increased from 1,024 lakh in March 2008, to 1,374 lakh by March 2009, registering a growth of 34% over previous financial year (2007-08).

The credit card base, however, reported a negative growth of 10.34% at 246.99 lakh as compared with 275.47 lakh during financial year 2007-08. Interestingly, the debit card market is tentatively grown at 26% to cross the 1,732 lakh mark in the country by March 2010. On the other hand, the credit card base is almost fall further in 2009-10 to about 226 lakh. The credit card business, however, is witnessing a crunch. With the increasing delinquency rate in the country, banks and card issuers are hesitant to issue new credit cards. Many banks have been closing inactive and unproductive accounts from their credit card portfolio. The research further said ICICI Bank, HDFC Bank, HSBC Bank, SBI and Citibank have over 80% share of the Indian credit card industry. ICICI Bank has the largest credit card base in India with 70 lakh credit cards in the market as on March, 2009, followed by HDFC Bank and HSBC Bank with market share of 16% and 14%, respectively. SBI trail blazes with 11% market share. The market share of private banks has fallen to 47% in 2009 from 48% in 2008. Private banks have shown a decrease in their credit card base from 130.77 lakh cards in 2008 to 116.73 lakh cards by March 2009. The market share of foreign banks increased from 34% in 2008 to 37% in 2009. Public sector banks constitute 15% market share with 36.08 lakh credit cards. Other banks having card base of 2.13 lakh cover the balance 1% of market share.

Despite of decrease in the credit card base, spends at merchant point of sale (POS) terminals increased by 13% to ₹ 65,356 crore during the year 2008-09. However, it was lower than the 40% growth recorded in 2007-08. The average annual credit card spend has increased significantly to ₹ 26,461 during the year 2008-2009 from ₹ 21,049 during the year 2007-2008, reporting a growth of 26%, higher than the 18% recorded in the previous financial year. India has seen remarkable growth in its debit card market over the past few years. The surge in debit card usage can be attributed to the ongoing economic slowdown and the cautious attitude towards spending money.

SBI has emerged the leader in issuing debit cards with 30% of market share during the year 2008-2009, followed by ICICI Bank with 10% market share. AXIS Bank ranks third with a market share of 9%. The debit card spends at merchant POS terminals increased significantly by 48% to Rs 18,547 crore during the year 2009 from ₹ 12,521 crore during the previous financial year.

In the financial year 2008-09, the average annual debit card spend at merchant POS terminals increased by 10% to ₹ 1,350 from ₹ 1,222 in the year 2007-08, lower than the 12% growth of previous year.

Also, the average spend on debit card is much lower than the average spend on credit card. A study by Edgar, Dunn & Company (EDC) and India Cards Council (ICC) has revealed that unlike in the UK and Australia where 90% cards are active, there are only 56% active debit cards in India.

According to the research, the spread of ATMs has increased from 34,789 in March 2008 to 43,651 in March 2009, reporting a growth rate of 25%. The ATMs are tentatively grow by 35% during the year 2009-10, where SBI is increased their ATM outlets by around 75%. As per the RBI release, the volume of ATM transactions has increased from 17,797 lakh aggregating to ₹ 438,151 crore during 2007-08 to 23,530 lakh aggregating to ₹ 616,456 crore during 2008-09.

The usage of plastic money now is just 2.5 per cent of the USD 700 billion consumers are spending in India annually (PTI, May 5, 2010). The international average (of plastic money usage) is 9 per cent. This is after the bank had floated a Request For Proposal (RFP) for selection of joint venture (JV) partners for merchant acquiring business last year 2009. India's largest lender State Bank of India (SBI) said it has selected US-based Elavon Incorporation and Visa International as its joint venture partners for the merchant acquiring business. Two decades ago, the number of debit cards in circulation was approximately 19 million. This figure is projected to cross 34.4 million by 2016. The history of debit cards shows that they have largely been used to pay for food and drinks.

Huge Market Remains Untapped

The most promising part of the growth of India is that so much still remains to be covered. Only 2.4% of the working population in India owned a credit card in 2004. Compared to other Asian markets, Indian credit card market is still at a nascent stage. Credit cards per bankable population in India is 0.03 per person against 3 in South Korea, 2.66 in Taiwan, 2 in Hong Kong, 1.1 in Singapore and 0.4 in Malaysia. According to Mr. V. Vaidyanathan, senior general manager and head — retail products, ICICI Bank, an average Indian credit cardholder spends less than $500 on his card annually, compared to around $ 800 in Sri Lanka and over $ 3,000 in Hong Kong and Singapore. Outstanding dues on credit card are the lowest in the region. The outstanding balance in India is at $ 1.5 billion, compared to $ 90 billion in Korea, $ 10 billion in Hong Kong and US $ 2.5 billion in Malaysia. In other words, the credit card market in India could continue to register the current scorching growth in the medium to long term. According to McKinsey prediction, 35 million credit cards will be issued with an outstanding balance of over $ 7 billion by 2010.

WHAT IS CREDIT CARD REFORM ACT?

In the May of 2009, United States President, Barack Obama, requested the Congress to pass an enactment to improve the status of accountability in the credit creation sector. The actual name of the act is Credit Card Accountability Responsibility and Disclosure Act, 2009 and its genesis lies in the Bill 90 - 5 of the Senate, and Bill 361 - 64 of the House of Representatives. Though the enactment, Credit Card Reform Act of 2009, was passed in 20th of May 2009, it was enforced in February of 2010.

The main objective of the act is to protect and maintain public accountancy of consumers and also banned all unfair and consumer unfriendly practices that are imposed by credit creators to consumers. The credit card companies are required to maintain a policy of clear and simple disclosures. The advantage of such disclosures facilitates the consumers aware of the policies and charges that are imposed by the credit card companies. The effect of such reforms enable the credit card user consumers to know what they are exactly paying as an interest APR, charge and fee. This enhanced transparency in the structure of fees is further aided by the compliance of notice periods. The charges and terms and conditions of the credit card can be changed by the credit card companies at any given point of time. To eliminate the problems of consumers, regarding the rise of rates, the act creates compliance, in accordance of which the service provider has to notify the cardholder about the rise in rate, prior to the billing cycle. Furthermore, the compliance regarding the credit provided to the student community has been changed with a view to protect the youngsters from dire and unnecessary consequences of credit card debt.

Credit Card Reform Act of 2009: Features and Provisions

There are some important features of this act that every consumer should know:

Credit card companies are not permitted to raise the interest rate in the first service year. In addition to that, the company can hike the cost of credit, only if the payment of the bill is 60 days late. Upon the addition of interest rate, the account is to be reviewed, and in cases where the payment for last 6 months has been on time, the original lower rate of interest is to be levied. In accordance with the new legislation, the credit card company must intimate a notice of 45 days, before the interest rate is increased. Some essential changes regarding billing cycle have also been implemented. The first genuine change is the ban on double billing procedures. The interest levied upon a single bill plus, differential interest rates and APRs must be disclosed properly in the monthly bill. The statement and the said bill is to be mailed 21 days before the payment is due. In addition to that, charges for payments over Internet or cellphones are to be abolished. Debt settlement would also become an easier option, owing to the transparency of billing. Two drawbacks affecting the entire industry include the elimination of grace periods and revision in annual fees.

There has been an exponential growth in the debit cards' issuance and wage among the people. Today, the debit card segment is highly competitive with almost all the banks offering debit cards in association with international or master card. The popularity of debit card is mainly due to the fact that unlike the western world, where the culture is to live on loan, Indians are credit shy people. It is often said now that "credit shy Indians are going by debit card".

LITERATURE REVIEW

Hirschman (1979) focused her research on the influence of method of payment on purchasing behavior and found that cardholders are more likely to make bigger purchases than non-holders. This finding suggests that credit cards facilitate and induce purchases, as compared to cash. Kaynak and Ugur (1984) conducted a cross-cultural study of credit card usage behavior of Canadian and American cardholders. In the first stage of their research, cardholders' attitudes towards credit cards were evaluated. Both populations of cardholders agreed that credit cards are useful in a sense that cards are safer than cash and help making impulse buying payments. The finding was that both Americans and Canadians show similar patterns in attitudes toward ownership of credit cards, but their behavioral characteristics are different. Kanyak *et.al*, (1995) has conducted the study looked at credit card usage in. Turkey and their findings suggest that respondents with lower and middle income and with high school and less education who use credit cards are likely to value the credit feature more than the service features such as safety and convenience. Warwick and Mansfield (2000) study the attitudes of college students towards the aggressive promotion of credit card industry. Findings of the study shows that the majority of college students who own credit cards do not actively seek them out, but are aggressively pursued through the mail and on-campus by credit card issuers. With regard to students' knowledge of their credit card, the majority of students did not report knowing the interest rate they were paying. Worthington and Gerrad (2007) study seeks to extend knowledge about credit cards by investigating two matters relating to consumers who are multiple cardholders. The study found that that high income earners and higher educated respondents are making more use of their credit cards and value them in a more favorable manner and derive more satisfaction from their use. On the other hand, sex, age and employment are found to be insignificant factors in people's levels of satisfaction with their credit cards. These disputes lead researchers to focus attention on the credit card industry.

TAKE A SAMPLE SURVEY OF 400 CUSTOMERS TO IDENTIFY THE PRODUCT ATTRIBUTES THAT ARE IMPORTANT TO CUSTOMERS AND TO MEASURE THEIR RELATIVE IMPORTANCE

In this study, sample size of 400 customers is being taken for the study. Multidimensional Scaling technique is used to tests the brands which compete most directly with each other. The perceptual map technique has also been used to identify the underlying dimensions that differentiate customer perception of products and the position of existing products on the dimensions. The following method has been used to find out the number of dimensions and configuration of that dimensionality.

The similarity matrix from response matrix has been found out by the following formula:

$$sij = \frac{rij \times rji}{N}$$

Where N is total sample size; i=row and j=column

The distance between each brand is found out by using Euclidean distance formula:

$$dij = \left[\sum_{k-1}^{r} (x_{ik} - x_{ik})^2 + (y_{ik} - y_{ik})^2 \right]^{1/2}$$

Where X_{ik}, X_{jk} are the projections of points i and j on dimension k

(K= 1, 2 -------------r)

The stress value is calculated as a badness of fit at 10 per cent. So, any value below the value of allowable badness of fit is acceptable.

$$\text{Stress} = t - \frac{\Sigma d^2 ij}{\Sigma d^2 ij}$$

In the present study, out of the total respondents, 54.7% are salaried employees, 31% are businessmen and 14.2% are professionals. About 100% of the total respondents are coming under the income level of higher than ₹ 20, 000. The people who are very much aware of debit card are taking into consideration.

Analysis

The study has been made to know the preference and perception of customers towards the debit cards offered by the different banks. It is also found from the study that customers are preferring to the debit card of a bank whose number of facilities are more, i.e., more functionalities and mostly acceptable in any retail outlet of India. So from the informal discussion with customers, all the relevant variables are included in the study. Seven statements are generated for measuring respondents' opinion on a 5-point Likert scale for preferring debit card. Factor matrix and their corresponding factor loading after the varimax rotation are presented in the Table 1.

Table 1

Eigen Values and Cumulative %age

Statement. No.	*Attributes*	*Initial Eigen Values*	*% of Variance*	*Cumulative %*
S1	Convenience of debit card	2.846	20.332	20.332
S2	Availing No. of Facilities	2.470	17.646	37.978
S3	Limitation on withdrawal of Cash	1.942	13.872	51.850
S4	Least Interest Payable	1.402	10.015	61.865
S5	Service Behavior	1.193	8.521	70.387
S6	Acceptability	1.032	7.372	77.759
S7	Insurance Coverage	.830	5.931	83.689
S8	Theft Coverage	.522	3.725	87.414

S9	Availing Discount in Air travel	.466	3.329	90.743
S10	Hassles free	.369	2.634	93.377
S11	Innovative Features	.333	2.377	95.753
S12	Brand Image	.271	1.937	97.691
S13	Reliability of Customer/High Market Share	.229	1.635	99.325
S14	Friend/Relative Suggestion	.221	.675	100.000

Table 2

Loadings of Selected Variables on Key Factors (Loading Criteria >0.5

Statement. No.	***Attributes***	***Factor Loadings***					
		F1	***F2***	***F3***	***F4***	***F5***	***F6***
S1	Convenience of debit card	.902					
S2	Availing No. of Facilities	.871					
S3	Limitation on withdrawal of Cash		.559				
S4	Least Interest Payable				.646		
S5	Service Behavior		.812				
S6	Acceptability					.802	
S7	Insurance Coverage			.831			
S8	Theft Coverage			.872			
S9	Availing Discount in Air-Travel					.787	
S10	Hassles free				.854		
S11	Innovative Features		.701				
S12	Brand Image	.636					
S13	Reliability of Customer/ High Market Share		.782				
S14	Friend/Relative Suggestion						.947
Eigen Values		2.846	2.470	1.942	1.402	1.193	1.032
%age of Variance		20.332	17.646	13.872	10.015	8.521	7.372
Cumulative Variance		20.332	37.978	51.850	61.865	70.387	77.759

The grouping of variance with a factor coefficient is more than 0.5 is shown in the Table 2. Factor 1 has an eigen value of 2.846 and explains 20.332% of the total variance. The eigen value of Factor 2 is 2.470 and explains 17.646% of the total variance. Factor 3 has an eigen value of 1.942 and explains 13.872% of the total variance. Factor 4 has an eigen value 1.402 and explains 10.015% of the total variance. Factor 5 has an eigen value 1.193 and explains 8.521% of the total variance. Factor 6 has an eigen value 1.032 and explains 7.372% of the total variance. The total variance accounted for by all the six factors is 77%, which is quite high, and it establishes the validity of the study.

Table 3
Grouping of Factor Loadings for Identifying Key Factors

Statement. No.	*Attributes*	*Factor Loadings*					
		F1	*F2*	*F3*	*F4*	*F5*	*F6*
S1	Convenience of debit card	.902					
S2	Availing No of Facilities	.871					
S12	Brand Image	.636					
S5	Service Behavior		.812				
S11	Innovative Features		.701				
S13	Reliability of Customer/ High Market Share		.782				
S3	Limitation on withdrawal of		.559				
S7	Insurance Coverage			.831			
S8	Theft Coverage			.872			
S10	Hassles free				.854		
S4	Least Interest Payable				.646		
S6	Acceptability					.802	
S9	Availing Discount in Air-Travel					.787	
S14	Friend/Relative Suggestion						.947
Total factor Loadings		2.409	2.854	1.703	1.50	1.589	0.947

The factors are named after grouping the key variables and looking at the communality of the variables in explaining at typical attribute of credit card. The Table-4 represents the grouping of factors. The grouping of factors takes into consideration of the high factor loadings of statements under each factor.

Table 4
Factors of Customers Preference for Debit Cards

State ments	***F1 (Brand Association)***	***F2 (Service)***	***F3 (Security)***	***F4 (Risk free)***	***F5 (Accessi-bility)***	***F6 (Biasness)***
1	Convenience of debit card (Statement-1)	Service Behavior (Statement-5)	Insurance Coverage (Statement-7)	Hassles free (Statement-10)	Acceptability (Statement-6)	Friend/Relative Suggestion (Statement-14)
2	Availing No. of Facilities (Statement-2)	Reliability of Customer/High Market Share (Statement-13)	Theft Coverage (Statement -8)	Least Interest Payable (Statement-4)	Availing Discount in Air Travel (Statement-9)	

3	Brand Image (Statement-12)	Innovative Features (Statement-11)		₹	
4		Limitation on Withdrawal of Cash (Statement-3)			

The Table 5 depicts the variables under each of the six desired factors. The first factor identified with the convenience of debit card, the number of facilities associated with and the brand image has been grouped under F1 and termed as "Brand Association" factor. The second factor explains the number of offers, extra facilities and the extent of cash withdrawal. These are the core part of the debit card, which is the common expectation of any customer while purchasing the debit card in any bank. The second factor F2 is termed as "Service" factor. The third factor F3 explains the insurance coverage and theft coverage, which is associated with the safety part of the customer. The factor F3 is termed as "Security" factor. The fourth factor F4 explains the least interest payment and extended credit period associated with the credit card. The factor F4 is termed as "Risk" factor. The fifth factor F5 explains the acceptability in different services and discount in air travel. So, the factor F5 is termed as "Accessibility" factor. The sixth factor F6 explains the influence of friends and family members. So, it is a motivation factor associated with the factor 6, which is termed as "Biasness" factor.

Table 5

Ranking of Factors on Satisfaction Level

Factors	*Factor Loadings*	*Rank*
F1 (Brand Association)	2.409	2
F2 (Service)	2.854	1
F3 (Security)	1.703	3
F4 (Risk free)	1.50	5
F5 (Accessibility)	1.589	4
F6 (Biasness)	0.947	6

According to the ranking, the most prioritized factors can be known from the customers' response. In the Table 6, customers have given highest priority to the factor like "service" followed by brand association, security, accessibility, risk free and biasness respectively.

The correlation table is shown in Table 6. The values in correlation table are standardized and range from zero to one, positive and negative. Looking at the third column, it can be said that all the variables are highly correlated to compensation ranging from 0.784 to 0.901 except the "age" whose correlation is very low of 0.310. There is the highest correlation of 0.901 which is between the average monthly income and expenditure. This means that the independent variables have been chosen in a fairly good manner. This Table 6 is a one-to-one correlation of each variable with the other, so it will still have to multiple regressions with an independent variable showing low correlation with a dependent variable because in the presence of other variables this independent variable may become a good predictor of the dependent variable. This correlation is significant at both the 1% and 5% level. So, it is evident that the buying behavior of consumers is highly correlated with debit card.

Table 6

Correlation between the Buying Behavior of Consumers and Debit Card

Variables	*Exp.cred*	*Exp.incr*	*Age*	*Income*	*Expendit*
EXP.CRED	1.000				
EXP.INCR	.784	1.000			
AGE	.312	.310	1.000		
INCOME	.799	.853	.393	1.000	
EXPENDIT	.841	.883	.414	.901	1.000

The measure of strength of association in the regression analysis is given by the coefficient of determination denoted by R^2. This coefficient varies between 0 and 1 and represents the proportion of total variation in the dependent variable that is accounted for by the variation in the factors. From the table 8, the R^2 value is 0.721 which shows that 72% of the variation in expenditure through debit card can be explained by four independent factors. Adjusted R^2 is 0.677 which is the difference of one and the ratio of residual variance and sample variance. For a optimistic picture of fit of the regression, R^2 is taken rather than the adjusted R^2.

Table 7

Summery of Regression Analysis of Debit Card

Predictors	*Unstandardised*	*Unstandardised*	*Standardised*	*t*	R_2	*Adj* R_2	*F*
	B	*S.E.B*					
EXP.INCR	.107	.193	.131	.553	.729	.677	16.163*
AGE	-7.487	22.779	-.039	-.329			
INCOME	.026	.035	.186	.730			
EXPENDIT	.127	.064	.573	1.984			
CONSTANT	-236.597	915.930					

*Significant at 1% level

The value of F at this confidence level is 16.163, which is quite significant to indicate that the regression model is a good predictor. So, the use of debit card is highly related to the buying behaviour of consumers. It is being seen that t-tests for significance of individual dependent variables indicates that at the significance level of 0.10 (confidence level of 90%), only in average monthly "expenditure" is statistically significant in the model. The other three independent variables are individually not significant at 90% confidence level.

Multidimensional Scaling (MDS)

MDS is proposed to help understand people's judgments of the similarity of members of a set of objects. MDS pictures the structure of a set of objects from data that approximate the distances between pairs of the objects. Multidimensional scaling is based on similarity/dissimilarity approach. Here pairs of brands are taken to study the superiority of the brand through the ordinal scale. Four public sector banks are taken in a matrix form. Accordingly, the respondents have given their preference for the different banks. Final perceptual map is drawn to know the Euclidian distance among the different banks.

The dimensions calculated by the MDS analysis are able to generate the final perceptual map of the respondents. It is observed from Table 8 that the respondents have given highest rank to SBI and in dimension two the next highest rank to ICICI. This explains that respondents' weightage is highest to SBI credit card followed by ICICI credit card.

Table 8

	Risk Free	***Service***
SBI	.983	–.172
PNB	–.321	.298
IOB	–.829	.013
Canara Bank	–.184	–.143
UTI	.196	.319
ICICI	.259	–.262
IDBI	–.214	–.802
HDFC	.111	.748

The perceptual map is drawn by taking the preferences of respondents through the ranking scale. The location of different bank's position is purely based on the perceptual map of the respondents generated by the MDS. Euclidian distance is measured to know the gap among the different brands of credit cards.

Title
Object Points
Common Space

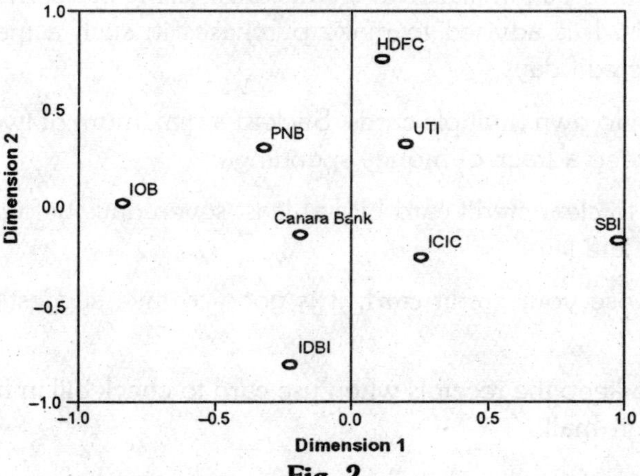

Fig. 2

Table 9

	SBI	*PNB*	*Canara IOB*	*Bank*	*UTI*	*ICICI*	*IDBI*	*HDFC*
SBI	.000							
PNB	1.385	.000						
IOB	1.821	.583	.000					
Canara Bank	1.167	.461	.664	.000				
UTI	.927	.517	1.069	.597	.000			
ICICI	.729	.806	1.122	.459	.585	.000		
IDBI	1.352	1.105	1.021	.660	1.193	.717	.000	
HDFC	1.267	.624	1.193	.938	.438	1.021	1.584	.000

Euclidian Distance

The distances from each brands of credit card is measured after plotting the perceptual map of the respondents. The measured distances from one brand to another of credit cards are represented in the Table 9. The Euclidian distance between State Bank of India (SBI) and Indian Overseas Bank (IOB) is the highest, which indicates respondents have given highest rank to SBI and least rank to IOB. But HDFC got next highest Euclidian distance from IDBI. The least distance between State Bank of India (SBI) and ICICI shows that respondents has given second rank to ICICI bank.

INFORMATION FOR PLASTIC CARDHOLDERS

- It is prudent to pay your bill before the due date. If it is not possible, use the transfer balance facility through which it is easy to transfer the balance amount on your bill to another credit card issuer and pay fewer charges.
- Do not use the cash advance feature unless it is very crucial. Otherwise, it imposed interest rate charges of 25-30 per cent per annum on such withdrawals.
- It is always better to be familiar with credit card's billing cycle, the actual date of when it begins and ends. It is advised to make purchases in such a manner that helps to get maximum free credit days.
- It is not essential to own multiple cards. Stick to a maximum of two cards. More than that it is difficult to keep a track of money spending.
- It is worthwhile to clear credit card bills at least seven days before the due date to avoid being hit with a late fee.
- Before you choose your credit card, it is good to take suggestions from your friends/ relatives.
- It is necessary to keep the receipts when use card to check bill in future when it is known/ informed through mail.

- Keep your card and your 16 digit credit card number confidential.
- It is better to carry only those cards if having more than one card.
- It is better to choose a card that gives the highest free credit period.

CONCLUDING OBSERVATION

This chapter signifies several identifiable consumer decision-making styles which are consistent across different income groups. Moreover, some differences are also identified related to income, age and facilities provided by the banks to the customers. There is a high inclination of customers towards debit card and less troublesome in financial transaction. Next priority they are giving to the amount of discount. So in the near future there will be a great demand for the debit card in order to avoid the transaction through cash. Besides that they are willing to get the advantage of discount on purchase. Therefore, customers are very much interested to get the advantage of the debit facilities with little expenditure and less effort.

The customers' perception about the debit card is different due to the different banks as so many features are related to it. Their preferences are strongly based on certain key features. They are giving priorities on the basis of amount of debit and number of facilities provided by each bank, also their importance relies on the service standard, innovative features. These features are also being associated with the market share of that brand of debit card. Recently, they are also giving the importance towards the theft coverage and insurance coverage which is a new dimension for the branding of debit card. This chapter also presents that the customers' preferences can be changed with the change in value-added services available with different brands of debit cards. The MDS has given the same result which is quite surprise. The MDS has given perceptual map of highest rank to SBI and ICICI respectively. This explains the changing economic scenario of the country and the changing features of different brands of debit cards. It is also observed from factors analysis that customers have given highest priority to the factors like risk-free factors and service. This chapter concludes that sometimes the brand image of the company gives major impact on the perception of the customer which indirectly makes the customer as a brand loyal one.

Today, the Indian mode of payment has shifted from money to electronic mode. This is due to the high money-valued transactions and more risk involvement. The new electronic payment and settlement act should follow the strict norms for banks and merchants to make secure payments and prevent money laundering as the transactions through plastic money.

REVIEW QUESTIONS

1. What is your opinion on the debit card vs. credit card? What do you think is more convenient to use and what are the pros and cons of using each of them?
2. Share your experiences of using credit cards and/ or debit cards in your day-today life.
3. Write briefly about history of plastic cards.
4. How many plastic cards are available? Briefly explain their features.
5. What are similarity and difference of debit and credit card?

6. What is Credit card reform act? Who introduce it? What are its features?
7. Quiz
   (a) _____ card is typically a card offering special benefits to users, e.g., discounts or rewards.
   (b) The plastic cards began to be widely used only after _____.
   (c) Plastic money has become an essential form of _____.
   (d) _____ are the physical carriers of electronic cash.
   (e) Which cards have tied up with a popular brand for the purpose of offering certain exclusive benefits to the consumer?
   (f) Which is well-known branded charge cards?
   (g) Which is called reloadable debit cards?
   (h) The use of credit cards originated in the _____ country.
   (i) Who invented the "Charge-it" program between bank customers and local merchants and in which year?
   (j) _____ head of the Hamilton Credit Corporation.
   (k) American Express issued their first credit card in _____ year.
   (l) The credit card market in India, which started in _____ year.
   (m) The Access Card was launched in the year _____ in _____ country.
   (n) The first credit card introduced by _____ Bank was _____ in the year _____.

18

Inclusive Growth: Role of Insurance Industry in India

The transition of the insurance industry from a public monopoly to a competitive environment now presents very interesting challenges both to the new players and to the customers. Customer today has an option to choose from policies offered by many insurers depending on their needs. This chapter explains that the insurance industry should design the product that should satisfy the personal needs of customers with ample degree flexibilities to create more vibrant and competitive industry with greater efficiency, choice of products and value to customers.

INTRODUCTION

There is a worldwide debate about the fast growing integration of financial services with the globalization of the economy. Manufacturing companies are entering the domain of financial services activities while the financial services provide is gradually diversifying into various sectors depending upon the market attractiveness. As a result, the extent of competition has reached a cut-throat level that is evident from the innovative products, competitive pricing, drastic promotional activities in the marketplace. A wide range of products customer-focused service and professional advice has become the mainstay of the industry. The insurance products are acting more as an umbrella for protection than as a financial instrument for saving and tax planning. With more and more customers demanding innovative insurance solutions to their problems, insurers are competing with each other. The entry of private players has enabled the industry to look at alternative distribution channels. To get the maximum pie of the premium, every insurance company is adopting new distribution and marketing strategies. In the last couple of years, the economy has witnessed some fundamental changes in the Indian insurance industry. The transition of the insurance industry from a public monopoly to a competitive environment now presents very interesting challenges both to the new players and to the customer. Not only the new players have an opportunity to test out their various hypotheses and apply learnings from overseas markets, the customer is also having a greater choice when it comes to choosing a provider or a solution for their needs. The Indian insurance market grew by 22.1% in 2009 to reach a value of $63,825.4 million presented in Table 1and Fig. 1.The compound annual growth rate of the market in the period 2005-09 was 26.6% revealed in Table-1.

Table 1
Compound Annual Growth Rate of Insurance Market

Year	*$ million*	*Rs million*	*% Growth*
2005	24842.3	1213547	
2006	40140.1	1960844	61.60%
2007	47457.9	2318317	18.20%
2008	52273.5	2553558	10.10%
2009	63825.4	3117867	22.10%
CAGR (2005-2009)			26.60%

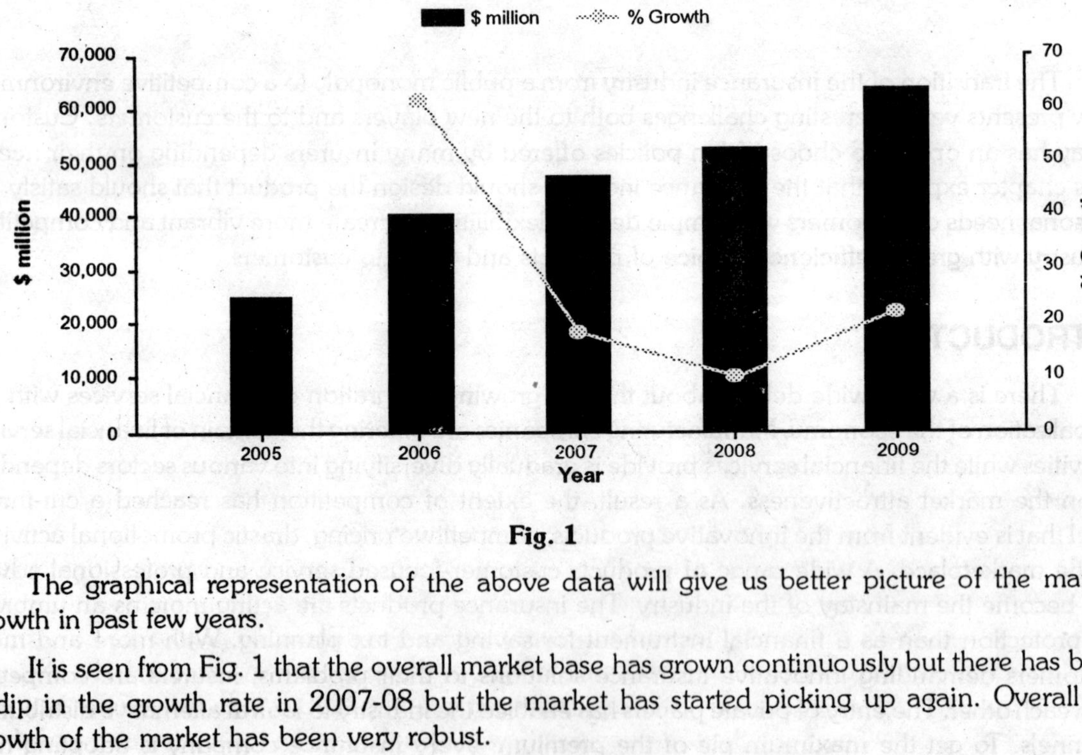

Fig. 1

The graphical representation of the above data will give us better picture of the market growth in past few years.

It is seen from Fig. 1 that the overall market base has grown continuously but there has been a dip in the growth rate in 2007-08 but the market has started picking up again. Overall the growth of the market has been very robust.

HISTORY OF INSURANCE SECTOR IN INDIA

The history of general insurance came to India as a legacy of British occupation. 1818 saw the advent of life insurance business in India with the establishment of the Oriental Life Insurance Company in Calcutta. This company however failed in 1834. In 1829, the Madras Equitable had begun transacting life insurance business in the Madras Presidency. General Insurance in India has its roots in the establishment of Triton Insurance Company Ltd., in the year 1850 in Calcutta by the British. 1870 saw the enactment of the British Insurance Act and in the last three decades of the nineteenth century, the Bombay Mutual (1871), Oriental (1874) and Empire of India (1897) were started in the Bombay Residency. This era, however, was dominated by foreign insurance offices which did good business in India, namely Albert Life Assurance, Royal Insurance, Liverpool and London Globe Insurance and the Indian offices were up for hard competition from the foreign companies. In 1907, the Indian Mercantile Insurance Ltd. was set up. This was the first company to transact all classes of general insurance business. Though there has been immense growth from 1907, still 80% of the population is not insured. The insurance industry in India can be broadly classified into pre-nationalization, nationalization and post-nationalization phases.

Pre-nationalization Phase

Pre-nationalization

Year	Milestone
1912	The Indian Life Assurance Companies Act enacted as the first statute to regulate the life insurance business
1928	The Indian Insurance Companies Act enacted to enable the government to collect statistical information about both life and non-life insurance business
1938	Earlier legislation consolidated and amended to by the Insurance Act with the objective of protecting the interests of the insuring public.

In 1914, the Government of India started publishing returns of Insurance Companies in India. The Indian Life Assurance Companies Act, 1912 was the first statutory measure to regulate life business. In 1928, the Indian Insurance Companies Act was enacted to enable the Government to collect statistical information about both life and non-life business transacted in India by Indian and foreign insurers including provident insurance societies. In 1938, with a view to protecting the interest of the Insurance public, the earlier legislation was consolidated and amended by the Insurance Act, 1938 with comprehensive provisions for effective control over the activities of insurers. The Insurance Amendment Act of 1950 abolished Principal Agencies. However, there were a large number of insurance companies and the level of competition was high. There were also allegations of unfair trade practices. The Government of India, therefore, decided to nationalize insurance business.

Nationalization Phase

An Ordinance was issued on 19th January, 1956 nationalizing the Life Insurance sector and Life Insurance Corporation came into existence in the same year. The LIC absorbed 154 Indian, 16 non-Indian insurers as also 75 provident societies — 245 Indian and foreign insurers in all. The LIC had monopoly till the late 90s when the Insurance sector was reopened to the private sector. 1957 saw the formation of the General Insurance Council, a wing of the Insurance Association of India. The General Insurance Council framed a code of conduct for ensuring fair conduct and sound business practices. In 1968, the Insurance Act was amended to regulate investments and set minimum solvency margins. The Tariff Advisory Committee was also set up then. In 1972 with the passing of the General Insurance Business (Nationalization) Act, general insurance business was nationalized with effect from 1st January, 1973. 107 insurers were amalgamated and grouped into four companies, namely National Insurance Company Ltd., the New India Assurance Company Ltd., the Oriental Insurance Company Ltd. and the United India Insurance Company Ltd. The General Insurance Corporation of India was incorporated as a company in 1971 and it commenced business on January 1, 1973.

Nationalization

Year	Milestones
1956	245 Indian and foreign insurers and provident societies taken over by the central government and nationalised. LIC formed by an Act of Parliament,viz. LIC Act, 1956, with a capital contribution of Rs. 5 crore from the Government of India.
1957	General Insurance Council, a wing of the Insurance Association of India, frames a code of conduct for ensuring fair conduct and sound business practices
1968	The Insurance Act amended to regulate investment and set minimum solvency margins and the Tariff Advisory Committee set up.
1972	The General Insurance Business (Nationalisation) Act, 1972 nationalised the general insurance business in India with effect from 1st January 1973. 107 insurers amalgamated and grouped into four companies viz. the National Insurance Company Ltd., the New India Assurance Company Ltd., the Oriental Insurance Company Ltd. and the United India Insurance Company Ltd. GIC incorporated as a company.

Post-nationalization Phase

This millennium has seen insurance come a full circle in a journey extending to nearly 200 years. The process of reopening of the sector had begun in the early 1990s and the last decade and more has seen it been opened up substantially. In 1993, the Government set up a committee under the chairmanship of R. N. Malhotra, former Governor of RBI, to propose recommendations for reforms in the insurance sector. The objective was to complement the reforms initiated in the financial sector. The committee submitted its report in 1994 wherein, among other things, it recommended that the private sector be permitted to enter the insurance industry. They stated that foreign companies must be allowed to enter by floating Indian companies, preferably a joint venture with Indian partners. Following the recommendations of the Malhotra Committee report, in 1999, the Insurance Regulatory and Development Authority (IRDA) was constituted as an autonomous body to regulate and develop the insurance industry. The IRDA was incorporated as a statutory body in April, 2000. The key objectives of the IRDA include promotion of competition so as to enhance customer satisfaction through increased consumer choice and lower premiums, while ensuring the financial security of the insurance market. The IRDA opened up the market in August 2000 with the invitation for application for registrations. Foreign companies were allowed ownership of up to 26%. The Authority has the power to frame regulations under Section 114A of the Insurance Act, 1938 and has from 2000 onwards framed various regulations ranging from registration of companies for carrying on insurance business to protection of policyholders' interests. In December, 2000, the subsidiaries of the General Insurance Corporation of India were restructured as independent companies and at the same time GIC was converted into a national reinsurer. Parliament passed a bill delinking the four subsidiaries from GIC in July, 2002. Today there are 24 general insurance companies including the ECGC and Agriculture Insurance Corporation of India and 23 life insurance companies operating in the country.

Post-nationalization

Year	Milestones
1956	Economic Reform Process — Malhotra Committee
1957	IRDA passes
1968	Insurance sector opened up for private companies
1972	Four public non-life insurers — 73.47% market share Private sector — 26.53% market share
Current	Growth of 15.2% annually

PRESENT SCENARIO

The insurance sector is an immense one and is growing at a speedy rate of 15-20%. Together with banking services, insurance services add about 7% to the country's GDP. A well-developed and evolved insurance sector is a boon for economic development as it provides long- term funds for infrastructure development at the same time strengthening the risk-taking ability of the country.

The life insurance sector of India has added up to 4.1% of the GDP in 2009; a considerable growth was recorded since the time the sector was opened for the private companies. The contribution in FDI by the life insurance segment was recorded at US $ 1.3 billion, even though the government is likely to increase the FDI cap limit from 26% to 49%, a bill of which is pending at the Rajya Sabha. The year 2009-10 also saw private sector insurance company, Aviva Life Insurance establishing nine unit-linked plans, in line with the recent IRDA guidelines featuring enhanced and higher internal rate of return (IRRs).As per the data provided by the IRDA, the businesses of the life insurance companies had a growth of 22% at US $ 12 billion in April-November 2009-10, in comparison to the US $ 9.8 billion during the same period last year. Such a huge sale of single premium policies led the industry to record a raise of 53.25% in November 2009 alone.

With the registration of India, First Life Insurance Company Limited, a joint stake life insurance company encouraged by Bank of Baroda, Andhra Bank of India and Legal and General Middle East Limited, UK. The total number of life insurers registration with the Insurance Regulatory Development Authority (IRDA) has increased to 23. According to industry body, Life Insurance Council, the life insurance industry had earlier been anticipated to grow by 15% in the year 2009 - 10 and surpass the US $ 54.1 billion mark in total premium income by March-end of 2010. This growth in premium income includes new business as well as renewals, driven by increasing awareness on the value of getting insured. The US $ 41- billion Indian insurance industry made a grand return with better performances in the April-November 2009 period. Life insurance in India recorded the first year premium (inclusive of Single Premium) segment accounting to US $ 24 billion.

The potential of Indian insurance sector is immense and unprecedented growth of over 200% is likely to be seen in Indian insurance business by 2010-11 in which private insurance business would grow 2.40 times. On account of intense marketing strategies adopted by private insurance players, the market share of state-owned insurance companies like General Insurance Corporation of India (GIC), Life Insurance Corporation of India (LIC) and others have already come down to 70% in last 4-5 years from over 97%.

The Life Insurance Corporation of India (LIC) is the largest state-owned life insurance company in India, and also the country's largest investor base. It is fully owned by the Government of India. It also funds close to 24.6% of the Indian Government's expenses. It has assets estimated of Indian rupee 9.31 trillion (US $ 211.34 billion). It was founded in 1956 with the merger of more than 200 insurance companies and provident societies. The recent Economic Times Brand Equity Survey rated LIC as the No. 1 Service Brand of the Country. The Analysis of Income is presented in Fig. 2.

The major growth of India Insurance sector was from Life Insurance with a total Gross Premiums of $ 56 billion and thus gaining 87.8% of the market's overall value. While the Non-life Insurance sector contributed only $ 7.8 billion and thus managed a market share of 12.2%. So it is evident that majority of the insurance earning is achieved through the life insurance sector and there is still a lot of development that is yet to be witnessed in the Non-Life insurance sector. The Non-life insurance sector has 22 players out of which, 7 belong to public sector while 15 belong to private sector. In the public sector, most players have experienced growth by formulating aggressive growth strategies and capitalizing on their distribution network to target the retail segment. In the private sector, non-life insurance players outperform their public sector counterparts in service quality.

The premium income grew at a CAGR of 17.6 per cent between 2002-03 and 2008-09 and the segments covered include auto, health, fire, marine and engineering, among others. The share of the private sector in total premiums increased from 9.5 per cent in 2002-03 to 41.1 per cent in 2008-09. Auto insurance had the largest share in 2008-09 (43.2%) while Health segment recorded a growth of 21.3 per cent in 2008-09. The public sector companies have a dominant share in the marine insurance segment.

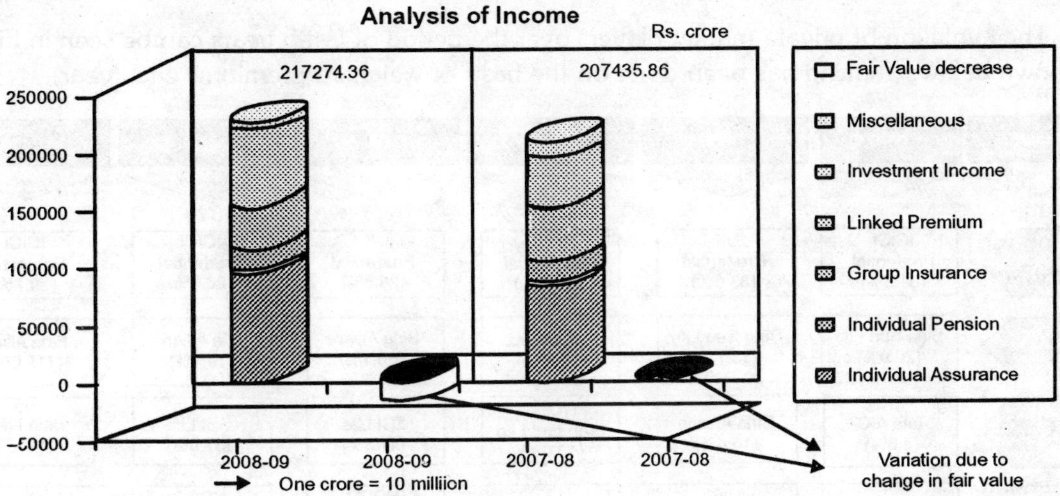

Fig. 2

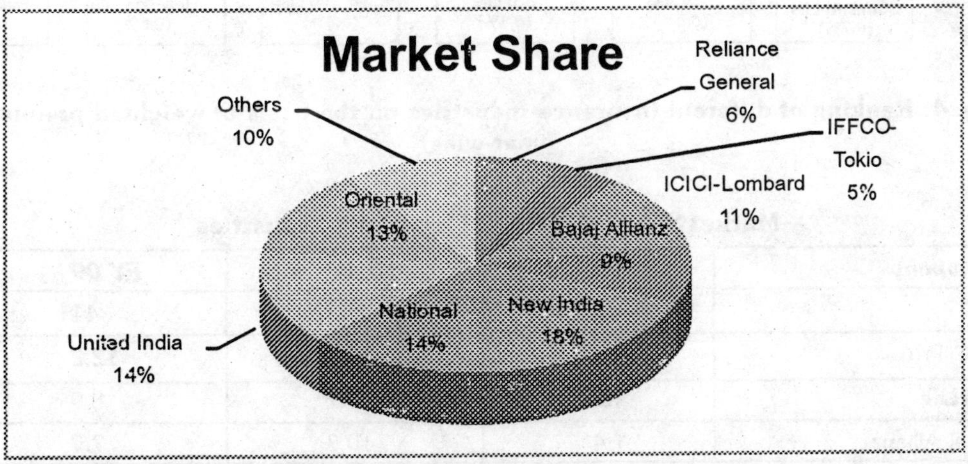

Fig. 3: Market Share of Different Players in Non-life Insurance Segment

PRIVATE PLAYERS IN THE MARKET

It is seen that state-owned LIC is the market leader in most of the aspects. Other companies like ICICI Prudential and SBI Life insurance are the major private market players. Despite the advent of the private market players, LIC has grown much faster than the private sector and commands a significant market share. It boasts of one of the most diverse product profile. The general trend in the industry has been the falling market share of single premium, but LIC on the contrary has been able to hold on 66% of the premiums. The persistency ratio is as high as 90% and the entire expenses ratio are well below 10% which are pretty healthy signs for any insurance company. It garners 2/3rd proportion of renewal premiums and all the capital requirements are funded by internal accruals.

The evolution of private market players over the period of last 5 years can be seen in Fig. 4 as shown below: (ranking has been done on the basis of weighted premiums each year).

Rank	2004	2005	2006	2007	2008	2009
1	ICICI Prudential (31.3%)	ICICI Prudential (33.6%)	ICICI Prudential (30.2%)	ICICI Prudential (28.5%)	ICICI Prudential (26.3%)	ICICI Prudential (20.7%)
2	Birla Sun Life (20.9%)	Birla Sun Life (13.7%)	Birla Allianz (17.4%)	Birla Allianz (20.1%)	Birla Allianz (19.9%)	Birla Allianz (15.0%)
3	Tata AIG (8.6%)	Birla Allianz (10.4%)	HDFC Standard Life (10.6%)	SBI Life (11.3%)	SBI Life (11.9%)	Birla Allianz (113.1%)
4	Birla Allianz (7.8%)	HDFC Standard Life (9.0%)	Birla Sun Life (8.2%)	HDFC Standard Life (8.3%)	HDFC Standard Life (7.9%)	Reliance Life (9.8%)
5	HDFC Standard Life (6.7%)	Tata AIG (6.8%)	SBI Life (6.3%)	Birla Sun Life (5.3%)	Reliance Life (6.6%)	Birla Sun Life (9.0%)

Fig. 4: Ranking of different insurance industries on the basis of weighted premiums (year-wise)

Table 2

Market Share of Different Insurance Industries

Company	*FY 07*	*FY 08*	*FY 09*
LIC	63	48	41
ICICI Pru	10.6	13.7	12.2
SBI Life	4.2	6.2	8.9
Bajaj Allianz	7.4	10.3	7.7
Reliance Life	1.7	3.4	5.8
Birla Sun life	1.9	3.4	5.3
HDFC Standard	3.1	4.1	4.5

Most of the companies except LIC, ICICI Prudential and Bajaj Allianz have seen a decline over the years. Apart from these two, all the other private players have witnessed a gradual increase in the market share with time. Most of the private insurance companies have formed joint venture partnering well with recognized foreign players across the globe revealed in the Table 3.

Table 3

Private Players in the Indian Insurance Market

Company	*Indian Partner*	*Foreign Insurer*	*Area*
Birla Sunlife	Aditya Birla Group	Sunlife, Canada	Life
Om Kotak	Kotak Mahindra Finance	Old Mutual, South Africa	Life
HDFC-Standard Life	HDFC	Standard Life UK	Life
Royal Sundaram	Sundaram Finance	Royal Sun, UK	Life & Non-life
ICICI-Prudential	ICICI	Prudential, UK	Life
Max New York Life	Max India	New York Life USA	Life
Tata-AIG	Tata Group	AIG, USA	Life & Non-life
ING Vysya	Vysya Bank	ING Insurance, Netherlands	Life
Aviva	Dabur	CGU Life, UK	Life
Metlife India	Jammu & Kashmir Bank	Metlife, USA	Life
Bajaj Allianz	Bajan Auto	Allianz	Life & Non-life
AMP Sanmar	Sanmar Group	AMP, Australia	Life
SBI Life Insurance	SBI	Cardiff, France	Life

Also, the premium earned by LIC as compared to other private companies is huge as can been seen from Fig. 5.

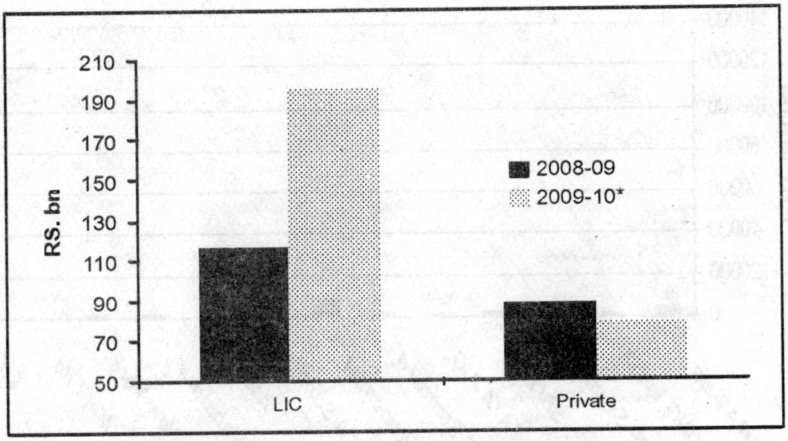

Fig. 5: Premium Earned in JAS (LIC vs Private)

The market share amongst the private companies over the last two financial years is shown in Fig. 6.

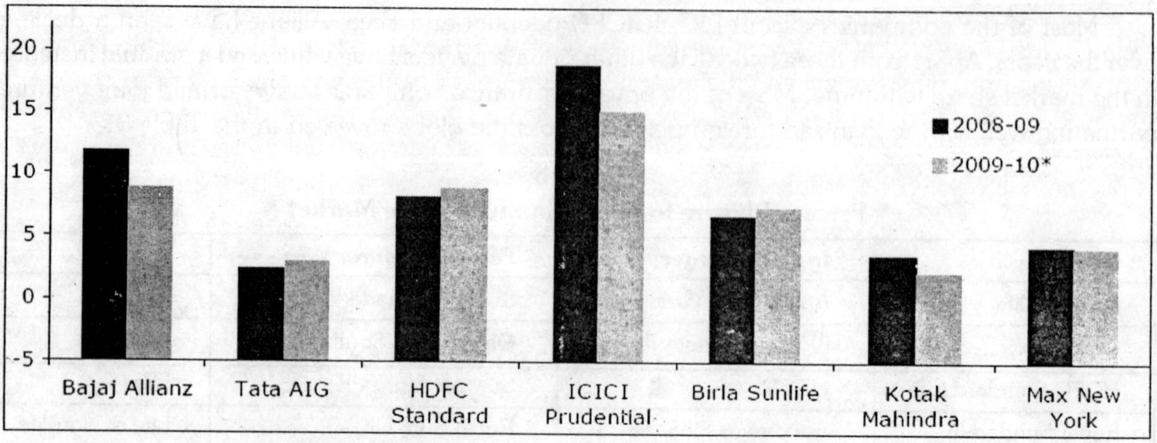

Fig. 6: Market Share of Private Companies in JAS

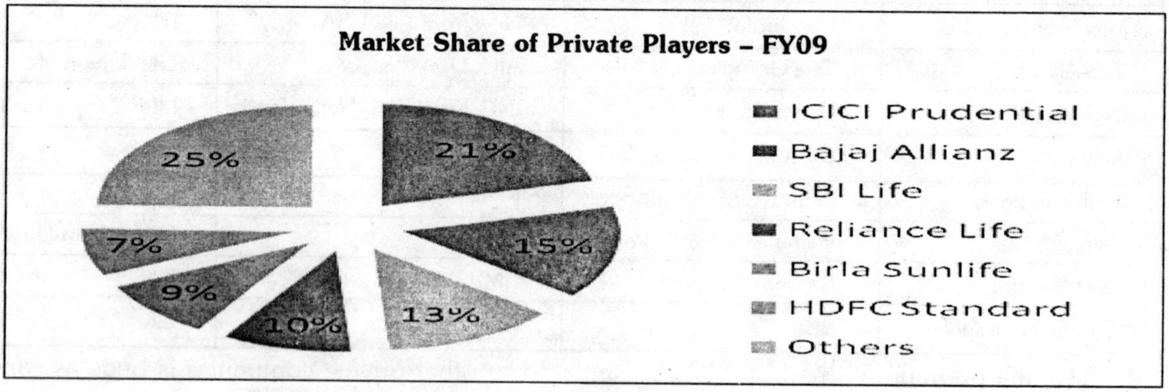

Fig.7: Comparison Between Players

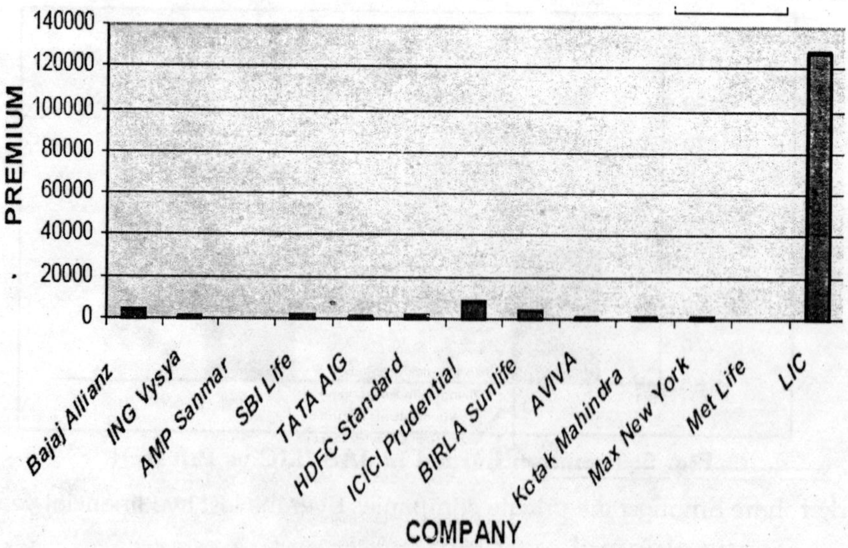

Fig. 8:

The insurance markets have witnessed a dynamic change, which includes presence of a fair number of insurers both life, and non-life segment. The new insurance companies used all channels of advertising from newspapers and the television to insurance agents and direct mailers. The new companies focused their campaigns primarily on building an image of trustworthiness and reliability for themselves. Their advertisement focused on insurance as an investment option and not a mere tax saving tool. Most of these advertisements carried messages like the family's happiness.

Factors Driving Change

At the end of 2003, the Indian insurance market (in terms of premium volume) was the 19th largest in the world, only slightly bigger than Denmark and comparable to that of Ireland (Swiss Re, Sigma No. 3/2004). This was despite India being the second most populous country in the world as well as the 12th largest economy. Yet, there are strong arguments in favor of sustained rapid insurance business growth in the coming years, including India's robust economic growth prospects and the nation's high savings rates (Dreaming with BRICs: The Path to 2050", Goldman and Sachs, Global Economics Paper). The dynamic growth of insurance buying is partly affected by the (changing) income elasticity of insurance demand. It has been shown that insurance penetration and per capita income have a strong non linear relationship. Based on this relation and other considerations, it can be postulated that by 2014 the penetration of life insurance in India will increase to 4.4% and that of non life insurance to 0.9%.

Some of the factors that will drive positive change in the sector are as under:

- Increasing Gross Financial Household Savings
- Deregulation in the Indian Insurance Market
- Increase in Dependency Ratio

PEST ANALYSIS

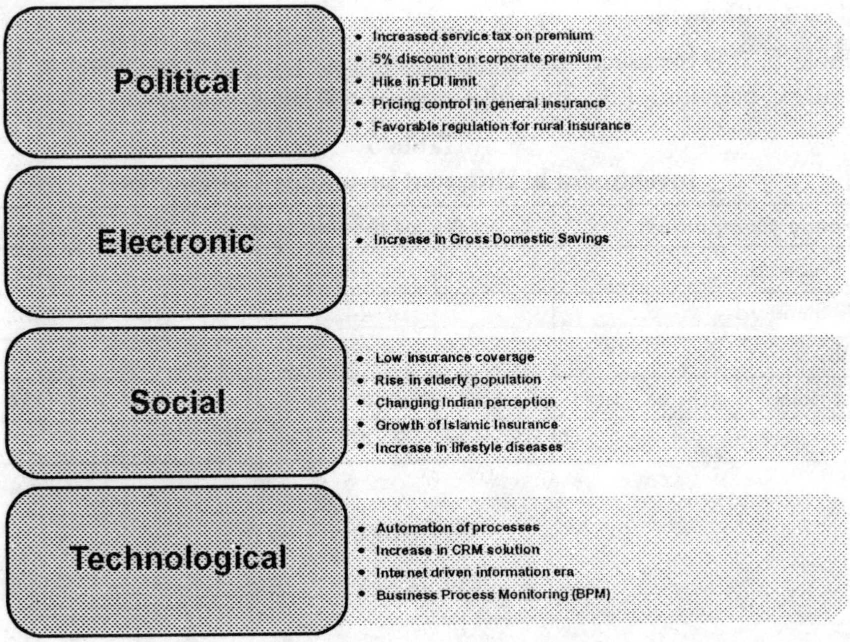

LET'S TAKE SAMPLE SURVEY OF 225 CUSTOMERS TO FIND THEIR PERCEPTION TOWARDS INSURANCE COMPANY THROUGH MARKET VARIABLES

The discussion in this chapter is based on the results of a survey of individual customers and individual agents. In order to determine the objective of this chapter, multidimensional scaling technique has been used to identify the product attributes that are importance to investors and to. measure their relative importance. The perceptual map technique has also been used to identify the underlying dimensions that differentiate customer perception of products and the position of existing products on the dimensions.

ANALYSIS

Insurance is an essential service to make life meaningful, dignified and worth living. The citizens of this country have a right to know and freedom of access to any information about the working of Insurance Companies. More information flow will lead to better transparency. More information means consumers can make an informed choice. The first and foremost change required is that it must learn to provide a competitive service in the market responding to public outcry.

Table 4

Investor of Private/Public Sector Insurance Company

Opinion	*Total response*	*Percentage*
Private Sector insurance Company	116	58
Public Sector Insurance Company	84	42

It is observed from the Table 4 that 58 per cent investors like to invest in private sector insurance companies. The main reason is that they are maintaining choice of product, servicing of policy and claims settlement.

From Table 5, it is observed that majority of customer prefer to invest in ICICI prudential followed by HDFC Standard, LIC, Tata AIG, and Allianz Bajaj.

Table 5

Investment in Different Insurance Companies

Insurance Companies	*No. of Respondent*	*Percentage*
ICICI Prudential	48	24
HDFC Standards	44	22
Tata AIG	32	16
Allianz Bajaj	36	18
LIC	40	20

Table 6
Sources of Awareness to Invest in Insurance Companies

	Number	*Percentage*	*Rank*
Financial Journal/Business Magazines	48	24	2
Reference Groups	40	20	3
Television	25	12.5	5
General/Business Newspapers	58	29	1
Brokers/Agents/professional Consultant	29	14.5	4

The Table 6 shows that 24 per cent of investors use financial journals and business magazines for investment decision. Majority of consumers use newspapers as the source of information for their investment. It is also evident that reference groups do play a vital role in influencing the decision on investment.

Table 7
Factors Influencing Consumer Decision

	Ranking Response					*Total Score*	*Mean Score*
	1	2	3	4	5		
High reputation	-	18	90	58	34	708	3.54
Good CRM		24	68	64	30	688	3.44
Good promotion	6	24	114	46	4	600	3.00
More facilities	6	32	84	58	16	634	3.17
Relationship with Agent	96	78	16	-	-	300	1.50

The Table 7 shows that the response of the respondents regarding the factors which influence to invest their funds in a particulars insurance company. It clearly shows that the two factors, i.e., high reputation and good customer relationship management to be the important criteria for investing in insurance companies. More facilities and Good promotion are also equally important to them. These results clearly reveal the investment psychology of the respondents.

Table 8
Brand Loyalty of Customers

Opinion	*Total Response*	*Percentage*
Always	36	18
Sometimes	80	40
Often	44	22
Seldom	40	20
Never	0	0

The Table 8 depicts that 40 per cent investors have given their opinion that they sometimes invest in a particular type of insurance company. Only 18 per cent customer says that they invest always in a particular type of insurance company. So, it is concluded that respondents are investing indifferent type of insurance companies on the basis of different factors.

Table 9
Difficult Faced in Selling

Factors	*Total Response*	*Percentage*	*Rank*
Lack of Awareness of Products	55	27.5	1
Lack of more options	28	14	4
Flexible Mode of payment	44	22	2
Multiple channels	18	9	6
Transparency	25	12.5	5
Custom made Products	30	15	3

It is inferred from the Table 9 that 27.3 per cent customers are unaware of the different products lunched by the insurance companies, 22 per cent investors are dissatisfied due to not availablility of flexible mode of payment of premium through credit cards, smart cards, Internet etc, 14 per cent customers gave their opinion that policies are not offered according to their needs, 15 per cent customers are dissatisfied due to not design the products by the company to a targeted segments, 9 per cent opinion that there is lack of multiple channels like brokers, bancassurance, corporate agents for professional approach towards customers. So while developing a marketing programme, one has to design the product as well as promotion strategy to solve customer problems as hinted during the study.

Perceptual Map of Insurance Companies

Samples of 200 respondents were asked to rank the different Insurance Companies and the dominance matrix has been obtained.

Table 10
Preference Matrix

Preferred than	*HDFC*	*ICICI Prudential*	*TATA AIG*	*Allianz Bajaj*
HDFC	0	108	40	80
ICICI Prudential	92	0	28	32
TATA AIG	160	172	0	132
Allianz Bajaj	120	168	68	0

Table 11
Similarity Matrix

Preferred than	*HDFC*	*ICICI Prudential*	*TATA AIG*	*Allianz Bajaj*
HDFC	0	49.68	32	48
ICICI Prudential	-	0	24.08	26.58
TATA AIG	-	-	0	44.58
Allianz Bajaj	-	-	-	0

To obtain the matrix of dissimilates, the simple approach of ranking is used. In order words, the natrix data are converted into non-matrix data.

Table 12
Dissimilarity Matrix

Preferred than	*HDFC*	*ICICI Prudential*	*TATA AIG*	*Allianz Bajaj*
HDFC	0	1	4	2
ICICI Prudential	-	0	6	5
TATA AIG	-	-	0	3
Allianz Bajaj	-	-	-	0

To obtain points are plotted in an arbitrary graph. The plotted four brands dimensions are:

Perceptual Map 1

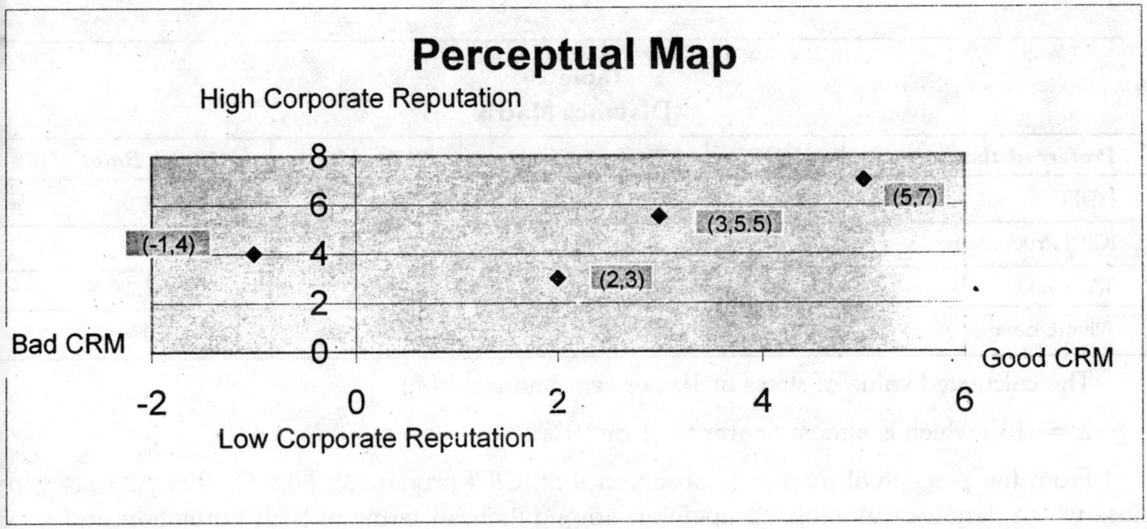

Table 13
Distance Matrix

Preferred than	*HDFC*	*ICICI Prudential*	*TATA AIG*	*Allianz Bajaj*
HDFC	0	2.5	4.27	2.69
ICICI Prudential	-	0	6.7	5.0
TATA AIG	-	-	0	3.16
Allianz Bajaj	-	-	-	0

Now the calculated value of stress at 10 per cent badness of fit

Z = .19 > .10

Perceptual Map 2

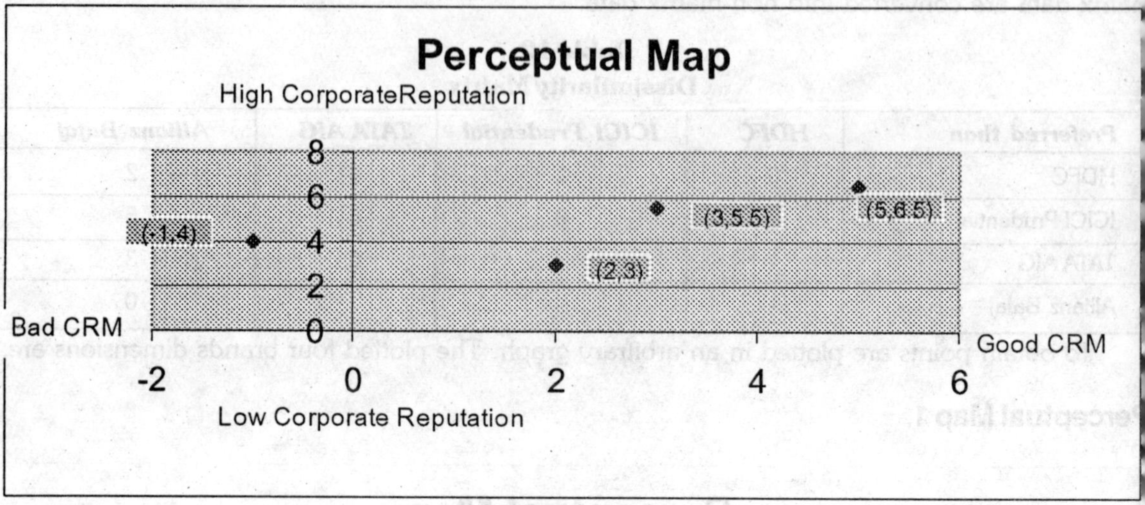

Table 14
Distance Matrix

Preferred than	*HDFC*	*ICICI Prudential*	*TATA AIG*	*Allianz Bajaj*
HDFC	0	2.23	4.27	2.69
ICICI Prudential	-	0	6.5	4.6
TATA AIG	-	-	0	3.16
Allianz Bajaj	-	-	-	0

The calculated value of stress at 10 per cent badness of fit

Z = .125 which is almost nearer to .1 or 10%

From the perceptual map, it is observed that ICICI prudential, HDFC, Tata AIG are lying close which denotes a notable competition among them in terms of high reputation and good customer relationship management. But ICICI emerged as the highest competent among others insurance companies. But Allianz Bajaj is lack of good customer relationship management even it it creates a good reputation in the market. The configurations of the brands are also within the accepted badness of fit.

QUALITATIVE ANALYSIS OF THE MARKET: 5 FORCE MODEL

The five forces that can help the insurance sector in India are: Buyer Power, Degree of Rivalry, New Entrants, Substitutes, and Supplier Power.

Buyer Power

The market comprises of Insurance companies as players and both individuals and corporate as buyers. As the base of the market has increased and there are many individual customers acting as the part of the market, the individual bargaining power of the customers has reduced tremendously. This means the impact of losing one customer is not much for the companies. Additionally high switching costs have to be incurred by the customers to switch between various companies. Thus, the amount of buying power has reduced tremendously over the years.

Degree of Rivalry

The Indian Insurance market is highly saturated with LIC being the market leader. As the private as well as foreign players have increased, the rivalry in the market is also increased. Most of the players also have similar products and business model which leads to price competitions and rivalry in the market.

New Entrants

Entrance to the Indian insurance market can be achieved in several ways. Either a new company can be established, an existing company can diversify their operations into the insurance business, or acquirement of an already existing insurance company or geographical expansion into another country. Overall, the new entrants force in the market is moderate.

Substitutes

Due to rules and regulations, there is no possible substitute for the Insurance Sector in India.

Suppliers

The Indian insurance market is supplied by ICT manufacturers and software houses. Insurance companies rely on sophisticated computer systems which are equipped with a range of specialist programs. This allows the company to manipulate large quantities of data. This means that suppliers within the ICT industry hold considerable sway over insurance companies. Thus, the supplier power is very high in the Insurance sector.

CONCLUDING OBSERVATION

To achieve success in the marketing of the insurance products, the entire business environment is required to be considered. The strategies are to be adopted based on the dynamics of the market trends observed. As the market moves from an emerging to the emerged, a change in approach is necessary. So in order to have good market performance, customer awareness about insurers' prices, products and financial strength should be enhanced. The company should have a clear vision and mission that should be known to all the stakeholders like employees, agents, customers, business associates etc. and an accordingly each one should clearly directed. The company should design the product, which should satisfy the personal needs of customers with an ample degree of flexibilities. To achieve greater insurance penetration, private sector insurance companies are to create a more vibrant and competitive industry, with greater efficiency, choice of products and value to customers. Insurance has today become a mainstay of any market economy since it offers plenty of scope for garnering large sums of money for long periods of time. A well-regulated insurance industry, which moves with the times by offering its customers tailor-made products to satisfy their financial needs is, therefore, essential if we desire to progress towards a worry-free future.

REVIEW QUESTIONS

1. Briefly explain the history of Insurance Sector in India.
2. What is the present scenario insurance industry of India?
3. Quiz
   (a) The five forces that can help the insurance sector in India are: ____, ____, ____, ____, ____ and ____.
   (b) Insurance services add about ____ to the country's GDP. Insurance has assets estimated of Indian rupee ____ trillion.
   (d) The Indian insurance market grew by ____ in 2009 to reach a value of ____ million.
   (e) An Ordinance was issued on ____ month, ____ year nationalizing the Life Insurance sector ____ was incorporated as a company in 1971 and it commence business on January 1, 1973.
   (f) Today, there are ____ general insurance companies and ____ life insurance companies operating in the country.
   (g) India Insurance sector gaining ____ of the market's overall value, while the Non-life Insurance sector managed a market share of ____.
   (h) Who rated LIC as the No. 1 Service Brand of the country?
   (i) Who was the first statutory measure to regulate life business?

REFERENCES

1. Andersen, T. G. and Bollerslev (1997), "Intraday Periodicity and Volatility Persistence in Financial Market," Journal of Empirical Finance, 4, 115-158.
2. Abdulla, ISA and V. Murinde (1997), "Exchange Rate and Stock Price Interactions in Emerging Financial Markets: Evidence on India, Korea, Pakistan, and Philippines," Applied Financial Economics. 7, 25-35.
3. Ajayi, R.A. and M. Mougoue (1996), "On the Dynamic Relation between Stock Prices and Exchange Rates," Journal of Financial Research, 19, 193-207.
4. Agarwal, R.N. (1997), "Foreign Portfolio Investments in Some Developing Countries: A Study of Determinants and Macroeconomic Impact", Indian Economic Review, Vol. XXXII, No. 2, 217-229.
5. Alexakis, P. (2007), "On the Effect of Index Futures Trading on Stock Market Volatility", International Research Journal of Finance and Economics, Vol. 11, 7-20.
6. Afsal E.M. and Mallikarjunappa, T. (2007), "Impact of Stock Futures on the Stock Market Volatility", The ICFAI Journal of Applied Finance, Vol. 13, No. 9, 54-75.
7. Antoniou, A. and P. Holmes (1995), "Future Trading, Information and Spot Price Volatility: Evidence for the FTSE-100 Stock Index Futures Contract using GARCH", Journal of Banking and Finance, 19(1), 117-129.
8. Antoniou, A., P. Holmes, and R. Priestley (1998), "The Effects of Stock Index Futures Trading on Stock Index Volatility: An Analysis of the Asymmetric Response of Volatility to News, " Journal of Futures Markets, 18(2), 151-166.
9. Antoniou, A., G. Koutmos, and A. Pericli (2005), "Index Futures and Positive Feedback Trading: Evidence from Major Stock Exchange", Journal of Empirical Finance, 12(2) 219-238.
10. Aitken, M.; Frino, A. and Jarnecic, E. (1994), "Option Listings and the Behaviour of Underlying Securities: Australian Evidence", Securities Industry Research Centre of Asia-Pacific (SIRCA) Working Paper, Vol. 3, 72-76.
11. Alif Darrant, Shafiqur Rahman, Maosen Zhong (2002), "On the Role of Futures Trading in Spot Market Fluctuations: Perpetrator of Volatility or Victim of Regret?", The Journal of Financial Research, Vol. xxv, No. 3, 431-444.
12. Apolinario, R.M.C.; Santana, O.M.; Sales, L.J. and Caro, A.R. (2006), "Day of the Week Effect on European Stock Markets", International Research Journal of Finance and Economics, Issue 2, 53-70.
13. Arora, V., and Das, S., (2007), "Day of the Week Effects in NSE Stock Returns: An Empirical Study". Available at SSRN: http://ssrn.com.
14. Apte, PG. (2004), "Derivatives — What Time India", Chartered Financial Analyst, Jan.
15. Agarwal, Anan (2001), "Derivatives — Ware of the Future", Finance India, Vol. XV, No. 2, June.
16. Allen, F. and Faulhaber, G. (1989), "Signaling by Underprice in the IPO Market", Journal of Financial Economics, Vol.1, 303-323.
17. Allen F. and R. Michaely (1995), "Dividend Policy", in Handbooks in Operations Research and Management Science, Vol. 9.

18. Ajinkya, B. and Gift, M. (1984), "Corporate Managers, Earnings Forecast and Symmetrical Adjustments of Market Expectations", Journal of Accounting Research, Autumn.

19. Angel J. (1997), "Tick Size, Share Price, and Stock Splits", Journal of Finance, Vol. 52, pp. 655-681.

20. Agarwal, Vipin (1995), "MFs — The Unnoticed Silver Line", The Economic Times, Calcutta, August 11.

21. Ahuja, R. (2004), "Health Insurance for the Poor", Economic and Political Weekly, Vol. XXXIX, No. 28.

22. Bhattacharya, Basabi and Jaydeep Mukherjee (2003), "Causal Relationship Between Stock Market and Exchange Rate, Foreign Exchange Reserves and Values of Trading Balances: A Causal Study for India", National Conference on Money and Finance, Indira Gandhi Institute of Development and Research, Mumbai.

23. Bhattacharya, Prakash (2002), "Pension Products: A Marketing Perspective", Insurance Chronicle, Oct.

24. Baura, Samir (1996), "Portfolio Management the Ways and the Means", Chartered Financial Analyst Jan. Bhat, U.R. (1995), "Mutual Funds", The Economic Times, Calcutta, July 31.

25. Brown, P. (1970), "The Impact of Annual Net Profit on the Stock Market", The Australian Accountant, July.

26. Budhraja, I., Paresh, P., and Singh, T. (2004), "Empirical Study on Market Reaction Around the Bonus and Stock Split", www.Indiainfoline.com.

27. Bhosle, Meenal and Umesh, Adhikary (1994), "Risk-Return Analysis of Mutual Fund Growth Scheme", Indian Management, August.

28. Barclay M.J., C.W. Smith and R.L. Watts (1995), "The Determinants of Corporate Leverage Policy and Dividend Policy", Journal of Applied Corporate Finance, Bank of America, Vol. 7, No. 4, Winter, 4-19.

29. Bennet, M. and R. Donnelly (1993), "The Determinants of Capital Structure: Some UK Evidence", British Accounting Review, 43-59.

30. Brittain, J. (1964), "The Tax Structure and Corporate Dividend Policy", American Economic Review, 272-287.

31. Brittain, J. (1966), Corporate Dividend Policy, The Brookings Institution, Washington.

32. Batty, R. & Ritter, J.R. (1986), "Investment Banking Reputation and Underpricing of Initial Offerings", Journal of Financial Economics.

33. Basher, S.A. and Sadorsky, P. (2000), "Day-of-the-Week Effects in Emerging Stock Markets", Applied Economics Letters, Vol. 13, 621-628.

34. Bekaert, G. and Harvey, C.R. (2003), "Emerging Market Finance", Journal of Empirical Finance, Vo. 10, 3-56.

35. Bekaert, G.; Harvey, C. R. and Lundblad., C. (2003), "Equity Market Liberalization in Emerging Markets", Journal of Financial Research, Vol. 26, 275-299.

36. Bekaert, G.; Harvey, C. R. and Lundblad, C. (2007), "Liquidity and Expected Returns: Lessons from Emerging Markets", Review of Financial Studies, Vol. 20, 1783-1831.

37. Bildik, R. (2004), "Are Calendar Anomalies Still Alive? Evidence from Istanbul Stock Exchange", (2008) Social Science Research Network, http://ssrn.com/abstract=59894. Accessed on February 12.

38. Blaxter, L., Hughes, C. & Tight, M. (2002), "How to Research", Viva Books Private Limited, New Delhi, India.

39. Bose, Suchismita & Bhaumik, S.K. (2007), "Impact of Derivative Trading on Emerging Capital Market: A Note on Expiration Day Effects in India", William Davidson Institute, Working paper 863.

40. Bae, S.C., T.H. Kwon, and J.W. Park (2004), "Future Trading, Spot Market Volatility and Market Efficiency: The Case of the Korean Index Futures Market", Journal of Futures Markets, 24(12), 1195-1228.

41. Bernd, E.K., B. Hall, R. Hall, and J.A. Hausman (1974), "Estimation and Inference in Non-linear Structure Models", Annals of Economic and Social Measurement, 3-4, 63-665.

42. Bologna, P. and L. Cavallo (2002), "Does the Introduction of Stock Index Futures Effectively Reduce Stock Market Volatility?, Applied Financial Economics, 12(3), pp. 183-192.

43. Butterworth, D. (2000), "The Impact of Futures Trading on Underlying Stock Index Volatility: The Case of the FTSE Mid 250 Contract", Applied Economics Letters, 7(7), pp.439-442.

44. Black F. (1976), "Studies of Stock Price Volatility Changes", Proceedings from American Statistical Association, Business and Economics Statistics Section, American Statistical Association, pp.177-181, Washington, DC.

45. Benilde Mania Do Nascimen Oliveora and Mannel Jose da Rocha Armada (2001), "The Impact of the Futures Markets on Portuguese Stock Market", Finance India, Vol. XV, No. 4, 1251-1278.

46. Board John, Sandman Gleb and Sutcliffe Charles (2001), "The Effect of Futures Market Volume on Spot Market Volatility", Journal of Business Finance and Accounting, Vol. 28, No. 7&8, 799-819.

47. Bollerslev, T. (1987), "A Conditional Heteroscedasticity Time Series Model for Speculative Prices and Rates of Return, " Review of Economics and Statistics, 69, 542--547.

48. Bollerslev, T., R.F. Engle and D.B. Nelson (1994), "ARCH Models," in R.F. Engle and D. McFadden (eds.), Handbook of Econometrics, Vol. 4, pp. 2959-3038, North-Holland.

49. Basal, V. K.; Pruitt, S.W. and Wei, K. C. J. (1989), "An Empirical Re-examination of the Impact of COBE Option Initiation on the Volatility and Trading Volume of Underlying Equities: 1973-1986", Financial Review, Vol. 24, 19-29.

50. Batra, Amita (2003), "The Dynamics of Foreign Portfolio Inflows and Equity Returns in India", Seventh Annual Capital Market Conference, UTI Institute of Capital Markets Conference, UTI Institute of Capital Markets, Mumbai, 18-19.

51. Bollersleve, T. (1986), "Generalized Auto Regressive Conditional Hetroscedasticity", Journal of Econometrics, 31, 307-327.

52. Brooks, C. (1996), "Testing for Non-linearity in Daily Sterling Exchange Rates", Applied Financial Economics, 6, 307-317.

53. Box, U.P. and U.M. Jenkins (1978), Time Series Analysis: Forecasting and Control, Revised edition, San Francisco: Holden Day.

54. Bhoi, B.K. and S.C. Dhal (1998), "Integration of Financial Markets in India: An Empirical Evaluation", Reserve Bank of India, Occasional Papers, Vol. 19, No. 4, 345-80.

55. Broca (1994), Volatility Shifts in Stock Market Returns: A Look at Emerging Markets, Vikalpa, 19, Jan-March.

56. Broca (1995), Monitoring Volatility Changes on the Bombay Bourse: A Control Chart Approach, Vikalpa, 20, July-September.

57. Black, F. (1976), "Studies of Stock Price Volatility Changes", In Proceedings of the 1976 American Statistical Association, Business and Economical Statistics Section,. Alexandria, VA: American Statistical Association, 177-181.

58. Baillie, T. and T. Bollerslev (1991), "Intraday and Inter-market Volatility in Foreign Exchange Rates", Review of Economic Studies, 58, 565-585.

59. Chaudhri, Swapan Kanti (1992), "The New Breed of Bourses", Chartered Financial Analyst, Hyderabad, April.

60. Chakraborti, R. (2001), "FII Flows to India: Nature and Causes", Money and Finance, October-December, 61-81.

61. Campbell, J.Y. and L. Hentschel (1992), "No News is Good News: An Asymmetric of Changing Volatility in Stock Returns", Journal of Finance and Economics, 31, 281-318.

62. Conrad, J. (1989), "The Price Effect of Option Introduction", Journal of Finance, 44(2), pp. 487-498.

63. Covrig V. and Melvin M. (2001), "Asymmetric Information and Price Discovery in the FX Market: Does Tokyo Know More About the Yen?", Journal of Empirical Finance, Vol. 9, 271-285.

64. Christiane Good Fellow and Christian A. Salm (2008), "Do Individual Investors on the Future Market Induce Higher Spot Market Volatility", Working Paper, Westfalische Wilhelms, Munster University, Germany.

65. Cox C.C. (1976), "Futures Trading and Market Information", Journal of Political Economy, Vol. 84, pp.1215-1237.

66. Chan, K., (1992), "A Further Analysis of the Lead-Lag Relationship Between the Cash Market and Stock Index Future Market", Review of Financial Studies, 5, 123-152.

67. Chan, K.K.C. Chan and G.A. Karolyi (1991), "Intraday Volatility in the Stock Index and Stock Index Future Market", Review of Financial Studies, 4, 657-684.

68. Chakrabarti R., and R. Roll (2002), "East Asia and Europe During the 1997 Asian Collapse: A Clinical Study of a Financial Crisis", Journal of Financial Markets, Vol. 5, No. 1, pp. 1-30.

69. Chow, Y., Yung H. and H. Zhang (2003), "Expiration Day Effects: The Case of Hong Kong", Journal of Futures Markets, 23, 67-86.

70. Corredor, P., Lechón P. and R. Santamaría (2001), "Option-Expiration Effects in Small Markets: The Spanish Stock Exchange", Journal of Futures Markets, 21, 905-928.

71. Chaudhury, S.K. (1991), "Seasonality in Share Returns: Preliminary Evidence on Day-of-the-Week Effect", Chartered Accountant, Vol. 40 (November), 107-109.

72. Chia, R.C.; Liew, V.K. and Wafa, S.A.W.S.K. (2008), "Day-of-the-Week Effects in Selected East Asian Stock Markets", Economic Bulletin, Vol. 7 (5), 1-8.

73. Choudhry, T. (2000), "Day-of-the-Week Effect in Emerging Asian Stock Markets: Evidence from GARCH Model", Applied Financial Economics, Vol. 10, 235-242.

74. Chapeare, J.P.D. (1979), "Dividend Policy Revisited: Within and Out-of-sample Test", Journal of Business Finance and Accounting, 6(3).

75. Chawla, D. and Srinivasan, G. (1987), "Impact of Dividend and Retention on Share Price — An Econometric Study", Decision, July-September.

76. Conrad J. S. and Conroy R. M. (1994), "Market Microstructure and the Ex-date Return", Journal of Finance, Vol. 49, 1507-1519.

77. Carlson, R. (1977), "Aggregate Performance of Mutual Funds, 1948-1967", Journal of Financial and Quantitative Analysis, 1-31.

78. Chandra, Prasanna (1993), "The Investment Game: How to Win", Tata McGraw-Hill Publishing Company, New Delhi.

79. Chandra, Subhas, and Mahajan, Mukesh (1992), "Perceptions of Investors Towards Mutual Funds: An Investigation", The Indian Journal of Commerce, Calcutta, June. Dronbusch, R. and S. Fischer (1980), "Exchange Rate Accounts", American Economic Review, Vol. 70, 960-971.

80. Dharmaja, N.L. (1976), "Corporate Dividend Practices and Policies", Productivity, October-December.

81. Diz. F. & Finucane. T.J. (1908), "Index Option Expirations and Market Volatility", Journal of Financial Engineering, 7, 1-23.

82. Damodaran, A. and J. Lim (1991), "'The Effects of Option Listing on the Underlying Stocks' Return Process", Journal of Banking and Finance, 15(3), 647-664.

83. Danthine, J.P. (1978), "Information, Futures Prices and Stabilizing Speculation", Journal of Economic Theory, 17(1), 79-98.

84. Dennis, P.J. and J.P. Weston (2001), "Who's Informed? An Analysis of Stock Ownership and Informed Trading", Working Paper. Available Under http://ssrn.com/abstract=267350.

85. Dyl, E. A. and Martin, S. A. (1985), "Weekend Effects on Stock Returns: A Comment", Journal of Finance, Vol.40, 347-349.

86. Dronbusch, R. and S. Fischer (1980), "Exchange Rate Accounts", American Economic Review, Vol.70, 960-971.

87. Dhankar, R.S. (1991), "Empirical Tests of the Efficiency of Indian Stock Market", Journal of Financial Management and Analysis, Vol.4, No.2.

88. Dennis, P.J. and Strickland, D. (2002), "Who Blinks in Volatile Markets, Individuals or Institutions? The Journal of Finance, 57(5), 1923-1949, Financial Dailies.

89. Daniel, Glamouridis, and Michael, Tamvakis (2001), " The Relation Between Return and Volatility in the Commodity Markets", Journal of Alternative Investments, Vol. 22, No.1, 54-62, Summer. Available at SSRN: http://ssrn.com/abstract=566421.

90. Devlin. J.F., Worthington S. and Gerrard P. (2007), "An Analysis of Main and Subsidiary Credit Card Holding and Spending", International Journal of Bank Marketing, Vol. 25, No. 2, pp. 89-101.

91. Doost. R.K. (1997), "Why We Need to Use Credit Cards: A University Experience", Managerial Auditing Journal, Vol.12, No.2, 105-106.

92. Dickey David and Wayne A. Fuller (1979), "Distribution of Estimates for Autoregressive Time Series with a Unit Root", Journal of American Statistical Association, Vol.74, 427-31.

93. Ely, David P. and Robinson, Knneth, J. (1997), "Are Stocks a Hedge Against Inflation?", International Evidence Using a Long-run Approach, Journal of International Money and Finance, Vol. 16, No.1, 1997, 141-167.

94. Engle, R.F. (1982), "Autoregressive Conditional Hetroscedasticity Estimates of the Variance of UK Inflation," Econometrica, 50, 987-1008.

95. Edwards, F.R.(1988), "Does Future Trading Increase Stock Market Volatility?", Financial Analysts Journal, 44 (1), 63-69.

96. Edwards, F.R. (1988b), "Futures Trading and Cash Market Volatility: Stock Index and Interest Rate Futures", Journal of Futures Markets, 8(4),421-439.

97. Engle R.F. and Ng V.K. (1993), "Measuring and Testing the Impact of News on Volatility", Journal of Finance, Vol.48, 1749-1778.

98. Eriotis N. and D. Vasiliou (2003), "Dividend Policy: An Empirical Analysis of the Greek Market", International Business & Economics Research Journal, 2004, Vol. 3, No. 3, 49-57.

99. Fama, F.F. (1974), "The Empirical Relationship between the Dividend and Investment Decisions of Firms", American Economic Review, June.

100. Feldstein, M. and Green, J. (1983), "Why Do Companies Pay Dividend?", American Economic Review, March.

101. Fama, E. F. (1970), "Efficient Capital Markets: A Review of Theory and Empirical Work", Journal of Finance, Vol. 25(2), 283-417.

102. Frankfurter G.M. and B.G. Wood, Jr., (2002), "Dividend Policy Theories and their Empirical Tests", International Review of Financial Analysis, Vol. 11, Issue 2, 111-138.

103. Fama E.F. and H. Babiak (1968), "Dividend Policy: An Empirical Analysis", Journal of the American Statistical Association, 63, 1132-1161.

104. Figleewski. S., (1981), "Futures Trading and Volatility in the GNMA Market", Journal of Finance, 36 (May): 445-456.

105. Fama, E.F. and Schwert, G.W. (1997), "Asset Returns and Inflation", Journal of Financial Economics, (Nov.). Frank, P and Young, A. (1972), "Financial Management", Winter, 66-73.

106. Fung, Joseph K.W. and Yung, Haynes (2007), "Expiration-Day Effects-An Asian Twist", HKIMR Working Paper No. 1/2007. Available at SSRN: http://ssrn.com/abstract=1007150.

107. Feinstein S.P. and W. Goetzmann, (1988), "The Effect of the Triple Witching Hour" on Stock Market Volatility", Economic Review, 2-18.

108. Fama E.F., Fisher L., Jensen M. and Roll (1969), "The Adjustment of Stock Prices to New Information", International Economic Review, Vol. 10, 1-21.

109. Frank, M., and Jaganathan, R. (1998), "Why Do Stock Price Drop by Less than the Value of the Dividend? Evidence from a Country without Taxes", Journal of Financial Economics, Vol.47, 1998, 161-188.

110. Friend, Irwin and Vickers, Douglas (1965), "Portfolio Selection and Investment Performance", The Journal of Finance, Vol.XX, No. 3, Sept., 391-415.

111. Fock. H.K.Y, Woo. K. and Hui. M.K. (2005), "The Impact of a Prestigious Partner on Affinity Card Marketing", European Journal of Marketing, Vol. 39 No. 1/2, 33-53.

112. Fama, E. (1972), "Components of Investment Performance", Journal of Finance, 2-7, 551-567.

113. Gupta, Ramesh (1992), "Portfolio Management for an Individual Investor", The Management Accountant, March.

114. Goyal, A. (2004), "Role of Supplementary Services in the Purchase of Credit Card Services in India", Asia-Pacific Journal of Marketing and Logistics, Vol.16, No.4, 36-51.

115. Gurbandini, Kaur and Rao, D.N. (2009), "Do the Spot Prices Influence the Pricing of Future Contracts? An Empirical Study of Price Volatility of Future Contracts of Select Agricultural Commodities Traded on NCDEX (India)". Available at SSRN: http://ssrn.com/abstract=1469700.

116. Gupta, Pradeep and Bhyana, Sanjay (2002), " Insurance Sector: Challenges and Strategies" JIMS 8 M, Oct-Dec.

117. Granger C. W. J. and Huang B. (1998), "A Bivariate Causality between Stock Prices and Exchange Rates: Evidence from Recent Asia", Quarterly Review of Economics and Finance, Vol. 40, 337-354.

118. Glosten, L.R., R. Jagannathan and D. Runkle [1993], "On the Relation between the Expected Value and the Volatility of Nominal Excess Returns on Stocks", Journal of Finance, 48, 1779-1801.

119. Gulen, H and S. Mayhew (2000), "Stock Index Futures Trading and Volatility in International Equity Markets", Journal of Futures Markets, 20(7), 661-685.

120. Gibbons, M.R. and Hess, P. (1981), "Day-of-the-Week Effect and Asset Returns", Journal of Business, Vol. 54, 579-596.

121. Gordon J. and P. Gupta (2003), "Portfolio Flows into India: Do Domestic Fundamentals Matter?", IMF Working Paper, Number WP/03/02.

122. Grinblatt Market and Titman Sheridin (1989), "Mutual Fund Performance: An Analysis of Quarterly Portfolio Holdings", Journal of Business, Vol.62, No.3, 393-416.

123. Goodart, C. A. E. and M. O'Hara (1997), "High Frequency Data in Financial Markets: Issues and Applications", Journal of Empirical Finance, 4, 73-114.

124. Granger, C.W. (1988), "Some Recent Developments in a Concept of Causality", Journal of Econometrics, 39, 199-211.

125. Gristin, J.M. and R.M. Stulz (2001), "International Competition and Exchange Rate Shocks: A Crosscountry Industry Analysis of Stock Returns", Review of Financial Studies, 14, 215-241.

126. Ghose, Dipak, Levin, E.J., Macmillan, Peter and Wright, R.E. (2002), "Gold as an Inflation Hedge", Dept. of Economics, University of St.Andrews in its Series Discussion Paper Series, 2002.

127. Gallant, A.R., Rossi, P.E. and Tauchen, G.E. (1992), "Stock Prices and Volume", Review of Financial Studies, Vol.S, 199-242.

128. Golaka C. Nath, G.P. Samanta (2003), "Dynamic Relation Between Exchange Rate and Stock Prices-India".

129. Gordon M.J. (1963), "Optimal Investment and Financing Policy", Journal of Finance, May, 264-272.

130. Hooi, T.S., Lee, C.L and Roy, K.W.L. (2001), "Testing for Proxy Effect Hypothesis from Malaysian Pre and Post Crisis Eras", Multimedia University, Sept, FBL Economics Working Paper Series, WP. Harris, L. (1989), " A Day-end Transaction Price Anomaly", Journal of Financial and Quantitative Analysis, March, Vol. 24. 29-45.

131. Haque, Mainul and Somchai Harhirun (1993), "Time Series — Analysis of Causality Between Aggregate Merger and Stock Prices: The Case of Canada", Economic Affairs, 38(2), 73-81.

132. Huizinga, John (1981), An Empirical Investigation of the Long-run Behaviour of Real Exchange Rates", Carnegie-Rochester Conference Series on Public Policy, 27, 149-214.

133. Hsieh, D. A. (1991), "Testing for Non-linear Dependence in Daily Foreign Exchange Rates", Journal of Business, 62, 329-368.

134. Hence, H. and S.Voronkova (2005), "Price Limits on a Call Auction Market: Evidence from the Warsaw Stock Exchange", International Review of Economics and Finance, 14(4), 439-453.

135. Hiraki, T., E.D. Maberly, and N. Takezawa (1995), "The Information Content of End-of-the Day Index Futures Returns: International Evidence from the Osaka Nikkei 225 Futures Contract", Journal of Banking and Finance, 19(5), 921-936.
136. Haris L. (1989), "The October 1987 S&P 500 Stock-Futures Basis", Journal of Finance, Vol.44, 77-99.
137. Heta M. Saria Nupur and Sovan Deb Saikat (2003), "Impact of Index Futures on Indian Stock Market Volatility: An Application of GARCH Model", Proceedings of the International Conference on Business and Finance, ICFAI University Press, Hyderabad, 291-306.
138. Hensler, Douglas. Rutherford, Ronald, D., Springer, and Thomas, M. (1997), "The Survival of Initial Public Offerings in the Aftermarket", The Journal of Financial Research, Vol.XX, No.1, Spring, 93-110.
139. Hensler, D. (1995), "The Over/Underpricing of Initial Public Offerings", Managerial and Decision Economics, 16, 11-28.
140. Hancock. G.D. (1993), "Whatever Happened to the Triple Witching Hour?", Financial Analysts Journal, 66-71.
141. Herbst. A.F. and Mabeily, E-D. (1990), "Stock Index Futures — Expiration Day Volatility and the "Special" Friday Opening: A Note", Journal of Futures Markets, 10, 323-325.
142. Hagelin, Niclas and Alkeback, Per. (2004), "Expiration Day Effects of Index Futures and Options: Evidence from a Market with a Long Settlement Period", Applied Financial Economics, Vol. 14, pp. 385-396. Available at SSRN: http://ssrn.com/abstract=432560.
143. Harsh Vardhan, Deepika and Sehgal Rajen (1994), 'FIIs — Waiving the Magic Wand', Chartered Financial Analyst, Hyderabad, April.
144. Gangadhar V., and Yadagiri, M. (1996), "Diversities in Foreign Direct Investments in India", The Management Accountant, Vol. 31, No.1, Jan.
145. Gupta, Amitabh (2000), "Investment Performance of Indian Mutual Funds: An Empirical Study", Finance India, Vol. XIV, No.3, Sept., 833-866.
146. Gulti, Swati (2002), "Currency Options: Indian Debut", Chartered Financial Analyst, Nov.
147. Goel, N.G. (2007), Foreign Exchange Derivatives in India: Status and Prospects. Gavini, Augustine. L. and Athma Prasanta (1997), "Customer Service in Commercial Banks — Expectation and Reality", Indian Journal of Marketing.
148. Lakshman, Ramesh (1997), "Derivative Instruments: Managing Volatility", The Chartered Accountant, May.
149. Irwin Friend, Marshall Blume and Jean Crockett (1970), "Mutual Funds and Other Institutional Investors: A New Perspective", McGraw-Hill Book Company.
150. Ibotson, R.G., Sindelar, J.L., and Ritter, J.R. (1994), "Initial Public Offerings", Journal of Applied Corporate Finance, Vol. 1, 6-14.
151. Iqbal, Badar Alam (1997), "FDI Inflows Scenario is not Bright One", Monthly Commentary Ippolito, Richard. A. (1993), "On Studies of Mutual Fund Performance, 1962-1991", Financial Analysis Journal, January-February, 43.
152. Jaffe, J. and Westerfield, R. (1985), "The Weekend Effect in Common Stock Returns: The International Evidence", Journal of Finance, Vol. 40, 433-454.
153. Joannos J. and N. Filippas (1997), "Dividend Policy of Firms Listed in the Athens Stock Exchange: An Empirical Analysis", Spoudai, Vol. 47, No. 3-4, 249-285, (in Greek).

154. Joy, O.M. Litzenberger, R.H. and Mc Enally, R.W. (1997), "The Adjustment of Stock Prices to Announcements of Unanticipated Changes in Quarterly Earnings", Journal of Accounting Research, Autumn, 1997.

155. Jack L. Treynor, (1965), "How to Rate Management of Investment Funds", Harvard Business Review, 43, No.1, January-February, 63-75.

156. Jenson, M.C. (1968), "The Performance of Mutual Funds in the Period 1945-1964", Journal of Finance, 23, No. 2.

157. Johanse, S. (1991), "Estimation and Hypothesis Testing of Cointegration Vectors in Gaussian Vector Autoregressive Models", Econometrica, 58, 165-188.

158. John G. McDonald (1974), "Objectives and Performance of Mutual Funds 1960-1967", Journal of Financial and Quantitative Analysis, June, 311-333.

159. Jaideep, Sarkar and Sudipta Majumdar (1994), "Performance Evaluation of Mutual Funds in India", NMIS Management Review, Vol. VI, No. 2, July-Dec., 64-78.

160. James R.F. Guy (1978), "The Performance of the British Investment Trust Industry", Journal of Finance, Vol. XXX, No. 2, May, 443-455.

161. Kunz, R. M., and Agarwal, R. (1994), "Why Initial Public Offerings are Underpriced: Evidence", Switzerland Journal of Banking and Finance, Vol. 18, 705-723.

162. Kumar, S. and Khurana, P.K. (1984), "Policy Orientation of Dividends in Indian Industry", The Management Accountant, October.

163. Kwan, C. (1981), "Efficient Market Tests of the Information Content of Dividend Announcements: Critique and Extension", Journal of Financial and Quantitative Analysis, June.

164. Kumar, S.S. (2001), "Does the Indian Stock Market Play to the Tune of FII Investments?: An Empirical Investigation", The ICFAI Journal of Applied Finance, Vol. 7, No. 3, 36-44.

165. Karpoff, J.M. (1986), "A Theory of Trading Volume", Journal of Finance, December, Vol. 41, 1069-1088.

166. Karpoff, J.M. (1987), "The Relation between Price Changes and Trading Volume", Journal of Financial and Quantitative Analysis, March, Vol. 22, 109-126.

167. Kiran Kumar Kotha and Mukhopadhyay (2003), "Impact of Futures Introduction on Underlying NSE Nifty Volatility", Proceedings of the International Conference on Business and Finance 2003, ICFAI University Press, Hyderabad, 326-42.

168. Kumar, A.; Sarin, A. and Shastri, K. (1995),"The Impact of Listing of Index Options on the Underlying Stocks", Pacific-Basin Finance Journal, Vol. 3, 303-317.

169. Kawaller I.G., Koch P. D., and Koch T. W. (1987), "The Temporal Price Relationship between S&P 500 Futures and the S&P 500 Index", Journal of Finance, Vol. 42, 1309-1329.

170. Keef, S.P. and Roush, M.L. (2005), "Day-of-the-Week Effect in the Pre-holiday Returns of the Standard and Poor's 500 Stock Index", Applied Financial Economics, Vol. 15, 107-190.

171. Kim, J. & Charles W. M. (1989), "Introduction to Factor Analysis: What it is and How to do it" Newbury Park, CA: Sage Publications Series, Number 07-013.

172. Lakonishok, J. and Levi, M. (1982), "Weekend Effects on Stock Returns: A Note", Journal of Finance, Vol. 37, 883-889.

173. Lee, Sang Bin & Ohk, Ki Yool (1992), "The Effects of Future Trading on the Stability of the S&P 500 Returns", Journal of Future Markets, 12(5), 493-509.

174. Ljung, U. M. & GPE Box (1978), "On a Measure of Lack of Fit in Time Series Models", Biometrka, Vol. 66, 66-72.

175. L.O., A.W. and Mackenlay, A.C. (1988), "Stock Market Price Do Not Follow Random Walks: Evidence from a Simple Specification Test", The Review of Financial Studies, 1, 41-66.

176. Lessep M. and Morrel J.U. (1997), "Forecasting Exchange Rate: Theory and Practice", The Henley Centre for Forecasting, London.

177. Lintner J. (1962), "Dividends, Earnings, Leverage, Stock Prices, and the Supply of Capital to Corporations", Review of Economics and Statistics, August, 243-269.

178. Lintner, J. (1956), "Distribution of Incomes of Corporations among Dividends, Retained Earnings and Taxes", American Economic Review, May, 97 - 113.

179. Lintzenberger R.H. and K. Ramaswamy (1979), "The Effects of Personal Taxes and Dividends on Capital Asset Prices", Journal of Financial Economics, June, 163-196.

180. Lamour C. G. and Poon P. (1987), "The Market Reaction to Stock Splits", Journal of Finance, Vol. 42, 1347-1370.

181. Lawson, R. and A. Watt (1983); "Market Oriented Pricing for U.K. Banks", International Journal of Bank Marketing, Vol. 1, No. 2.

182. Rao, Nageshwar (1987), "Customer Service on Banks must Improve", Yojna, Vol. 31, No. 13, July 16-31.

183. Lewis, B. and Smith, A.M. (1984), "Customer Care in Financial Service Organizations", International Journal of Bank Marketing, Vol. 7, No. 5, 13-22.

184. Muralidharan, S. (2004), "Distribution Strategies: New Avenues", Chartered Financial Analyst, Feb.

185. Masse, I., Hanrahn, J.R., and J. Kushner (1997), "The Effect of Canadian Stock Splits, Stock Dividends and Reverse Splits on the Value of the Firm", QJBE, Vol. 36.4 (Autumn), 51-62.

186. Madhusoodanam, T. P., and Thiripalraju, M. (1997), "Underpricing in Initial Public Offerings: The Indian Evidence", Vikalpa, Vol. 122, No. 4, October-December.

187. McInish, T.H. and Wood, R.A. (1990a), "An Analysis of Transactions Data for the Toronto Stock Exchange: Return Patterns and End-of-the-Day Effect", Journal of Banking and Finance, Vol.14, 441-458.

188. M.A., K.C., and Kao, G.W. (1990), "On Exchange Rate Changes and Stock Prices Reactions," Journal of Business Accounting, Vol. 17 (3), Summers, 441-449.

189. Mohsen Bahmano OSKooee, Ahmad Sohrabian (1992), "Stock Prices and the Effective Exchange Rate of Dollar", Applied Economics, Vol. 24, 459-464.

190. Mittal, R.K. (1995), "New Findings on Price Change and Trading Volume Relationship in the Indian Stock Market", Finance India, Vol. 9 (2), pp. 337-342.

191. Macdonald R., Taylor M.P. (1993), "The Monetary Approach to the Exchange Rate", IMF Stall, Papers, 40, 89-107.

192. Meese, R. Rogott, R. (1983a), "Exchange Rate Model of the Seventies: Do they fit out of the Sample?", Journal of International Economics, 14, 3-24.

193. Merton, Robert C. (1987), "A Simple Model of Capital Market Equilibrium with Incomplete Information", Journal of Finance, Vol. 42(3), 483-510.

194. Ma, C.K. and G.W. Kao (1990), "On Exchange Rate Changes and Stock Price Reactions", Journal of Banking Finance and Accounting, Vol. 117: 441-449.

195. Mikiyo Kii Niizeki (2003), "Cash Stock Volatility and the Option Volume: Empirical Tests in the Japanese Markets", Working Paper, Doshisha University.

196. Mayhew Stewart (2000), "The Impact of Derivatives on Cash Markets: What We Have Learned", www.terry.ugaedu/finance/research/workingpaper/infact.pdf.

197. Miller, M. (1990), "International Competitiveness of US Futures Exchange", Journal of Financial Service Research, 4, 387-408.

198. Min, J.H., and Najand, M. (1999), "A Further Investigation of the Lead-Lag Relationship between the Spot Market and Stock Index Futures: Early Evidence from Korea", Journal of Futures Markters, 19, 217-232.

199. Baura, S., and M. Jayadev (1995), "Performance of Growth Oriented Mutual Funds: An Evaluation", The ICFAI Journal of Applied Finance, Vol.1, No.1, January, pp.1-14.

200. Miller M. and F. Modigliani (1961), "Dividend Policy, Growth, and the Valuation of Shares", Journal of Business, October, 411-133.

201. Michel, A. (1979), "Industry Influence of Dividend Policy", Financial Management, Autumn.

202. Muralidhar, S. (2000), "MFs Match FII's Financial Night in Stock Markets", The Financial Express, February 4.

203. Nath & Samanta (2003), "Dynamic Relation between Exchange Rate and Current Accounts", American Economic Review, Vol. 70: 960-971.

204. Nelson, D.B. [1991], "Conditional Heteroscedasticity in Asset Returns: A New Approach," Econometrica, 59, 347-370.

205. Nagaraju K.S. and Kiran Kumar Kotha (2004), "Index Futures Trading and Spot Market Volatility: Evidence from an Emerging Market", The ICFAI Journal of Applied Finance, Vol. 10, No. 8, pp. 5 -16.

206. Nag, A.K. and Amit Mitra (1999-2000), "Integration of Financial Markets in India: An Emperical Investigation," Prajanan, Vol. XXVIII, No. 3, 219-41.

207. Nath, Golaka C. and G.P Samanta (2003), "Dynamic Relation between Exchange Rate and Stock Price - A Case for India", NSE News, National Stock Exchange of India Limited (NSEIL), Feb. 2003, 15-18.

208. Nath, Golaka C. and Tulsi, Lingareddy (2008), "Commodity Derivative Market and its Impact on Spot Market". Available at SSRN: http://ssrn.com/abstract=1087904.

209. Nakagawa, Shinobu and Osawa Naoto (2000), "Financial Market and Macroeconomic Volatility — Relationships and Some Puzzles", May, Working Paper Series of the Research and Statistics Depts., Bank of Japan (2000).

210. Nascimentoo Liveria, Benilde Maria and Armada Manueljose Da Pocha(2001), "The Impact of the Futures Markets Indroduction of the Conditional Volatility of the Portuguse Stock Market", Finance India, Vol. XV, No. 4, Dec.

211. Narasimhan, M.S. and Ramana, L.V. (1995), "Pricing of Initial Public Offerings: Indian Experience with Equity Issues", Journal of Applied Finance, 26-39.

212. Obaidullah, M. (1992), "How Do Stock Prices React to the Bonus Issues?", Vikalpa, 17(1), 17-22.

213. Obaidullah, M. (1991), "Earning, Stock, Prices and Markets Efficiency.-The Indian Evidence", Securities Industry Review, Journal of the Singapore Securities Research Institute, Oct.

214. Obaidullah, M. (1994), "Portfolio Optimization — Some Practical Problems", Chartered Financial Analyst, Jan.

215. Peasnell, Skerratt and Taylor (1979), "An Arbitrage Measurable for Tests of Mutual Fund Performancès", Journal of Business Finance and Accountings, Autumn.

216. Peter Oertmann, and Heinz Zimmermann (1996), "US Mutual Fund Characteristics across the Investment Spectrum", The Journal of Investing, Fall, 56-67.

217. Prake, P. D. and Vdetsuypens, M.R. (1993), "Under Pricing and Insurance Against Legal Liability", Financial Management, 22, 64-73.

218. Pagon A. and Schwert G.W. (1990), "Alternative Models for Conditional Stock Volatility", Journal of Econometrics, 45, pp.267-290.

219. Poterba, James, M. and Lawerence H. Summers (1998), "Mean Reversion in Stock Prices: Evidence and Implications", Journal of Financial Economics, 22, 27-59.

220. Prasuna C.A. (2000), "Determinants of Foreign Institutional Investment in India", Finance India, Vol.XIV, No.2, 411-421.

221. Patsouratis, V. (1989), "Corporate Taxation and Dividend Behavior: An Empirical Analysis", Greek Economic Review, 323 -338.

222. Poon, Ser-Huang, and Clive W. J. Granger (2003), "Forecasting Volatility in Financial Markets: A Review", Journal of Economic Literature, 41, 478-539.

223. P. Roy, Debasis (1996), 'Promising Unlisted Firms Attract FIIs Investment', The Economics Times, New Delhi, July 30.

224. Pettengill, G. N. (2003), "A Survey of the Monday Effect Literature", Quarterly Journal of Business and Economics, Vol. 42, 3-27.

225. Phylaktis, K. and Ravazzolo F. (2005), "Stock Market Linkages in Emerging Markets: Implications for International Portfolio Diversification", Journal of International Financial Markets, Institutions and Money, Vol. 15, 91-106.

226. Roy, M.K. and Karmarkar, M. (1995), "Stock Market Volatility: Root and Results", Vikalpa, 20, Jan-March. Robinson, G. (1993), "The Effect of Futures Trading on Cash Market Volatility", Bank of England Working Paper No. 19, www.ssrn.com./Abstract id=114759.

227. Raju M.T. and Kiran Karande (2003), "Price Discovery and Volatility on NSE Futures Market" SEBI Bulletin, 1(3), 5-15.

228. Ross, S.A. (1989), "Information and Volatility: The No-arbitrage Martingale Approach to Timing and Resolution Irrelevancy", Journal of Finance, 44(1), 1-17.

229. Rai, K. and N. R. Banumurthy (2003), "Determinants of Foreign Institutional Investments in India: The Role of Return, Risk and Inflation", JEL Classification, Vol. 44, 415-411.

230. Rai Kulwant and Bhanumurthy, N.R. (2004), " Determinants of Foreign Institutional Investment in India: the Role of Return, Risk and Inflation", The Developing Economics, 42(4), 479-93.

231. Ravo Li, ar, M.A. (1993), " Hedging – The Emergence of Derivatives Market" IBA Bulletin, June.

232. Roy, S.P., and Chung, J. K. (1985), "Target Payout and the Association between Dividends and Share Price", Accounting and Finance, 25(2).

233. Roa, S.N. (1994),"The Adjustment of Stock Prices to Corporate Financial Policy Announcements", Finance India, Vol. 32 (2), 161-182.

234. Rankine, G.P., and Stice, E.K. (1997), "The Market Reaction to the Choice of Accounting Methods for Stock Splits and Large Stock Dividends", Journal of Financial and Quantitative Analysis, Vol. 32(2), 161-182.

235. Ray, Alok (1994), "Foreign Capital in Asia and Pacific Region-Trends, Problems and Prospects", Economic and Political Weekly, Oct. 22.

236. Rangnekar, Sharif, D. (1996), "FIIs to Go in for Broad Buy", The Economic Times, New Delhi, April 19.

237. Richard A. Ippolito (1993), "On Studies of Mutual Fund Performance, 1962-1991", Financial Analysis Journal, January-February, 42-50.

238. Rao, K.V., and Venkateswarlu, R. (1998), "Performance Evaluation of Mutual Funds: A Case Study of Unit Trust of India", Indian Capital Market: Theories and Empirical Evidence, Quest Publications, 219-233.

239. Ramachandran, G. (1998), "Pitfalls in Portfolio Performance Measures and their Implications to Mutual Fund Industry", Indian Capital Markets: Theories and Evidence, Quest Publications, 234-274.

240. Rao, C.S. (2004), "Insurance Industry: The Happening Sector", Chartered Financial Analyst, February.

241. Roy, Dilip & Banerjee, Saikat (2003), "Some Aspects of Insurance in the Context of Risk Management: The Vision", The Journal of Business Perspective, Jan-June.

242. Rai Kulwant and Bhanumurthy, N.R. (2004), "Determinants of Foreign Institutional Investment in India: The Role of Return, Risk and Inflation", The Developing Economics, 42(4), 479-93.

243. Rajendra, K. (1995), "Scaling New Heights", The Economic Times, July 31.

244. Ravi, A. B., and Krishnadevan, V. (1994), "Mutual Funds — Future Stock", Business India, Oct 24-Nov. 6.

245. Srinivasan, R. (1993), "Security Price Behavior Associated with Rights Issue Related Events", Unpublished Doctoral Dissertation, IIM, Ahmedabad.

246. Shankar, D. (1975), "Dividends and Stock Price — The Indian Experience", Economic and Political Weekly, September.

247. Smirlock, M. and Marshall, W. (1983), "An Examination of the Empirical Relationship between the Dividend and Investment Decisions: A Note", Journal of Finance, December.

248. Short H., H. Zhang, and K. Keasey (2002), "The Link between Dividend Policy and Institutional Ownership", Journal of Corporate Finance, 8, 105-122.

249. Reilly, F. K. (1977), "New Issues Revisited", Financial Management, Winter, Spyrou, S. I. (2005), "Index Futures Trading and Spot Price Volatility", Journal of Emerging market Finance, Vol. 4, 151-167.

250. Sarris, A.H. (1984), "Speculative Storage, Futures Markets and the Stability of Commodity Price", Economic Inquiry, 22(1), 80-97.

251. Skinner, D. (1989), "Option Markets and Stock Return Volatility", Journal of Financial Economics 23(1), 61-78.

252. Stein, J.C. (1997), "Informational Externalities and Welfare-reducing Speculation", Journal of Political Economy, 95(6), 1123-1145.

253. Stoll H.R. and Whaley R.E. (1990), "The Dynamics of Stock Index and Stock Index Futures Return", Journal of Financial and Quantitative Analysis, Vol.25, 441-467.

254. Schwarz, T.V., and Laatsch, F. (1991), "Price Discovery and Risk Transfer in Stock Index Cash and Future Markets", Journal of Futures Markets, 11,669-683.

255. Stennis E.A., Pinar M. and Allen A.J. (1983), "The Futures Market and Price Discovery in the Textile Industry", American Journal of Agricultural Economics, Vol.65, No.2, 308-310.

256. Shenbagaraman, P. (2003), "Do Futures and Options Trading Increase Stock Market Volatility?", NSE Research Initiative, Paper No. 20.

257. Sharma, J.L. and E. Kennedy (1977), "A Comparative Analysis of Stock Price Behaviour on the Bombay, London and New York Stock Exchanges", Journal of Financial and Quantitative Analysis, September.

258. Summers, Lawrence H. (1986), "Does the Stock Market Rationally Reflected Fundamental Values?", Journal of Finance, 41, 591-601.

259. S. Berkowitz, L. Finney and D. Logue (1988), "The investment Performance of Corporate Pension Plans", New York, Quorum Books.

260. Seth A.K. and Saloni G. (2005), "Understanding Volatility at BSE: A Quality Control Approach", 32, Decision, Jan-June.

261. Solnik, B. (1987), "Using Financial Prices to Test Exchange Models — A Note", Journal of Finance, Vol.42.

262. Stoll, H.R. and R.E. Whaley (1997), "Expiration-day Effects of the All Ordinar Share Price Index Futures: Empirical Evidence and Alternative Settlement Procedures", Australian Journal of Management, 22, 139-174.

263. Sandhya, Srinivasan (2008), "Futures Trading in Agricultural Commodities". Available at SSRN: http://ssrn.com/abstract=1197602.

264. Schulltz, P. (1993), "Unit Initial Public Offerings", Journal of Financial Economics, 34, 199-229.

265. Suri, Kamla (1994), "Can India Sustain Flow of Foreign Investment?", The Economics Times, Friday, July 8.

266. Tripathy, Naliniprava (1997), "Testing of Price Behaviour of Indian GDRs", Udyog Pragati, Vol.XXI, No.4, Oct.-Dec.

267. Tripathy, Naliniprava (2010), "Indian Stock Market Reaction to International Cross-listing: Evidence from Depository Receipts", China-USA Business Review, Vol. 9, No.10, October.

268. Samir K. Barua, *et al.* (1991), "Master Shares: A Bonanza for Large Investors", Vikalpa, Vol.16, No.1, Jan-March, 29-34.

269. Shah, Ajay and Thomas Susan (1994), "Performance in Evaluation of Professional Portfolio Management in India", A Paper Prepared by CMIE, 10 April.

270. Schiffman, Leon.G. & Kanuk Leslie Lazar (1995), "Consumer Behaviour", Prentice-Hall of India Private Limited, New Delhi, India.

271. Sahu, S. (1993), "Evolving a Marketing Strategy for Optimal Functioning of Mutual Funds", Sankalpa, Vol. No.1 Jan-June.

272. Satyendra, and Nayak, S. (1994), "Mutual Funds: A More Efficient Vehicle of Creation of Wealth", The Journal of the Indian Institute of Bankers, Vol. 65, No.3, July-Sept.

273. Sindhwani, Sanjay. (1995), "A Chance for Mutual Benefit", The Economics Times, Investor Guide, 28th August 3, Sept.

274. Subramanyam, M. J. (1993), "Mutual Funds: The Link between the Investors and the Capital Market", Indian Banking Today and Tomorrow, Dec.

275. Suchard, Hazel, T. Polonsky, Micha, ETJ., and Chan, Ricky Yec-Kwong (1996), "The Environment Buyer Behaviour Model — A Comparative Analysis of Consumer Environmental Behaviour", Marketing Management, Anmol Publishing Pvt. Ltd., New Delhi.

276. Tripathy, Naliniprava (2005), "Emerging Scenario of Indian Banking Industry", Mahamaya Publishing House, New Delhi.

277. Tinic, S. M. (1988), "Anatomy of Initial Public Offerings of Common Stock", Journal of Finance, September.

278. Trivedi, P. and A. Nair (2003), "Determinants of FII Investment Inflow to India", Presented in Fifth Annual Conference on Money and Finance in the Indian Economy, Indira Gandhi Institute of Development Research, Jan. 30-Feb. 1.

279. Turnovsky, S.J. (1983), "The Determination of Spot and Futures Prices with Storable Commodities", Econometrica, 51 (5), 363-1387.

280. Thomas Sony and Thenmozhi M. (2004), "Impact of Index Derivatives on S&P CNX Nifty Volatility, Information Efficiency, and Expiration Effects", Proceedings of the International Conference on Business and Finance, ICFAI University Press, Hyderabad, pp. 264-290.

281. Thenmozhi M. (2002), "Futures Trading, Information and Spot Price Volatility of NSE-50 Index Futures Contract", NSE Research Initiative, Paper 59.

282. Turkington J. And Walsh D. (1999), "Price Discovery and Causality in the Australian Share Price Index Future Market", Australian Journal of Management, Vol. 24, 97-113.

283. Tarun, M.S., Suneja, Ajay and Bodla, B.S. (1996), "Price Behaviour of Indian GDRs — An Analysis", The Indian Journal of Commerce, Vol. XLIX, No. 186-187, June.

284. Tripathy, Naliniprava (1996), "Innovative Growth Oriented Mutual Funds", Innovative in Asian Management, Delta Publishing House, Delhi, 384-391.

285. Tripathy, Naliniprava (1998), "Investors Behaviour Model in Stock Market — An Empirical Insight on Mutual Funds in India", Management of Development Growth with Equity, Excel Books.

286. Thiripalraju, M., and Patil, Prabhakar R. (1998), "Micro and Macro Forecasting Abilities of Indian Fund Managers", Indian Capital Markets: Theories and Empirical Evidence, Quest Publication, 205-218.

287. Tripathy, Naliniprava (1996), "An Empirical Evaluation of Growth-oriented Mutual Funds: A New Innovation of Financial Services", Management Innovations in South Asia, April.

288. Tripathy, Naliniprava (1995), "Mutual Funds in India — A Financial Service to Capital Market", Finance India, Vol. X, No.1, March.

289. Tilton, Jessica H. (2002), "The Development of Onshore Derivative Markets", Treasury Management, Aug.

290. Vasal, Virandra Kumar. (1997), "Financial Innovations and Derivatiives in Capital Markets", Udyog Pragati, Oct-Dec.

291. Vasiliou D. and N. Eriotis (2003), "The Determinants of Dividend Policy: Some Greek Data", Paper Presented in the European Applied Business Research Conference, Venice, Italy, 2003, 1-5.

292. Victor Murinde (1997), "Exchange Rate and Stock Price Interactions, in Emerging Financial Markets: Evidence on India, Pakistan and Philippines", Applied Financial Economics, Vol. 7, 25-35.

293. Wu. B. (1995), "Model-free Forecasting for Non-linear Time Series (with Applications to Exchange Rates)", Journal of Business and Economics Statistics, 5, 87-98.

294. Warther, Vincent A. (1995), "Aggregate Mutual Fund Flows and Security Return", Journal of Financial Economics, Vol.39, 209-235.

295. William F. Sharpe, (1966), "Mutual Fund Performance", Journal of Business, 39, No.1, Jan., 119-138.

296. Y.P. Singh and S. Bhatia, (2006), "Does Futures Trading Impact Spot Market Volatility? Evidence from Indian Financial Markets", Decision, Vol. 33, No. 2, July-Dec. 41-62.

297. Yan B. and Zivot E. (2004), "The Dynamics of Price Discovery", AFA, 2005, Philadelphia Meeting Posted on Social Science Research Network (SSRN).

298. Yadav, R.A., and Mishra, Biswadeep (1996), "Performance Evaluation of Mutual Funds: An Empirical Analysis", MDI Management Journal, Vol.9, No.2, July, 117-125.

299. Yamini Karmarkar, G. Kawadia (2002), "The Relationship Between Stock Index and Exchange Rate: Empirical Evidence Based on Indian Stock Markets", ICFAI Journal of Applied Finance, Vol. 8, No. 2, 51-56.

300. Zakoian, J.M. (1994), "Threshold Heteroskedasticty Models", Journal of Economics Dynamics and Control, Vol.18, 931-994.

301. Factors Infuencing the Indian Currency Market, In The Chartered Accountant (pp. 768- 71), 2006.

302. RBI (2006-07), Non-deliverable Foreign Exchange, Mumbai.

303. RBI (2009-10), Foreign Currency — Rupee Options, Mumbai.

304. Triennial Central Bank Survey (December 2007), Bank for International Settlements.

305. PNB Monthly Review, March, 1994.

306. IOB Quarterly News Review, April-June 1995.

307. Business India, March, 1995.

308. Facts for You, Vol.17, No.5, Oct. 1995.

309. Productivity, Vol.35, No.2, July-Sept. 1994.

310. Jain, S.K., "Indian Euro Issues — Boom or Depression" Financial Services, The Economic Times, March, 1995.

311. State Bank of India Monthly Review, 1995.

312. Economic Times, Special Issue, August 13, 1996.

313. Business World, March 1997.

314. The Economics Times, March 14, 1997.

315. Times of India, April 4, 1997

316. The Business Age, April 8, 1997

317. AMFI UP Date, July-September, 1999

318. Chartered Financial Analyst, Nov. 2004.

319. Bringing Card Usage Down to Earth — Raghu Mohan, Economic Times — Oct.8, 1999.
320. Credit Card Users' Association Launched, The Hindu, April 26, 2007.
321. Indian Credit Card Holders are Poor Users — Times New Network, July 21, 2003. The Economic Times, Online.
322. The Financial Express, Aug. 16, 2001.
323. The Economics Times, Aug. 12, 2001.
324. European Journal of Marketing, Vol. 39, No. 1/2, 2005, pp. 33-53.
325. http://www.eurojournals.com/finance.htm.
326. http://www.fmc.gov.in/.
327. http://finance.indiamart.com/markets/commodity/nmceil.html.
328. http://business.mapsofindia.com/india-market/commodity.html.
329. http://www.tradingpicks.com/beginners_guide.htm
330. http://www.indiancommodity.com/lic.htm.
331. http://ncdex.com/Aboutus/profile.aspx.
332. http://www.indiancommodity.com/trader.htm
333. http://business.mapsofindia.com/india-market/commodity.html.
334. http://isid.org.in/pdf/WP1003.PDF.
335. http://www.ftkmc.com/markets-commodities.html.
336. http://www.banknetindia.com/banking/80628.htm.
337. http://economictimes.indiatimes.com/
338. http://www.meditari.org.za/docs/2003/243_254.pdf
339. http://www.law.upenn.edu/academics/institutes/ile/PNYUPapers/2010/Lambrecht&Myers,%20Dividends.pdf.
340. http://www.bseindia.com/
341. http://www.investopedia.com/terms/l/lintnersmodel.asp.
342. http://www.nseindia.com.
343. http://www.sebi.com
344. http:// www.bseindia.org
345. http:www.nseindia.com
346. http://www.clickindia.com/detail.php?id=2581256
347. www.personalfn.com
348. www.iimk.digitallibrary.ac.in
349. www.economywatch.com/india-credit-cards/types/ - 30k
350. http://www.thefreedisctionary.com
351. http://www.indiaonestop.com/insurance/insurance.htm
352. http://www.paisawaisa.com/
353. www.economywatch.com and www.economypedia.com

354. http://www.creditcards.com/credit-card-news
355. http://articles.economictimes.indiatimes.com/2008-03-31/news/28486327_1_credit-card-management-consultancy-multiple-cards-citibank
356. http://www.moneycontrol.com/news/business/plastic-money-gaining-credenceindia-a-report_213440.html
357. HDFCBankcreditcards.co.in.
358. http://www.buzzle.com/articles/credit-cards-for-bad-credit-history.html
359. http://www.buzzle.com/articles/credit-card-reform-act-of2009.html
360. http://www.shvoong.com/books/1634429-advantages-disadvantages-relevant-possess-plastic/#ixzz1MU6gpiqX
361. http://www.articlealley.com/article_570428_19.html?ktrack=kcplink